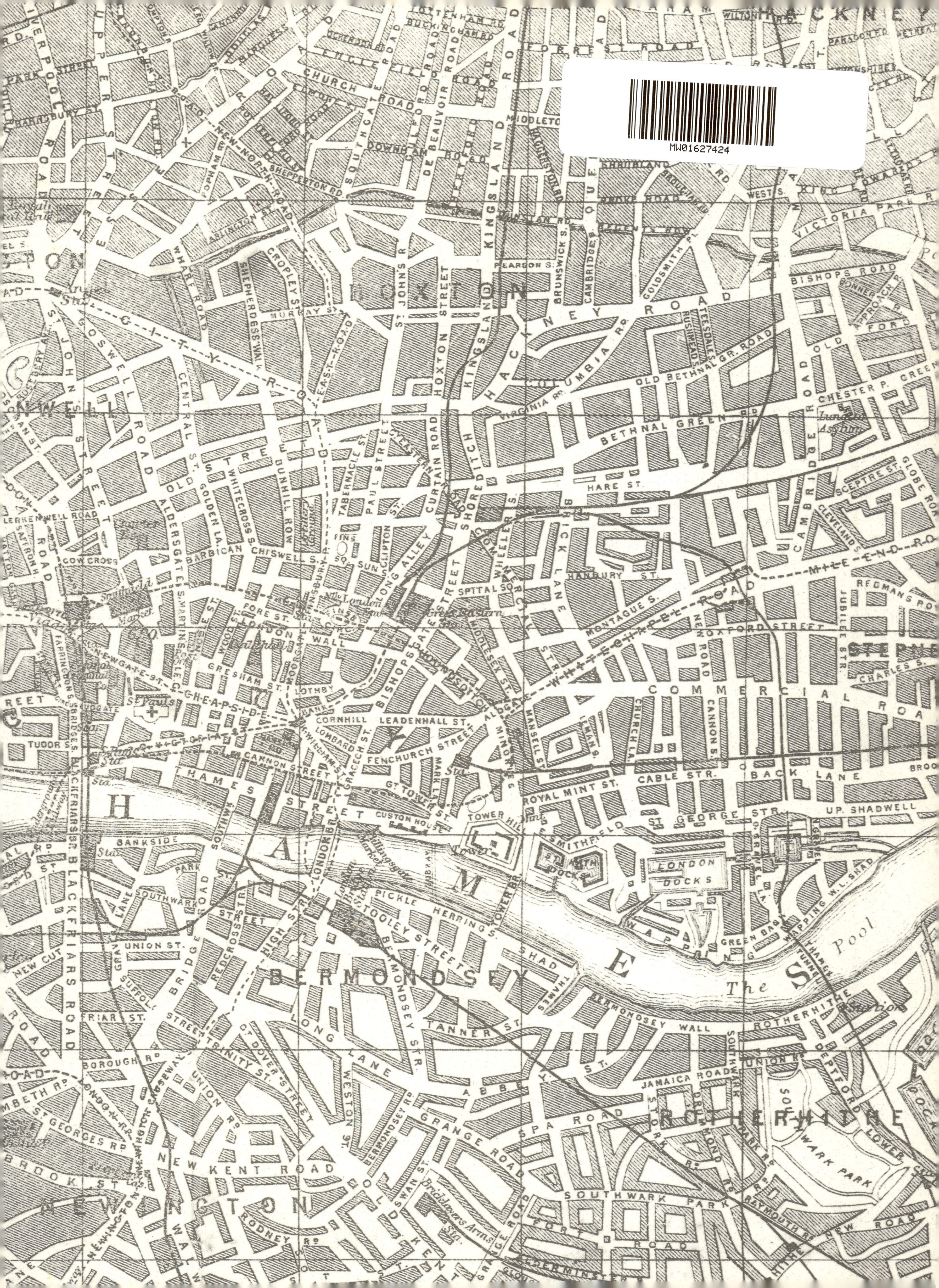
HACKNEY
HOXTON
KINGSLAND ROAD
HACKNEY ROAD
CITY ROAD
GOSWELL ROAD
BETHNAL GREEN RD
OLD BETHNAL GR. ROAD
COLUMBIA RD
VICTORIA PARK RD
BISHOPS ROAD
CAMBRIDGE ROAD
MILE END ROAD
WHITECHAPEL ROAD
COMMERCIAL ROAD
STEPNEY
SHOREDITCH
CURTAIN ROAD
OLD STREET
BRICK LANE
HANBURY ST.
BISHOPSGATE STREET
CHEAPSIDE
CORNHILL
LEADENHALL ST.
FENCHURCH STREET
CANNON STREET
THAMES STREET
TOWER HILL
ROYAL MINT ST.
CABLE STR.
BACK LANE
ST GEORGE STR.
LONDON DOCKS
WAPPING
The Pool
BERMONDSEY
TOOLEY STREET
BERMONDSEY WALL
ROTHERHITHE
JAMAICA ROAD
SPA ROAD
GRANGE ROAD
LONG LANE
TANNER ST.
BOROUGH RD
UNION ST.
BLACKFRIARS ROAD
NEW CUT
NEW KENT ROAD
NEWINGTON
SOUTHWARK PARK
BANKSIDE
HIGH ST.
LONDON BR.
TOWER BR.
CLERKENWELL ROAD
ALDERSGATE S.
BARBICAN
LONDON WALL
MINORIES
ALDGATE
MANSELL ST.
SPITAL SQ.
CHURCH LA.
CANNON ST.
CUSTOM HOUSE
PICKLE HERRINGS
SHAD THAMES
DEPTFORD LOWER RD
REDCROSS ST.
TRINITY ST.
GREAT DOVER STREET
RODNEY RD
ST GEORGES RD

THE STREETS OF LONDON

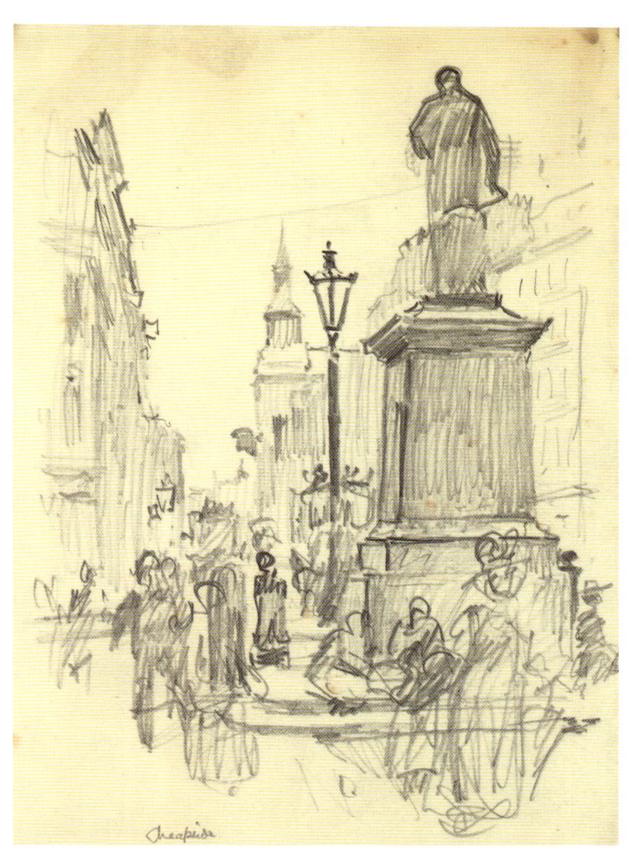

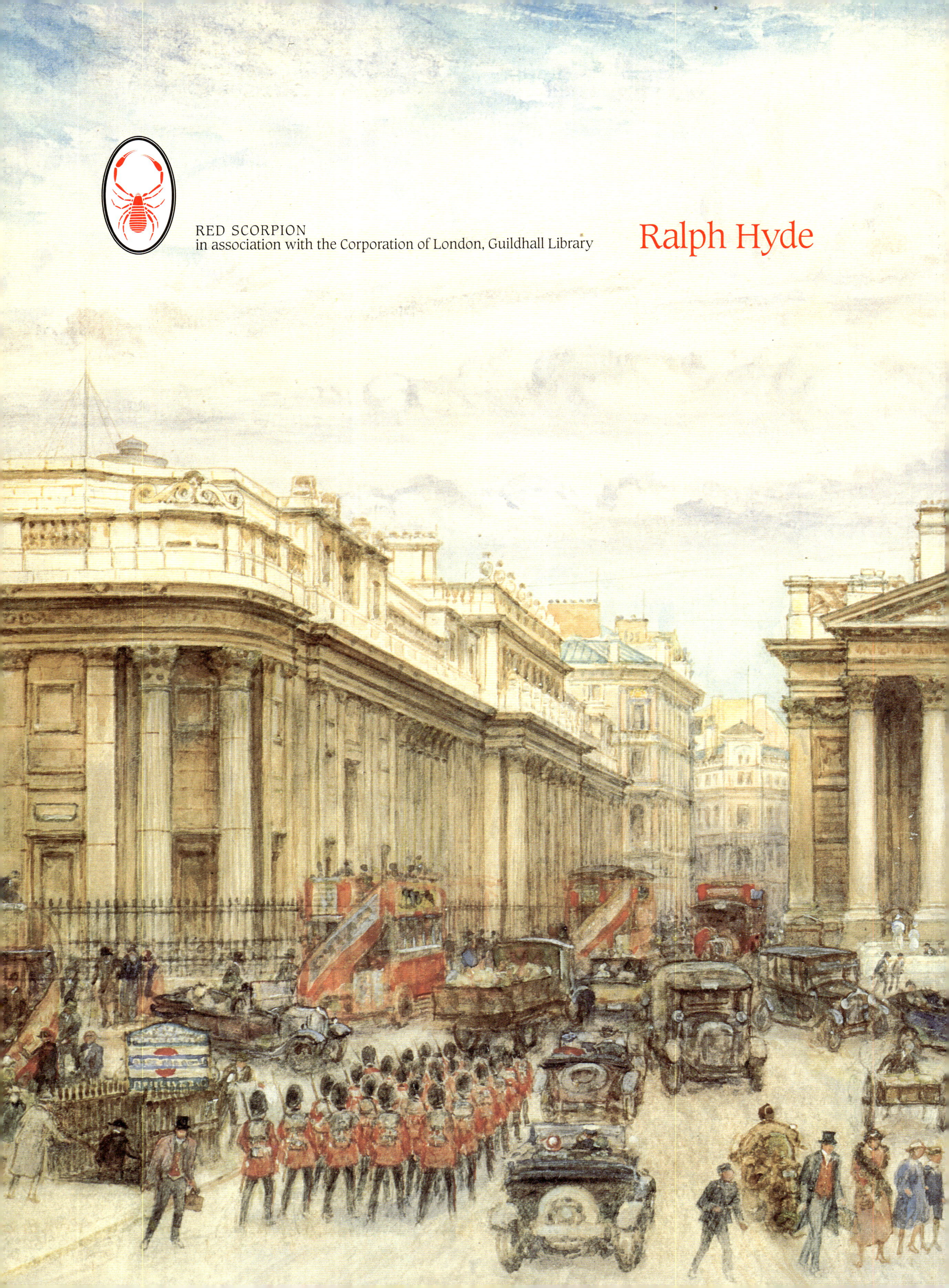

RED SCORPION
in association with the Corporation of London, Guildhall Library
Ralph Hyde

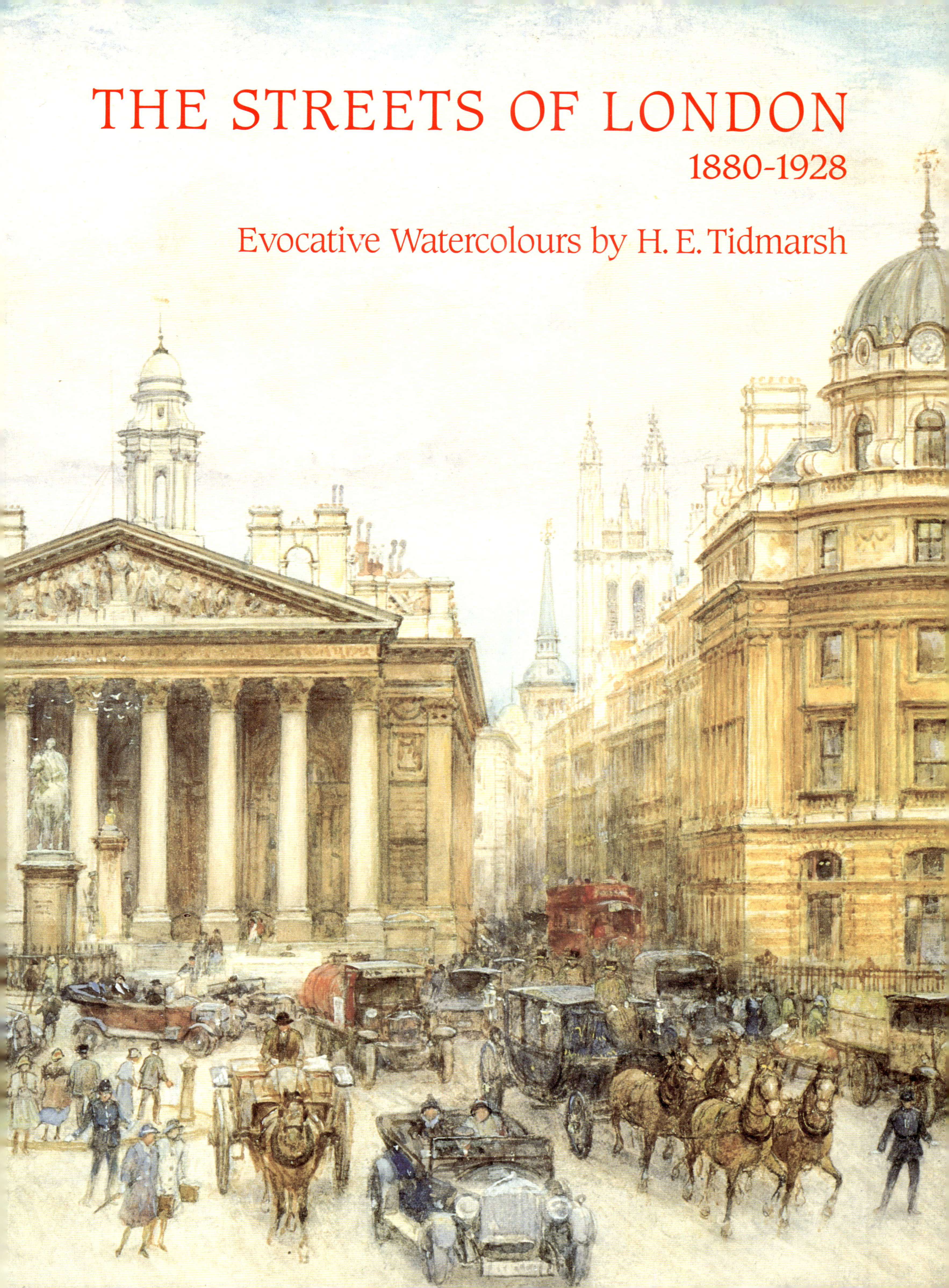

THE STREETS OF LONDON

1880-1928

Evocative Watercolours by H. E. Tidmarsh

First published in Great Britain in 1993 by Red Scorpion Publishing Limited, Bromans Farm, Bromans Lane, East Mersea, Colchester, Essex CO5 8UE

A CIP catalogue record for this book is available from the British Library

PUBLISHER
Brian Bell

DESIGN AND PRODUCTION CONSULTANT
David Milbank Challis

ORIGINATION CONSULTANT
John Parfitt

REPRODUCTION CONSULTANT
Philip Moore

DESIGN AND PRODUCTION ASSISTANTS
Sharon Crocker
Michele Dowley

PRODUCTION TEAM
Eric Lewis
Paul Gardner
Phil Hampshire
Mark Francis

TYPEFACE
TSI Caxton (light/book)

PAPER
Consort Royal Silk Tint

TYPESETTING
Paragraph Typesetting Limited

ORIGINATION
John Parfitt Facsimile and Fine Print
Principal Image
Scanner, Dainippon Screen 608 Mk II
Screen, 100 lines per centimetre

PRINTED IN ENGLAND AT
The Cloister Press, Cambridge

BOUND BY
Hunter & Foulis Limited

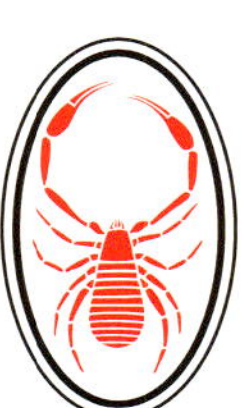

A
RED SCORPION
BOOK

ISBN 0 898414 00 9

ILLUSTRATION CREDITS

Archway Methodist Central Hall, 139; Barnet Archives and Local History Collection, 17; Guildhall Art Gallery, Corporation of London, 94, 96; Museum of London, 16, 138; National Library of Wales, 9, 10, 11; and private collectors, 4, 5, 6, 7, 8, 18, 19, 20, 21, 22, 23, 24, 25, 26, 27, 28, 29, 30, 31, 32, 35, 41, 51, 58, 68, 77, 81, 98, 110, 111, 116, 117, 119, 122, 125, 135, 136, 139. All the other illustrations are from the Print Room of Guildhall Library, Corporation of London.

PUBLISHER'S PREFACE

I am delighted to be publishing this book of Tidmarsh watercolours; I have been enthusiastic about the idea since the exhibition of his London watercolours first aroused my interest. I must thank all the people who have worked together on this publishing project: first Guildhall Library, whose close collaboration has made the whole venture possible; then Ralph Hyde, whose customary diligence and enthusiasm makes him a pleasure to work with; also the Tidmarsh family for assisting Ralph with his research; and not least the production team, who have combined to produce this superb volume.

Brian Bell

ACKNOWLEDGEMENTS

The author has been particularly indebted to Bernard Adams, who meticulously catalogued the Guildhall Library's extensive holdings of Tidmarsh drawings, identifying buildings, and carefully recording the staffage. His superb cataloguing proved invaluable in compiling the captions for this volume. Without his preliminary work this book would not exist. Barrington Gray, the Museum of London staff photographer, was responsible for skilfully photographing all the non-Guildhall Tidmarsh watercolours. David Milbank Challis both designed and edited the book, and was a stimulating colleague. Jeremy Smith, Print Room Assistant at Guildhall Library, acted with characteristic enthusiasm as the author's right hand man throughout the project.

Book scorpions (*Cheiridium museorum*), which are red, eat the book mites that eat books. Brian Bell, Publisher of Red Scorpion, proved to be a real friend to this particular book, and is thanked for lavishing it with his attention.

The following also provided the author with invaluable help and freely gave of their time: Lorraine Buckland, Mary Cosh, Alan Day, Graham Dibben, Jean Dibben, Roland Dibben, Brian Ellings, John S. Ellis, Chris Ellmers, John Fisher, Keith Fletcher, Revd Ronald Frost, Mary Hallett, Douglas Hyde, Betty Monro, Joy Monro, C. J. Nicholson, Elizabeth Petty, Dr Ann Saunders, Margaret Swarbrick, John Tidmarsh, Muriel Tidmarsh, Peter A. Tidmarsh, Pieter van der Merwe, Mike Wadsworth, and Barry Winter. Several branches of the Tidmarsh family made relevant family papers available and were ever warm and welcoming.

Endpapers

Detail from 'Cook's Map of London', 1911

Half title page

Cheapside looking East from behind the Robert Peel statue, c.1900

[1] *Pencil sketch, 200 × 142 mm*

Title spread

'Bank', 1927

[2] *Detail from plate 41*

CONTENTS

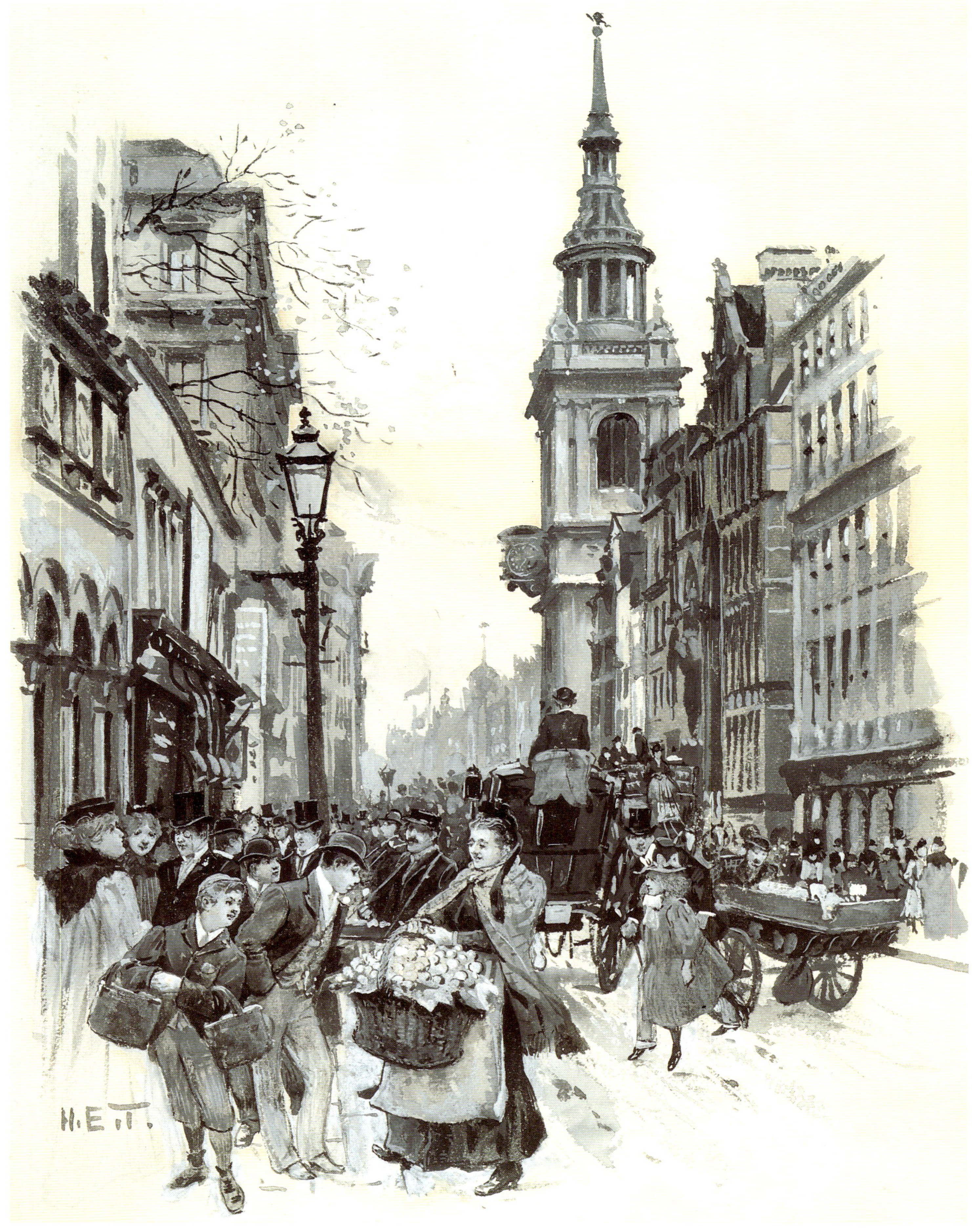

Cheapside seen from the St Paul's end, c.1900

[3] *Wash drawing, heightened by body colour, 279 × 212 mm (sight)*

FOREWORD

It can be embarrassing to come across an artist, close to home and worthy of a lavishly illustrated monograph, of whom one has never even heard. But Ralph Hyde assures me there is no shame in not having heard of H. E. Tidmarsh. Why not? Because nobody has.

How pleasant, then, for Ralph to be able to introduce Tidmarsh to the world in this volume. And how fortunate for Tidmarsh, however late in the day, to have Ralph as his proposer for wider recognition. There is no one better qualified, as I know from personal experience. In the late 1970s, when planning a book on the prints of Richmond, I first benefited from the warm welcome and expert advice which Ralph has offered researchers at the Guildhall for 28 years now. He is the best possible guide to interpret the topographical and social significance, as part of London's recent history, lying beneath the charm of Tidmarsh's images.

The charm itself needs no introduction, being evident as soon as one opens this book. But I also very much like the solemnity of Tidmarsh's approach to buildings. Here is someone recording the London he loved, apparently just for his own satisfaction (the finished paintings were rarely sold or exhibited, but were hung all round his home in frames which he made for them), and doing so with the meticulous thoroughness of a man who might never have heard of a camera - a machine which makes the task of record at once so much easier and so much duller.

Tidmarsh is a natural archivist, adding for example to his 1895 painting of St Giles Cripplegate the note: 'In 1903 the shops were removed' - not in faint pencil on the back, but in his bold brown lettering in the foreground of the image itself. In the same way he excuses a touch of artistic licence at St Botolph Bishopsgate with the equally prominent announcement: 'Near railings left out.'

Over the 50-year span of these paintings, there is the pleasure of the changing face of London's street life in Tidmarsh's very convincing scenes, as broad-brimmed Victorian and Edwardian bonnets give way to cloche hats, the open-topped horse-drawn doubledecker omnibus is gradually replaced by the motorized version (surprisingly little changed in its outward appearance by the 1920s), and traffic jams begin to consist of Morris and Austin rather than hackney and hansom.

If I have one regret about these delightful scenes, it is their respectability. Compared to the scenes of a century earlier in *Microcosm of London*, one does rather miss the gross paunches, vulgar flounces, and suggestive leers with which Rowlandson peopled Pugin's careful architectural settings. That is a comment not on the admirable Tidmarsh but on his admirable times. Even so, is there perhaps a faint promise of something improper in a painting of 1899 [134]? In front of a different church (St Saviour's Southwark instead of St Paul's Covent Garden), and 14 years before the writing of *Pygmalion*, a real-life Higgins seems to notice his Eliza. Who knows what may happen next?

Bamber Gascoigne

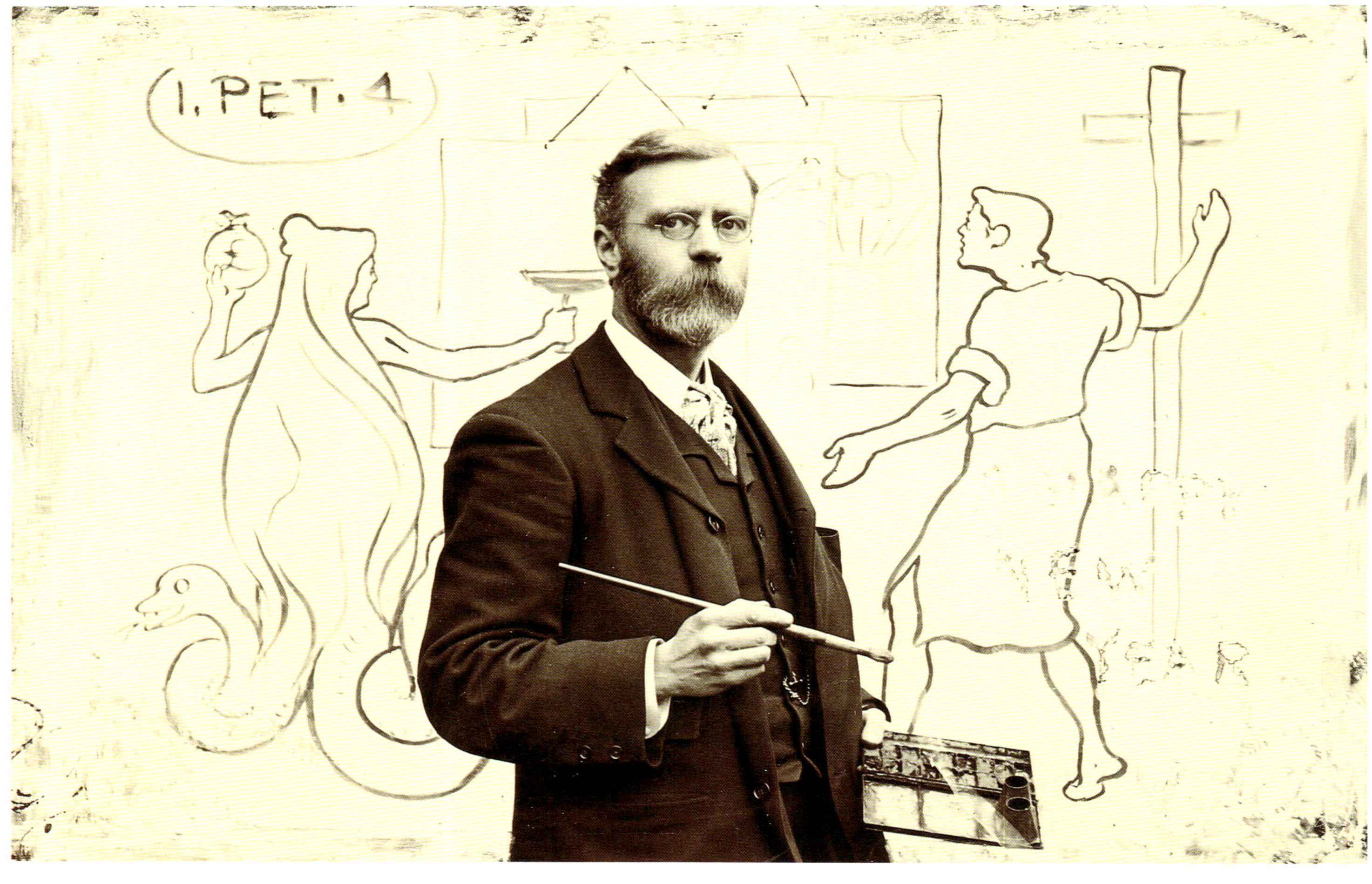
I. PET. 4

THE ARTIST

H. E. Tidmarsh at work, c.1895
[4] *Family photograph.*

Look at Tidmarsh's view of the Tower of London [136] and you will see 1
that a girl listening to a yeoman warder holds behind her back a small cane. A cane? How very curious. But why not? If that small girl was really holding a cane then this particular artist felt obliged to show her doing so. The same goes for the telegraph wires in the financial heart of the City of London. Untidy they may be but they were there. Truth for Tidmarsh was paramount. What he saw in the streets of London is what you get.

Tidmarsh's watercolours are full of such truths. As you would expect in topographical drawings, the architecture is respectfully recorded. But so too are the people. The figures are not there in order to complete the picture. They are there because this particular artist loved humanity, singly and collectively. The people are not tailors' dummies or stock figures as in most topographical images, put there to lend scale and proportion. Each person included is an individual with his or her own dignity, doing something or going somewhere with a purpose. It is this that distinguishes Tidmarsh from almost all the other artists who have recorded the London scene, and it puts him in the same lofty category as George Scharf Senior, Robert Blemmel Schnebbelie, George Sidney Shepherd, and Thomas Shotter Boys, and in our own day Dennis Flanders and Geoffrey Fletcher.

Henry Edward Tidmarsh was born on 4 February 1854 in Islington, North London. The Islington Tidmarshes were carpenters and sturdy Methodists who hailed from Icomb in the Cotswolds. H. E. Tidmarsh's grandfather, Charles Tidmarsh, was a carpenter on the local estate at Icomb. Although he was the parish clerk, he took to attending chapel at nearby Stow-on-the-Wold. Having an enthusiastic Methodist convert, prone, we may suspect, to evangelising fellow servants, displeased the squire. His bailiff ordered Tidmarsh to stop it or leave. Charles followed his conscience and went. There was no alternative job in Icomb. On 17 April 1828, therefore, Charles, with his wife (the household's laundress), their children, and a nephew called George, set off for an uncertain future in the great metropolis.

In fact, Islington, where they settled, was still a village though linked at this date by ribbon development to London proper. In Islington the family could worship in freedom. Methodism flourished there. Calvinistic Methodists worshipped at the Islington Tabernacle in Providence Place; Wesleyan Methodists had a chapel on the east side of Liverpool Road, opened in 1826; and the Independent Methodists were at the New Islington Chapel on the corner of Upper Street and Church Street. The Independents also ran a School of Industry. John Wesley's Chapel was not too far away in the City Road. Mrs Tidmarsh laundered, and George, it seems, soon made money. An extended Methodist tract, *Plain Facts in a Country Dress*, by 'a farmer', published in London in 1861 records, with much religious excitement and gratitude to a providential God, that Charles 'became possessed of considerable property, so much so that for many years past he has been living independent of business, and his family are all doing well.' Islington directories confirm the family's progress: a galaxy of Tidmarshes are listed living and working in the area - William Tidmarsh, carver and gilder; C. and S. Tidmarsh, watchmakers; James Tidmarsh; George Tidmarsh; Tidmarsh & Sons, carpenters and undertakers....

Henry's father, Joseph, was the owner of Tidmarsh & Sons. His works were at 10 Steyman's Row in Holloway. By 1866 the firm was describing itself as 'carpenters and blind-makers', and operating at 226 Upper Street. The firm's account books reveal that blind- and shutter-making had been a speciality of theirs from the start, but now it was becoming their principal concern. (Later, in about 1890, Henry would produce a huge illustrated trade card for his father carrying a pair of views of the shop, sixteen views of the processes involved in manufacturing blinds in Tidmarsh's works, two views showing blinds being fixed, and two pairs of views showing the windows of contented customers before and after Tidmarsh blinds had been fitted. The firm still manufactures blinds and shutters at its Transanna Works, Laycock Street, west out of Upper Street - essentially the same address - today).

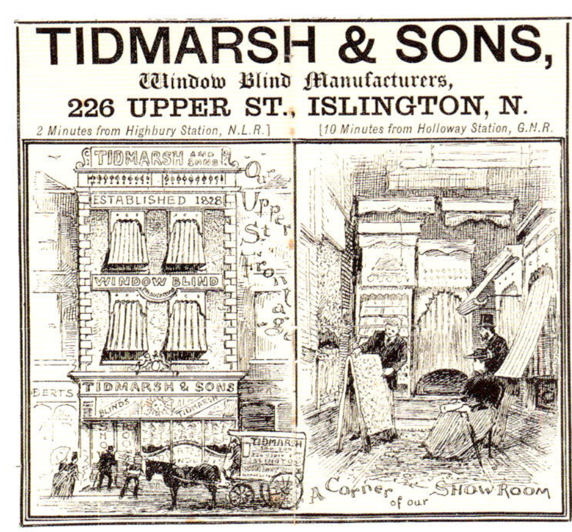

Tidmarsh & Sons' showroom at 226 Upper Street, Islington, 1890

[5] *Detail from trade card*

Henry was brought up with his brothers and sisters, Jane, Elizabeth, Thomas, and Frederick. It was very much a Methodist environment: father was a teetotaller and a Sunday school superintendent, and chapel was the centre of their lives. Henry attended a private school in Islington, and whilst there obtained his first artistic success - a prize in the South Kensington examination for exceptional merit in design. His brothers, Thomas and Frederick, would join the family firm. Henry did not. Instead in c.1872 he enrolled at the National Art Training School in Kensington, today's Royal College of Art. Metal work, wood carving, and mural painting were his specialities. Two examples of his student's work survive, an attractive metal bowl, and a metal bracelet with the symbols of truth, mercy, grace and love.

On leaving the National Art Training School, Henry launched into his career. He painted murals in a new public building in Sheffield, and whilst there in 1878 turned down an offer from his father for a job with the family firm designed to utilise his artistic talents. It was in Sheffield that he fell in love with a young lady called Alice Burnby. His brother, Thomas, came to visit him, and he fell in love with Alice, too. Thomas and Alice married in 1889. Henry would remain a bachelor for another thirteen years.

In London Henry lived at his parents' house at 11 Upper Hornsey Rise, now Hillrise Road. The family lived comfortably. There was a cook and a housemaid. In the chandeliered drawing room there was a settee where people could sit back-to-back, flowers under domes, and an organ with a lot of pipes which Joseph did not - perhaps could not - play. (Both Henry and his father could and did play the violin). French windows led into a sizeable heated conservatory with a palm tree. Outside was a croquet lawn and a vegetable garden. Henry had his studio at the top of the house, and a darkroom for developing photographs somewhere at the back.

Henry was a young man with strongly held opinions. He was a keen Methodist, and by 1889 was a Methodist local preacher. He was a pacifist. For a while he was a vegetarian. He was an ardent teetotaller. And he was an ethical Socialist. John Burns, the first working man to become a cabinet minister in England, and the Fabian playwright, George Bernard Shaw, were his heroes. The Socialist body which received his support was the Independent Labour Party. Founded in Bradford in 1893 by the prophetic Keir Hardie and others, the youthful I.L.P. fought for votes for women, for independence for the colonies, and, above all, for the brotherhood of man. Their aim was to create a new and better world. The I.L.P. became affiliated to the Labour Party when it was

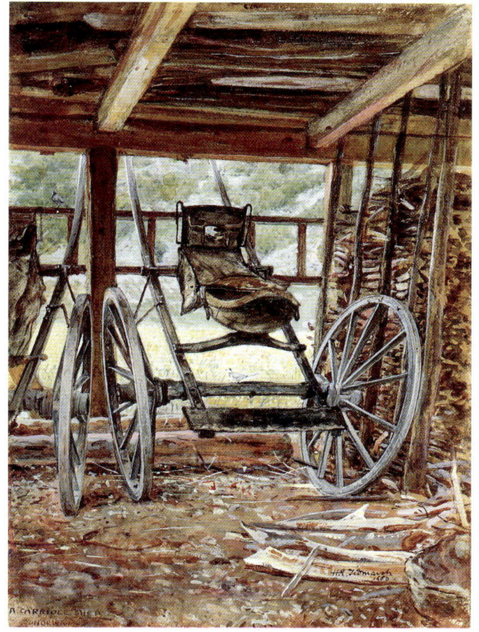

'A Carriole Shed, Norway', 1885

[6] *Watercolour drawing, 277 × 199 mm*

created in 1900. It opposed the Boer War and the 1914-1918 War. Dissatisfied with the Labour Party in government and opposition, it disaffiliated itself in 1932.

Tidmarsh always described himself modestly as a book illustrator. In the 1880s he contributed drawings to popular journals such as the *Graphic* and its rival the *Illustrated London News*. He also did work for *Cassell's Magazine*. In 1890 he collaborated with the Catholic convert and Medieval romantic, H. W. Brewer, in producing for the *Graphic* a long engraved panoramic view of Rome. Conceivably it was from Brewer that Tidmarsh acquired his enthusiasm for producing carefully observed watercolour drawings of Medieval cathedrals in Britain and on the Continent.

In 1885 Tidmarsh visited Norway, and two of his finest drawings were executed on that trip. In the winter of 1886-1887 he was the *Graphic's* 'special artist' in Montreux, Switzerland. When Christmas arrived, feeling home-sick, he attempted to keep his spirits up by producing and sending to the family an amusingly illustrated Christmas letter. He had been 'lugeing' (*luge* is the word the Swiss use for toboggan). It had given him satisfaction to speed past an attractive young woman; evidently she was impressed, but he had finished up detached from his toboggan, head stuffed into the snow, and mocked humiliatingly by a local. Pride before the fall. His Montreux drawings, with artist's notes, eventually appeared in the *Graphic* on 6 August 1887.

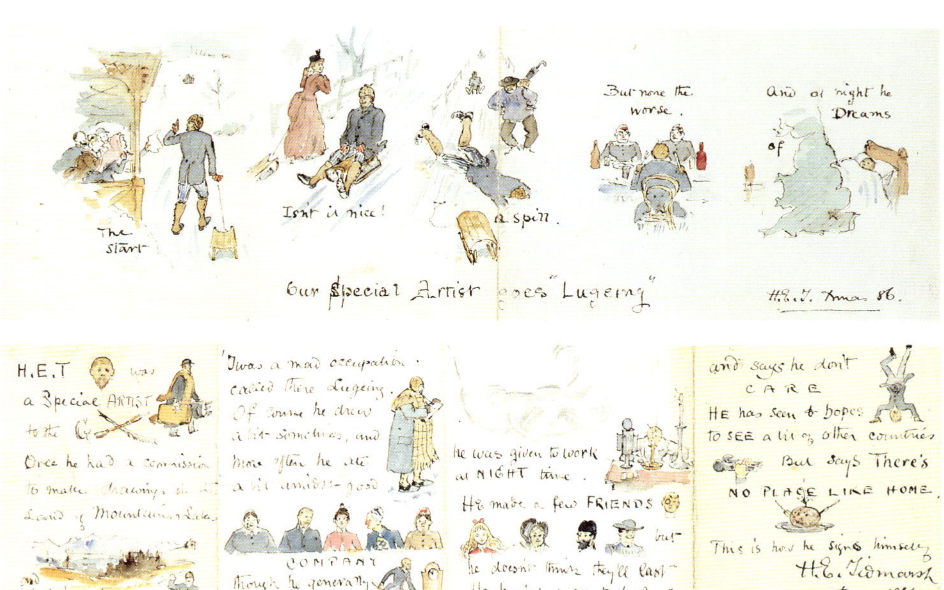

Letter home from Montreux, Christmas 1886

[7] *Manuscript illustrated with pen and ink and watercolour sketches, 90 × 280 mm*

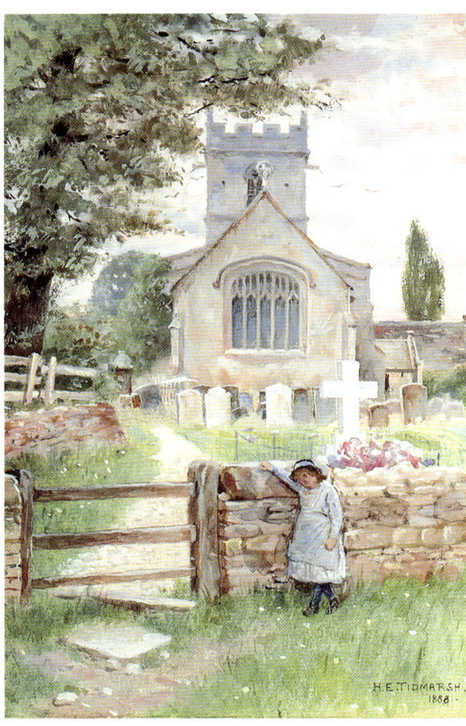

Combe Church, near Blenheim Palace, Oxfordshire, 1888

Probably the watercolour exhibited by Tidmarsh at the Royal Academy in 1888.

[8] *Watercolour drawing, 178 × 113 mm (sight)*

Back in England the *Graphic* sent him to Blenheim Palace. His drawings appeared in the issue for 12 and 19 February 1887. At the time of the Wesleyan Conference, he visited Wesley's Chapel in the City Road. The minister's wife, Helen McKenny, recorded in her diary:

'An old friend, Henry Tidmarsh of Archway Road, called to ask if he could take sketches of the curiosities and of our rooms, and the Chapel before the Conference for the *Graphic*. This was willingly granted him. Seized the opportunity of showing him my little attempts at sketching from Nature, and he read me a long lecture on 'horizontal lines' and 'right angles', which at the time partially enlightened me but still greatly mystified me. Took him into the Chapel, the vestry, the graveyard, and the vaults, then left him to sketch the Preacher's vestry before tea.... An animated discussion on vegetarianism (of which he is an ardent disciple) and a still more lively one on Home Rule. He is the first person I have met who believes in it. Told us much of interest about his tour in Norway, and how delightfully simple and trustful the people are there. He has also recently been to Woodstock and the Duke of Marlborough's palace at Blenheim.'

Tidmarsh's images of Wesley's Chapel and various Wesley relics (these included John Wesley's teapot) appeared in the journal on 24 July 1886. (He returned to the subject for the *Illustrated London News* on 28 February 1891). On 14 September in the following year Tidmarsh called at the Chapel again. 'Travel does make people entertaining', Mrs McKenny observed. 'He has been 10 months on the Continent roaming about. He was in Mentone [Menton on the French Riviera near the Italian border] during the earthquake - there for a fortnight - and actually made sketches of the ruins while people were screaming with fright around!' (*Graphic*, 5 and 19 March 1887). He had been to Italy and had accompanied the Baptist minister in Rome to a village outside the city. There they had insensitively attempted to evangelise the inhabitants, and had been stoned by boys who cried, 'Viva la Madonna!'

During this trip Tidmarsh was astonishingly industrious. He crammed hundreds of pencil, pen and ink, and wash sketches into sketchbooks, interspersing the sketches with details of expenses - even tips to porters. Most of these sketches are of landscapes, buildings, peasants, or townfolk, but some are pure reportage - 'The King and Queen [of Italy] Opening the Exhibition of Donatello's Works in the Bargello, Florence', for example - whilst others are historical and carry notes - 'Les Obliettes - Chillon: a staircase down which prisoners were tempted to escape and then fell into the lake and were drowned.'

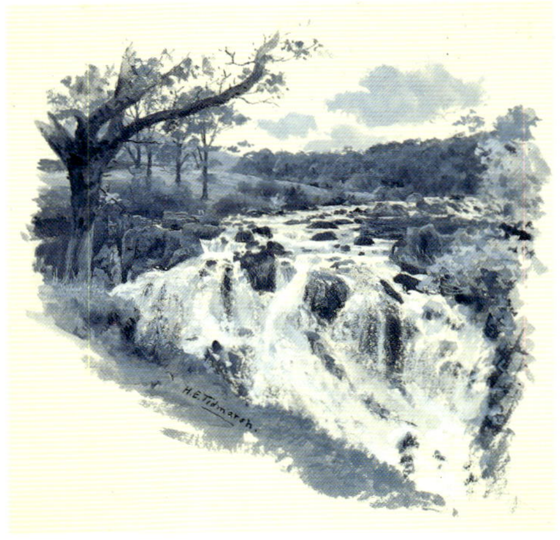

Upper Swallow Fall, 19 October 1884

[9] *Pen and wash with body colour, 228 × 290 mm*

In October 1884 Tidmarsh took himself to North Wales and tramped around Snowdonia, making a series of small vignetted views. Some of these were of local beauty spots - the Swallow Falls at Betws-y-coed, and the Roman bridge at Pandy, for instance - but others depicted local industry - lead mines, a water wheel for pumping mines, and a miners' bridge. These views, all drawn in wash with body colour, give the impression they were intended for a topographical work that was never published.

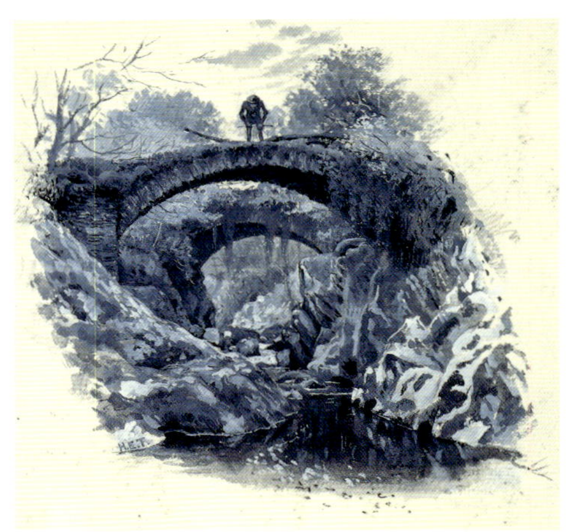

Roman Bridge, Pandy, 22 October 1884

[10] *Pen and wash with body colour, 228 × 290 mm*

A topographical venture that did materialise was Cassell's three-volumed book on Manchester. Cassell's were canvassing publishers, that is to say, their publications were marketed by large numbers of canvassers who went from door to door, interesting householders in new books and gathering subscriptions. Cassell's had already issued a five-volumed *Old and New London*, its text supplied by Walter Thornbury and Edward Walford, and this had been a resounding success. Now they planned parallel works for the principal provincial cities. For *Old and New London* they had copied miscellaneous prints and drawings, exploiting the private collection of the architectural decorator, Frederick Crace. All the images had been reproduced by wood engraving, a slow, labour-intensive process. By the 1890s wood engraving had been superseded by photographic methods - the line block and half-tone processes. These were the processes Cassell's would use for *Manchester Old and New*, by W. A. Shaw (1896). To give the book a consistent style a single artist would be commissioned to produce all the images. H.E. Tidmarsh got the job.

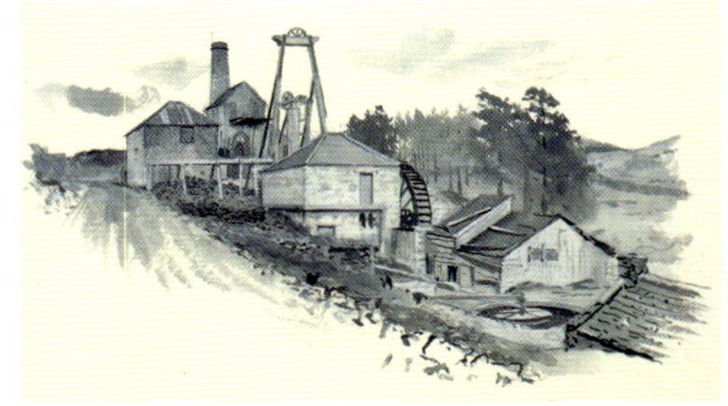

Lead Mine near Betws, 27 October 1884

[11] *Pen and wash with body colour, 215 × 332 mm*

Though Tidmarsh was what today we would call a graphic journalist, and therefore experienced at working under pressure, the scale of the Manchester commission must have been daunting. Approximately three hundred images were needed in a hurry to illustrate the work, and there

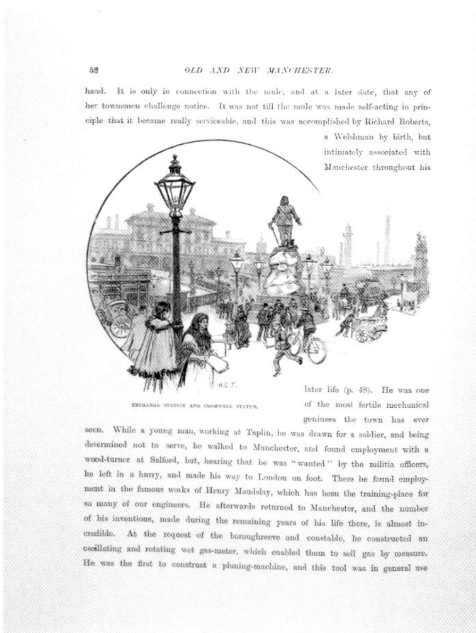

52 *OLD AND NEW MANCHESTER.*

hand. It is only in connection with the mule, and at a later date, that any of her townsmen challenge notice. It was not till the mule was made self-acting in principle that it became really serviceable, and this was accomplished by Richard Roberts, a Welshman by birth, but intimately associated with Manchester throughout his later life (p. 48). He was one of the most fertile mechanical geniuses the town has ever seen. While a young man, working at Taplin, he was drawn for a soldier, and being determined not to serve, he walked to Manchester, and found employment with a wood-turner at Salford, but, hearing that he was "wanted" by the militia officers, he left in a hurry, and made his way to London on foot. There he found employment in the famous works of Henry Maudslay, which has been the training-place for so many of our engineers. He afterwards returned to Manchester, and the number of his inventions, made during the remaining years of his life there, is almost incredible. At the request of the boroughreeve and constable, he constructed an oscillating and rotating wet gas-meter, which enabled them to sell gas by measure. He was the first to construct a planing-machine, and this tool was in general use

EXCHANGE STATION AND CROMWELL STATUE.

Page from volume 2 of Cassell's *Manchester Old and New,* (1896)

[12]

was a temptation to produce spin-offs. Nine views of Chetham Hospital and Library by Tidmarsh illustrated an article in the *Art Journal* (1894).

Whilst in Manchester a young niece came to stay. She later recalled a strange incident. Uncle Henry was sketching in a street outside a jeweller's shop. The jeweller took exception to him being there and ordered him to go away. Uncle Henry refused to move till he had finished his drawing. The jeweller called the police, and he was arrested. When Lloyd George visited Manchester Town Hall and was mobbed by the crowd, Uncle Henry found himself involved in the fracas. From the outset Manchester was a stronghold of the I.L.P. The party's newspaper, the *Clarion*, was published there. No membership lists exist, but it seems likely that it was in Manchester in 1894, during the Cassell assignment, that Tidmarsh first became involved with Socialist politics.

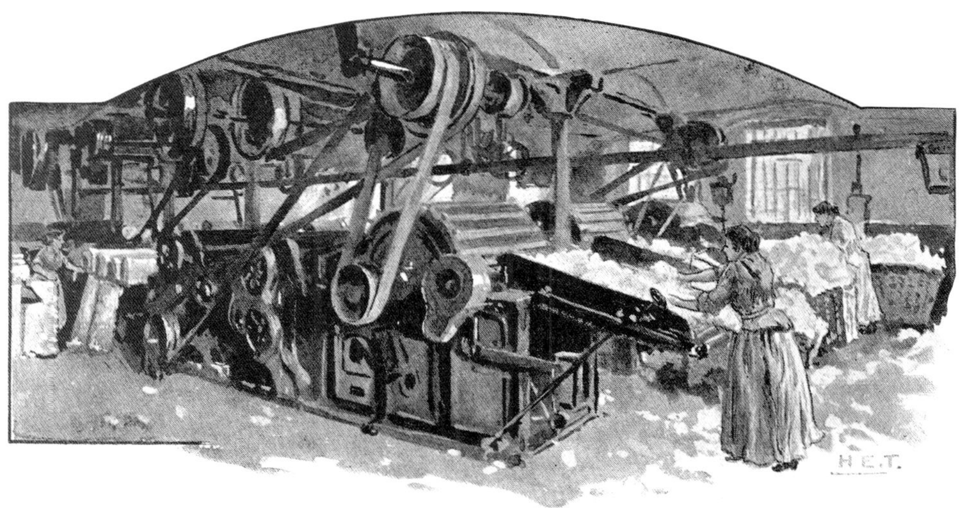

Scutching Room, c.1894

Scutching is the process of dressing cotton by beating. From volume 2 of Cassell's *Manchester Old and New* (1896).

[13] *Half-tone after pen and wash drawing, 70 × 126 mm*

Over 150 of Tidmarsh's pen and wash drawings for *Manchester Old and New* were purchased from Cassell's by Manchester City Art Gallery. They constitute a unique and invaluable record of Manchester topography and life at the end of the nineteenth century. Predictably, art in Manchester attracts his attention. A vignette shows school boys at work in the drawing room at Manchester Grammar School, and another shows students - mainly women - producing drawings in the Designing Room at the Municipal Art School. A pavement artist attracts a crowd under the Memorial in Albert Square. In Belle Vue pleasure gardens we see the open-air panorama for the current year, a feature of life at Belle Vue since 1852. Street scenes often highlight social contrasts. In Corporation Street a street orderly armed with dustpan and brush clears up horse manure, and news vendors stand in the gutter perilously close to traffic. The sensitive artist from London is shocked by the poverty he discovers in the streets of this northern industrial town - ragged, bare-footed children in Angel Meadow and St Chad's in the Cheetham Hill district, for example, and he is shocked too by the conditions under which women workers must labour in the cotton mills. W. A. Shaw's text for *Manchester Old and New* is often clinical and detached. Tidmarsh's illustrations - especially in 'Sale of Coke at the Gasworks' - present the reader with raw reality. Tidmarsh discreetly puts his own message across. Near the cathedral a seated bowler-hatted gentleman sells magazines which include one published by Cassell's; a poster on the wall behind him advertises the I.L.P.'s *Clarion*, and calls for strike action.

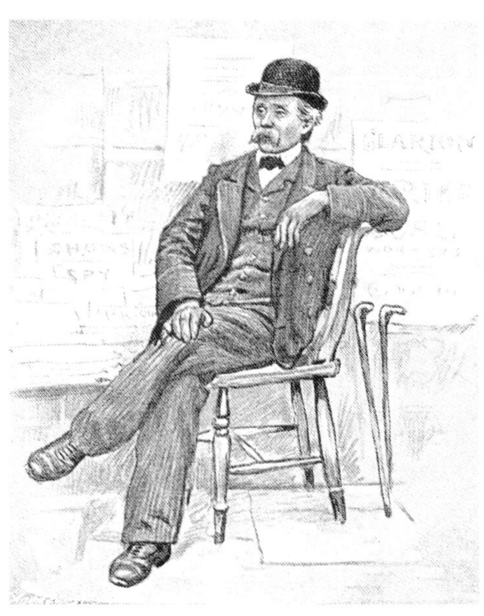

Newspaper vendor, c.1894

His wares include the *Clarion*, mouthpiece of the Independent Labour Party. From volume 1 of Cassell's *Manchester Old and New* (1896).

[14] *Half-tone after pen and wash drawing, 76 × 63 mm*

Tidmarsh's Manchester drawings are respectable examples of their type. Though similar in style and approach to those W. Luker, Junior provided for *London City* (1891) and *London City Suburbs as they are Today* (1893) - two works that may have influenced Tidmarsh - his images are more

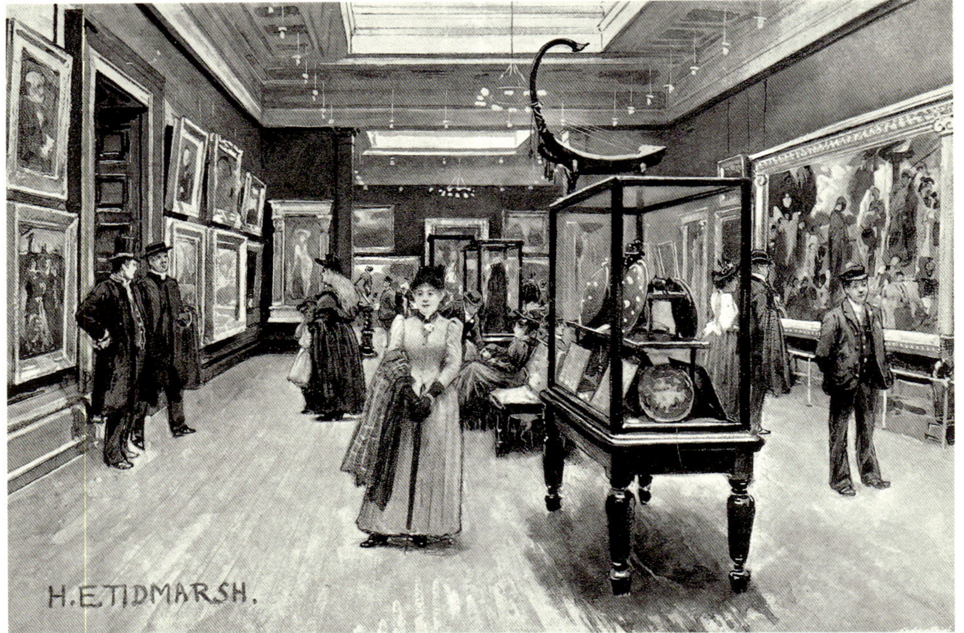

Manchester City Art Gallery, interior, 1894

From volume 3 of Cassell's *Manchester Old and New* (1896).

[15] *Half-tone after pen and wash drawing, 165 × 240 mm*

sharply delineated and the subjects more acutely observed. One or two of the drawings anticipate the better work that was to come - the view of the interior of Manchester City Art Gallery, in particular.

It must have been the *Manchester Old and New* venture that inspired Tidmarsh to start recording the street life of London. In the early 1880s he had produced topographical watercolours in the vicinity of London. They had included one of Putney Bridge, now in the Museum of London collection, one of Northolt Church, now in the Greater London Record Office, views of Chingford Church and Hadley Church for the *Art Journal* (1884), and a series showing rural East End (the district now known as East Finchley) which are in the Archives and Local Studies department of Barnet Public Libraries. Arriving back in London in 1895, he embarked on recording London topography, Wren churches in particular. Surprisingly it was not the inside of the London churches where people worshipped that interested him, though these, particularly with the Wren churches, were certainly worth recording. It was their often less promising exteriors. For it was the exteriors that gave him the scope that he needed. Exteriors meant showing the season, the weather, the time of the day. Exteriors meant indicating the pace of life characteristic to that part of town. Above all exteriors meant people.

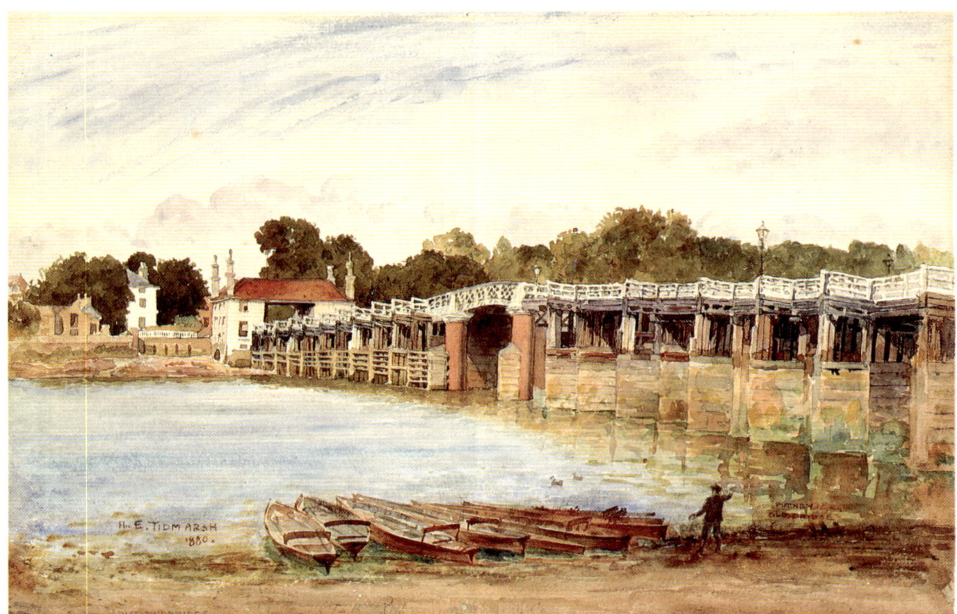

Putney Old Bridge, 1880

The bridge was rebuilt in stone 1884-1886.

[16] *Watercolour drawing, 446 × 365 mm*

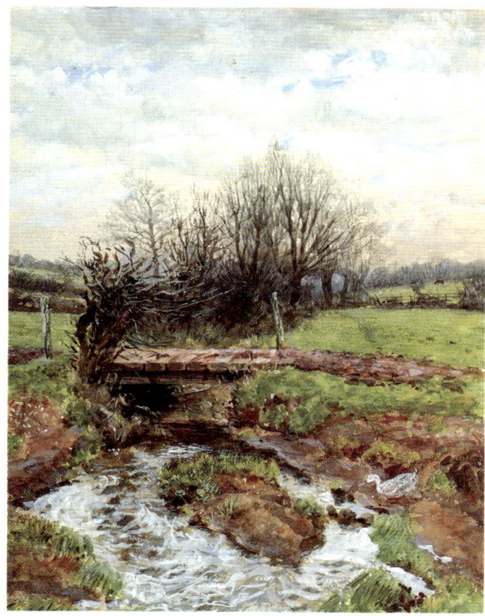

'Mymms', north of London, 1881

[17] *Watercolour, 290 × 230 mm*

There was nothing planned or systematic about Tidmarsh's series of London streets and churches. He appears to have done them when the spirit moved him - perhaps between commissions when he had time to spare. In a letter, J. L. Howgego, my predecessor as Keeper of Prints & Maps at Guildhall Library, remembers seeing H. E. Tidmarsh in action:

> 'I was a fourteen year old school-boy who on visits to the old [Guildhall] Art Gallery used to watch him sketching in Cheapside with his sketchboard slung round his neck and his paint box on a tray in front of him, while cart horses and motor buses sprayed him with mud as they rumbled past him in the rain!'

Very few of these London street scenes seem to have been sold. One or two of them were exhibited. It would seem he did them for pleasure, not for profit, and that he kept them because he liked them and they gave him pleasure too. There was no publication in prospect.

If we can consider the London churches and street views a series, then we can certainly consider his long views of London's townscape a series too. It is possible that these really were intended for publication. According to a member of the family, Joseph Swain & Son, who undertook colour printing for the *Illustrated London News* and whose works for colour printing were at High Barnet, reproduced several of Tidmarsh's long views of London, and also a long view that he made of Hong Kong from photographs. (I have not found any of Swain's reproductions unless a long view of the Bank, Royal Exchange, and Mansion House in the Guildhall Library collection is one of them). His roof-top view of Westminster looking north east (c.1913) [117] has a note on the support which says 'the copyright sold to Robinsons of Bristol for reproduction….' A long view entitled 'Tower Bridge and London' (1930) [139] belonging to Archway Methodist Central Hall carries a pencilled note: 'First study for the careful drawing afterwards reproduced in three colour.'

A third 'series' were his views of Gothic cathedrals. Every autumn, according to the family, when the leaves had fallen from the trees and the architectural detail was no longer obscured by foliage, he set off for a cathedral city and painted the cathedral. Cathedral drawings found in researching this book include Wells, Norwich, Lincoln, Ely, Durham, and Canterbury.

'Oranges and Lemons', 1929

With characteristic Tidmarsh border drawn on the window mount.

[18] *Six watercolour drawings mounted as one, 374 × 899 mm (overall)*

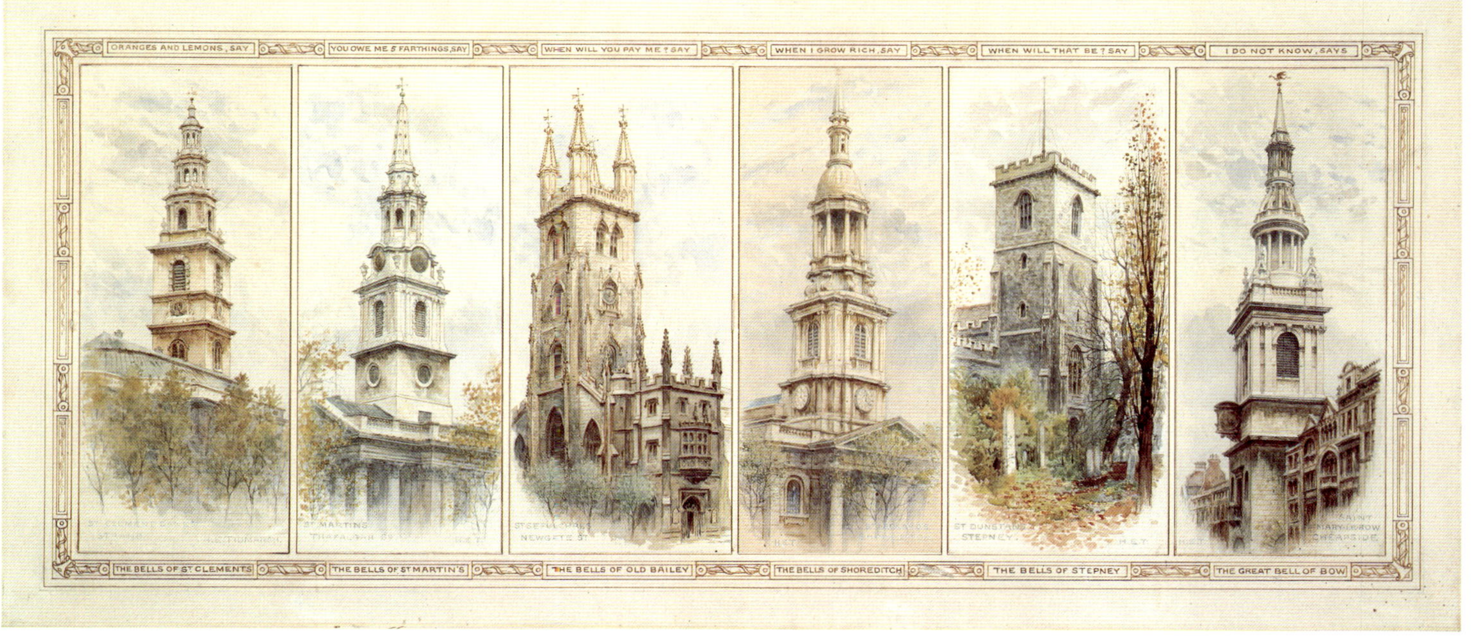

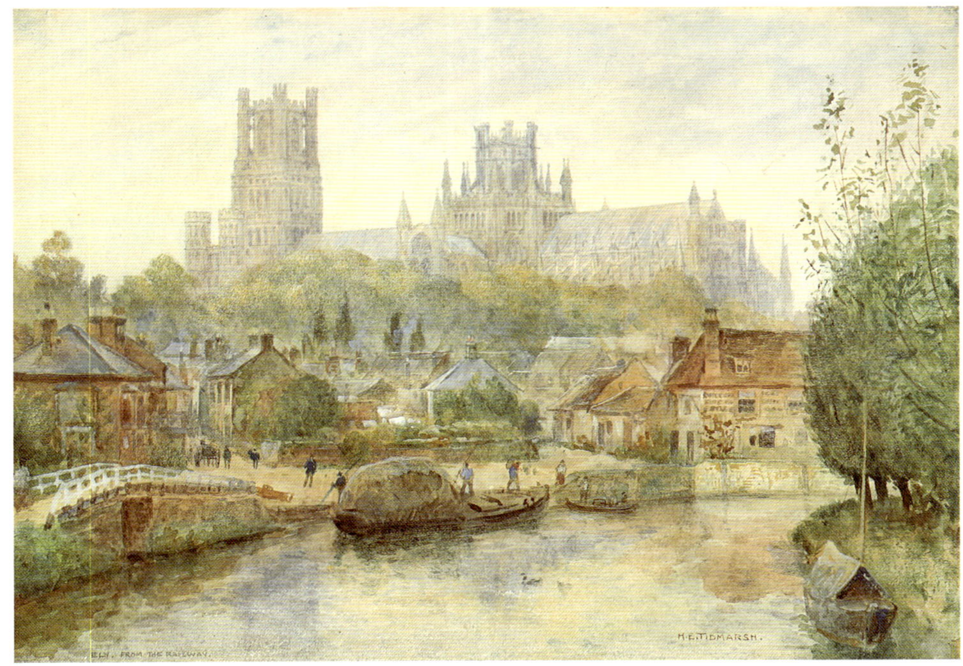

'Ely from the Railway', undated

[19] *Watercolour drawing, 276 × 387 mm (sight)*

Surviving watercolours demonstrate Tidmarsh's passion for foreign travel. These we can consider a fourth major category of his output. He paid frequent visits to Switzerland, France, Belgium, Holland, Spain, and Italy, repeatedly seeking out the cathedral cities. In 1895 he travelled to the United States where he visited and recorded the Niagara Falls and Saratoga Springs. He seems to have visited relatives (offspring from his father's brother, William) in Seattle.

A Tidmarsh watercolour drawing is incomplete without its distinctive gilded Tidmarsh frame. Henry would have learnt something of the craft of carpentry at his father's works in Islington. He now applied it to his art, and for the rest of his life made all frames for his drawings himself. A Tidmarsh frame is ornamented with gesso work. The date of the drawing is often modelled into the moulding at top centre, and a short title at bottom centre. His long watercolours often have mounts with decorative borders, drawn in sepia ink, and in these appear identifications of the principal landmarks. They are curious, but have a certain charm.

Tidmarsh was also concerned with how pictures were hung. He wrote a letter to *The Times* (14 July 1928) in which he compared hanging practices in Britain and the Netherlands. He had noticed that in the Netherlands important pictures were tilted towards the light. That is how they should be hung in Britain, he contended. And pictures should be hung lower than was customary in Britain, so as to be on the line of sight. In Britain pictures were invariably glazed; dark oil paintings became mirrors. He suggested at least occasionally removing the glass.

From time to time Tidmarsh exhibited in various British shows: the Royal Society of British Artists; the Royal Institute of Painters in Water Colours; the Dudley Gallery; and the Royal Academy. In all he exhibited twenty watercolours at R.A. summer shows. He contributed an article for *The Times* (29 April 1896) on Artists' Day at the Royal Academy. On this day artists whose work has been selected for the R.A.'s Summer Exhibition can come in and varnish their pictures. It is good descriptive journalism, conveying the bustle and the excitement of the occasion. As in his drawings it is the behaviour of individual human beings that matter.

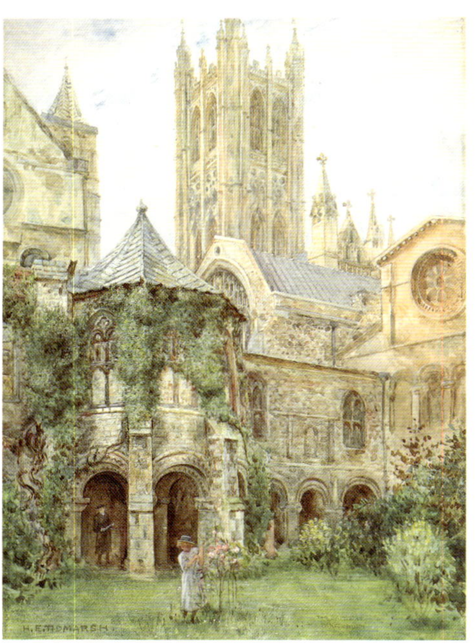

'The Baptistry, Canterbury', undated

[20] *Watercolour drawing, 381 × 273 mm (sight)*

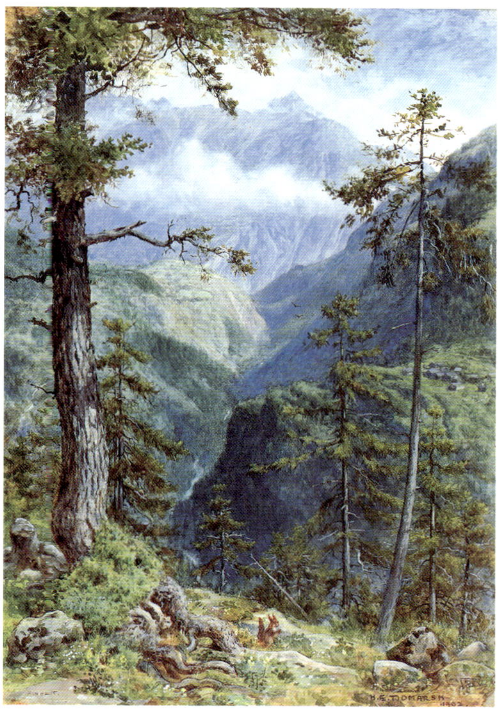

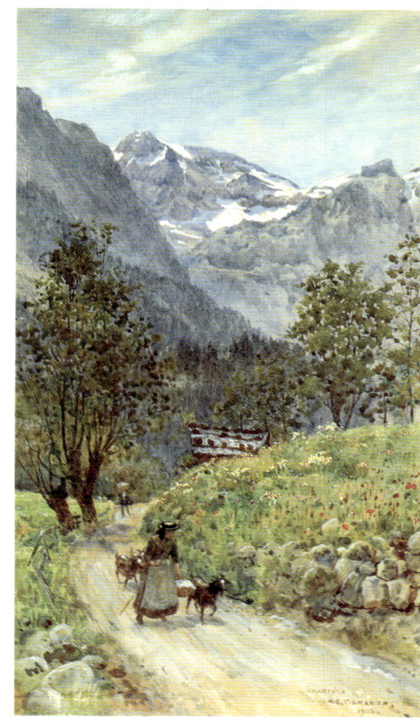

Finhaut, Switzerland, 1902

[21] *Watercolour drawing, 391 × 268 mm (sight)*

Champéry, Switzerland, 1902
(far right)

[22] *Watercolour drawing, 397 × 220 mm (sight)*

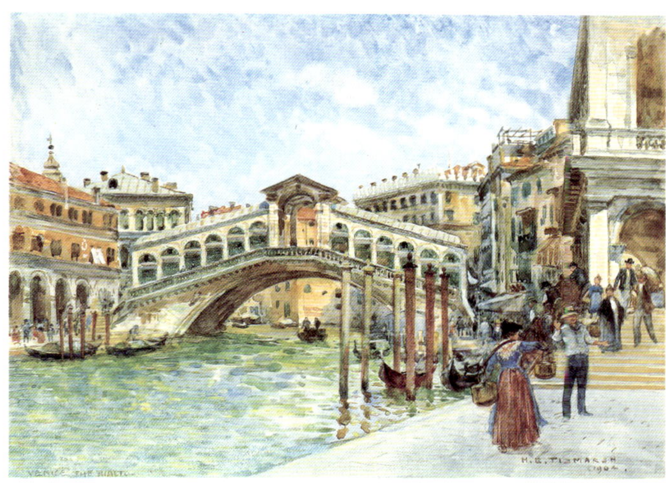

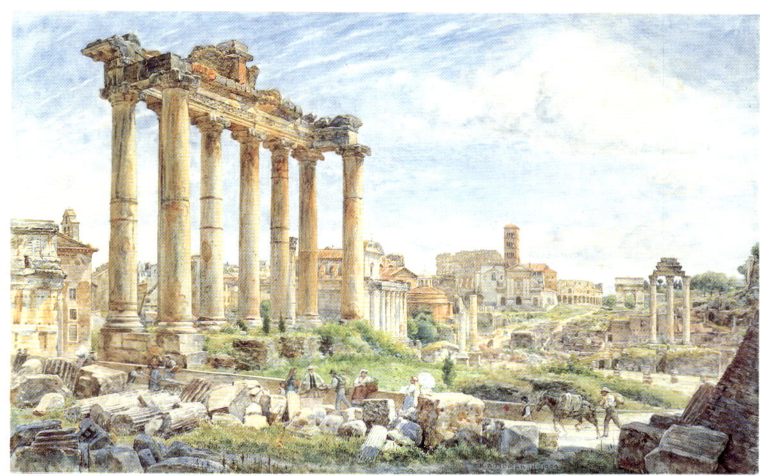

'Venice - The Rialto', 1904

[23] *Watercolour drawing, 207 × 281 mm (sight)*

The Forum, Rome, 1904
(far right)

[24] *Watercolour drawing, 366 × 560 mm*

Sheets from the official catalogue were set out on a trestle table in the entrance hall. Artists had to consult these to discover where their pictures were hung. Tidmarsh noted the position of his picture - in that year, 1896, he had submitted a watercolour of Westminster Abbey [116] - and mounted the stairs. Having shown his card to the porter at the top, he passed into the laughing, bowing, painting throng. In the centre of each room was a rough table covered in paint boxes. An artist was standing on a tall step ladder painting strength into a grey sky of a dark picture. Hung up near the skylight the soft effect of his image had been entirely lost. He was doing what he could to improve its looks from the floor which was so far below. One R.A. was painting in delicate clouds with his finger. Another had brought studies of figures and foliage, and was copying these on to his picture to finish the bits with which he was still unhappy.

'The courtly President is seen strolling through the rooms, and chatting with a few of his particular friends. Flat-brimmed French denote the presence of exhibitors from across the Channel. Pretty and fascinating misses flirt with susceptible and enthusiastic youths. Grey business-like matrons seek out their friends or scrub on varnish... Old men peer into their canvases and scrape off defects as contentedly as though in the quiet of their own homes. The smaller army of water-colourists, architects, etc. survey their productions, often regretting that

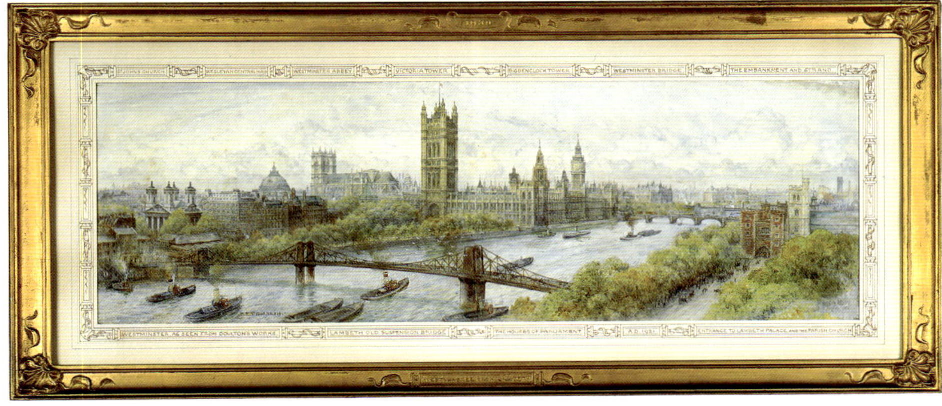

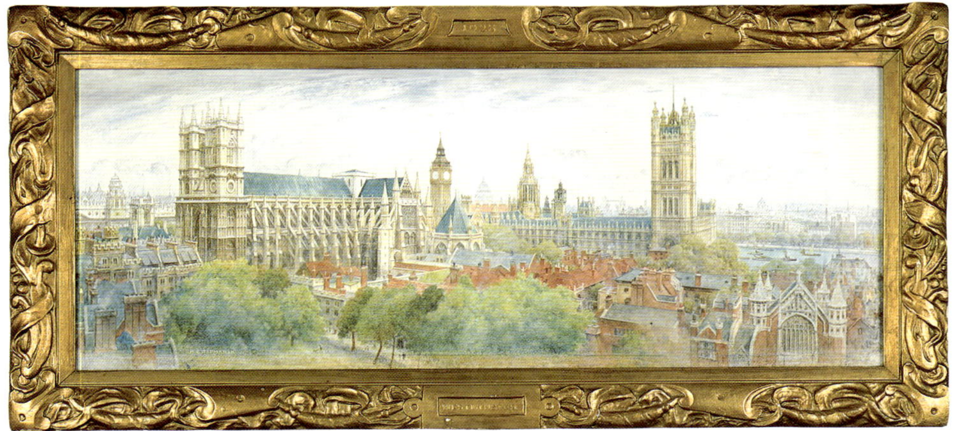

Examples of frames designed and made by H. E. Tidmarsh

[25/26]

they also cannot put on some finishing touches which the strong top light makes desirable, but which the covering glass makes impossible....' Tidmarsh was surprised by the number of women present on this occasion. Was it their colourful dresses that made them seem more numerous than they were? Or did as many women come to Artists' Day now as men? If this was the case, how was it the Royal Academy still had no women R.A.s or A.R.A.s? Dame Laura Knight would become the first woman R.A. in 1936.

On 8 May 1902, H.E. Tidmarsh, now aged forty-eight, was married. His bride, Ellen Louise ('Nellie') Tidmarsh, was a nurse. Henry made the wedding ring. The ceremony took place at the Baptist chapel in Holloway Road where Nellie was a Sunday school teacher. Nellie was the daughter of Henry's Uncle William, and thus Henry's first cousin. The two had been devoted to each other for years. Nellie shared Henry's passion for foreign travel: she had visited Fiji just after Christianity had seen off cannibalism. Both had a special rapport with children. Because of the blood relationship, marriage was sensibly delayed till Nellie could no longer have children. They moved to 20 Marriott Road in Barnet.

A copy of S. H. Widdicombe's *A Chat About Barnet and its History* (Barnet: Cowing & Son 1912) in the family's collection, has been extra-illustrated by Tidmarsh with pencil and watercolour sketches of local landmarks - Old Fold Manor House, the Boys' Grammar School, East Barnet Church Gate, Lawn House, and Christ Church in St Albans Road. At High Barnet Methodist Church Tidmarsh painted sepia frescoes representing the life and teaching of Christ. Sadly they have not survived, but the mural Tidmarsh is seen painting in the photographic portrait on page viii was probably one of them. It visually represents a passage of Scripture beloved of teetotallers - the first epistle of St Peter, chapter four, in which an early Christian community is enjoined to partake in Christ's sufferings, rejecting 'lasciviousness, lusts, excess of

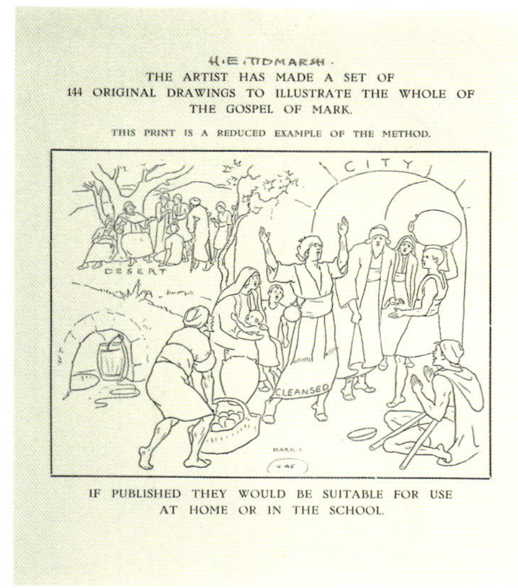

Handbill announcing Tidmarsh's intended gospel narrative cards

[27]

wine, revellings, banquetings, and abominable idolatries.' Like many Methodists of the time Tidmarsh was a dedicated teetotaller. He enrolled in the Barnet Temperance Council, and involved himself in providing the village with a well-equipped coffee tavern, a small but thoroughly practical way, as he saw it, of combatting the drink evil. On Sundays Tidmarsh ran a Bible class for young men at High Barnet Methodist church. During the week he instructed them in woodcarving and metalwork.

For Henry, art was a gift God had given him. It had to be put to His service. His niece, Dorothy Hallett, the daughter of Tidmarsh's elder sister, Jane, later recalled in five pages of 'Recollections' how Uncle Henry would sit at the Sunday dinner table with a large pad, water, and black paint, hastily finishing the pictures to illustrate his Sunday school lessons. 'I also recall larger work on a blackboard with which he illustrated his talks to the large Sunday school. He actually worked on these as he talked, as some artists do nowadays on television [e.g. Rolf Harris]. That certainly kept the attention.' We get some idea of his teaching style from the gospel narrative cards which he produced in large numbers. These he regarded as his most important works of art. They are full of conspiratorial fun - children and teacher are on the same side - and hidden messages abound, conveying the evil of drink, the wrongfulness of ill-distributed wealth ('Woe unto ye that are rich'), and the wickedness of war. They are certainly not to the modern taste, but to see them as a waste of an able artist's talent is entirely to misunderstand the Methodist spirituality of the time, and the priorities of an artist who was a committed Christian and Socialist. There were 144 original outline drawings to illustrate Mark's Gospel - these were left to the National Sunday School Union - and 244 to illustrate Luke. The Luke drawings, in a package neatly tied with string, are with a member of the Tidmarsh family. The package is urgently inscribed, 'VALUABLE DRAWINGS', and is addressed 'To any possible publisher in England or America.' The outlines were intended for parents and Sunday school teachers. Children could colour them. Tidmarsh explains:

'Every point in the narrative is introduced, and in such detail that it generally takes several sheets to illustrate each story. This has the merit of keeping the attention of the children. A picture that only suggests many things is often better than a highly finished painting, with nothing left to imagine.... H.E. Tidmarsh is not so anxious to make money out of them as to get the whole set completely published for the use of teachers - probably loose, not bound.'

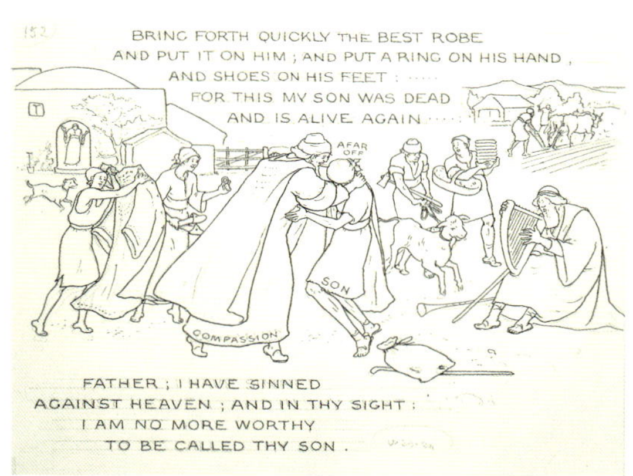

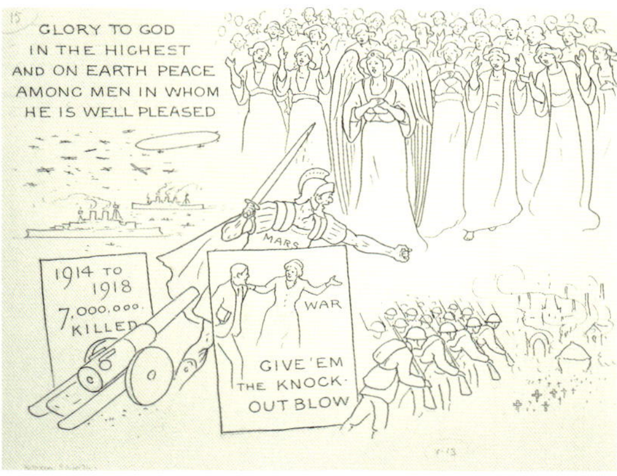

Examples of Tidmarsh's intended gospel narrative cards.

[28/29] *Ink outline on pencil, 240 × 316 mm (each)*

Henry's father, meanwhile, had retired, and with his wife had moved back to Icomb, the village he had left at the age of one. Their Cotswold home was called 'Vine Cottage' - it still has a vine growing across the front of it. In reality it was a sizeable house rather than a cottage. The village seems to have been caught in a time warp. Men still wore smocks for work, and milkmaids wore yokes to carry their pails. Children still bobbed and curtsied when the gentry spoke to them. The Tidmarshes, however, had advanced up the social ladder since their exodus some eighty years earlier. Henry's mother held tea parties in the orchard.

Henry and Nellie visited 'Vine Cottage' from time to time, and Henry got to know the squire and the parson. He encouraged the young men of the village to form a club in order to acquire musical instruments. The family's friend and 'help', Miss Ashdown, features in a pen and wash drawing, preparing a fire in 'Vine Cottage' [30]. Henry produced a drawing showing 'The Back of Vine Cottage & Church', and another which he classified as Category I, 'Icomb, 1908.'

The Tidmarshes' idyllic life was rudely jolted in 1914 by the outbreak of war. Henry's pacifist opinions were genuine and there was no room at all for compromise. Once more a Tidmarsh felt compelled to follow his conscience. Henry was unable to keep his opinions to himself - at this moment large numbers of young male I.L.P. members were being imprisoned for noncooperation. Members of the family became alarmed and embarrassed by the vigour with which he expressed his decidedly unfashionable feelings, and worried for his safety. Nellie persuaded him that till the war was over they should live with his parents at 'Vine Cottage.' At Icomb Henry was kept away from newspapers. He busied himself with projects intended to improve the villagers' lot, and grew food in the garden that he could distribute to needy locals. Henry's father died in 1915. Whilst at Icomb Henry painted at least two portraits of his mother, Caroline Tidmarsh. She died in 1916 at the age of 94.

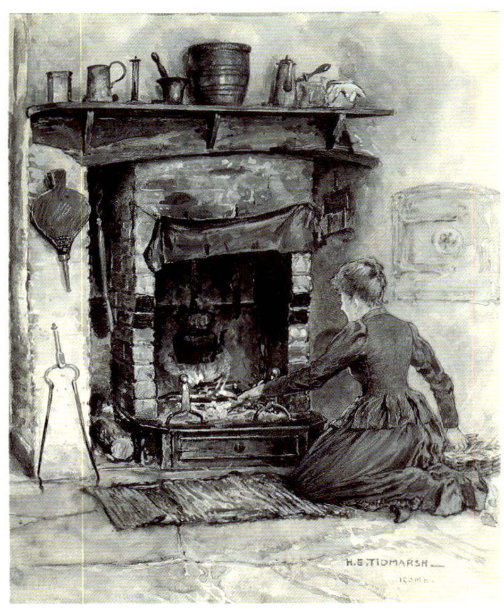

Making up the fire at 'Vine Cottage', Icomb, 1892

[30] *Wash drawing, heightened with body colour, 290 × 203 mm*

Following the declaration of peace the Tidmarshes returned to London, purchasing in c.1924 a three-storeyed terraced house at 48 Church Crescent, Muswell Hill. This was to be their home for the rest of their lives, and it is this house that is vividly remembered by several members of the various branches of the Tidmarsh family. On the ground floor were living rooms, and a workshop where Tidmarsh applied himself to metalwork and where he made his own very individualistic picture frames [25/26]. The studio was on the first floor. Framed watercolours lined the walls from ceiling to floor with little space in between them. The panels of the doors were decorated with biblical scenes. Above the couple's bed was a floating ceiling in which appeared the words of the Lord's Prayer, reminding the couple to make their devotions when they retired and when they woke up in the morning.

By all accounts, 48 Church Crescent was not a comfortable place. Henry had been a bachelor too long and it was difficult for him to break his bachelor habits. It was very much a bachelor's home, and reflected his interests and attitudes. It was thoroughly unpretentious.

Henry and Nellie Tidmarsh were not wealthy. Occasionally Henry would pay the bills by offering watercolours in lieu of cash. At the same time he was always alive to the needs of others. He made it his duty to go collecting door to door for the Methodists' National Children's Home. At Christmas it was his practice to buy a gargantuan turkey, carve slices onto grease-proof paper, and take it round to the poor.

Nellie Tidmarsh died on 2 October 1932. The funeral took place at the Friends Meeting House, Muswell Hill. Henry reorganised his home, making the top storey available for tenants. He presented two finished drawings of the India Museum and the South Kensington Museum to the Victoria & Albert Museum. And it was at this point too that he presented 176 drawings, including thirty of his finest and most vigorous watercolour drawings - those of the London churches - to Guildhall Library. The Corporation of London were delighted by the gift, and celebrated it by holding an exhibition of the church drawings in the Guildhall Art Gallery. This was the first exhibition of Tidmarsh's work to be held, and the first opportunity the public had been given to see most of his best watercolours. The *Times* (7 June 1934) carried a lengthy review. The writer remarked on the accuracy of Tidmarsh's draughtsmanship, the beauty of his colouring, and his mastery of atmospheric effect:

'Every one of Mr Tidmarsh's pictures is obviously the result of intimate study [he enthused]. There can be few pictures, be they oil or watercolours, which for accuracy of representation, quality of colouring, and sensitiveness to the relationship between bricks or stone, and the effects of light and shadow, can compete with these. They all seem to be of the same high quality and level of achievement, whether Mr Tidmarsh is treating the red-brick of St Benet's Paul's Wharf, or the stonework of St Mary-le-Strand; whether he is representing the combination of the two, as in the entrance to Christ Church, Newgate Street, or the lights and shadows about the portico of St Paul's Covent Garden, or the exquisite beauty that resides in the steeples of St Bride or St Mary-le-Bow, or the more archaic charm of the Temple Church and the gothic with which Wren clothed the steeples of St Dunstan-in-the-East and St Mary Aldermary, and St Michael Cornhill.'

Tidmarsh's drawings, the reviewer found, revealed beauties that could elude the eye when one looked at the actual objects.

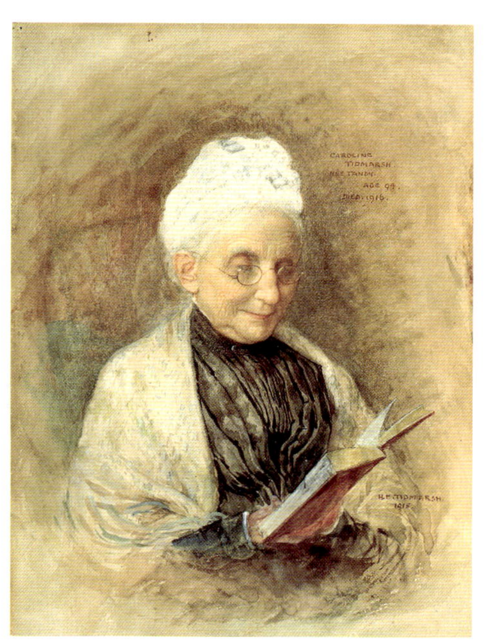

Henry's mother, Caroline Tidmarsh, née Tandy, aged 94, 1915

[31] *Watercolour drawing, 308 × 221 mm*

In 1936, Dorothy Hallett compiled a manuscript catalogue of the principal watercolour drawings - those hanging on the walls - at 48 Church Crescent, assigning each a correct title and providing dimensions. With Uncle Henry's approval she classified them into categories according to their 'general value' - I, II, and III. One hundred and sixty three drawings appear in this catalogue.

In 1935 Tidmarsh, now aged 80, embarked on his last big assignment - painting frescoes on walls in the recently opened Archway Methodist Central Hall, Upper Holloway. The new building was paid for by J. Arthur Rank, a keen Methodist. Its style was mildly art deco, and it resembled a J. Arthur Rank cinema. Indeed it had all the elements of one. A screen could be let down behind the pulpit, and behind the gallery there was a fully equipped projection room. The decoration in a border around the skylight in the ceiling is distinctly Tidmarshian, resembling the sepia ink decorative borders the artist delighted in drawing on the mounts of his larger watercolours. The rooms which he decorated were in the Sunday School - the Beginners' Room on the first floor, and the Intermediates' Schoolroom (the 'Inters' Room') on the second. The theme was true discipleship, and this was expressed in the Inters' Room in sixteen panels. Great-nephews and nieces recall being taken to see Uncle Henry, and watching him at work standing on planks stretched across two step-ladders. Between the windows he painted St Paul, St Augustine, St Francis of Assisi, George Fox (founder of the Society of Friends), John Bunyan, John Wesley, and William Booth (founder of the Salvation Army) - a generously ecumenical selection. According to one account the frescoes in the Beginners' Room were still there in 1969. According to another and probably more reliable account they were scraped off or painted over several years earlier. (By the 1960s the Inters' Room was already serving as a store for Home Grown Cereals, and its frescoes forgotten). The minister tells me that a few older members of his congregation still remember the Beginners' Room frescoes with affection, and lament their disappearance.

The Second World War was approaching, and Tidmarsh was caught up in the confusion widespread amongst pacifists at this time. Pacifists had felt at home in the Independent Labour Party, but no longer. In their enthusiasm to stop the advance of Fascism the I.L.P. sent a contingent to Spain to fight against General Franco's Nationalist forces. It was not with the International Brigade that this contingent fought but with Anarchists and atheistic Trotskyites. None of this would have pleased Tidmarsh. He was leaving money to the I.L.P. but a codicil in his will cancelled it. He remained a Methodist until the end, but was increasingly attracted to the quiet services of the pacifist Society of Friends (Quakers). Nephews and nieces visiting him on Sundays were taken along to a Quaker Meeting

House most conveniently opened a few doors away in the same street. (The meeting house is still there; on Saturdays it is used by the Seventh Day Adventists).

Henry Tidmarsh died in his sleep on 19 March 1939, having reached the age of 85. Mercifully he was spared the invasion of Poland and the outbreak of the Second World War. Following a brief service at the Friends Meeting House at Muswell Hill he was buried in the Islington Cemetery at Finchley. Employees of Tidmarsh & Sons, the blind-makers of Islington, formed a guard of honour. A tablet to his memory was unveiled in May at the Archway Methodist Central Hall. Its inscription reads: 'In affectionate memory of HENRY TIDMARSH who taught Christian truths to children through the medium of his pictures.'

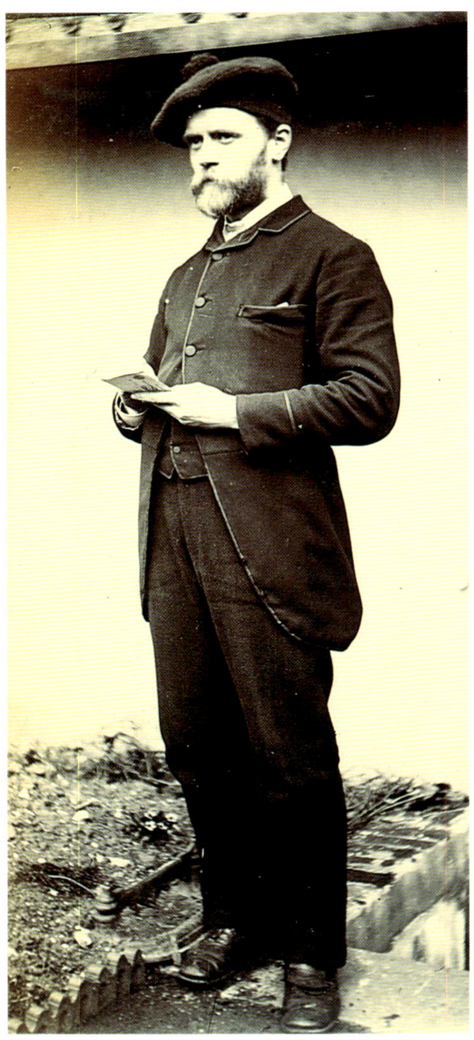

H. E. Tidmarsh, c.1900

[32] *Photograph probably taken by his brother, Thomas Tidmarsh*

Obituaries in the local newspapers and in the Methodist press described him as 'a man of real piety and utter conscientiousness, gentle, retiring, yet firm as a rock in his convictions.' Though he died over fifty years ago, those members of the family who were alive then still have vivid memories of him, climbing apple trees, riding his bicycle no hands, and getting them over excited and being chided by their parents for doing so. In the words of one of them, 'He was a thoroughly *good* man. He showed no *pride* in his art: he just enjoyed doing it.'

There were no clauses in Tidmarsh's will for the disposal of the drawings which filled 48 Church Crescent. Later in the year when a former teacher, Mrs Kathleen Duck, was buying the house, she found the walls still lined with the framed watercolours listed in Dorothy Hallett's catalogue. No doubt there were portfolios and sketchbooks in the house, too. Many of the framed items were distributed within the family. A view of Tower Bridge [139] listed by Dorothy Hallett hangs now at Archway Central Hall. A dozen more London drawings were handed to James Douthwaite, Librarian of Guildhall Library. He helped dispose of other items: 6 wash drawings of the interior of the South Kensington Museum were passed by Douthwaite to the Print Room of the Victoria & Albert Museum (they acquired 4 more in 1983), 21 vignettes of scenes in North Wales were sent to the National Library of Wales in Aberystwyth, and 189 sketches made by Tidmarsh during his trip to the Continent in 1886-1887 - including views of Montreux, the after-effects of the Riviera earthquake, and scenes in Rome - were passed to the Chief Librarian of Islington. (These Continental sketches can be consulted in the reference section of Islington Central Library). In 1945 two very large watercolour drawings of Fleet Street, looking respectively east and west, were presented to Guildhall Art Gallery by the widow of Henry's younger brother, Frederick.

The Guildhall Library's Tidmarsh watercolours have always excited interest. In 1992 the staff of the Print Room organised an exhibition of the Library's finest Tidmarsh watercolours which was held in the undercroft of St Mary Aldermanbury in Fulton, Missouri, and then at the Museum of London.

TIDMARSH'S LONDON

Tidmarsh recorded London during fifty years of radical change. The earlier London watercolours are of a horse-drawn city, and go as far as drawings are able to evoke the clatter and smells of late-Victorian street-life. Horse-drawn omnibuses, hansom cabs, landaus, and drays, gradually give way to motorcars and motorbuses. Networks of telegraph wires appear over the buildings.

Tidmarsh was a very able topographical artist with an especial interest in London churches, particularly those designed by Sir Christopher Wren. As a trained metal-worker he delights in showing City street lamps in all their splendid detail. What makes him rare and important, however, is his careful observation of the people who populate the streets, passing those splendid monuments of the past with scarcely a thought, preoccupied as they are with their own immediate business. People and vehicles when added to topographical drawings are called 'staffage.' Tidmarsh was truly a master of staffage.

Thus with H. E. Tidmarsh we can experience the streets of London at that time, with their fine buildings, certainly, but also with their bowler-hatted clerks, top-hatted stockbrokers, flower-girls, very vocal newspaper vendors, barristers, porters, costermongers, and the ubiquitous and necessary street orderly with his dustpan and brush.

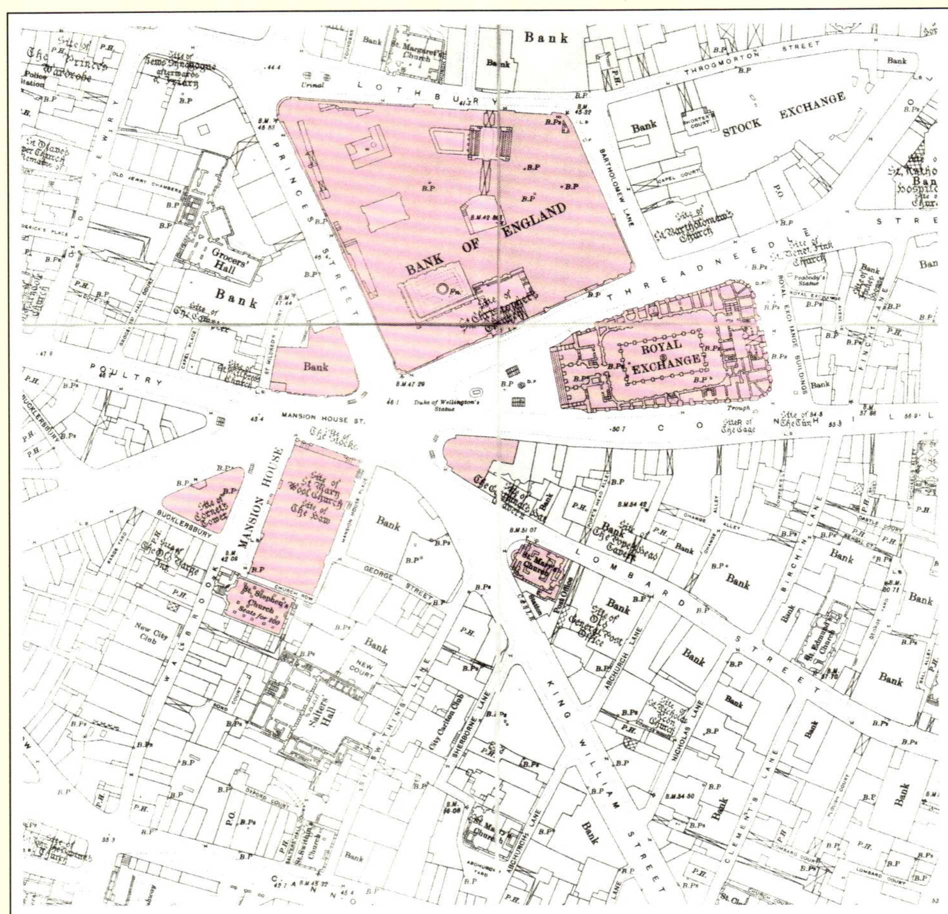

The Heart of the City

Detail from the Ordnance Survey Five Feet to One Mile Plan of London, V11.66, published 1916

St Stephen Walbrook *(right)*
[33] *Detail from plate 40*

The Heart of the City

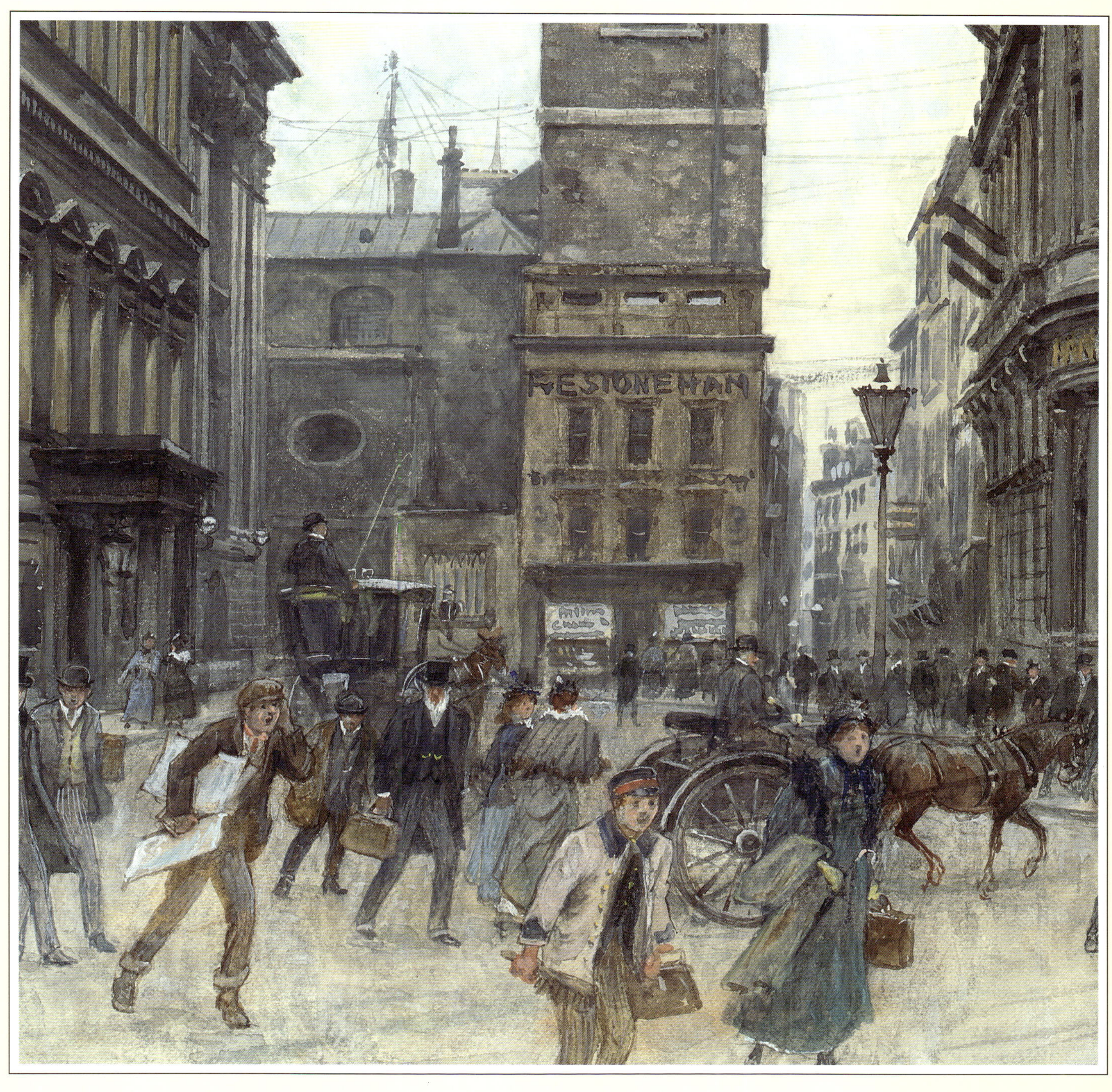

18 The Bank of England

1928

THE MANSION HOUSE STEPS

The Bank is viewed from the north end of Walbrook, with the Mansion House, the official residence of the Lord Mayor of London, on the right. On the left is the corner of the National Provincial Bank, Prince's Street, and an entrance to the Bank tube station. *Staffage:* a policeman, numerous pedestrians including a boy in knickerbockers, a small open motor car, and two omnibuses, one with a covered upper deck.

[34] *Watercolour drawing 380 × 265 mm*

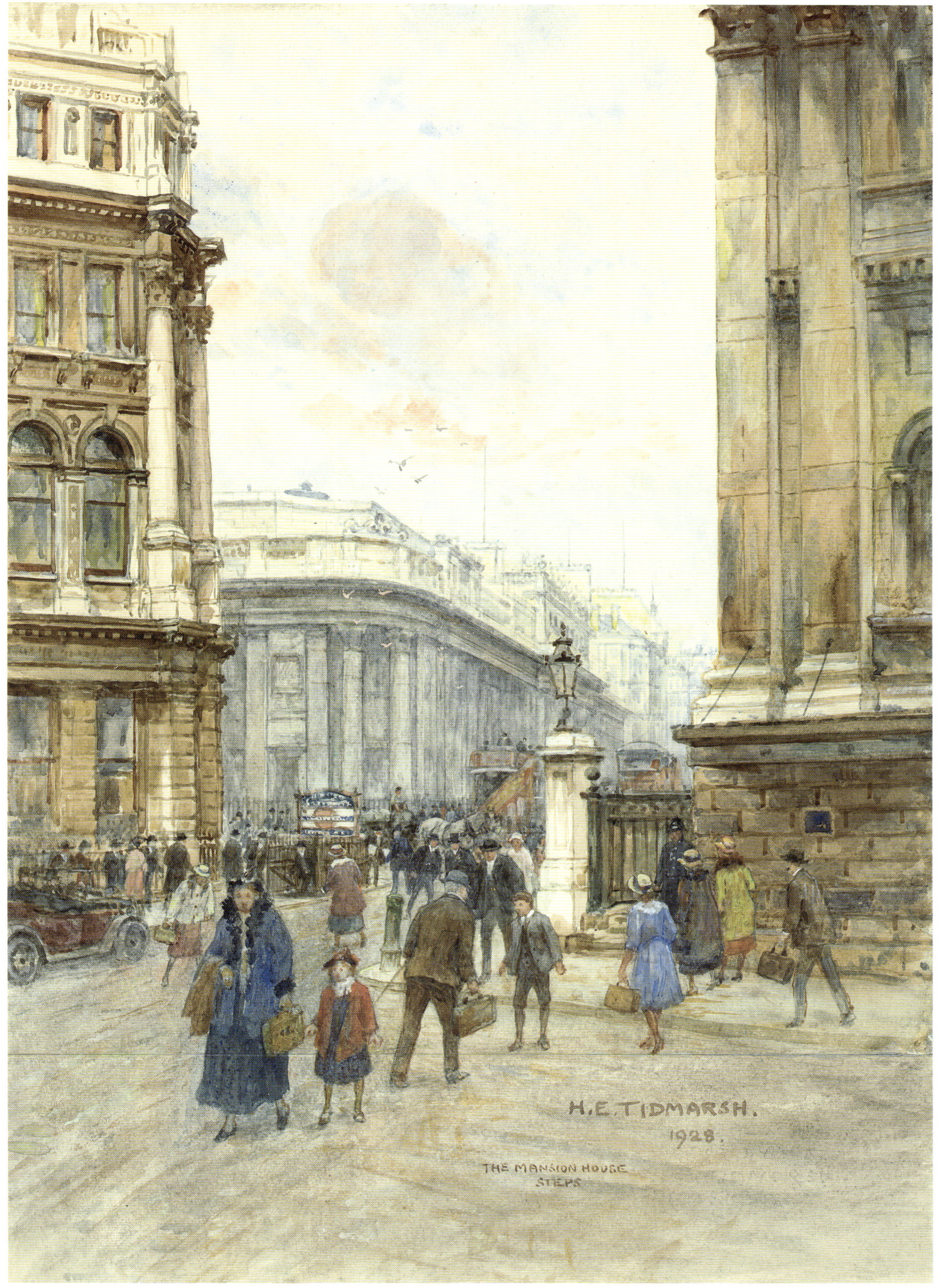
H.E. TIDMARSH.
1928.
THE MANSION HOUSE
STEPS

20 The Royal Exchange

c.1928

THE ROYAL EXCHANGE, LONDON (PAINTED ON THE SPOT)

View from Poultry showing the Princes Street corner of the Bank of England on the left, Threadneedle Street, and the Royal Exchange in the centre, and Cornhill with St Michael and the Globe Insurance Office on the right.

[35] *Watercolour drawing 252 × 385 mm (sight)*

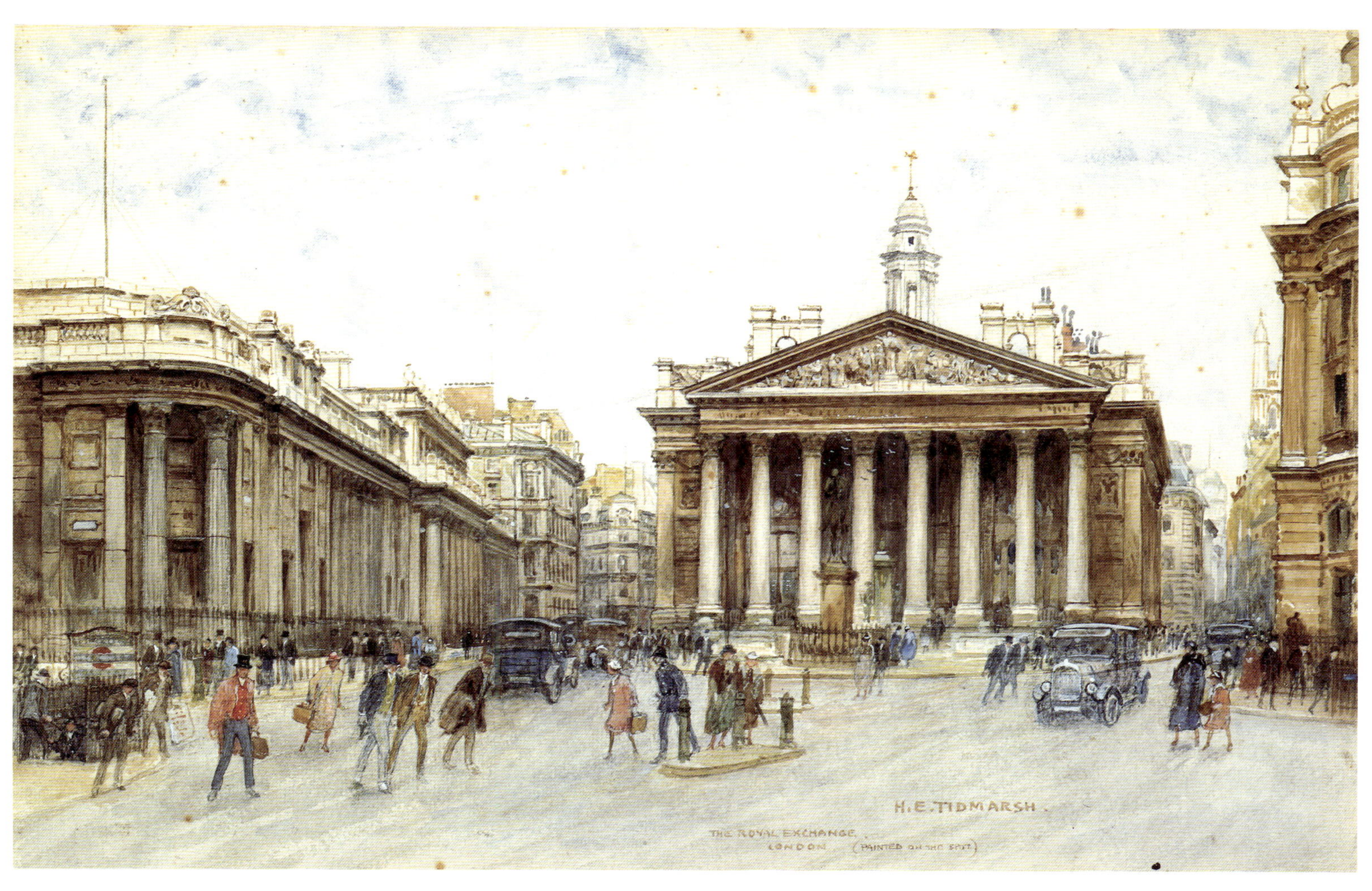
H.E. TIDMARSH.
THE ROYAL EXCHANGE.
LONDON. (PAINTED ON THE SPOT)

22 'Bank'

1927

OUTSIDE THE MANSION HOUSE, LONDON

The hub of the City of London, with half the facade of the Royal Exchange on the left, the Globe Insurance building in the centre, and the Mansion House on the right. In Cornhill, the street on the left, can be seen the Bank subway entrance, the spire of St Peter Cornhill, and the tower of St Michael Cornhill. In Lombard Street on the right are the churches of St Edmund the King and St Mary Woolnoth. *Staffage:* motorbus with a covered upper deck, a milk cart, private cars, a man with a coster's barrow, two postmen, a street sweeper, a policeman, and much else besides.

[36] *Watercolour drawing 280 × 390 mm*

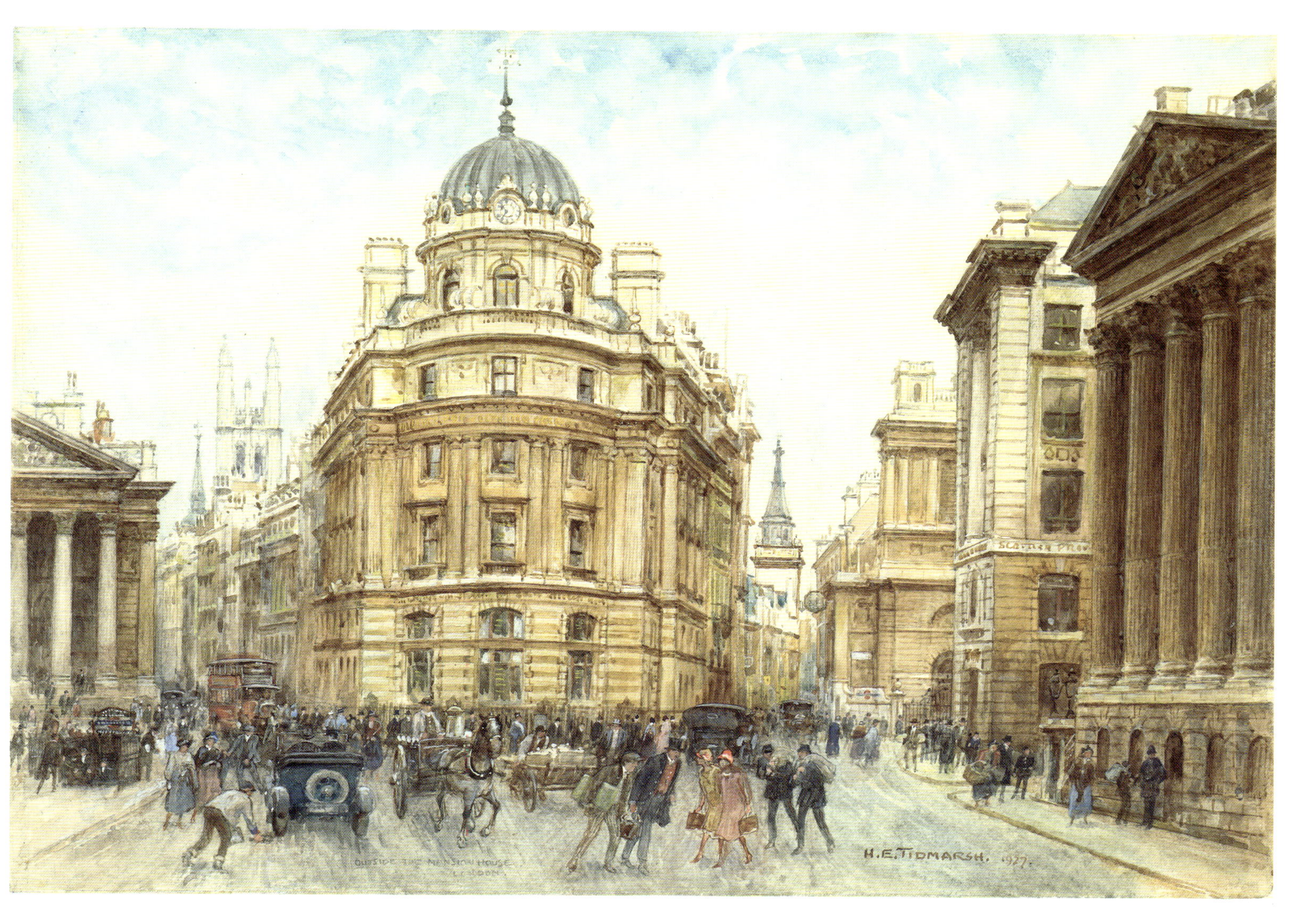
OUTSIDE THE MANSION HOUSE
LONDON
H.E. TIDMARSH. 1927.

24 St Mary Woolnoth

c.1896

ST MARY WOOLNOTH, KING WILLIAM STREET
(A HAWKSMOOR CH. 1716)

The west facade of the church, with vistas of Lombard Street to the left and King William Street to the right. *Staffage:* two horse buses, a hansom cab, a delivery cart, a newsvendor, a uniformed street cleaner, and top-hatted and bowler-hatted businessmen. In the foreground a nursemaid leads a small girl and holds a bouquet of flowers.

[37] *Watercolour drawing 385 × 270 mm*

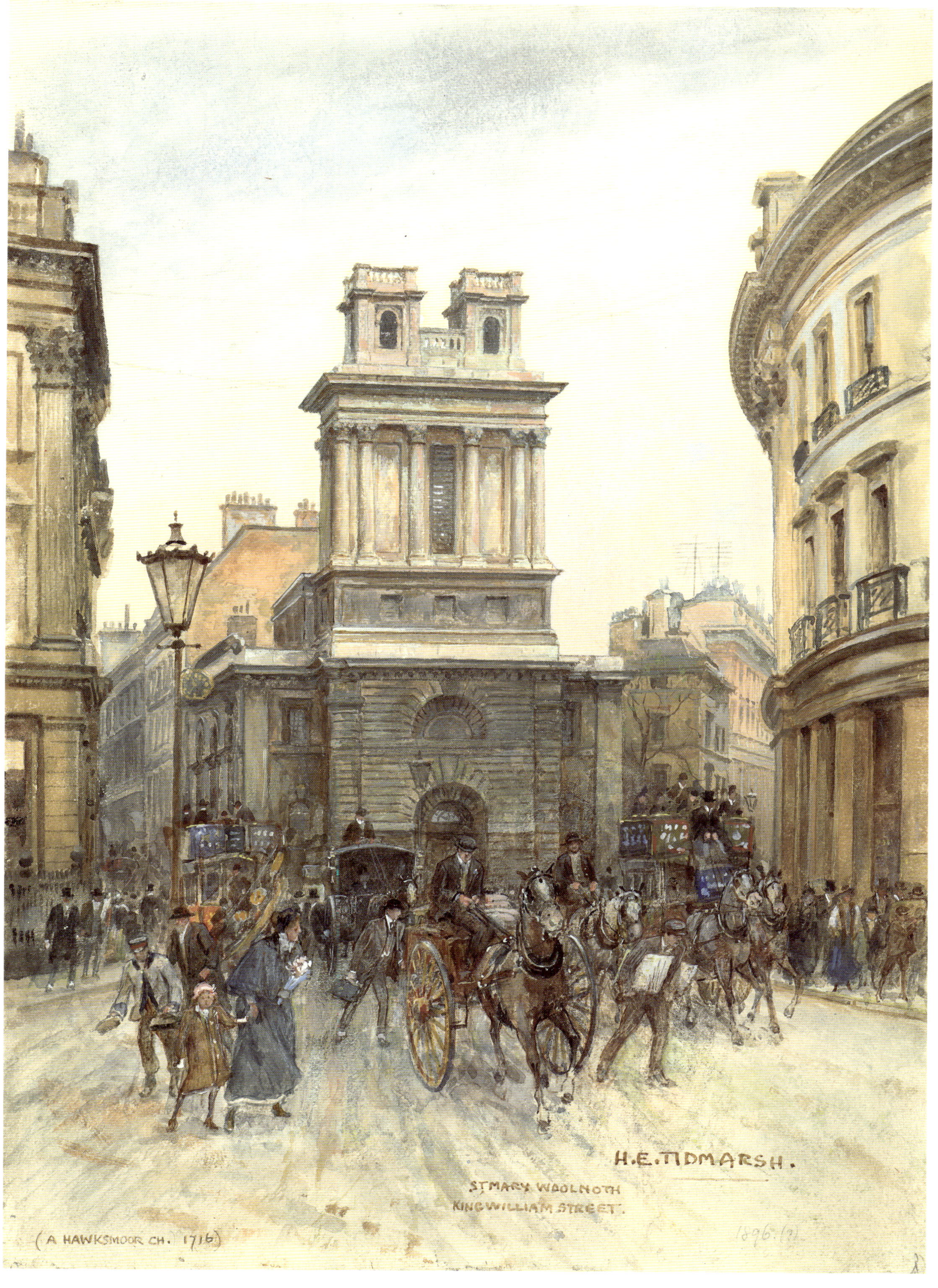
H.E. TIDMARSH.
ST MARY WOOLNOTH
KING WILLIAM STREET.
(A HAWKSMOOR CH. 1716)

The Mansion House

1927

THE MANSION HOUSE

View from Walbrook of the west side of the Mansion House with its impressive portico. Immediately beyond at no. 3 Lombard Street are the offices of the Scottish Provident Association, and beyond that can be identified the bracket clock fixed to the north face of St Mary Woolnoth. *Staffage:* a private car, a covered top bus, and pedestrians.

[38] *Watercolour drawing 278 × 252 mm*

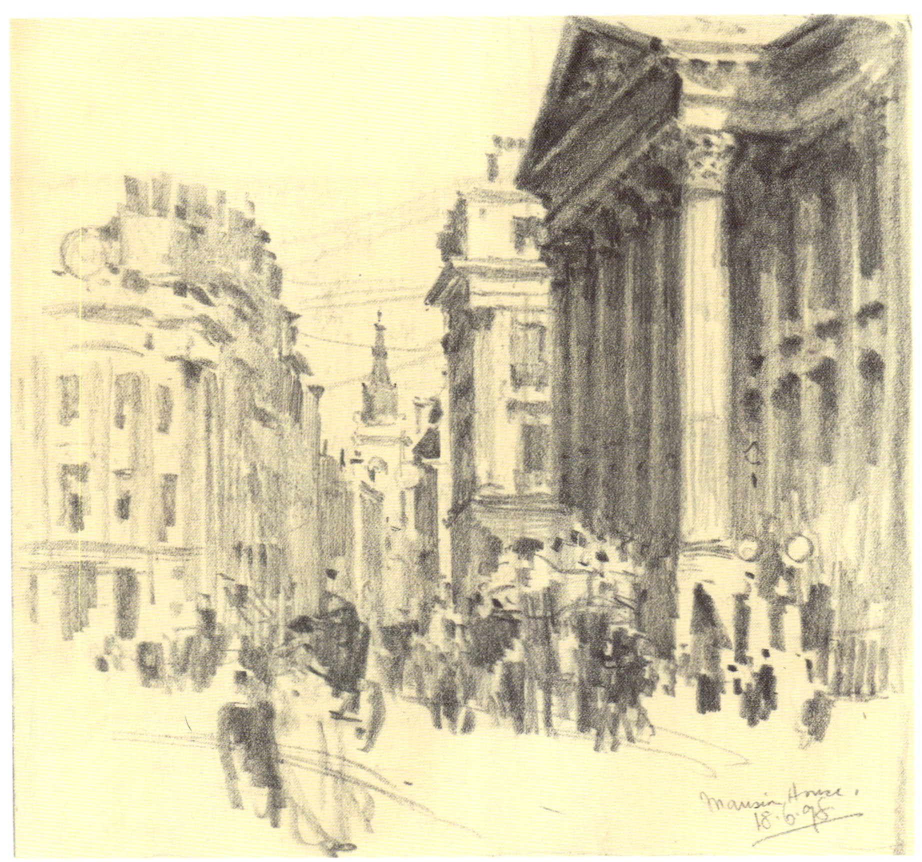

Mansion House, taken from virtually the same spot as for [38], 1898

[39] *Pencil sketch, 213 × 220 mm*

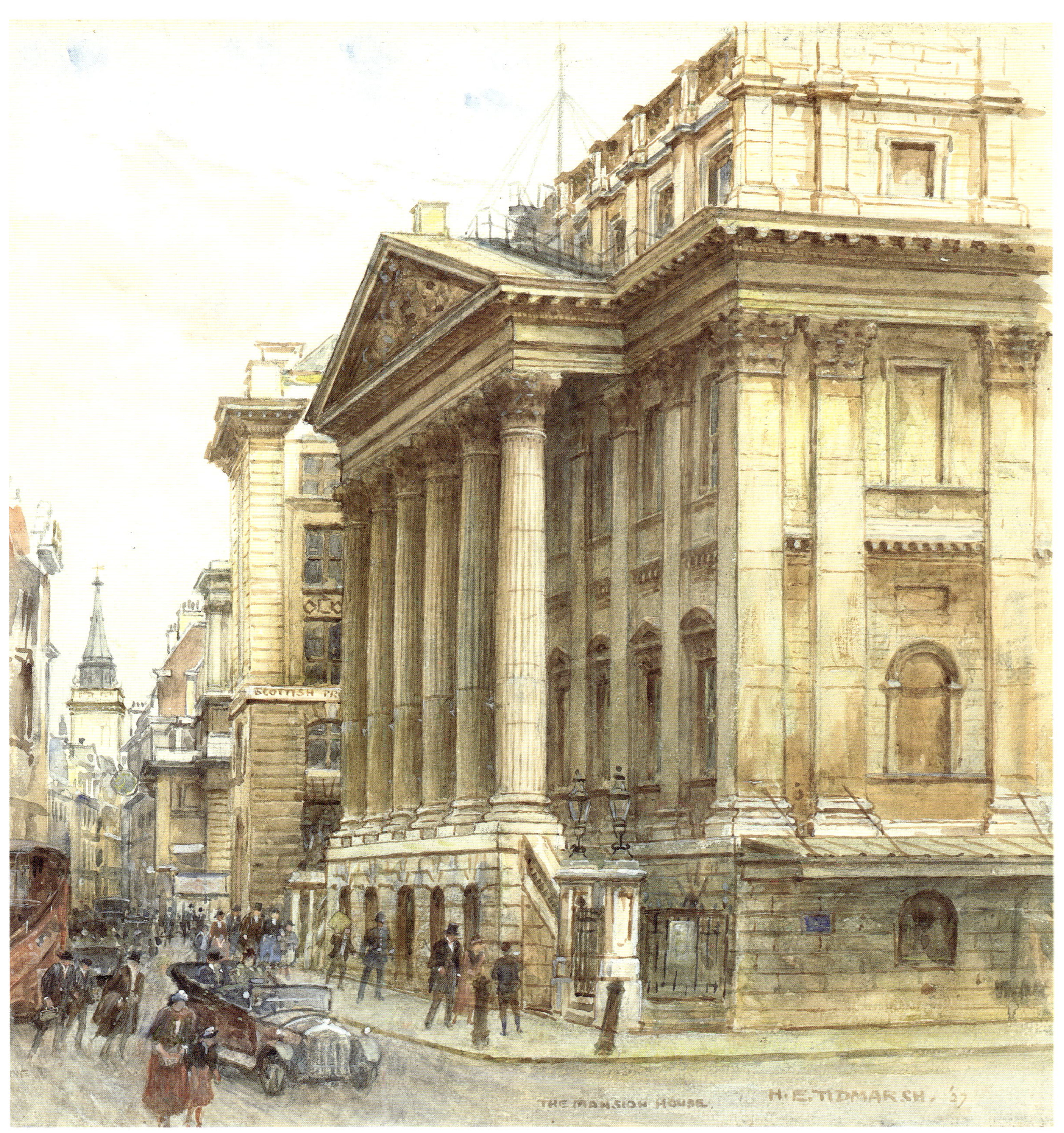
SCOTTISH PR
THE MANSION HOUSE
H.E.TIDMARSH. '27

St Stephen Walbrook

c.1895

ST STEPHEN WALBROOK AND MANSION HOUSE
A WREN CHURCH AND STEEPLE, 1672-9

The view down Walbrook, with the Mansion House on the left and St Stephen Walbrook beyond. The building on the right houses the Bank of New Zealand and the National Safe Deposit. Large mirrors attached to windows reflect light into offices. Above the roof tops can be seen a network of telegraph wires. It appears to be the morning rush hour; City businessmen scurry up Walbrook from Cannon Street Station. *Staffage:* a cab, a buggy, top-hatted and bowler-hatted gentlemen, a few women, a newsvendor, a uniformed street cleaner, and an errand boy.

[40] *Watercolour drawing 376 × 250 mm*

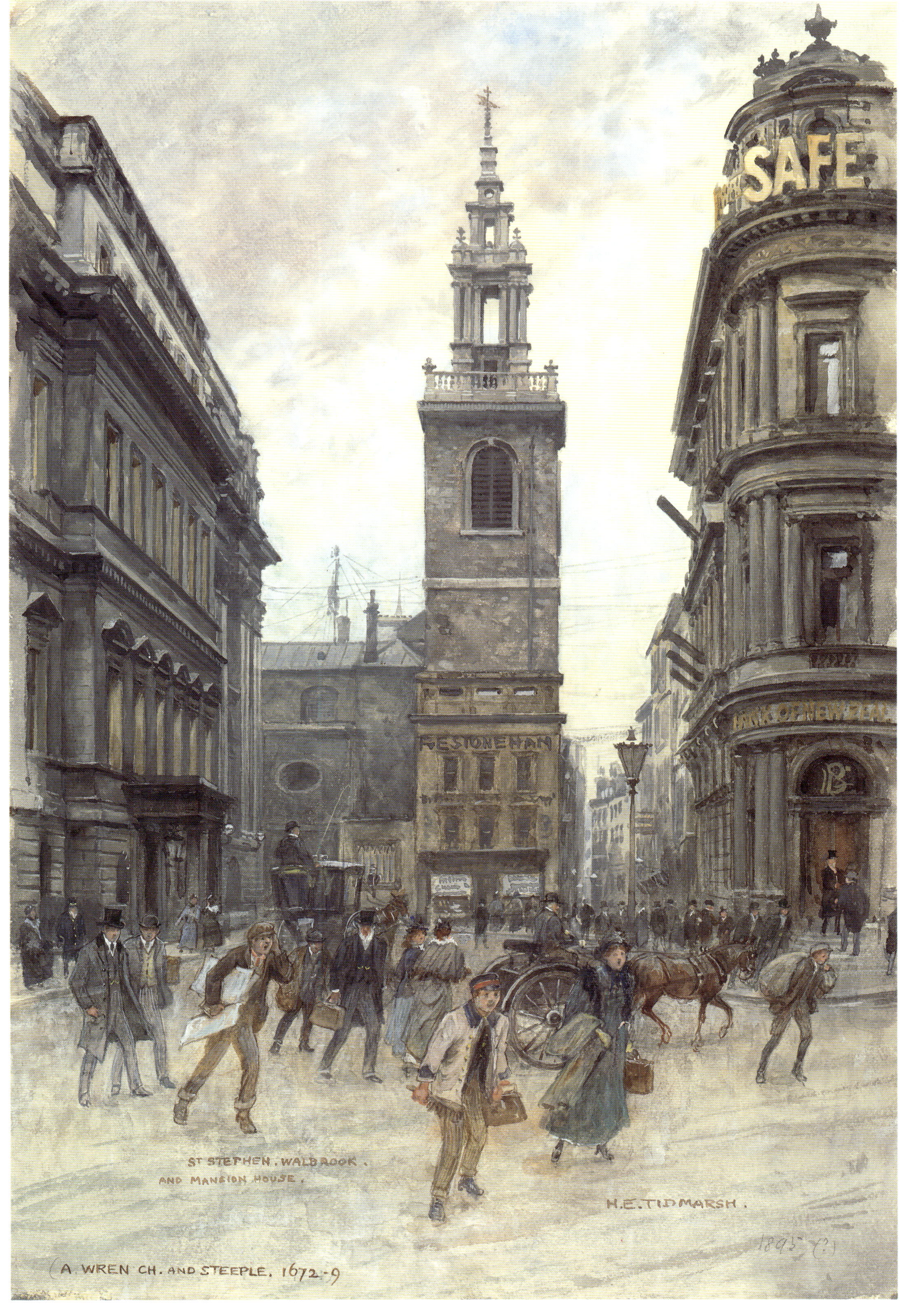
SAFE
ST STEPHEN, WALBROOK.
AND MANSION HOUSE.
H.E. TIDMARSH.
1895 (?)
(A. WREN CH. AND STEEPLE. 1672-9

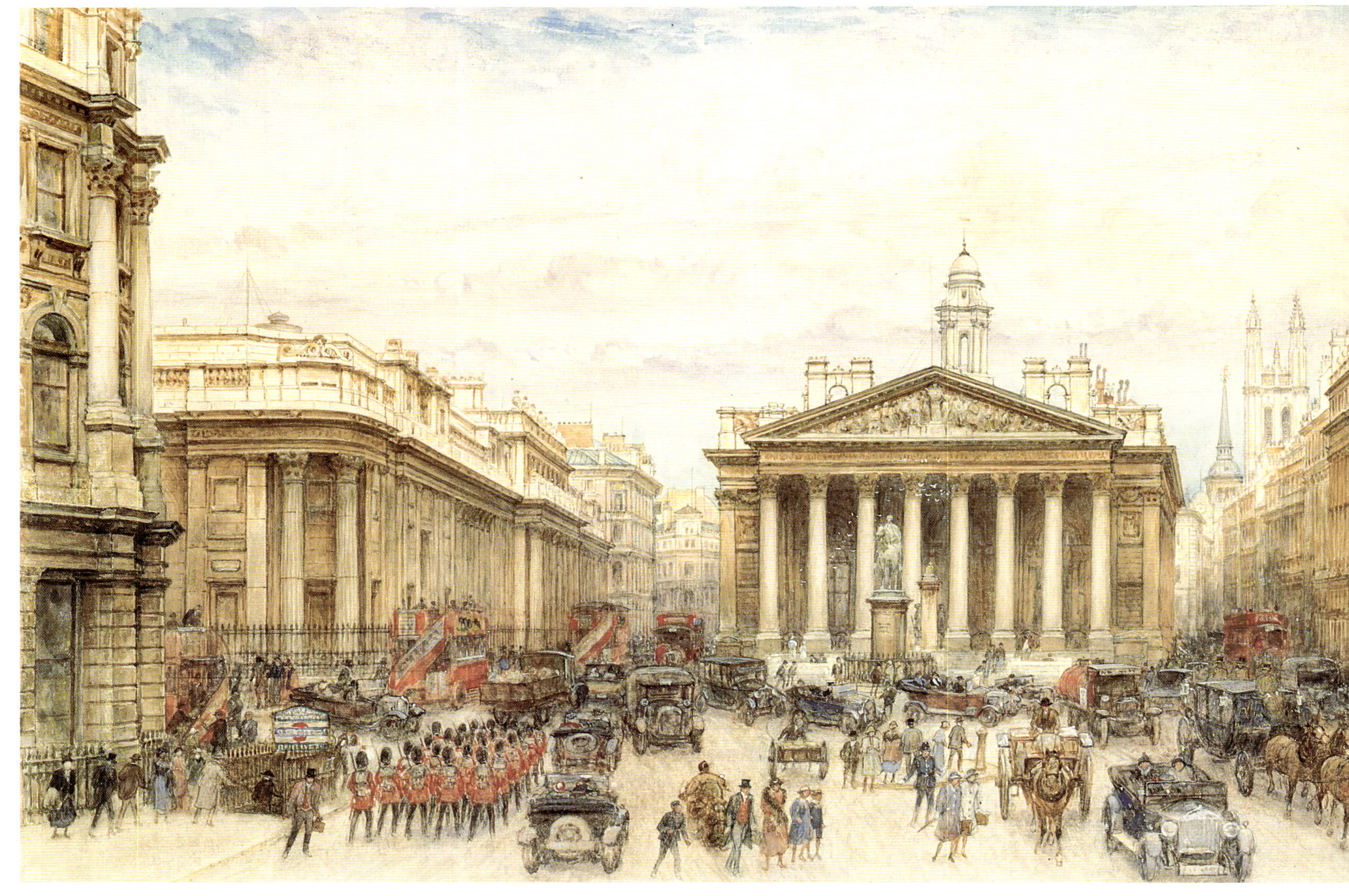

'Bank'

1927

THE HEART OF LONDON DEPICTED FROM CHEAPSIDE

The topography from left to right consists of the corner of the National Provincial Bank, Princes Street, the Bank of England, Threadneedle Street, the Royal Exchange, Cornhill with St Peter Cornhill and St Michael Cornhill, the Globe Insurance Office, Lombard Street with St Edmund the King and Martyr, St Mary Woolnoth, King William Street, the Monument, and the Mansion House. Guildhall Library has a contemporary colour art reproduction of this image, without imprint.

Staffage: advancing down Poultry towards the Bank of England, at an unlikely hour, is the Bank Picquet, provided by the Brigade of Guards. A variety of figures including City policemen, stockbrokers, a messenger boy, and intrepid lady pedestrians. The coach drawn by four horses which has emerged from Cornhill is the Lord Mayor's semi-state coach, built in 1902 and regularly used by the past Lord Mayor in the Lord Mayor's Show. The motor vehicles - poorly proportioned; the wheels are too small - include a Rolls Royce advancing towards us in the foreground, what appears to be a Shell petrol tanker, a Foden steam lorry with solid rubber tyres, and several taxi cabs and open-topped buses. The date that is moulded on the Tidmarsh frame (not reproduced) is 1928.

[41] *Watercolour drawing 264 × 790 mm sight*

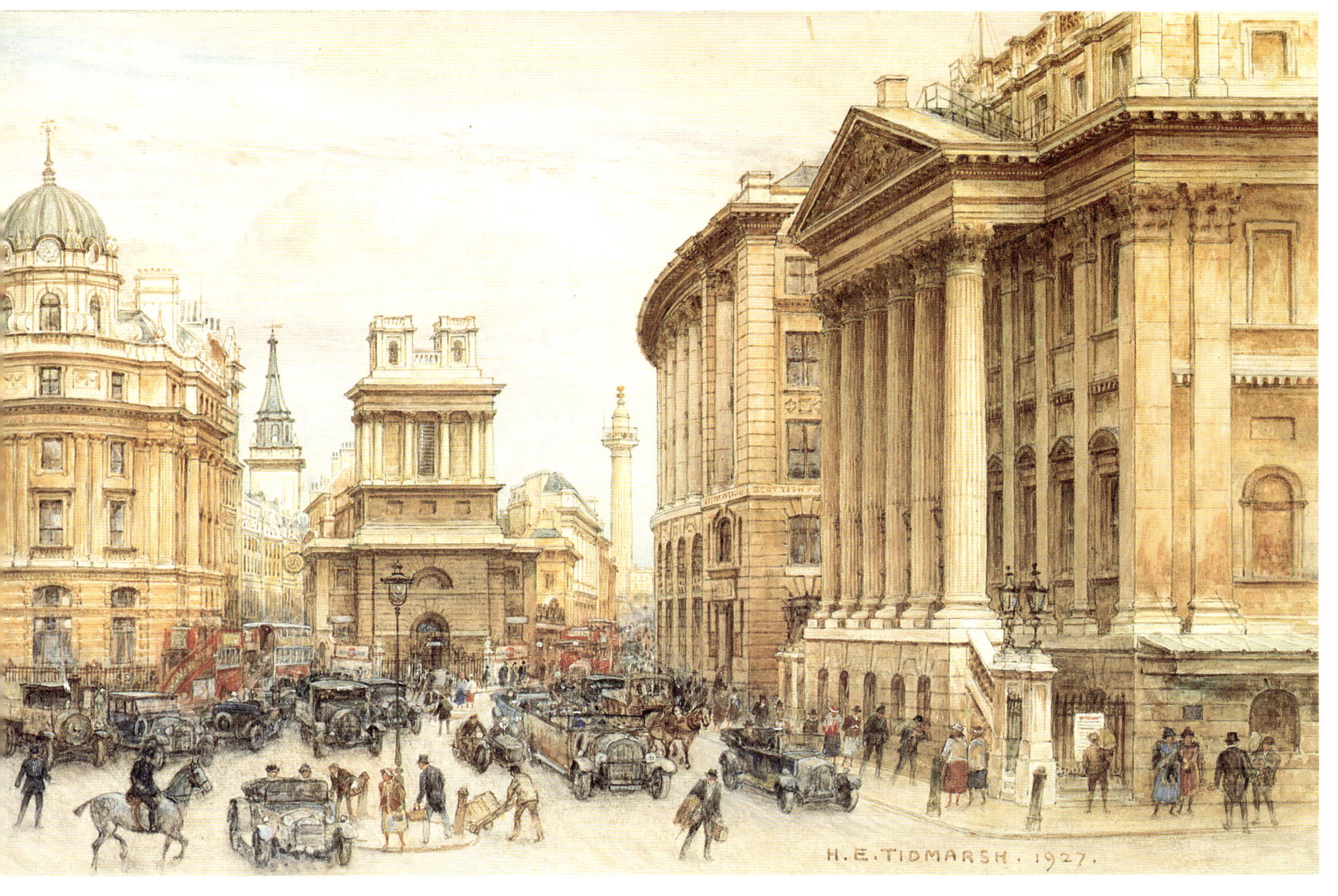
H. E. TIDMARSH . 1927.

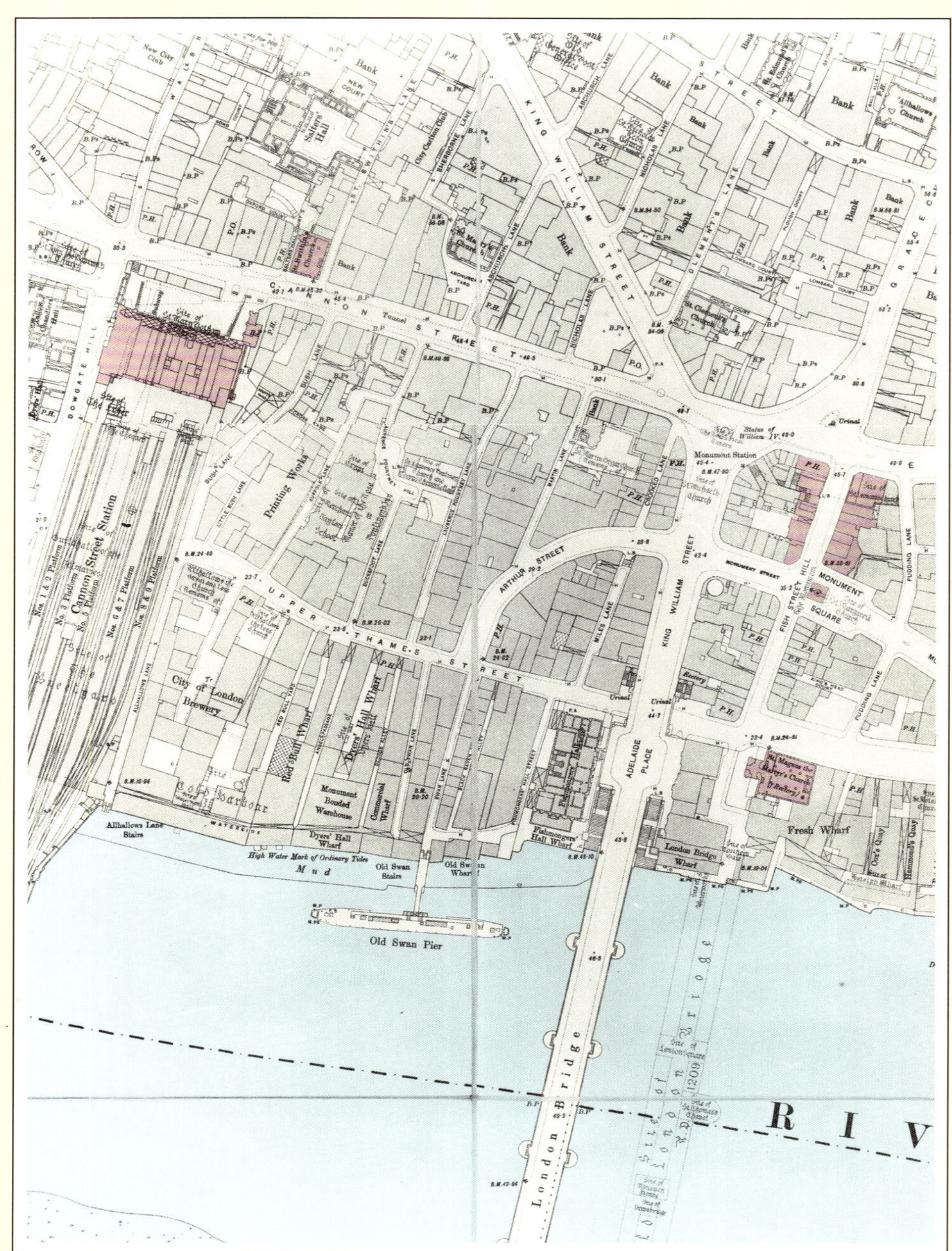

Heading East

Detail from the Ordnance Survey Five Feet to One Mile Plan of London, V11.66/76, published 1916/20

St Swithin London Stone *(right)*

[42] *Detail from plate 43*

Heading East

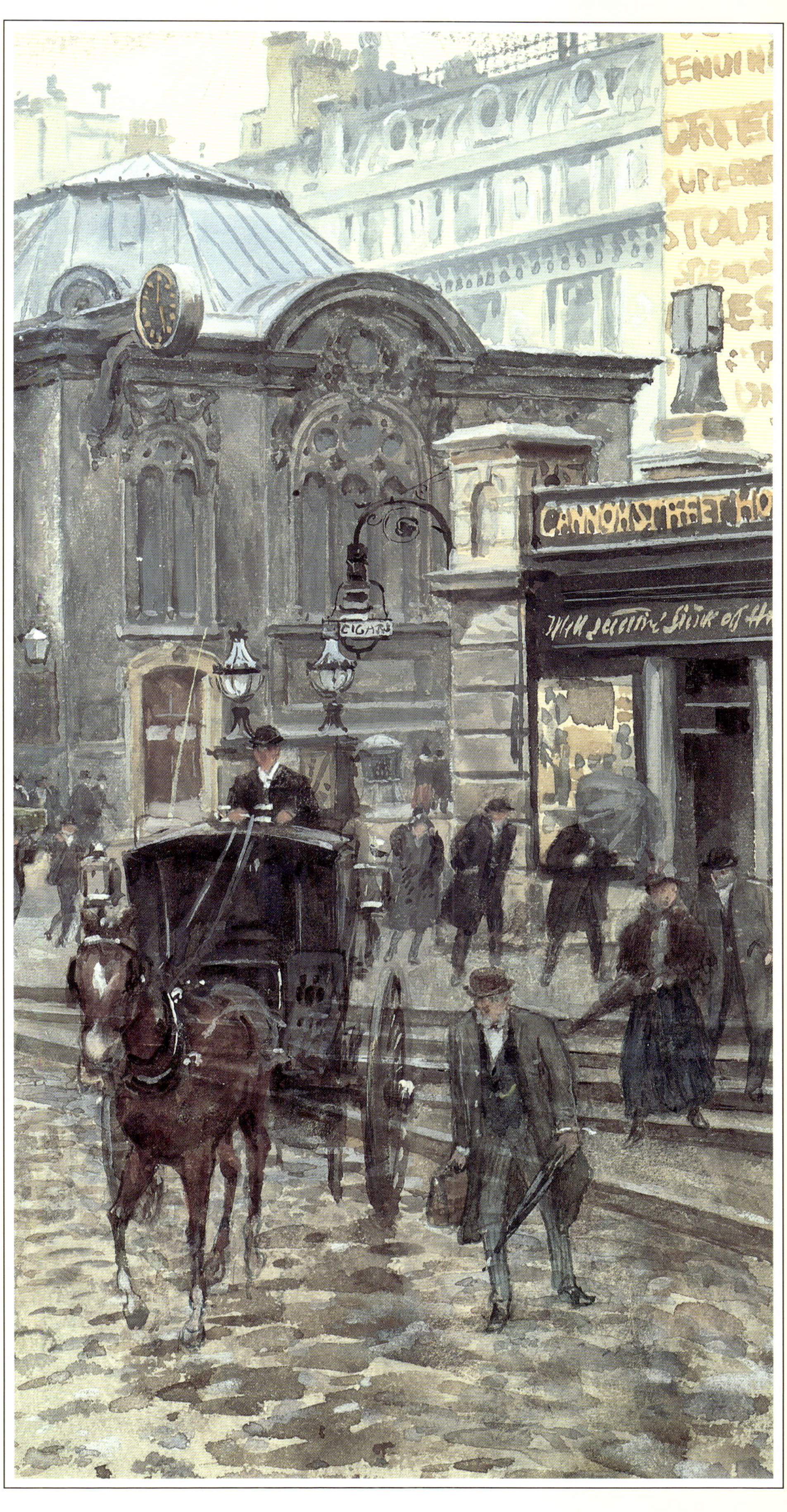

34 St Swithin London Stone

c.1895

ST SWITHIN'S CHURCH, CANNON ST. LONDON (A WREN CHURCH 1678)

The view from Cannon Street Station. It is 12.25 pm and a wet day. Set into the south wall of the church at pavement level can be spotted the niche containing London Stone. To the left of the church is Salters' Hall Court dividing it from 'The London Stone' pub; to the right notice the mansard roofs of St Swithin's Lane, and a network of telegraph wires. On the right is the Cannon Street Hotel Cigar Store. St Swithin, bombed in the Second World War, was demolished in 1962. *Staffage:* two hansom cabs arriving at the station, bowler-hatted and watch-chained business men, and a porter carrying a case on his back.

[43] *Watercolour drawing 400 × 280 mm*

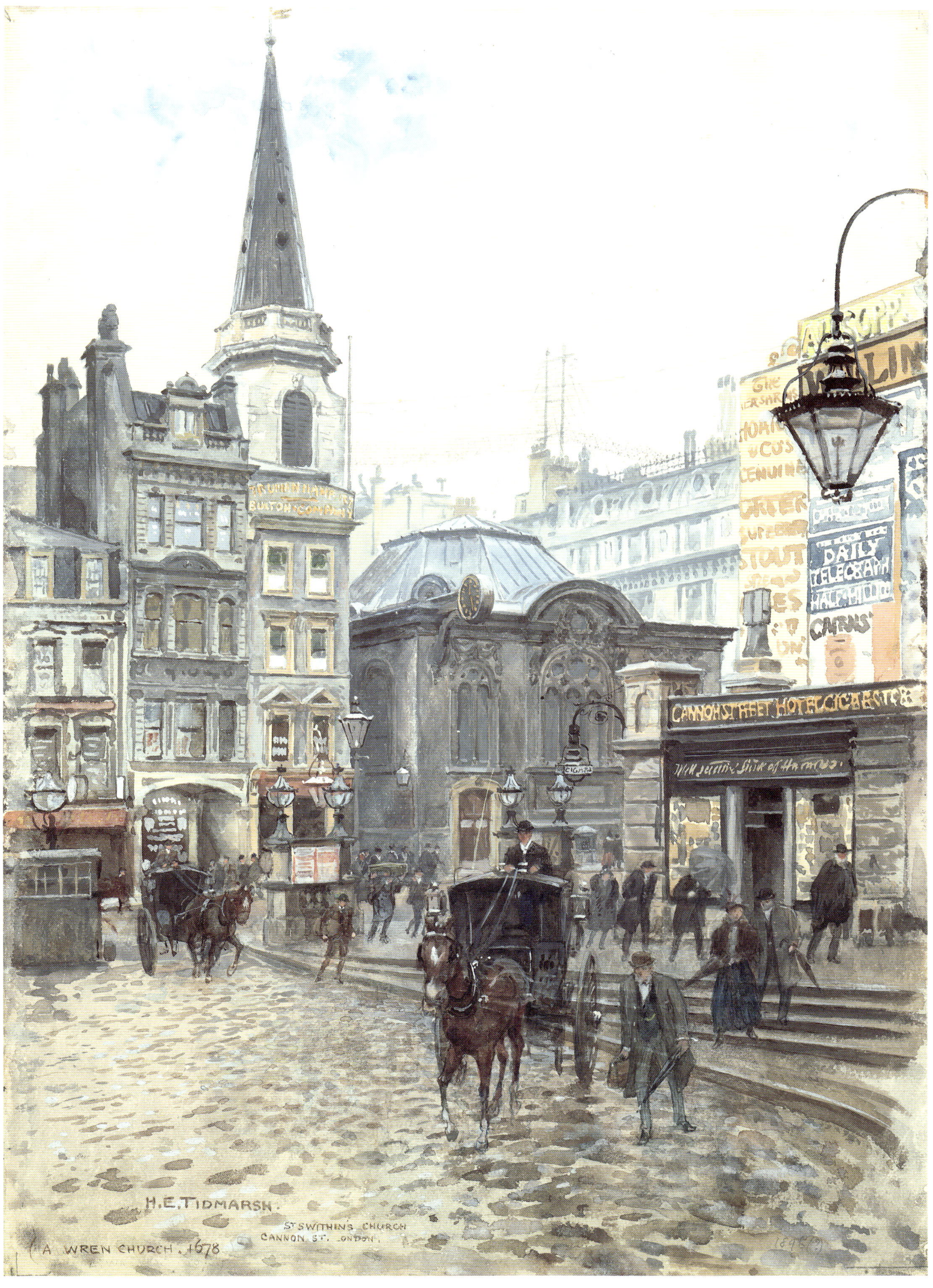
DAILY
TELEGRAPH
STOUT
CANNON STREET HOTEL CIGAR STORE
H.E. TIDMARSH.
St SWITHIN'S CHURCH
CANNON ST. LONDON.
A WREN CHURCH. 1678

36

Fish Street Hill

1898

ST MAGNUS CHURCH, AND THE MONUMENT, LONDON BRIDGE
A WREN CHURCH 1676, STEEPLE 1705

The view down Fish Street Hill from Monument underground station, and the foot of the Monument. Closing the vista are the tower and belfry of St Magnus the Martyr. In the foreground is a red pillarbox. *Staffage:* street vendors, a postman, a newsvendor, and pedestrians. On the verso of this drawing there are three studies of a male arm.

[44] *Watercolour drawing, heightened with body colour 385 × 273 mm*

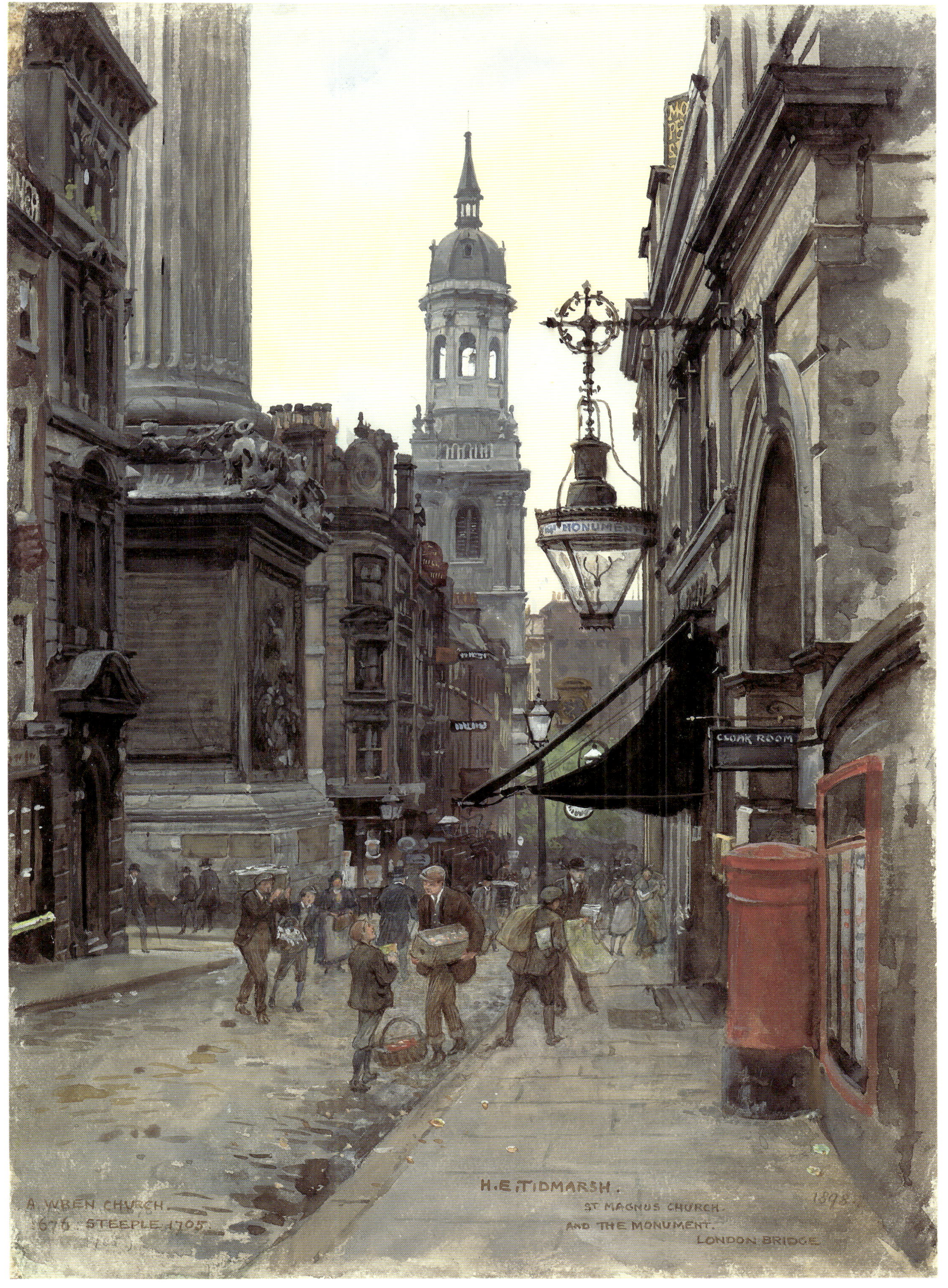
MONUMENT
CLOAK ROOM
A WREN CHURCH
1676 STEEPLE 1705
H.E. TIDMARSH.
ST MAGNUS CHURCH
AND THE MONUMENT.
LONDON BRIDGE
1898

St Dunstan in the East

1924

ST DUNSTAN IN THE EAST
A WREN STEEPLE 1671

A favourite view looking north from Thames Street up St Dunstan's Hill. On the east side at first level of no. 14 is the sign of Joseph Neal, printer. The tower and steeple of St Dunstan in the East were designed after the Great Fire by Wren. The church was rebuilt by David Laing in 1817 in the Gothic style, after it was discovered that the medieval walls had been forced out of perpendicular by pressure from the roof. *Staffage:* a small girl, a man with a porter's barrow, a street sweeper, etc.

[45] *Watercolour drawing 382 × 160 mm*

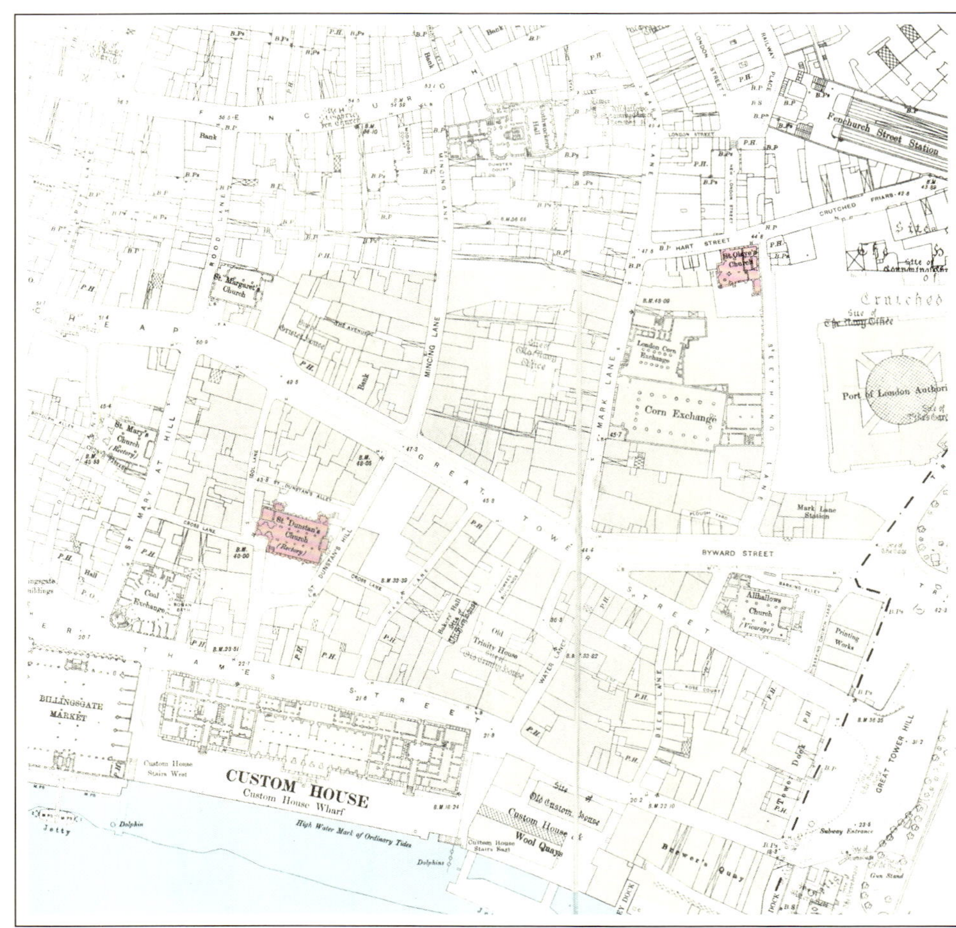

Detail from the Ordnance Survey Five Feet to One Mile Plan of London, V11.66/76, published 1916/20

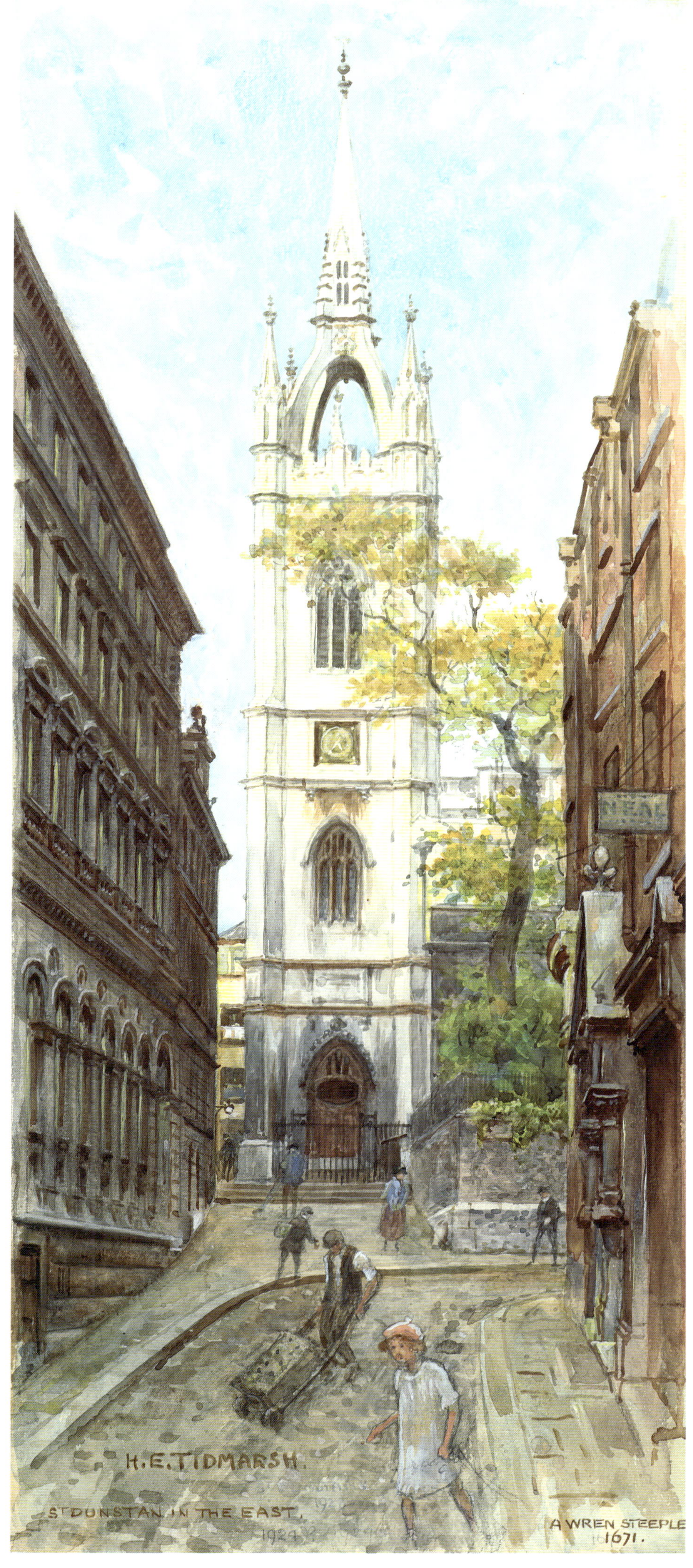
H.E.TIDMARSH.
St DUNSTAN IN THE EAST.
1924
A WREN STEEPLE
1671.

40

St Olave Hart Street

1900

ST OLAVES HART ST.
A PRE-FIRE CH. MID 15 CENT. PEPYS CH.

The north side of St Olave's - the church in which the diarist, Samuel Pepys, worshipped - viewed from New London Street. Three-storey buildings on either side, and, on the left at no. 1 New London Street, a hanging sign for W. A. Ratcliffe, tailor and hosier. *Staffage:* a woman with a girl, an errand boy in knickerbockers, a policeman, and City gentlemen wearing top hats or bowlers.

[46] *Watercolour drawing 390 × 205 mm*

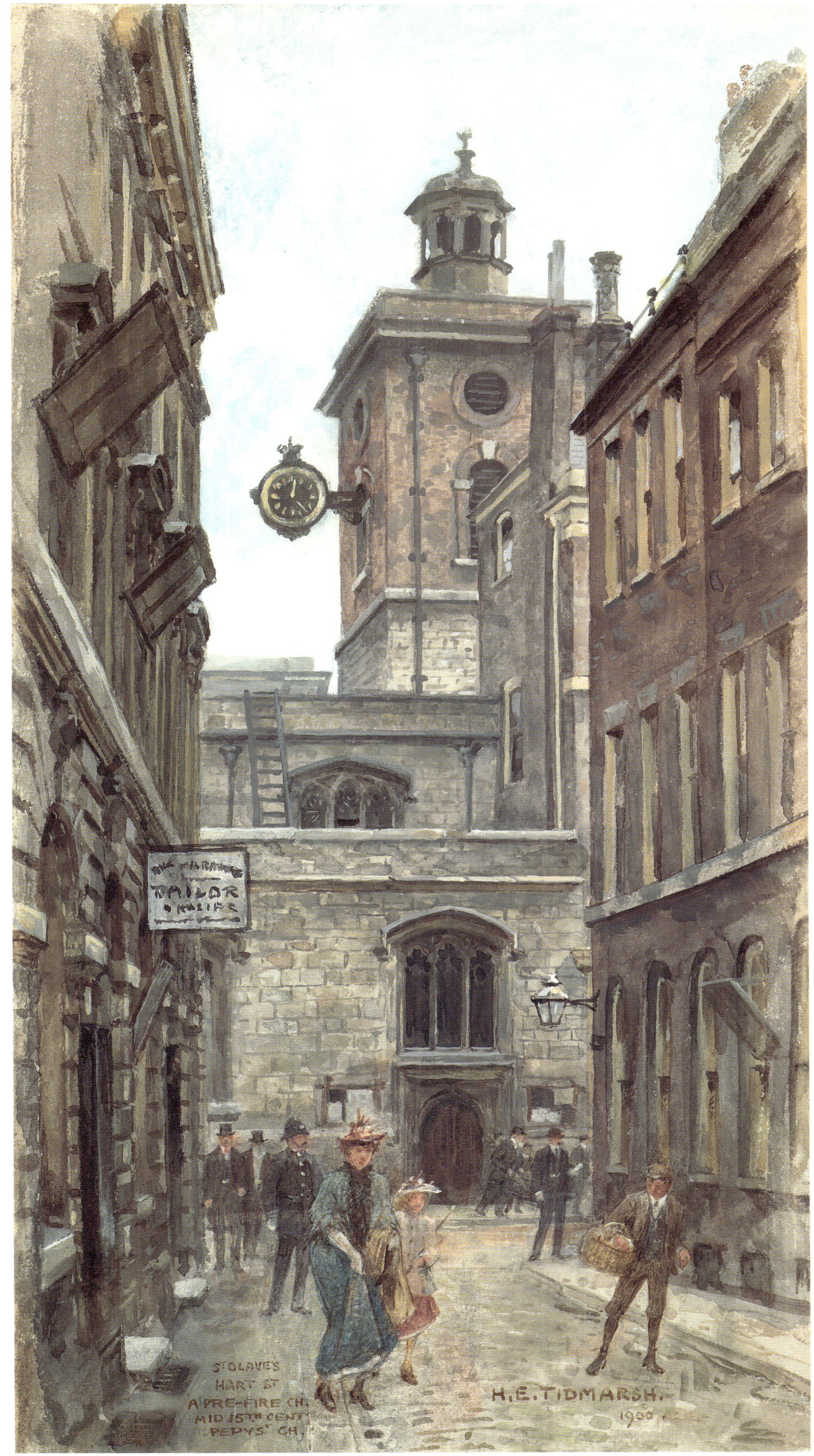
TAILOR
St OLAVE'S
HART St
A PRE-FIRE CH.
MID 15TH CENT
PEPYS' CH.
H.E.TIDMARSH.
1900.

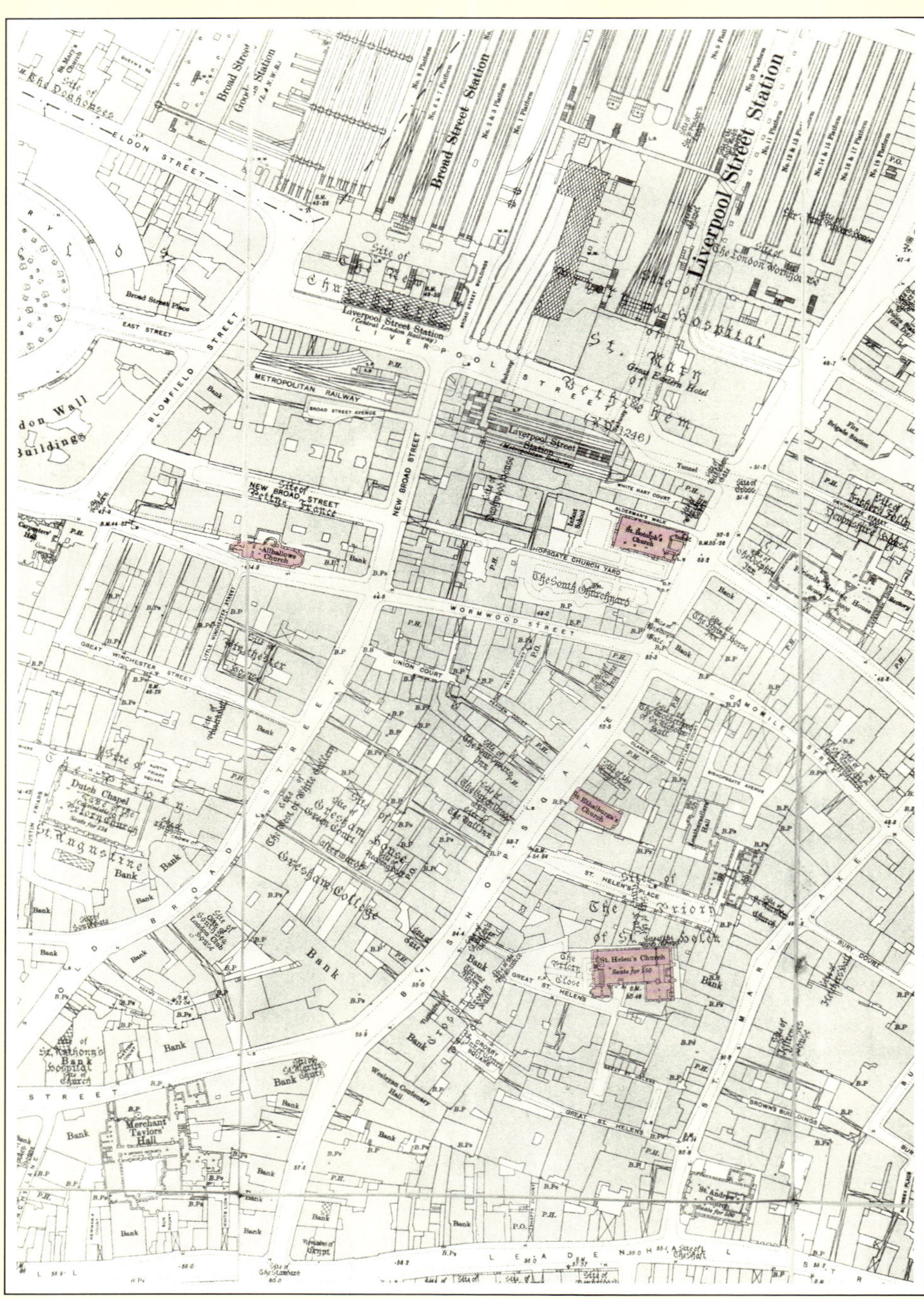

Bishopsgate and Cornhill

Detail from the Ordnance Survey Five Feet to One Mile Plan of London, V11.56/66, published 1916

St Peter Cornhill *(right)*

[47] *Detail from plate 53*

Bishopsgate and Cornhill

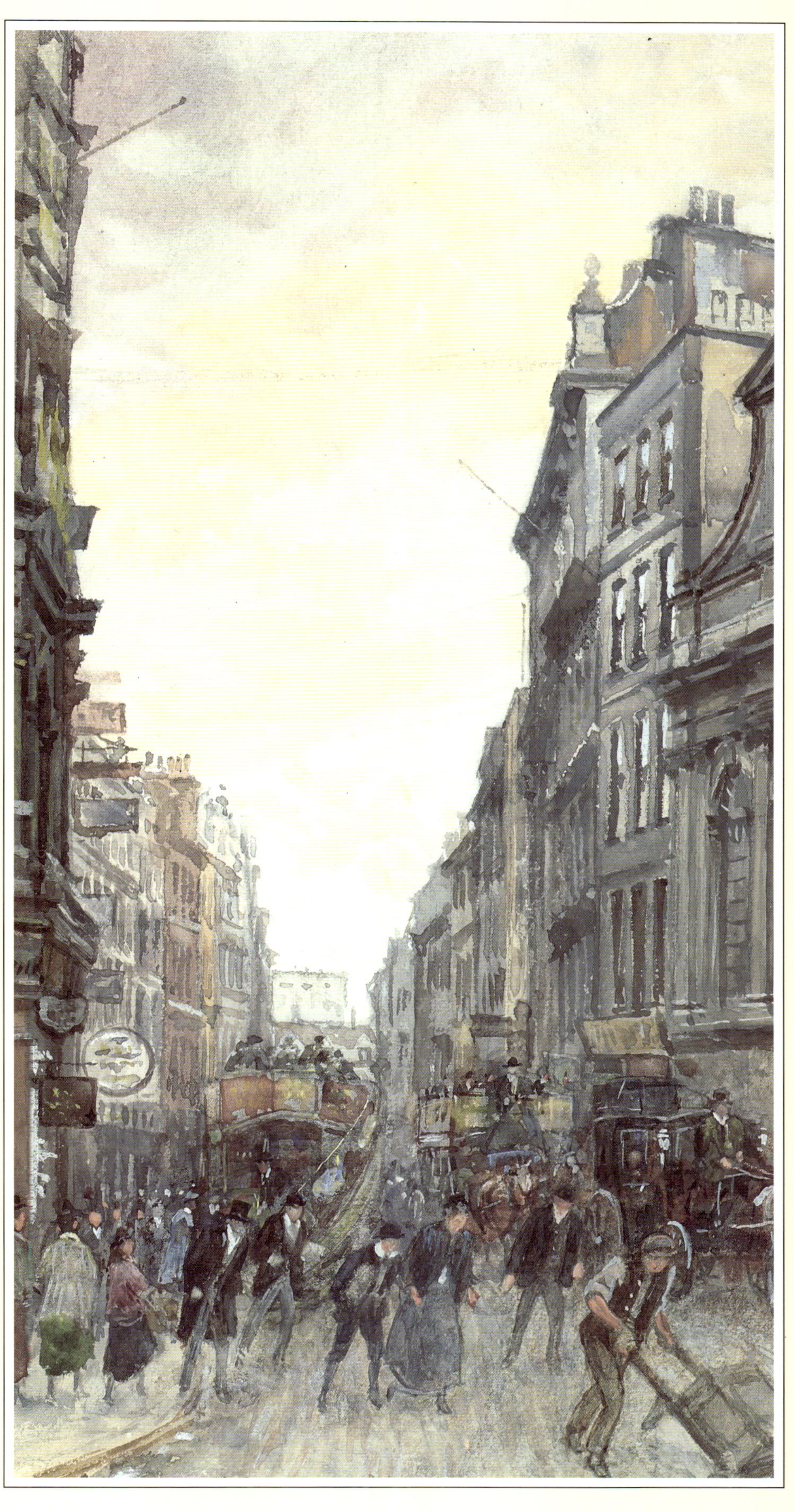

44

St Ethelburga

c.1910

ST ETHELBURGA'S CHURCH, BISHOPSGATE
(A 15TH CENTURY CH. MUCH ALTERED)

The west front of the church, the arch of its Perpendicular window almost entirely obscured by two two-storey shops tacked on to the front of the building. At this date they were tenanted by Edward Henry Robinson, optician. Three giant pairs of spectacles attached to the wall advertise his trade. The shops were removed by the Corporation of London in 1933 in order to make the pavement wider, revealing the rough ragstone wall of the 13th-century church. The church was destroyed by an I.R.A. bomb on 24 April 1993. *Staffage:* various male and female pedestrians dressed in Edwardian fashions.

[48] *Watercolour drawing 355 × 190 mm*

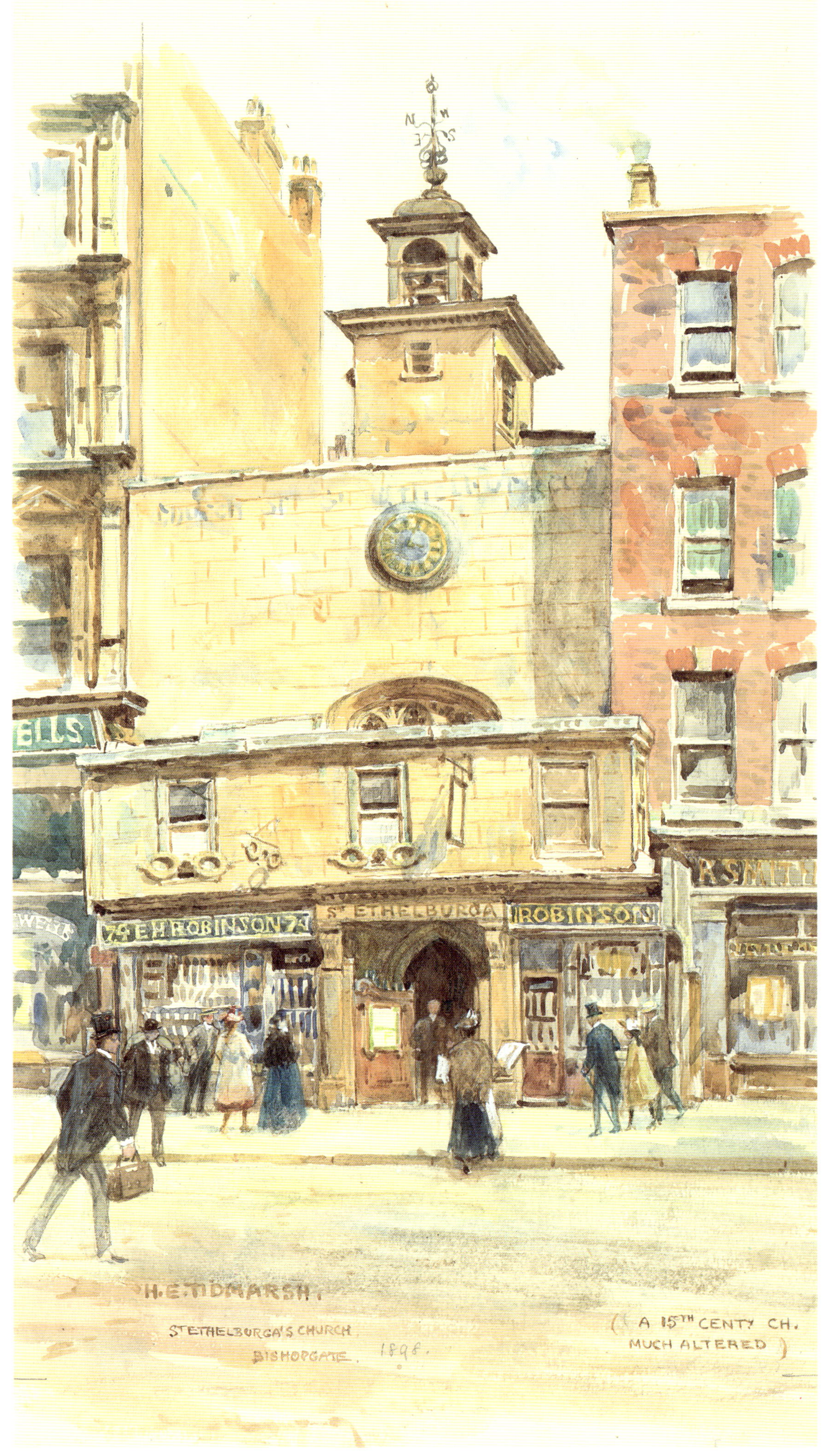
ELLS
79 E H ROBINSON 79
St ETHELBURGA
ROBINSON
R S SMITH
H.E.TIDMARSH.
ST ETHELBURGA'S CHURCH
BISHOPGATE. 1898.
(A 15TH CENTY CH.
MUCH ALTERED)

St Helen Bishopsgate

1922

ST HELEN'S BISHOPSGATE
(ANCIENT CHURCH MUCH ALTERED)

St Helen's viewed from the garden to the south. Tradition (not taken seriously) has it that the church was erected by the Emperor Constantine to the memory of his mother, St Helena. In the 13th century the parish church was given a conventual extension for a priory of Benedictine nuns. The building was restored on three occasions in the 19th century.

[49] *Watercolour drawing 358 × 212 mm*

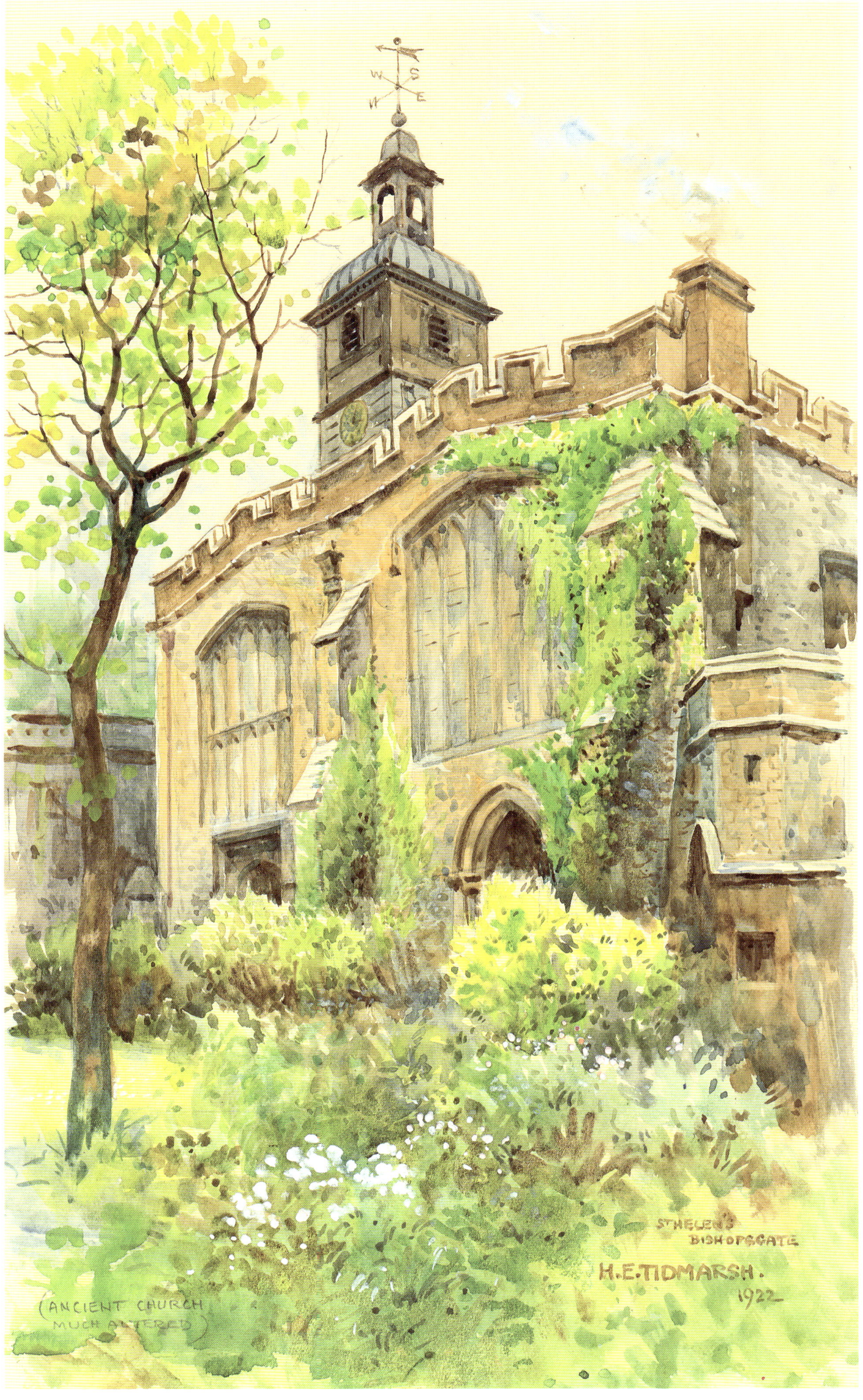
W
S
N
E
S[T] HELENS
BISHOPSGATE
H.E.TIDMARSH.
1922
(ANCIENT CHURCH
MUCH ALTERED)

St Botolph Bishopsgate

1922

ST BOTOLPH'S BISHOPSGATE (NEAR RAILINGS LEFT OUT)
REBUILT IN 1725 BY JAS GOLD

St Botolph's is viewed from the south west, outside the churchyard railings. A note on the reverse states that H. E. Tidmarsh drew the image in 1922, but retouched it in 1927. The church has been attributed to James Gold (or Gould), but no mention of the architect appointed appears in the parish records. *Staffage:* two workmen.

[50] *Watercolour drawing 390 × 225 mm*

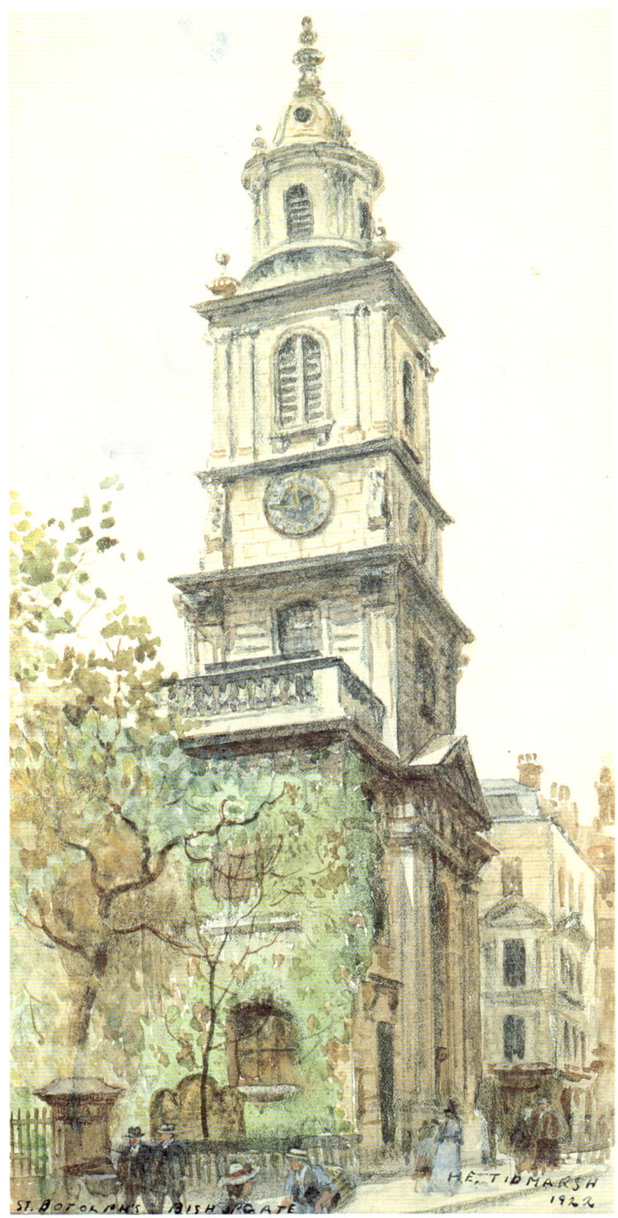

East front of St Botolph Bishopsgate

[51] *Watercolour drawing, 273 × 133 mm*

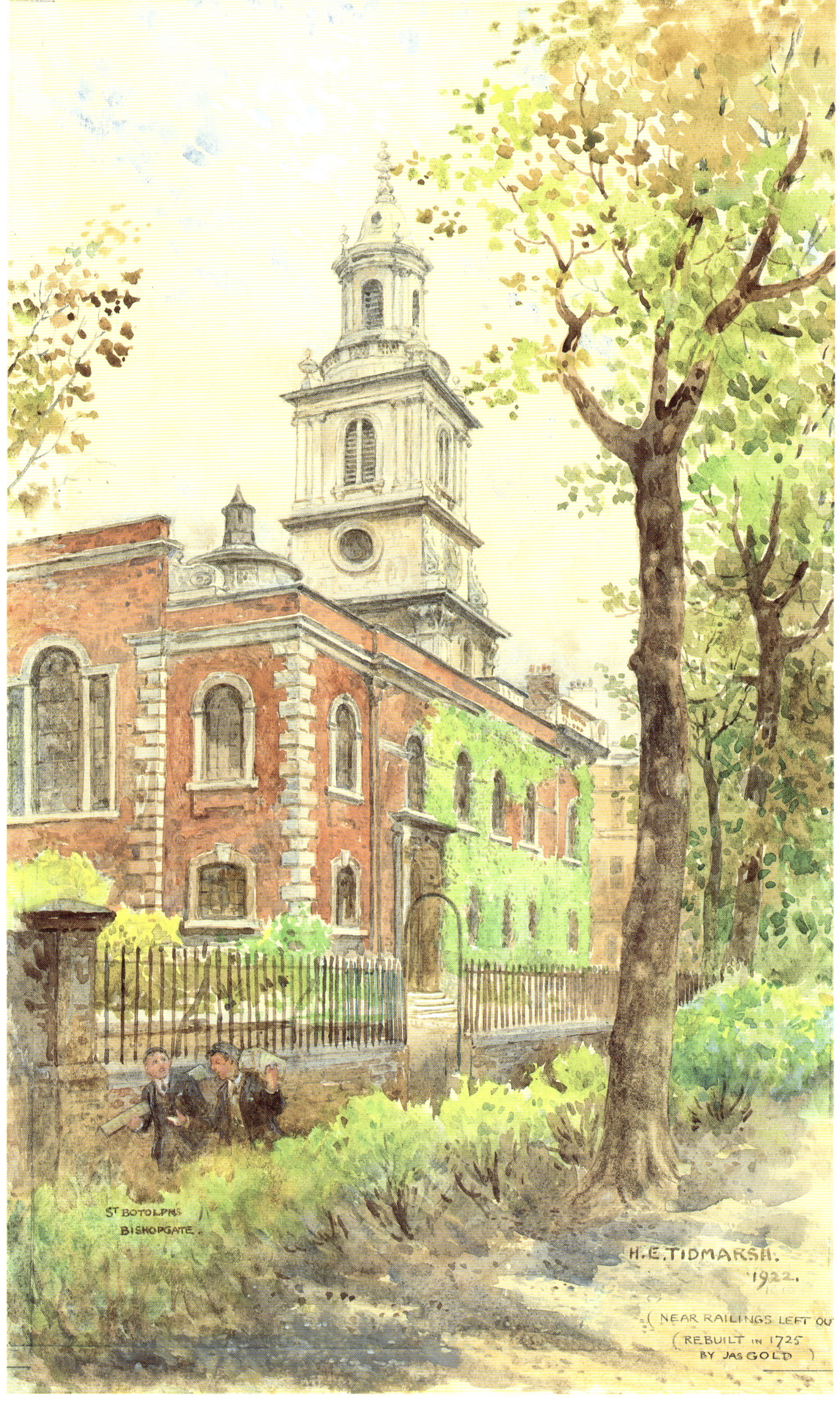
ST BOTOLPHS
BISHOPGATE.
H.E.TIDMARSH.
1922.
(NEAR RAILINGS LEFT OUT
(REBUILT IN 1725
BY JAS GOLD)

50

All Hallows London Wall

1899

ALL HALLOWS, LONDON WALL

This church, built right up against the ancient wall of the City, was designed by George Dance Junior, and consecrated in 1767. It was badly damaged in World War II, but carefully restored by David Nye. It is now the headquarters of the Council for the Care of Churches. Tidmarsh's watercolour views it down the narrow churchyard towards its west front. *Staffage:* a top-hatted man, a woman with a basket on her arm, and a man sitting on the steps, apparently sketching.

[52] *Watercolour sketch 375 × 202 mm*

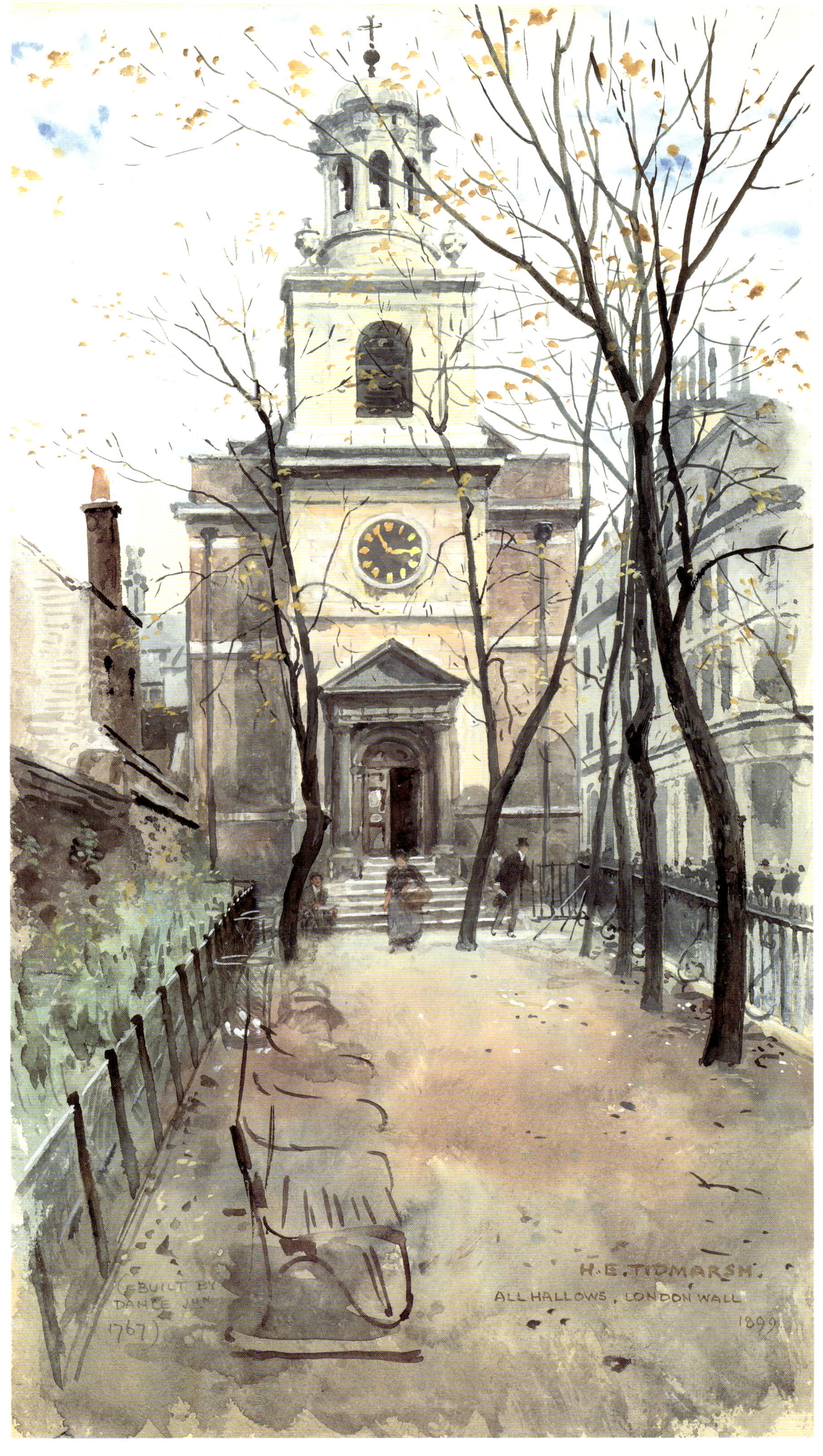
H. E. TIDMARSH.
ALL HALLOWS, LONDON WALL
1899
(REBUILT BY
DANCE JUN
1767)

52 St Peter Cornhill

c.1900

ST PETER'S CORNHILL AND GRACECHURCH ST.
(A WREN CHURCH, 1685)

The east end of St Peter's is seen on the right, looking south down Gracechurch Street. Higher up are nos. 59-60 Cornhill, the Cornhill Merchant Taylors' shop with, above it, the City branch of the Y.M.C.A. *Staffage:* two horse omnibuses passing each other, a four-wheeled cab, a porter and his barrow, and assorted pedestrians.

[53] *Watercolour drawing 280 × 293 mm*

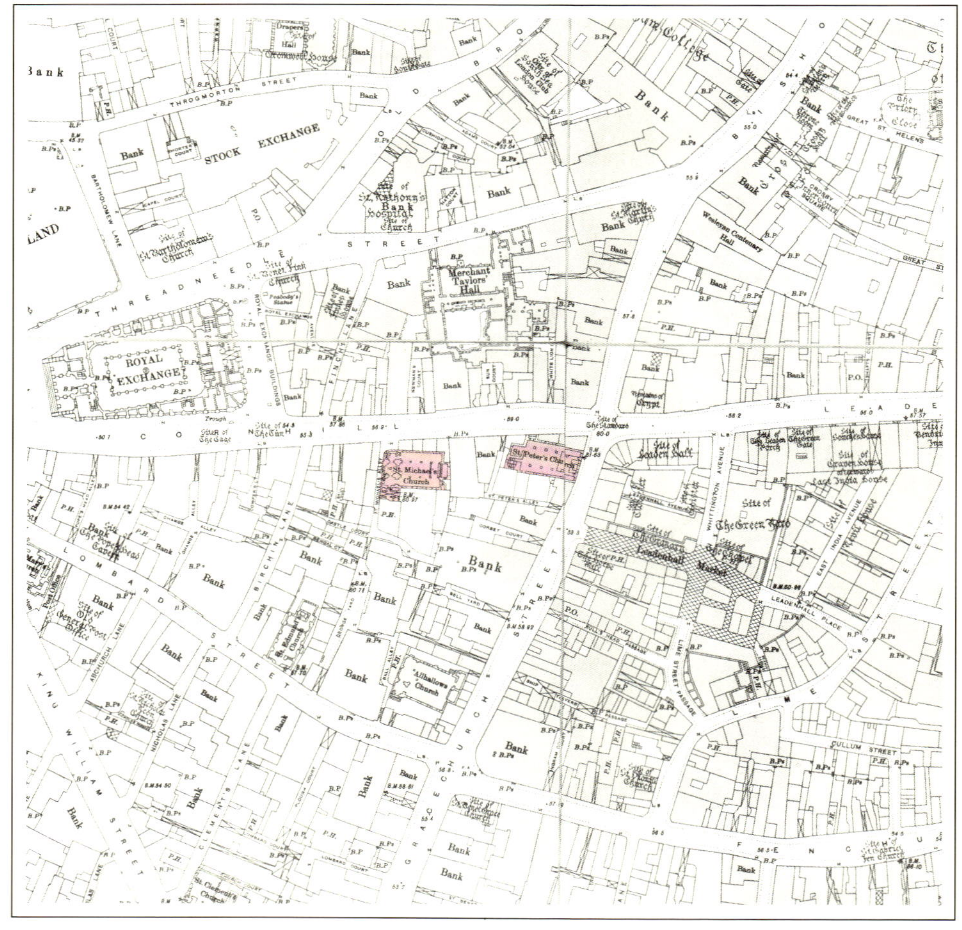

Detail from the Ordnance Survey Five Feet to One Mile Plan of London, V11.66, published 1916

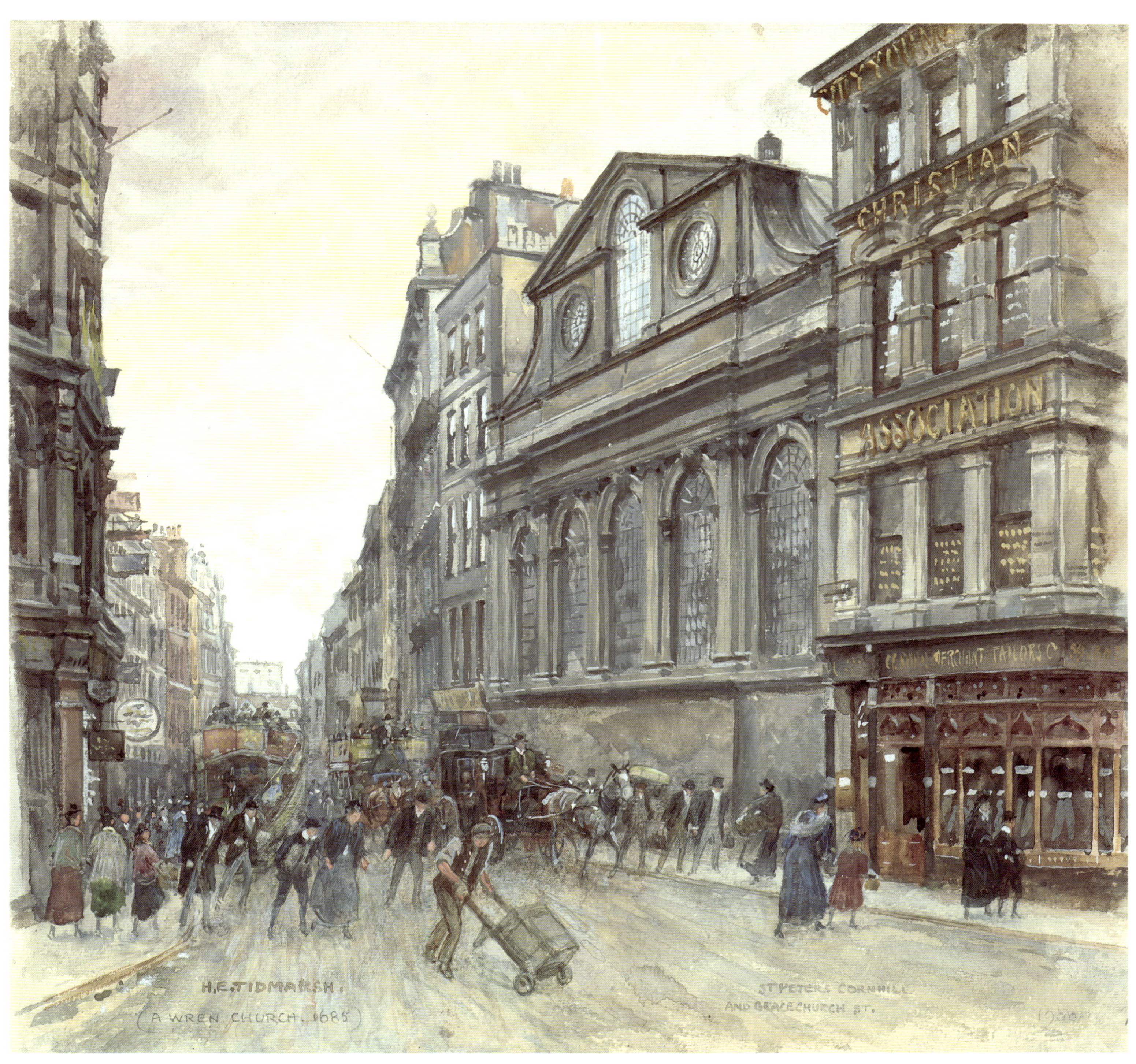
CHRISTIAN
ASSOCIATION
H.E. TIDMARSH.
(A WREN CHURCH. 1685)
ST PETERS CORNHILL
AND GRACECHURCH ST.

54

St Michael Cornhill

c.1920

ST MICHAEL'S CORNHILL
(A WREN TOWER IN HIS [sic] *OLD AGE)*

St Michael's was rebuilt after the Great Fire to designs by Sir Christopher Wren. The church was erected in 1670-1672. Due to a shortage of parochial funds, however, the tower (designed in fact by Nicholas Hawksmoor) was not added until 1722. Tidmarsh's watercolour shows the body of the church and tower as seen from the churchyard. In the foreground are plane trees and flowering shrubs.

[54] *Watercolour drawing 390 × 250 mm*

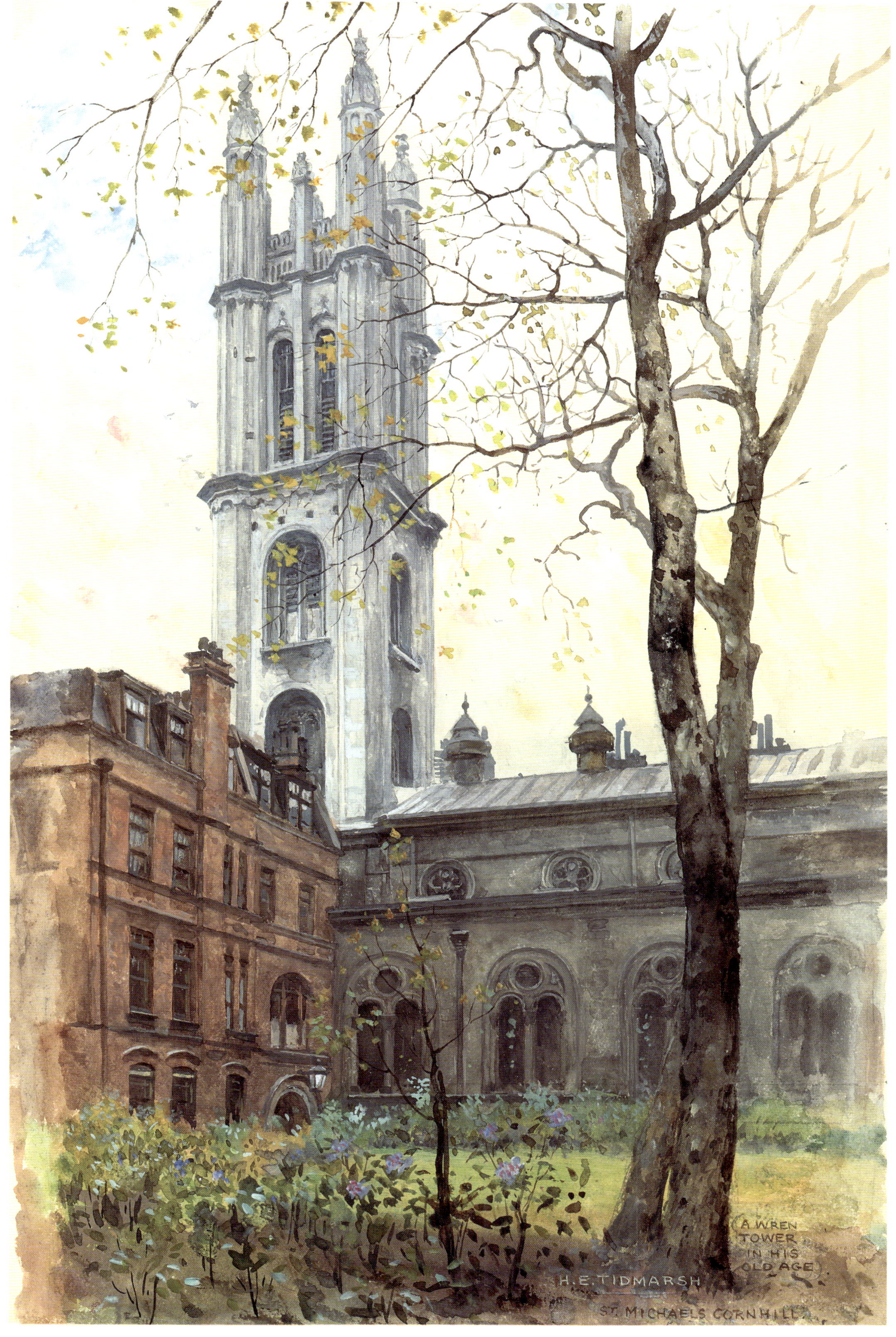
A WREN TOWER IN HIS OLD AGE
H. E. TIDMARSH
ST. MICHAELS CORNHILL

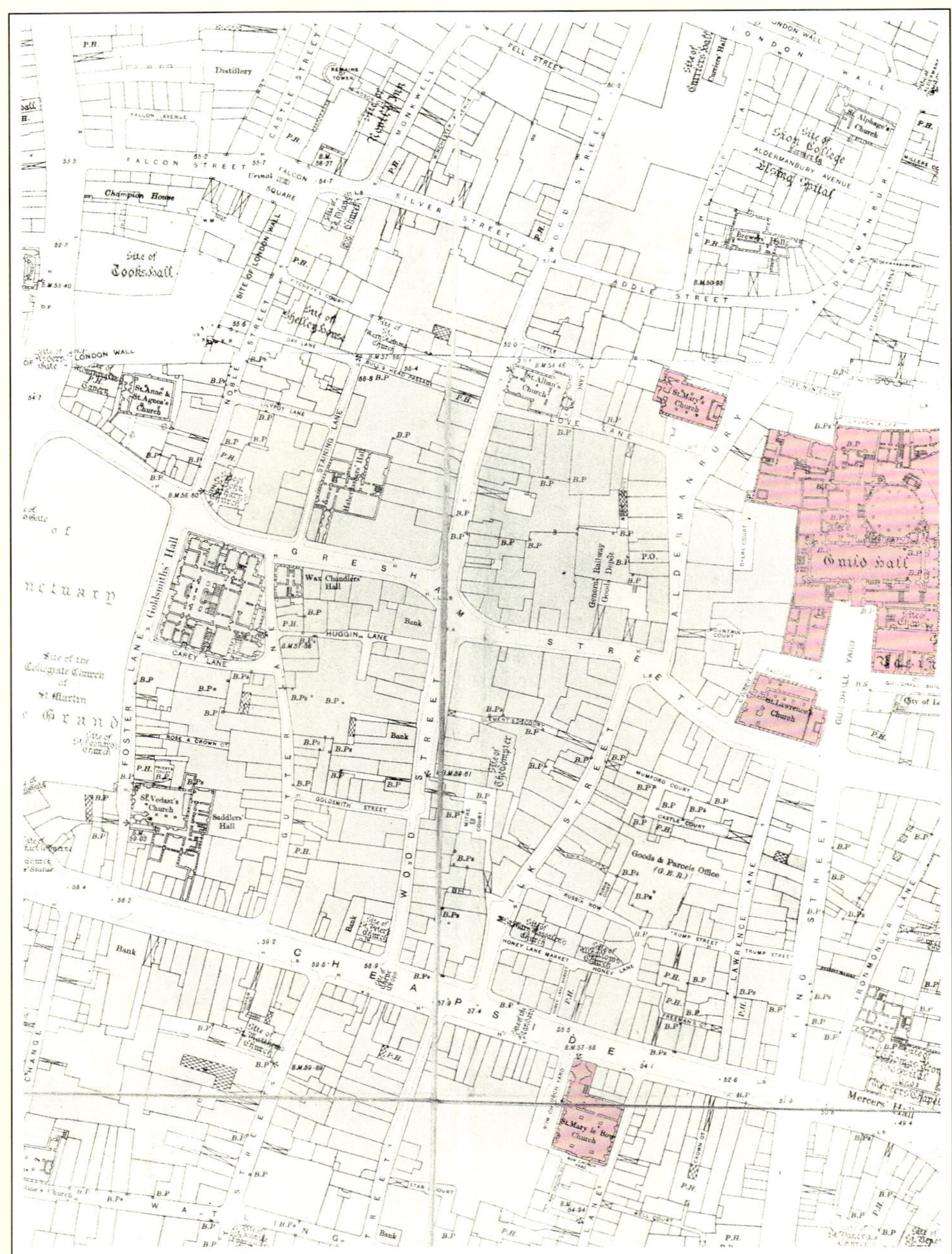

Wren Contrasts

Detail from the Ordnance Survey Five Feet to One Mile Plan of London, V11.55/65, published 1916/19

St Mary Aldermary *(right)*

[55] *Detail from plate 69*

Wren Contrasts

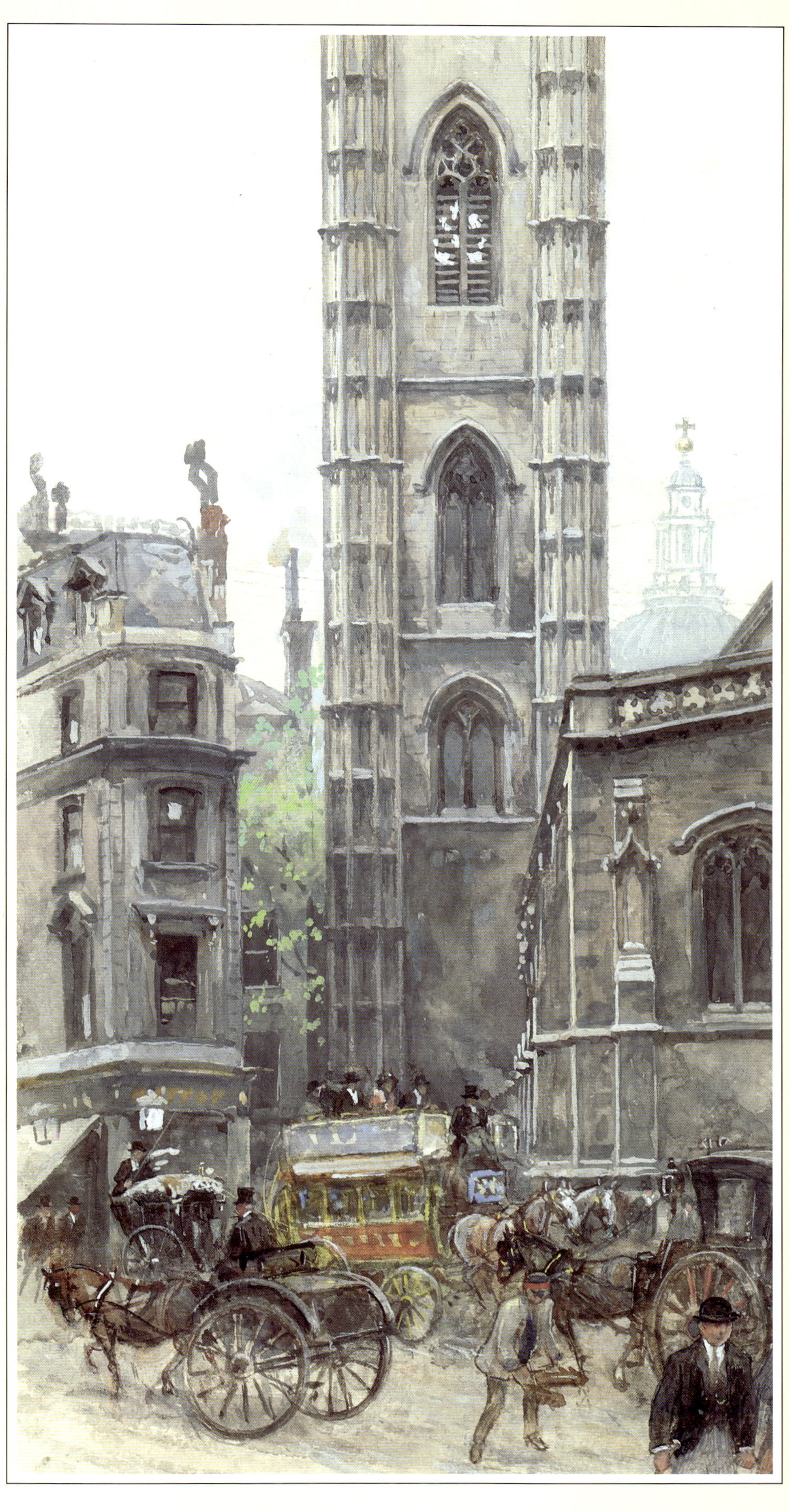

St Mary Aldermanbury

c.1897

ST MARY, ALDERMANBURY
WREN CH. 1678

The east side of the church with the railed churchyard and, beyond, a covered way leading to Love Lane. The view is from Aldermanbury (street). St Mary Aldermanbury, designed by Sir Christopher Wren and erected in 1672-1687, was severely damaged in World War II. It was re-erected on the campus of Westminster College, Fulton, Missouri in 1966-1969. An exhibition of Tidmarsh's watercolours was held here in 1992. *Staffage*: a market woman with a basket, a clergyman wearing a 'poached egg' hat who is accompanied by a boy, a postman, and a policeman who gives directions to a sailor.

[56] *Watercolour drawing 250 × 205 mm*

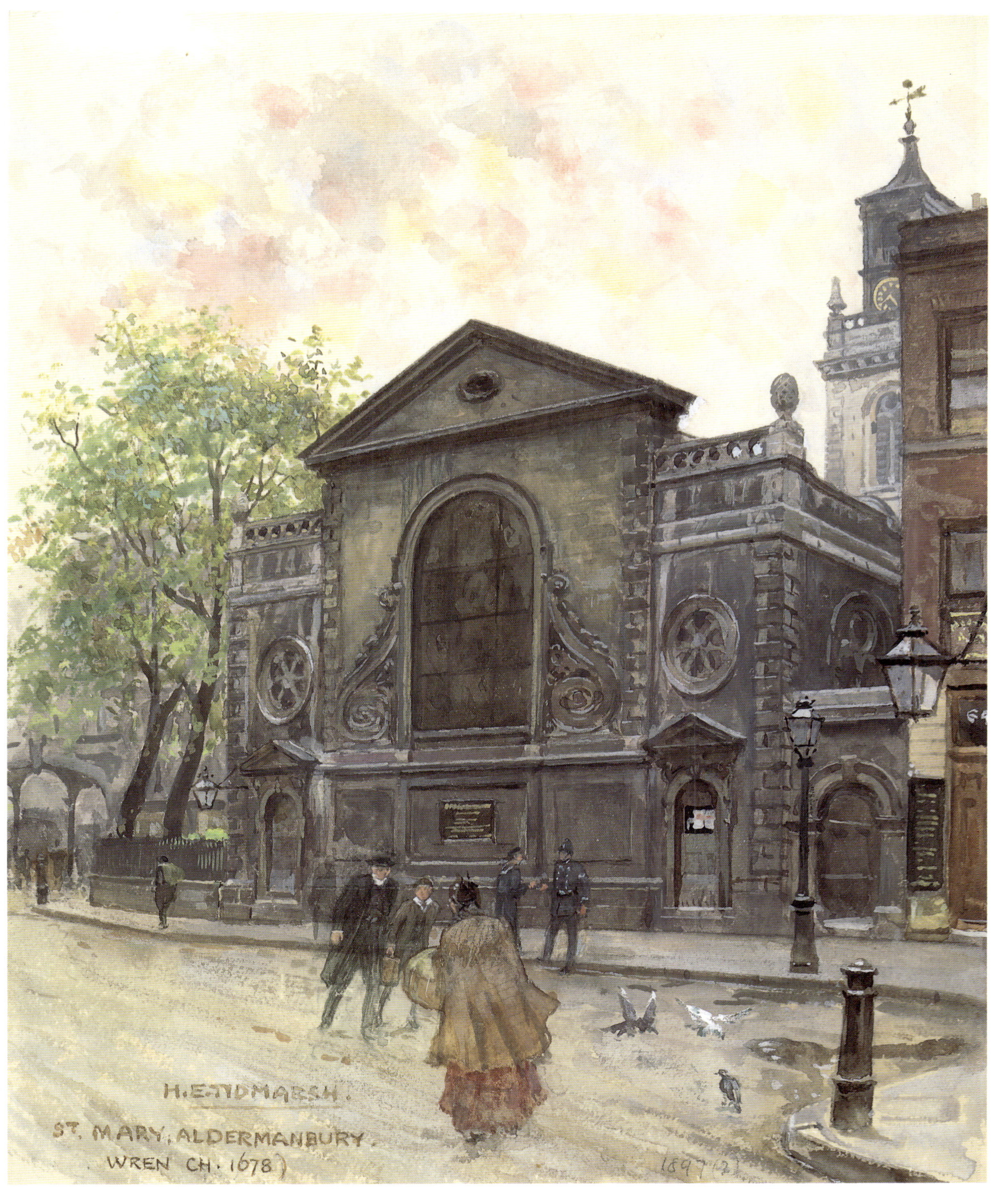
H.E.TIDMARSH.
ST. MARY, ALDERMANBURY.
WREN CH. 1678)
1897(?)

Guildhall and St Lawrence Jewry

c.1897

ST LAWRENCE JEWRY, AND THE GUILDHALL
AN EARLY WREN CHURCH 1676

View from the top of King Street looking towards Guildhall Yard. On the left is the east front of St Lawrence Jewry. On the right within Guildhall Yard is a building erected in 1823 to house the Law Courts, converted in 1886 to become Guildhall Art Gallery. *Staffage:* carriages, errand boys, business people, and a policeman.

[57] *Watercolour drawing 393 × 280 mm*

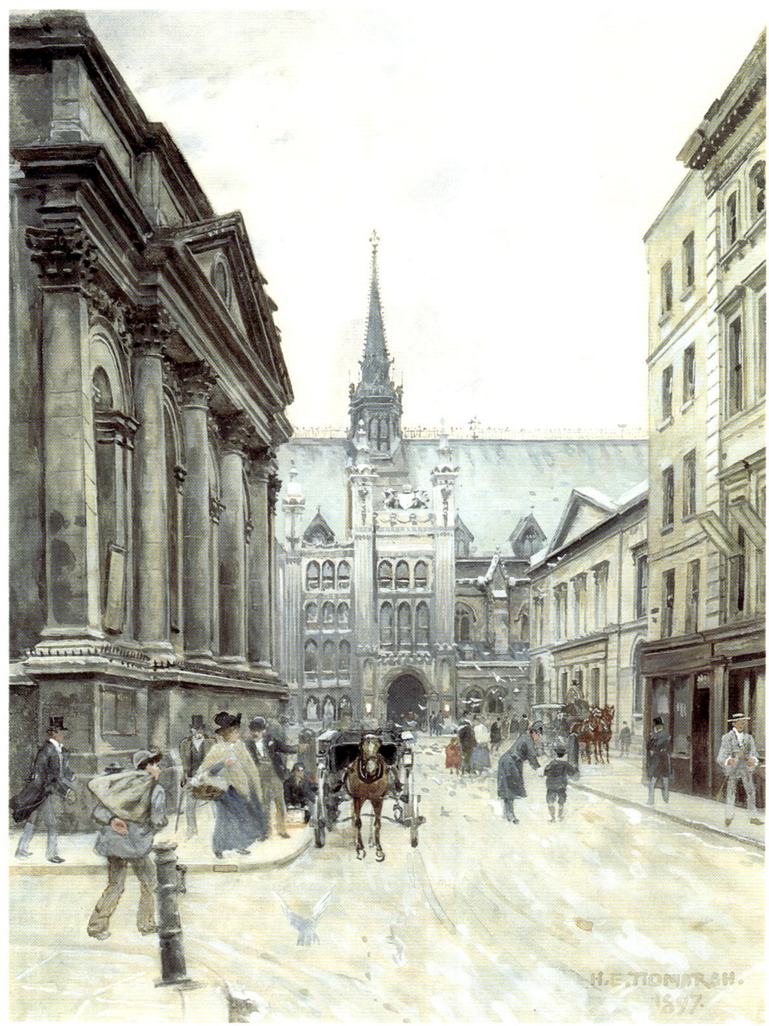

Another version of Tidmarsh's view of Guildhall and St Lawrence Jewry, 1897

The staffage differs: note the pigeon problem from which Guildhall then suffered. Probably the watercolour exhibited by Tidmarsh in the Royal Academy in 1897.

[58] *Watercolour drawing, 376 × 267 mm (sight)*

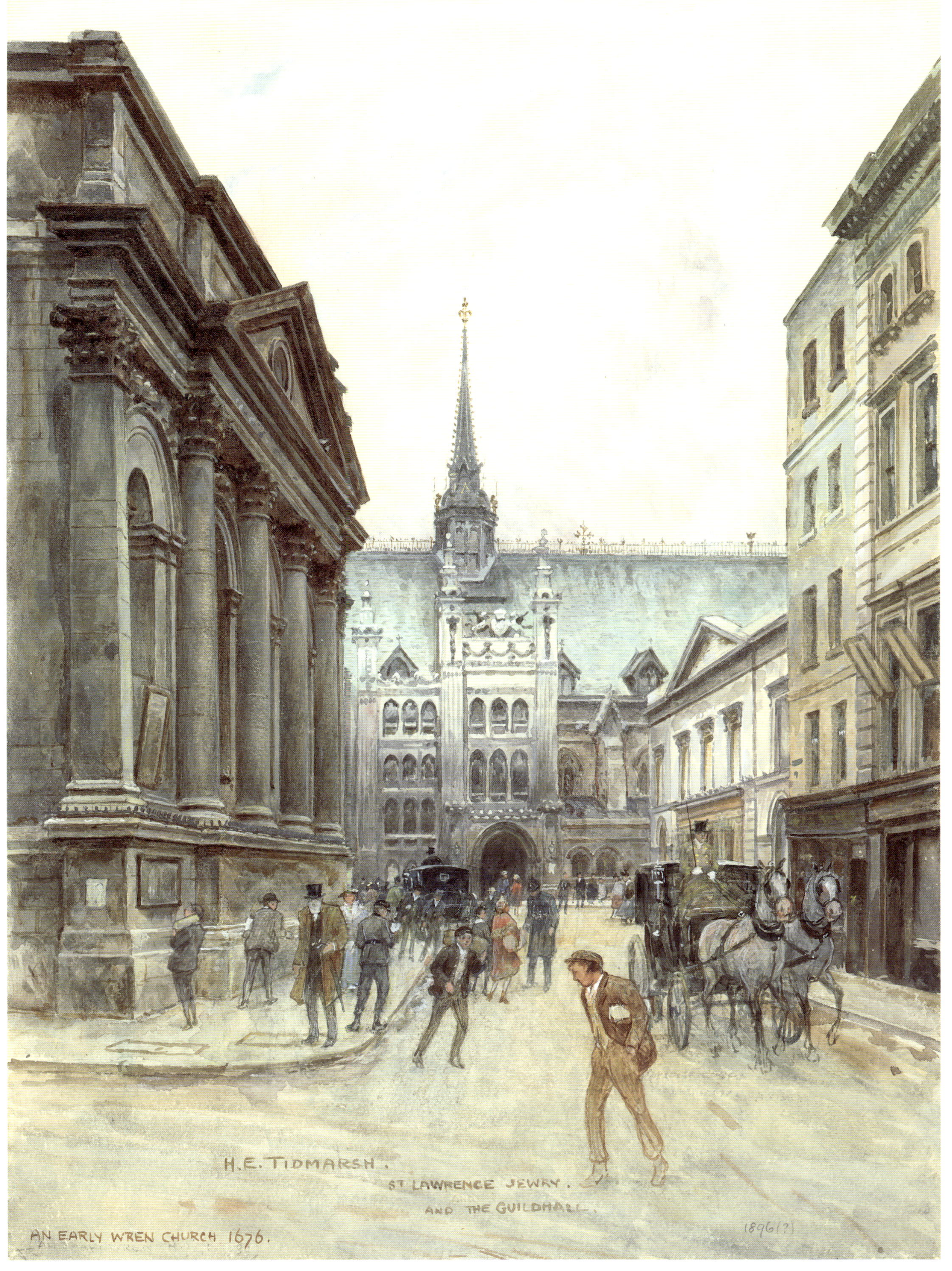
H.E. TIDMARSH.
ST LAWRENCE JEWRY.
AND THE GUILDHALL.
AN EARLY WREN CHURCH 1676.
1896(?)

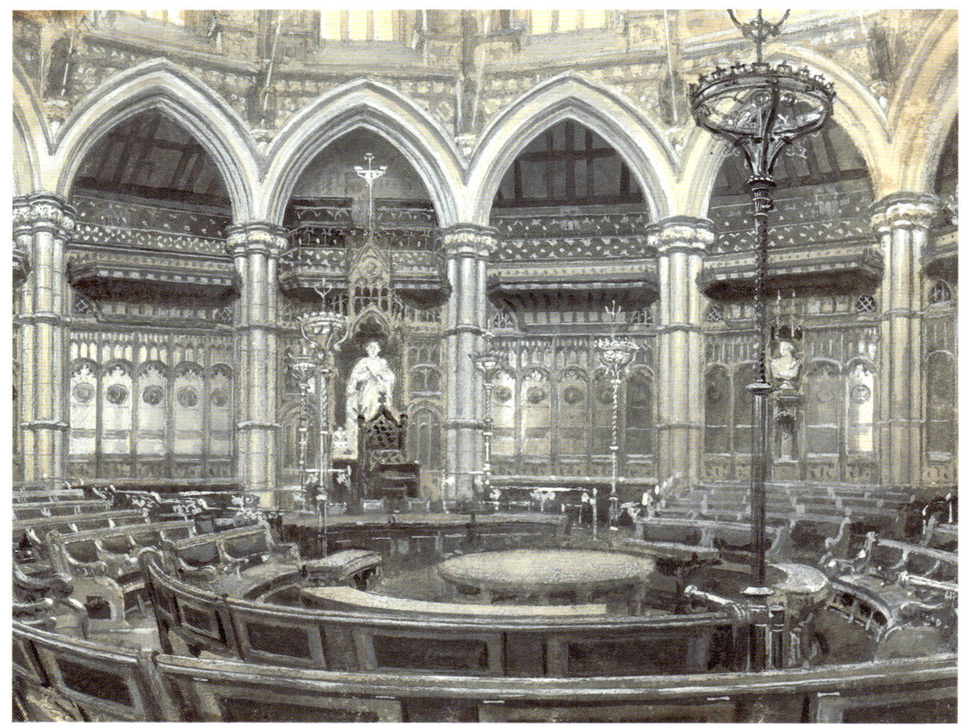

The interior of Guildhall Council Chamber, c.1900

The Chamber was designed by Sir Horace Jones. It was used by the Court of Common Council from 1884 until it was gutted in the air raid of 29 December 1940.

[59] *Wash drawing, heightened with body colour, 205 × 257 mm*

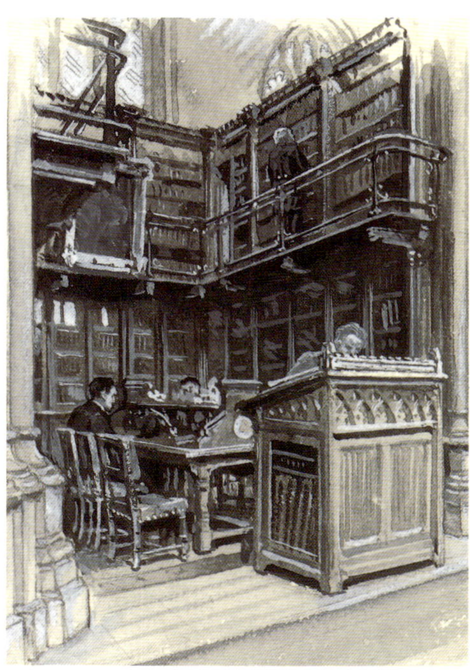

One of the bays in old Guildhall Library, c.1900

Readers are seated at the reading desk, standing at the reading slope, and examining books in the gallery above.

[61] *Wash drawing, heightened with body colour, 142 × 93 mm*

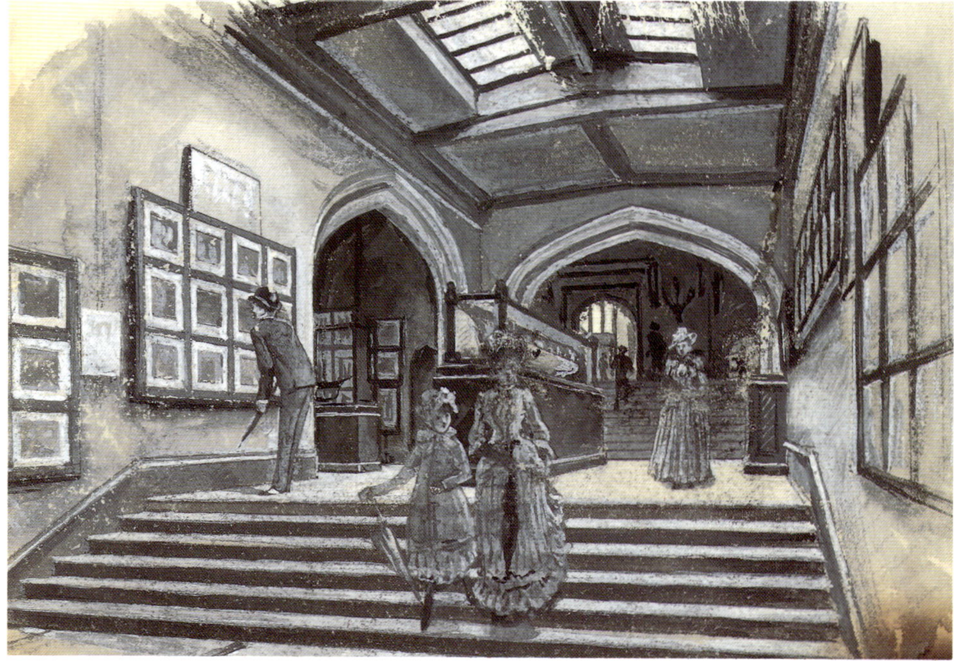

Corridor to Guildhall Library, c.1900
(above)

The Library was at the end of the corridor. Note the use of the corridor walls for displaying the Library's prints and drawings. The Library was designed by Sir Horace Jones, architect later of Tower Bridge. It opened in 1872.

[60] *Wash drawing, heightened with body colour, 108 × 160 mm*

Vestibule to Guildhall Museum and Guildhall Library from Basinghall Street, c.1900
(right)

The open door leads into a room that was called the Annexe.

[62] *Wash drawing, heightened with body colour, 125 × 115 mm*

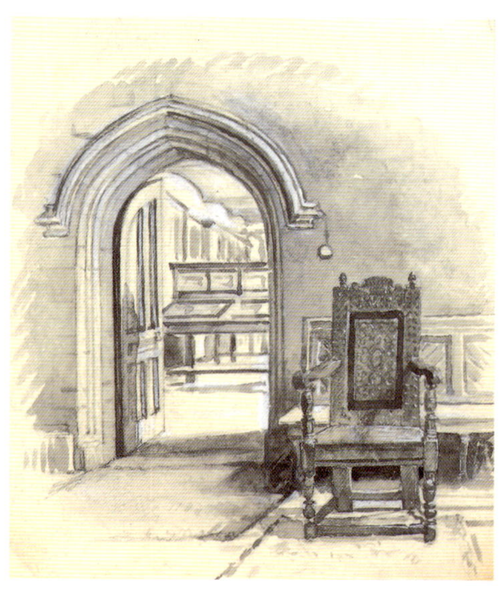

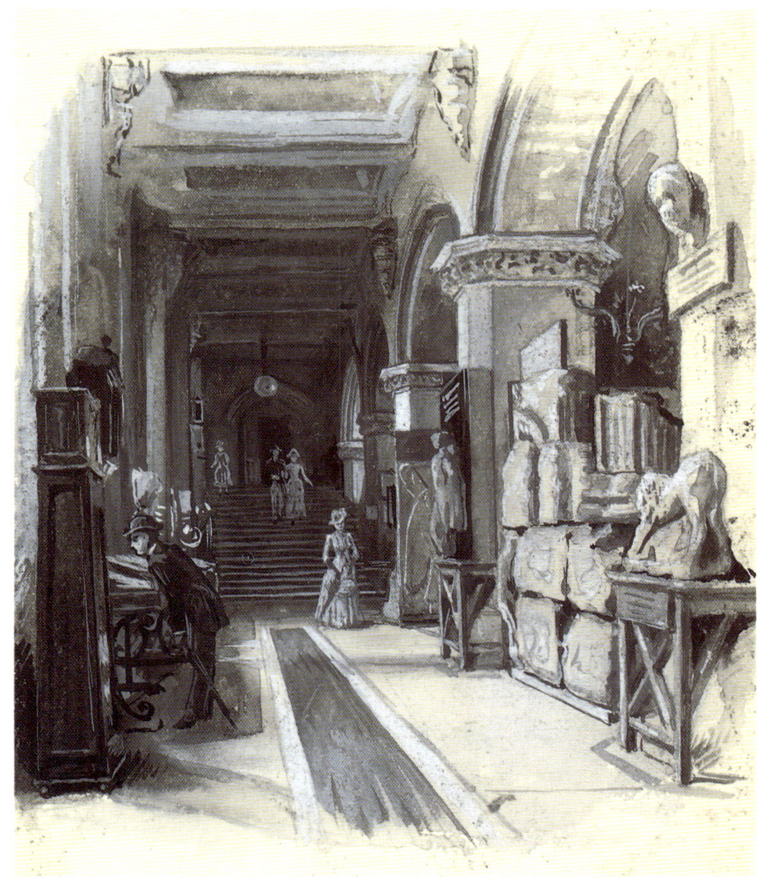

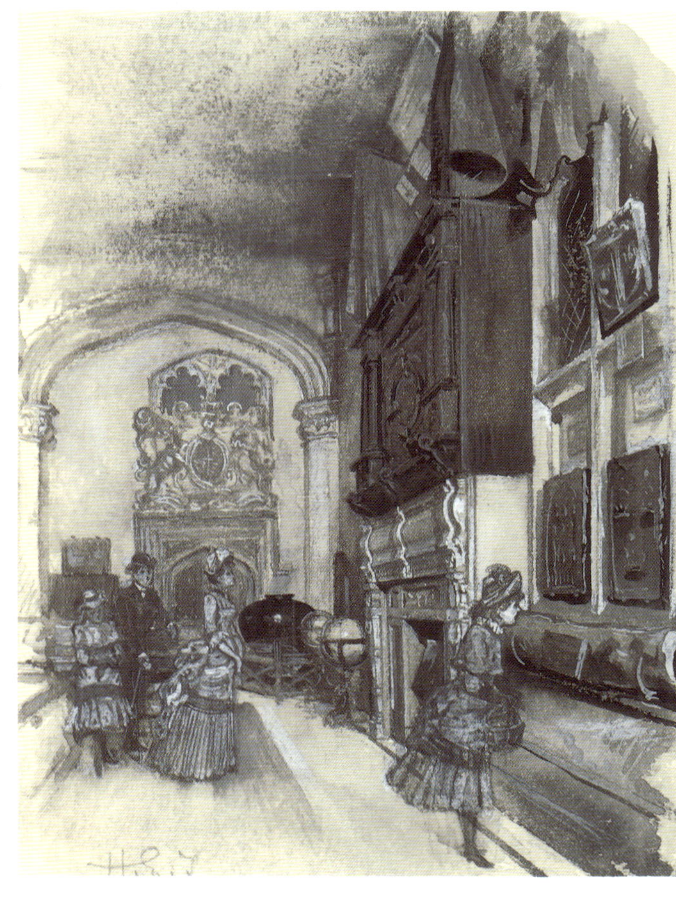

Guildhall Museum, c.1900
(above)

Looking along the east aisle to the south east staircase. The Museum was housed at basement level, below Guildhall Library.

[63] *Wash drawing, heightened with body colour, 166 × 135 mm*

The south end of Guildhall Museum
(above right)

[64] *Wash drawing, heightened with body colour, 168 × 122 mm*

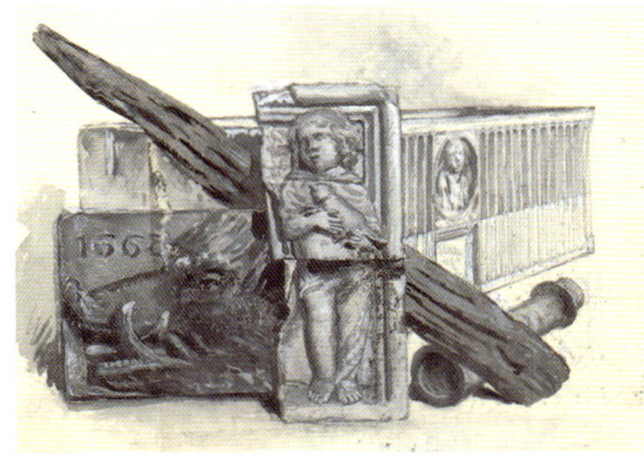

Objects on display in Guildhall Museum

The wood and stone fragments include a Roman sarcophagus found at Clapton, the sign of the Boar's Head from Eastcheap, and a putto holding a cat.

[65] *Wash drawing, heightened with body colour, 100 × 132 mm*

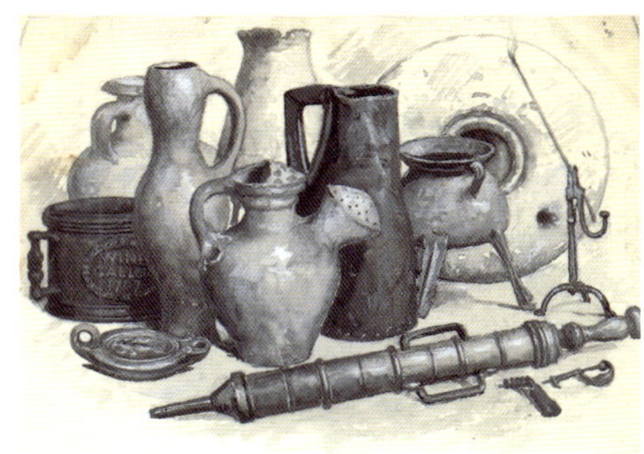

Drinking vessels, cooking utensils, a lamp, and a syringe exhibited in the Museum

[66] *Wash drawing, heightened with body colour, 98 × 135 mm*

St Mary-le-Bow

1922

ST MARY-LE-BOW, CHEAPSIDE

View in Cheapside looking west from the corner of King Street. On the left can be identified the premises of the self-publicist clockmaker, John Bennett. St Mary-le-Bow, noted for its elaborate and beautiful spire, was built to the designs of Sir Christopher Wren between 1670 and 1683. On the right a sign proclaims 'Tea Shop' (the Aerated Bread Co. at nos. 94-95). *Staffage:* a postman with his mailbag approaching the pillar box.

[67] *Watercolour drawing 387 × 140 mm*

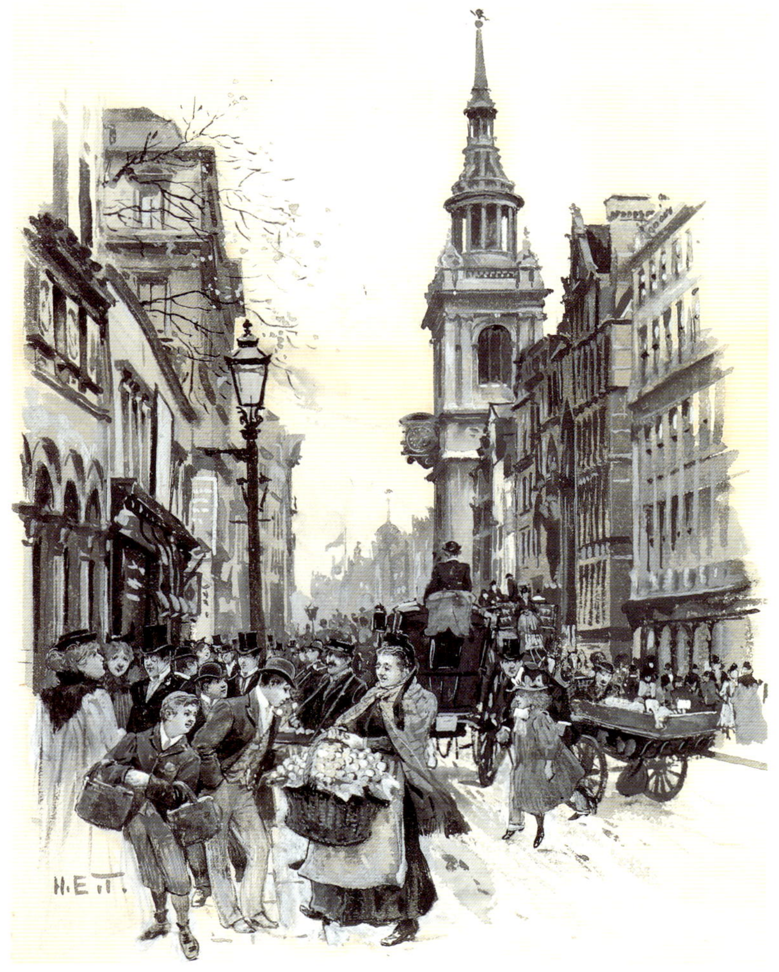

Cheapside looking east, c.1900

A customer wheels his barrow westwards; a flower lady and a row of other itinerant street traders offer their wares to well-heeled pedestrians.

[68] *Wash drawing, heightened with body colour, 279 × 212 mm (sight)*

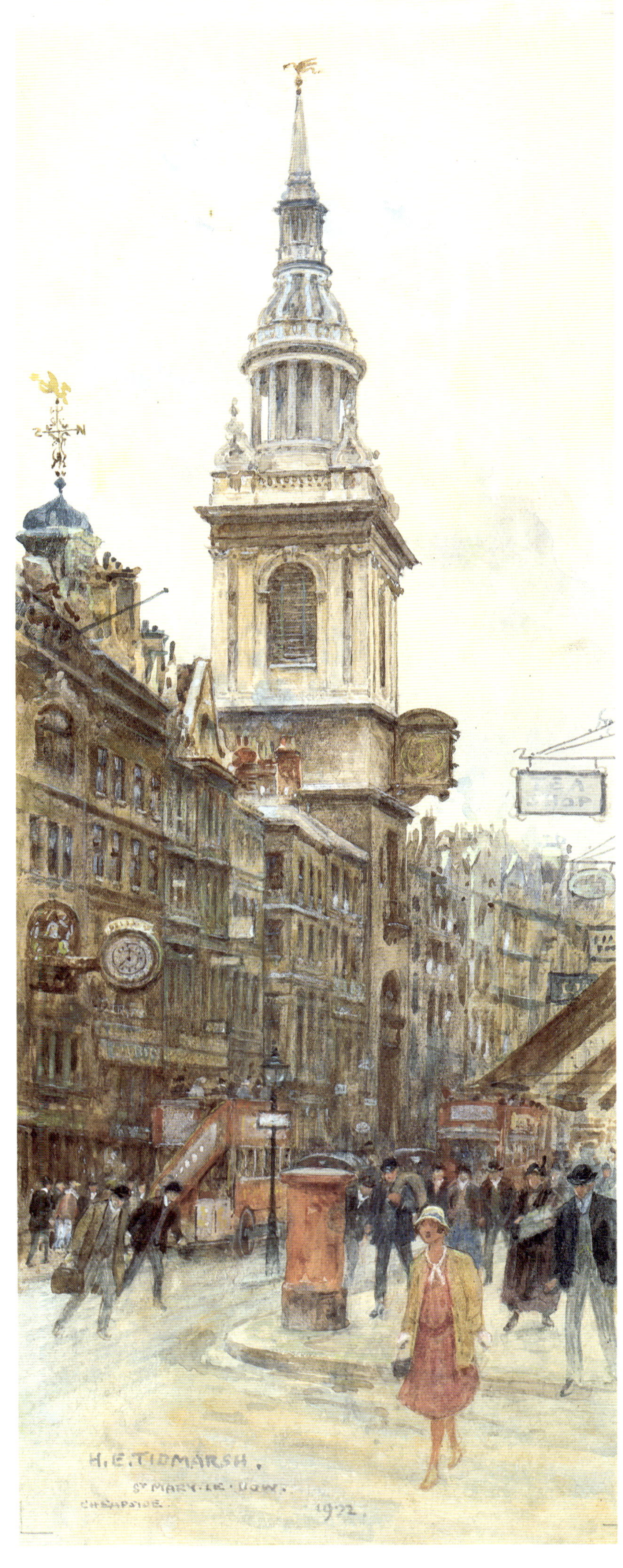
H.E.TIDMARSH.
St MARY-LE-BOW.
CHEAPSIDE.
1922.

St Mary Aldermary

c.1895

ST MARY ALDERMARY, QUEEN VICTORIA STREET

The tower and south aisle of St Mary Aldermary, as seen from Queen Victoria Street looking towards Watling Street and St Paul's Cathedral. The church today is used by the City's Roman Catholics. To the right is a shop with 'A. E. Long' on its blind. *Staffage:* hansom cabs, horse omnibuses, delivery carts, a uniformed street cleaner, and pedestrians.

[69] *Watercolour drawing 365 × 190 mm*

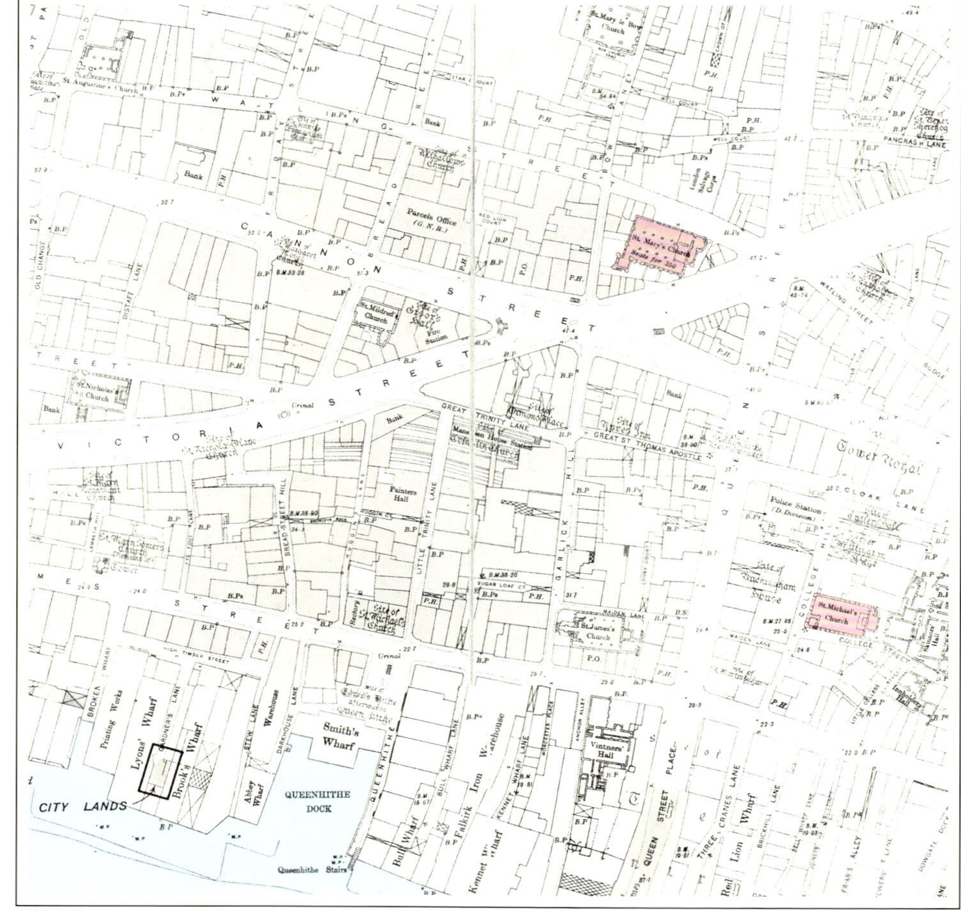

Detail from the Ordnance Survey Five Feet to One Mile Plan of London, V11.65, published 1919

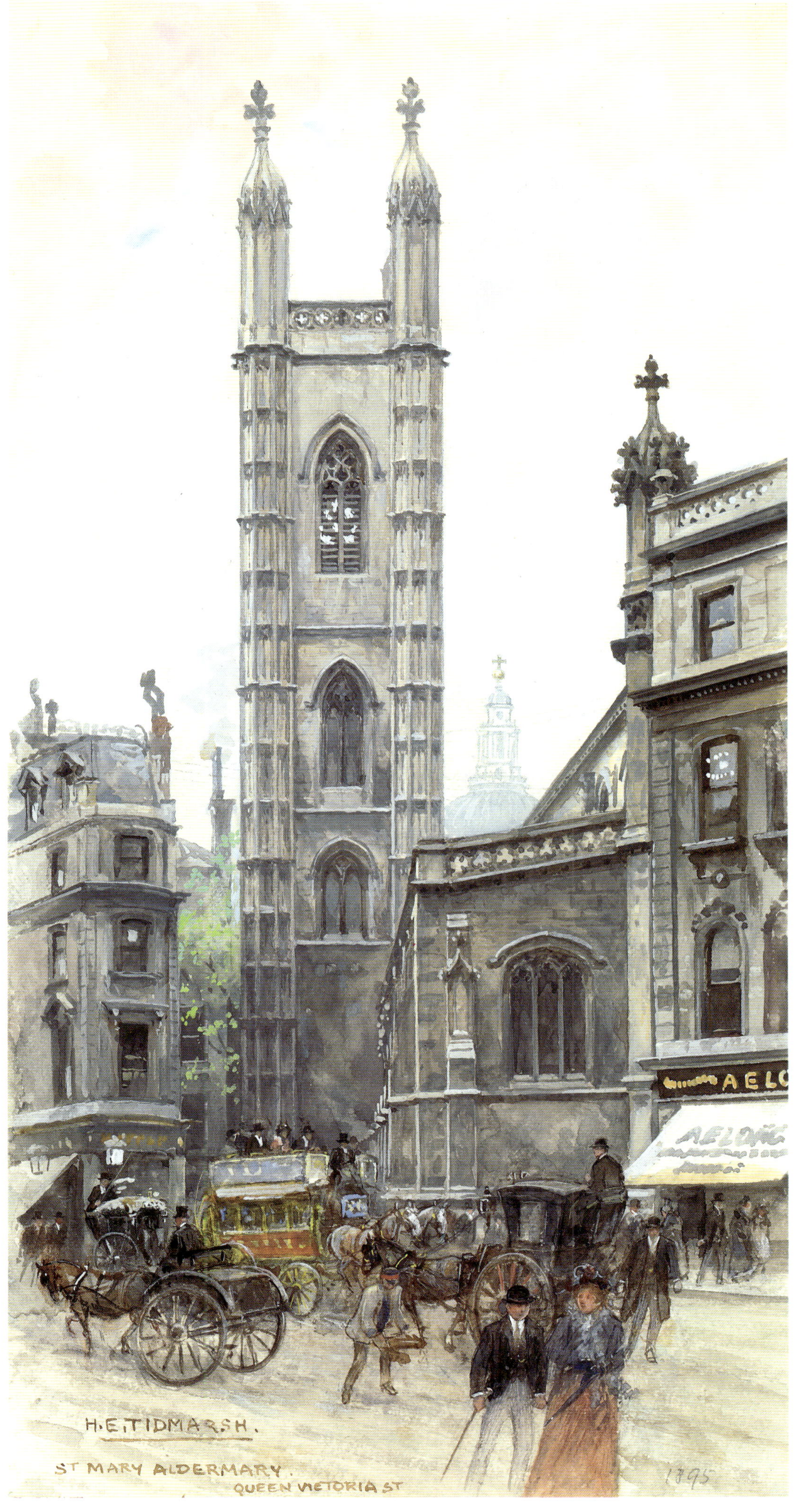
H.E. TIDMARSH.
ST MARY ALDERMARY.
QUEEN VICTORIA ST
1895

St Michael Paternoster Royal

c.1897

ST MICHAEL'S PATERNOSTER ROYAL COLLEGE HILL
A WREN STEEPLE 1713

View looking down College Hill towards Upper Thames Street. On the left of the street can be seen the former Whittington College and Mercers' School, and also the tower of St Michael's church. On the right, at the Cloak Lane corner, is the Cloak Lane Police Station guarded by a policeman. *Staffage:* a victoria, a covered cart, a porter, and two pairs of pedestrians.

[70] *Watercolour drawing, heightened with body colour 345 × 127 mm*

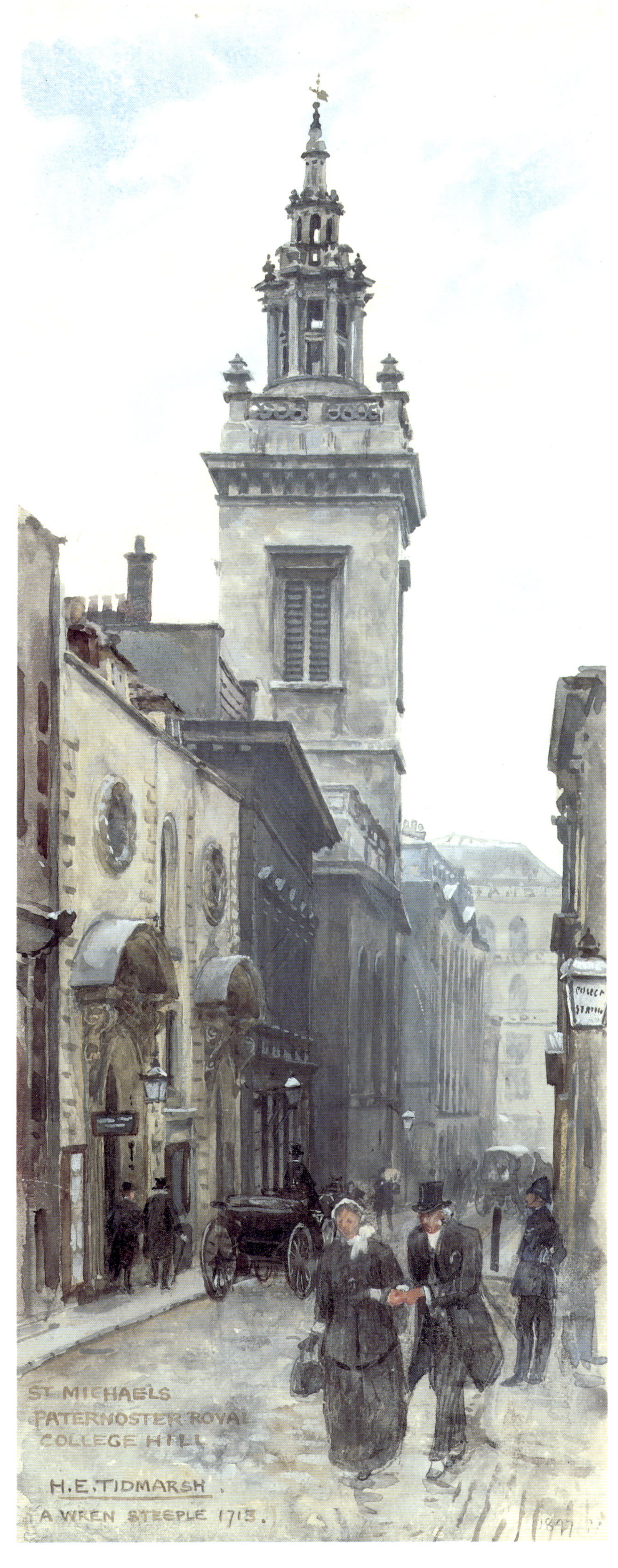
ST MICHAELS
PATERNOSTER ROYAL
COLLEGE HILL
H.E.TIDMARSH
A WREN STEEPLE 1713.

St Benet Paul's Wharf

c.1895

A WREN CHURCH, 1683

ST BENET PAUL'S WHARF, QUEEN VICTORIA ST.

St Benet's, designed by Sir Christopher Wren and erected in 1677-1685, is depicted here from the north. Today this attractive brick church is used by London's Welsh Episcopalians. *Staffage:* a fruit barrow pushed by a costermonger, a well-dressed lady wearing a feather boa, and a top-hatted City gentleman with a boy in an Eton suit.

[71] *Watercolour drawing 350 × 175 mm*

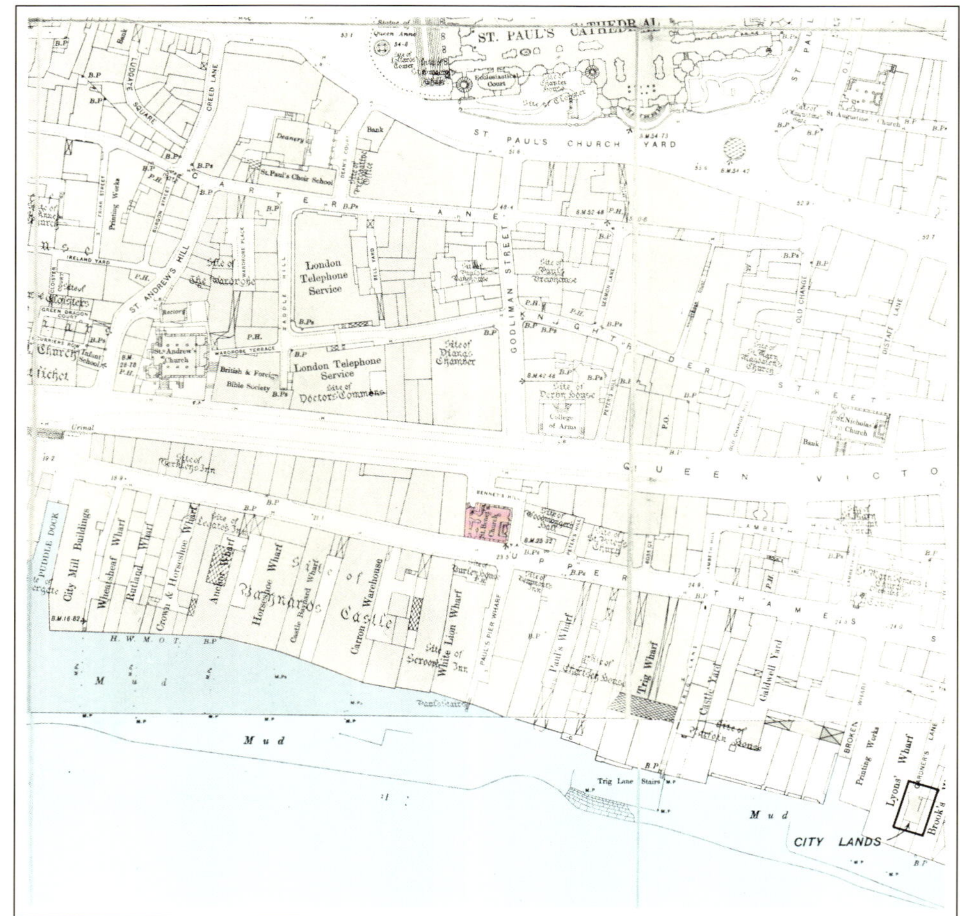

Detail from the Ordnance Survey Five Feet to One Mile Plan of London, V11.65/75, published 1919

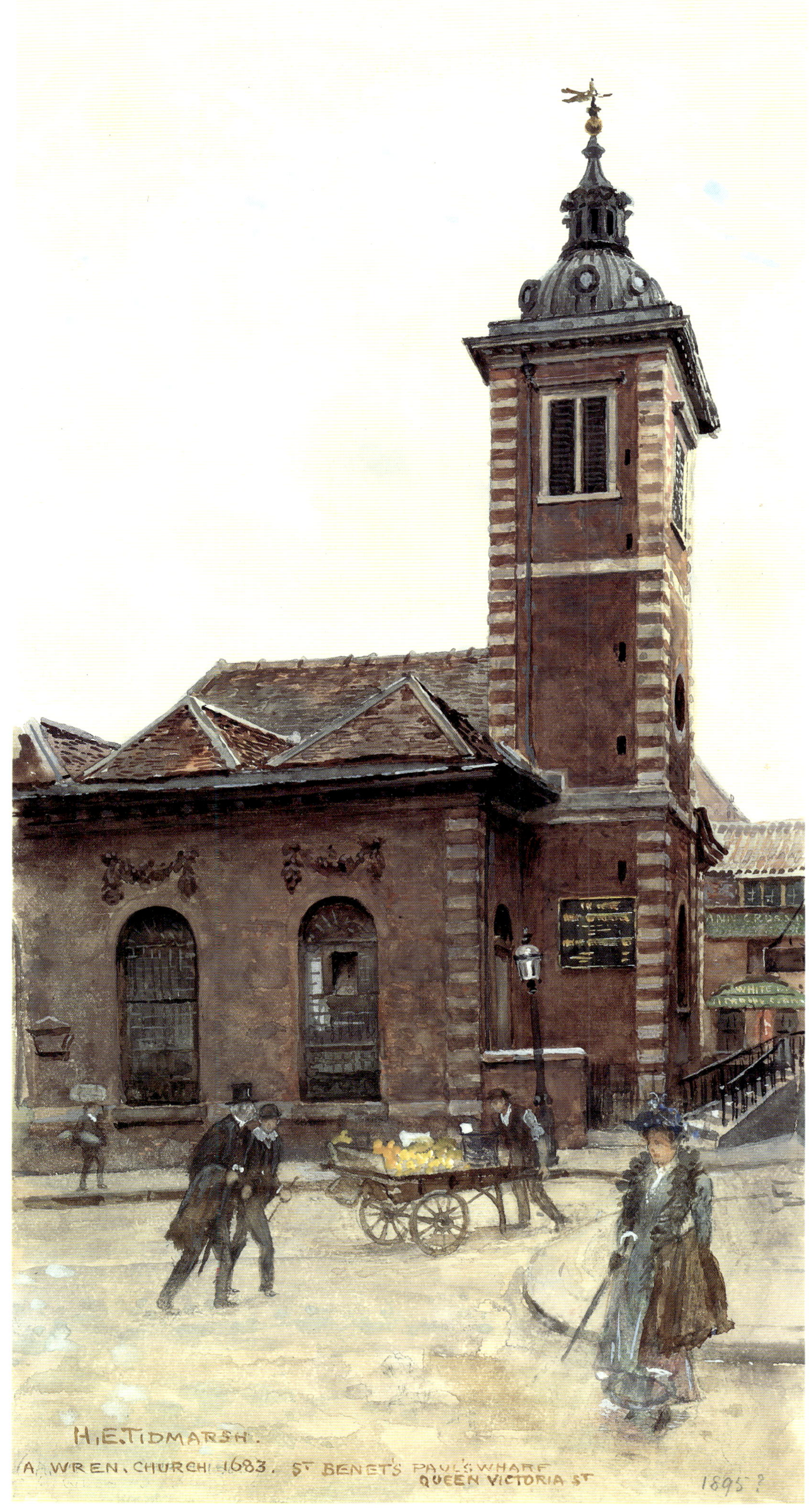
H.E.TIDMARSH.
A. WREN. CHURCH. 1683. ST BENET'S PAUL'S WHARF
QUEEN VICTORIA ST
1895?

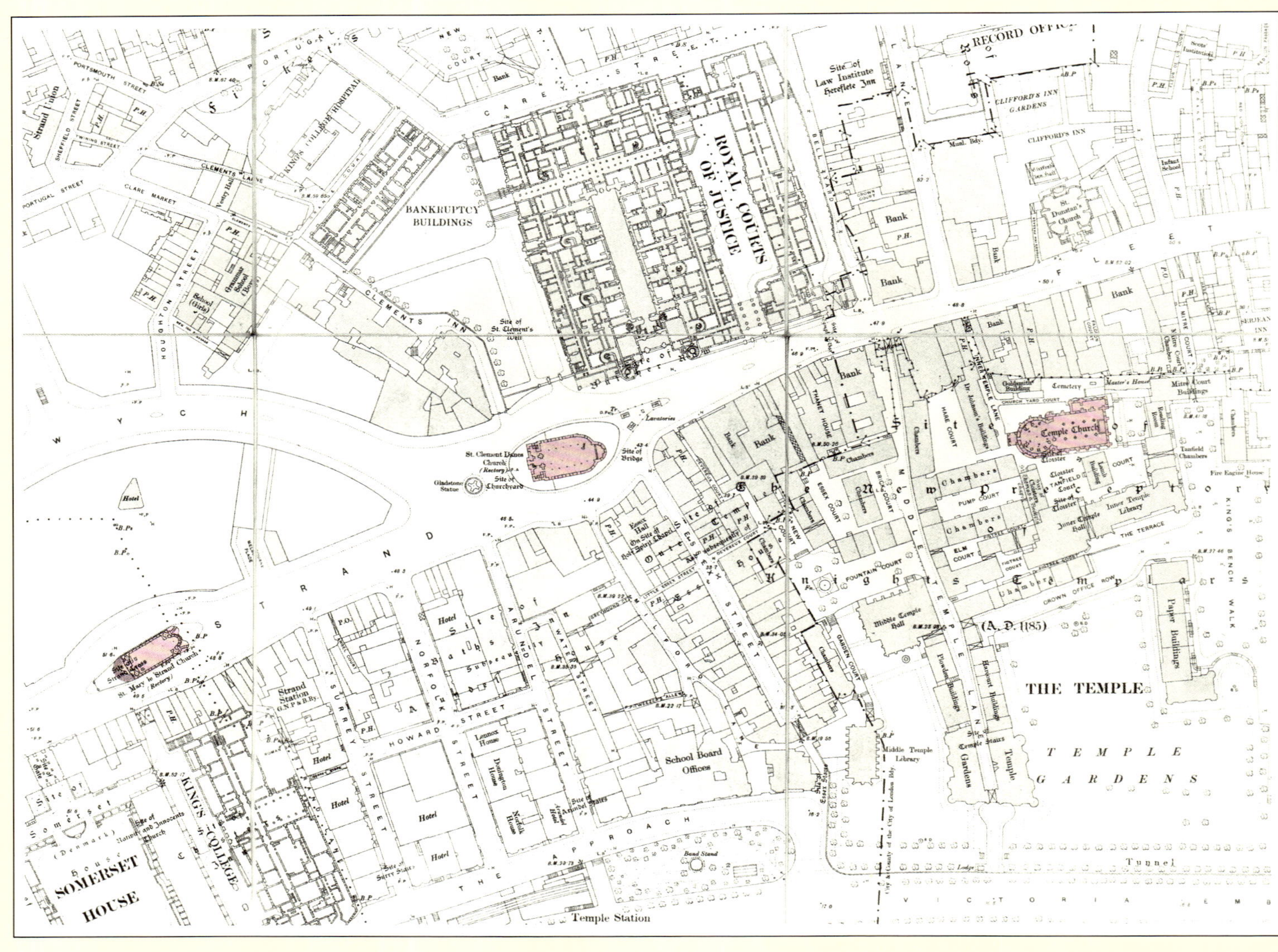

Heading West

Detail from the Ordnance Survey Five Feet to One Mile Plan of London, V11.64, published 1912

Trafalgar Square *(right)*

[72] *Detail from plate 81*

Heading West

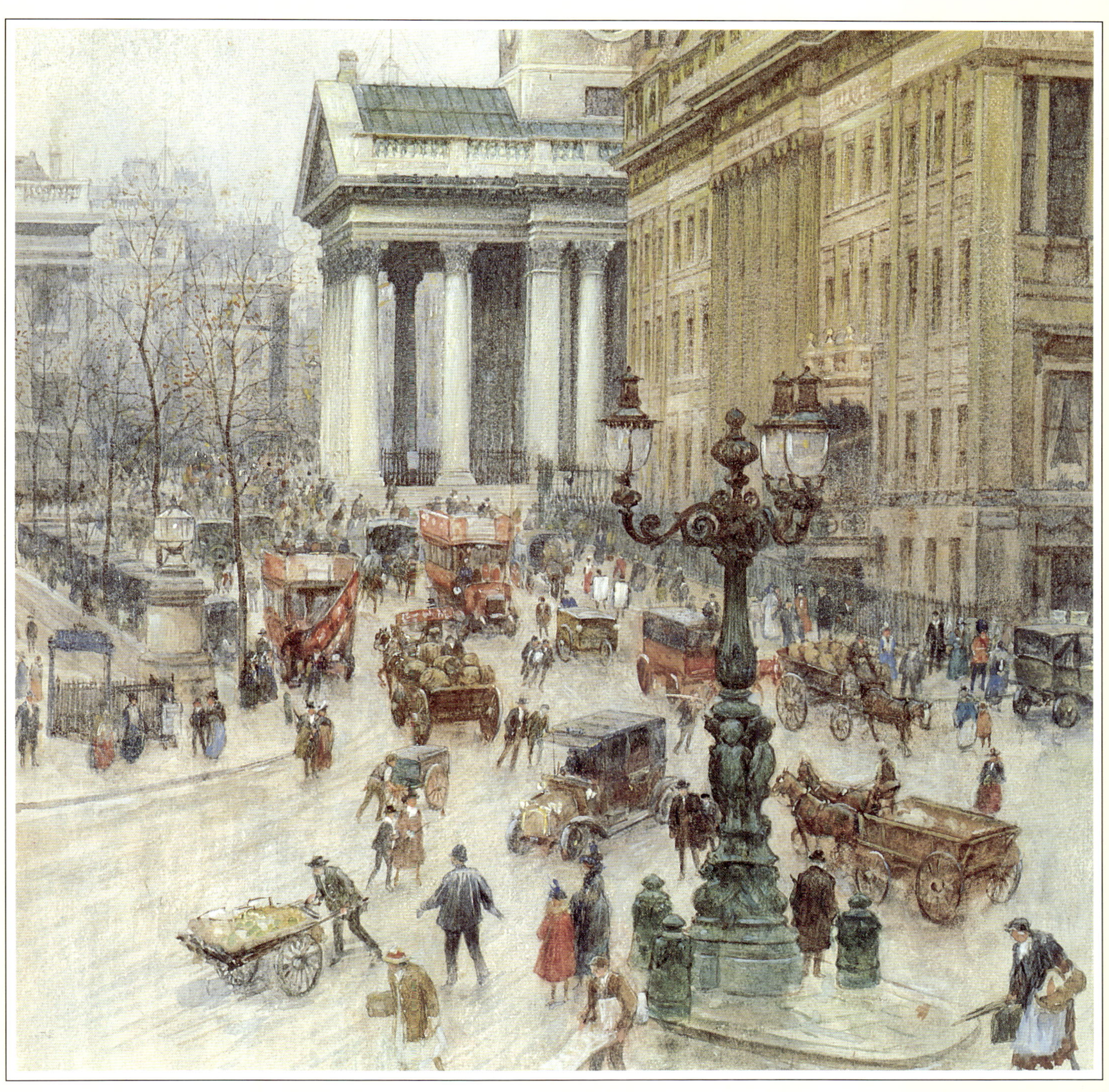

Temple Church

c.1900

THE TEMPLE CHURCH, FLEET ST. LONDON
A 'NORMAN' ROUND CHURCH 1185

The view is taken from the Inner Temple, with the 'round church' and its porch in the foreground. Temple Church, built in the 12th and 13th centuries, was originally the London house of the Order of Knights Templar. Today it serves as the joint chapel of the Societies of the Inner and Middle Temple, two of the four Inns of Court. *Staffage:* lawyers, one wearing a wig, and a woman accompanied by a small boy in knickerbockers holding a walking stick.

[73] *Watercolour drawing 275 × 393 mm*

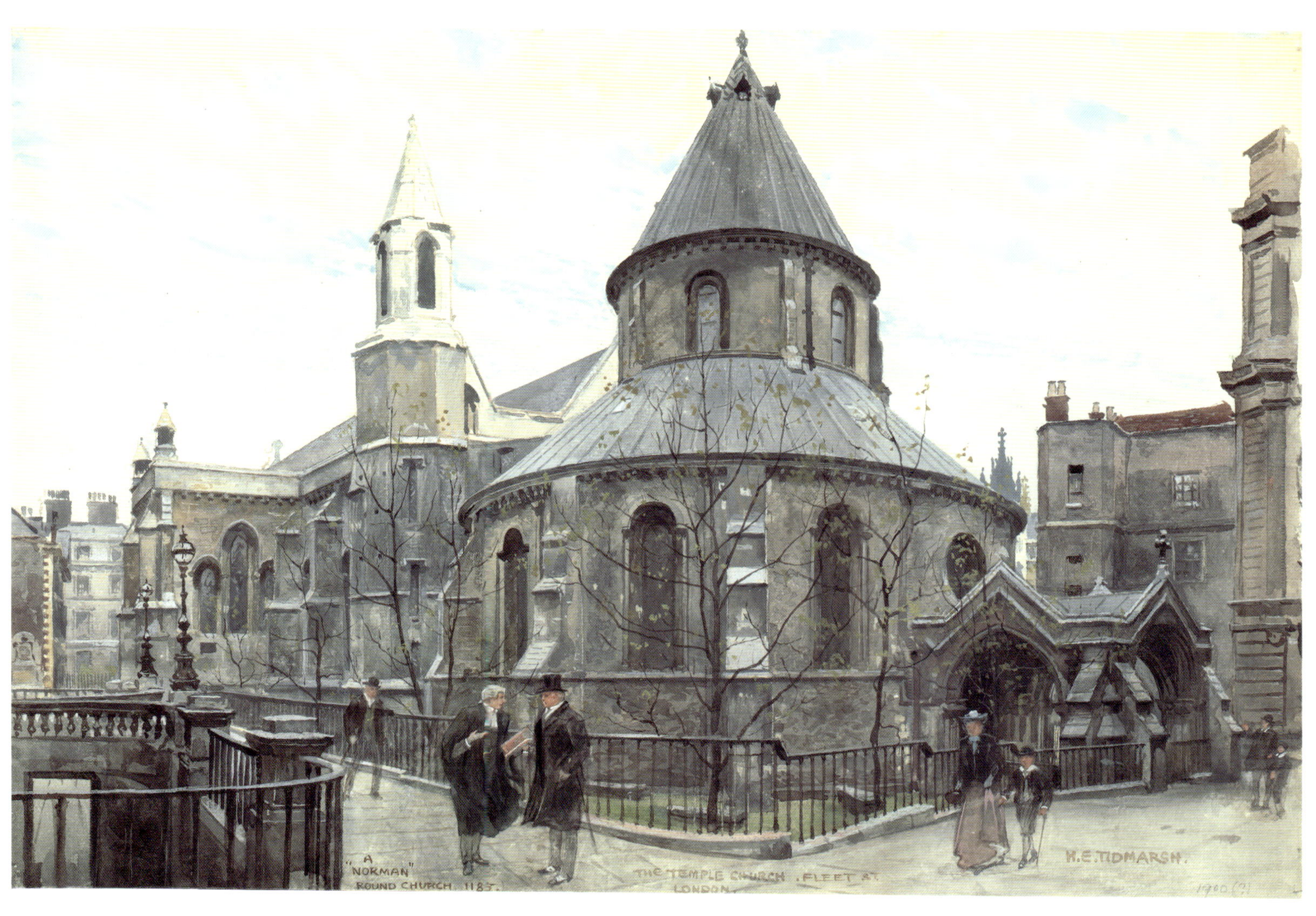
"A
"NORMAN"
ROUND CHURCH. 1185.
THE TEMPLE CHURCH. FLEET ST.
LONDON.
H.E. TIDMARSH.
1900(?)

St Clement Danes
c.1920

ST CLEMENT DANES, STRAND
A WREN CH. 1680. TOWER BY GIBBS 1719

The west facade of the church, and the Gladstone memorial in front. St Clement's, the only Wren church except St Paul's with an apse, was completed in 1682. James Gibbs' tower was finished in 1720. On the left can be seen the Law Courts, and the corona of St Dunstan in the West. On the right is the curve of Ingram House, and the junction with Essex Street. *Staffage:* taxis, motor buses, and a brewer's dray. Pedestrians include a bewigged lawyer, a postman, and an errand boy.

[74] *Watercolour drawing 280 × 390 mm*

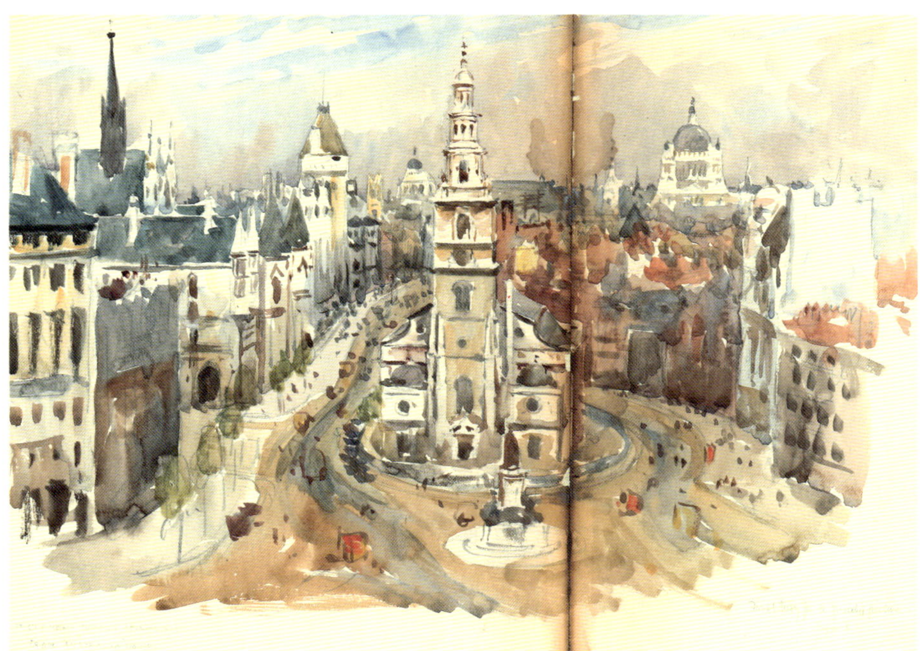

The Law Courts and St Clement Danes, looking east from a window in Australia House, c.1920

[75] *Watercolour sketch, 320 × 485 mm*

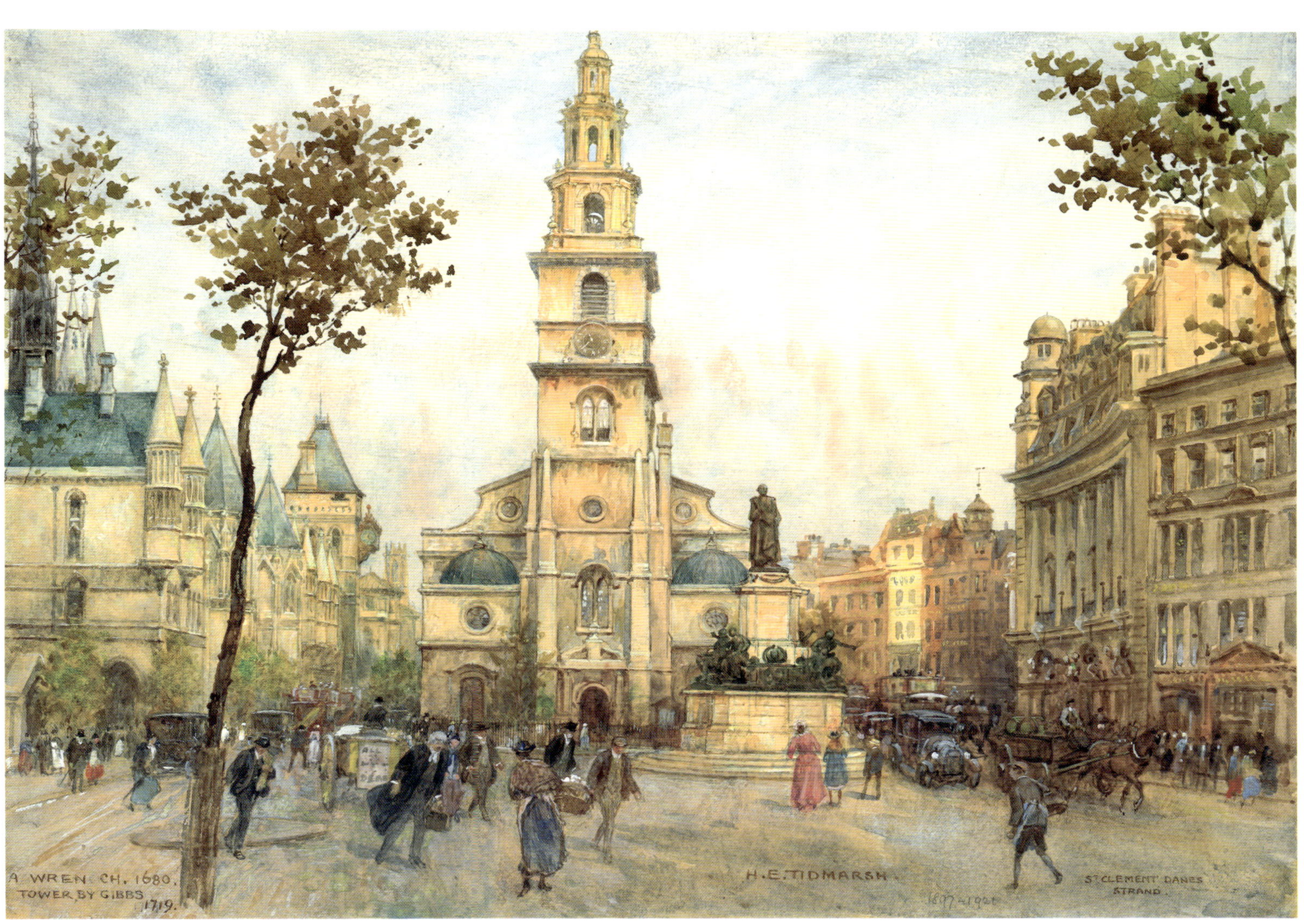
A WREN CH. 1680.
TOWER BY GIBBS
1719.
H.E.TIDMARSH.
ST CLEMENT DANES
STRAND.

St Mary le Strand

1927

ST MARY LE STRAND (BUILT BY GIBBS IN 1717)

St Mary's, designed by the Roman Catholic, James Gibbs, and consecrated in 1723, is viewed from the north west. The west facade is shown, but one and a half stages of the tower and cupola have been decapitated. *Staffage:* pedestrians only, including a well-dressed woman, a porter carrying a load, and a pedlar with a basket.

[76] *Watercolour drawing 395 × 250 mm*

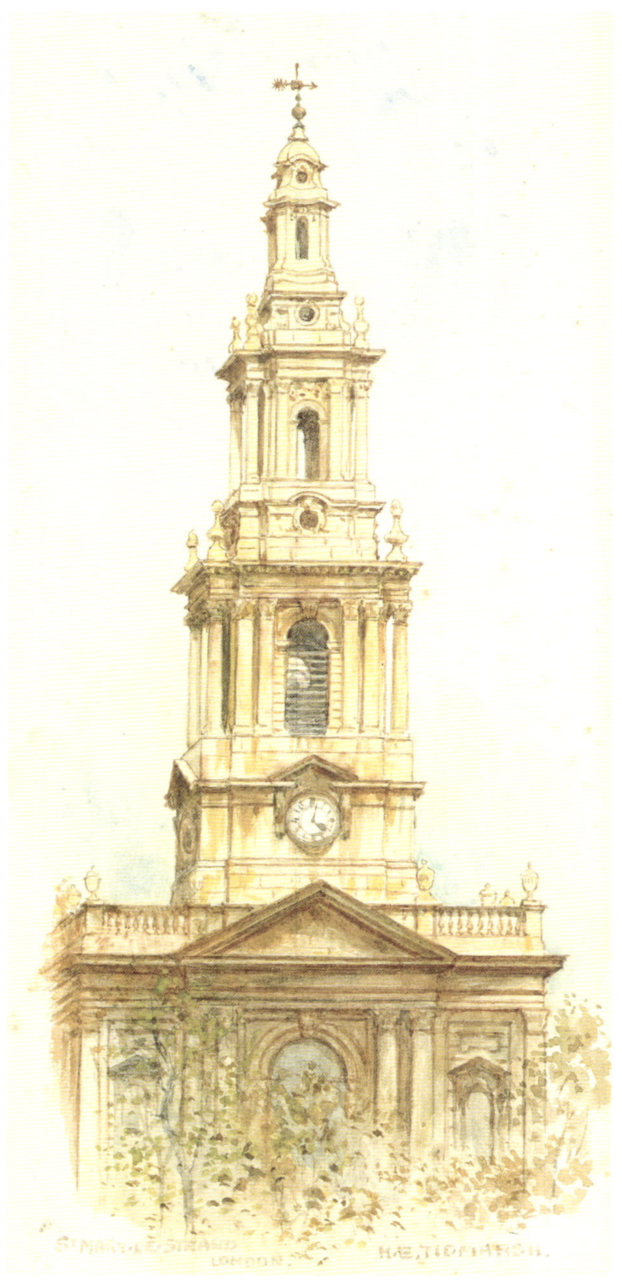

The tower of St Mary le Strand as seen from the west

[77] *Watercolour drawing, 303 × 140 mm (sight)*

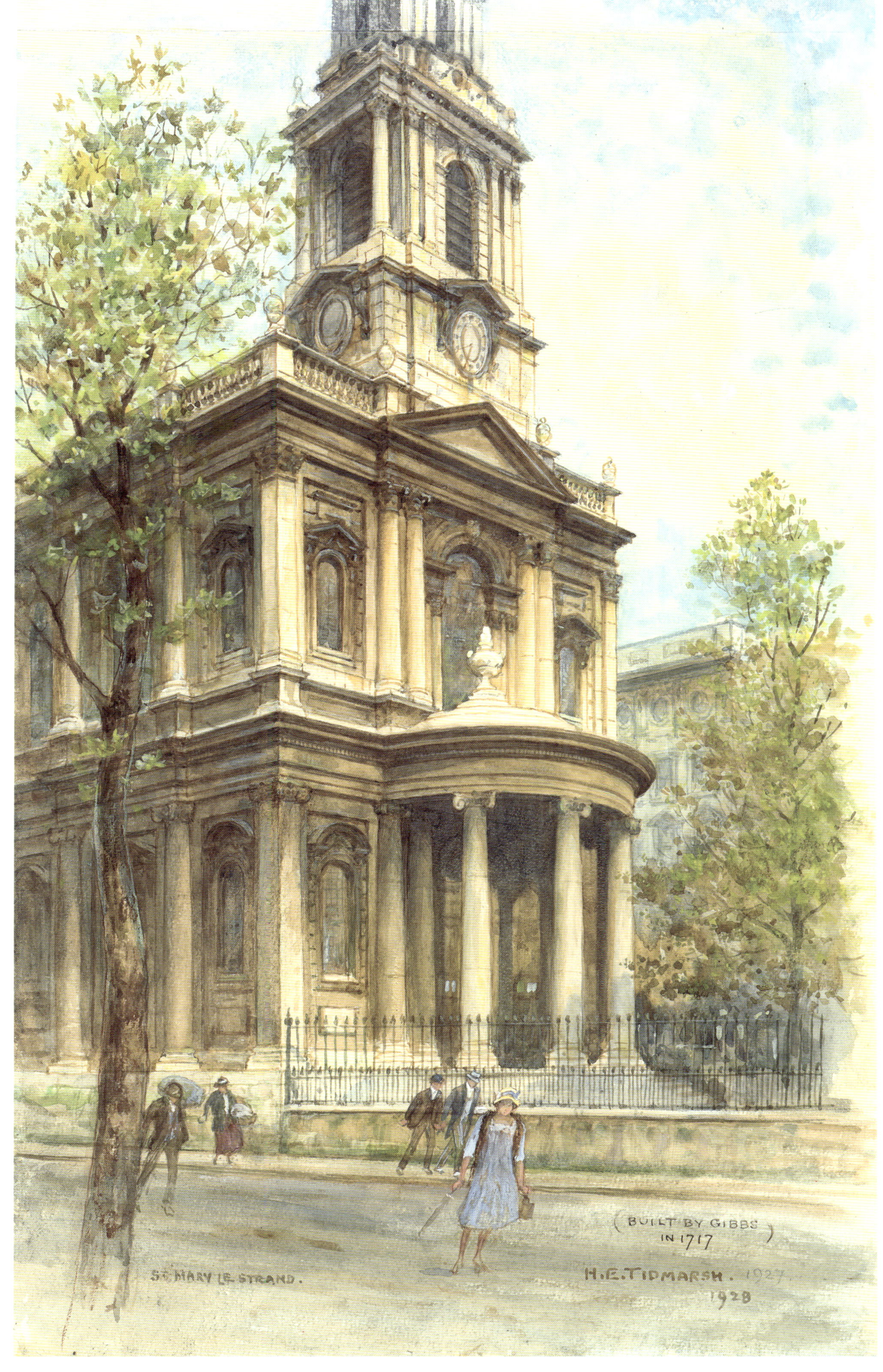
ST MARY LE STRAND.
(BUILT BY GIBBS IN 1717)
H.E. TIDMARSH. 1927
1928

St Paul Covent Garden

c.1915

ST PAUL'S, COVENT GARDEN
(BUILT BY INIGO JONES IN 1633)

The portico of this, the first Classical church in England, is seen from the north east through an arch of the covered piazza walk. Commissioned by the 4th Earl of Bedford, it was dubbed 'the handsomest barn in England.' *Staffage:* stallholders and porters carrying fruit baskets, and flower-sellers with their carts.

[78] *Watercolour drawing 394 × 260 mm*

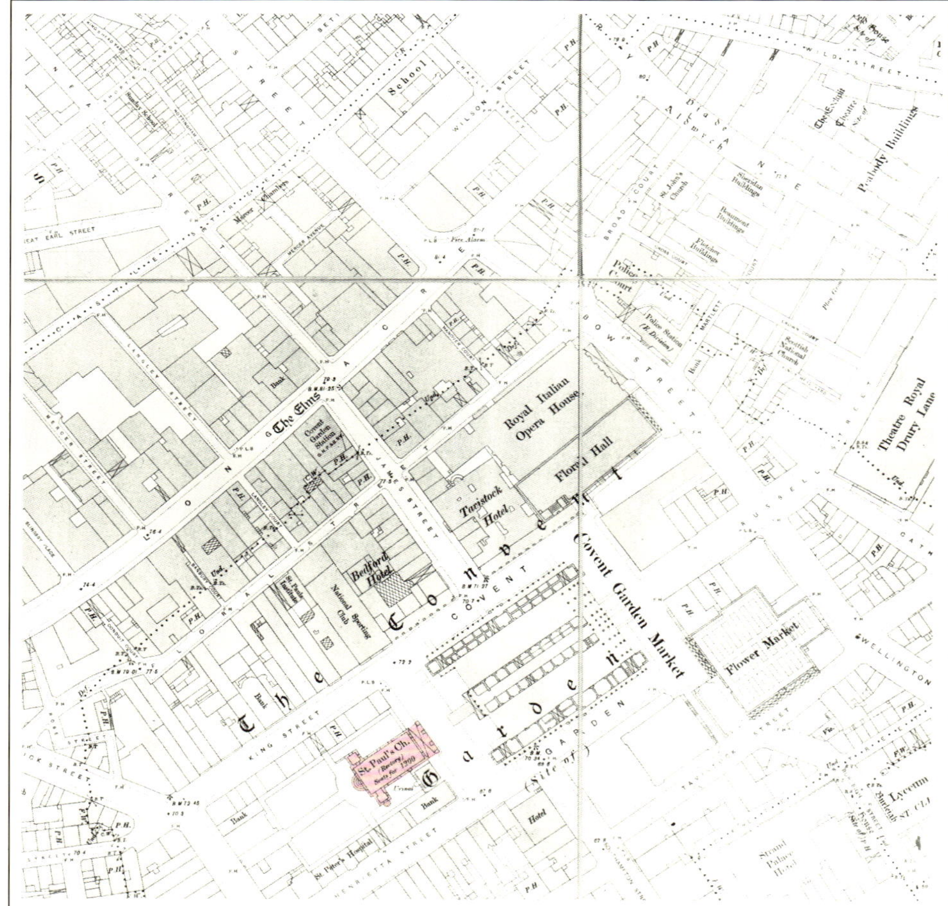

Detail from the Ordnance Survey Five Feet to One Mile Plan of London, V11.63, published 1911

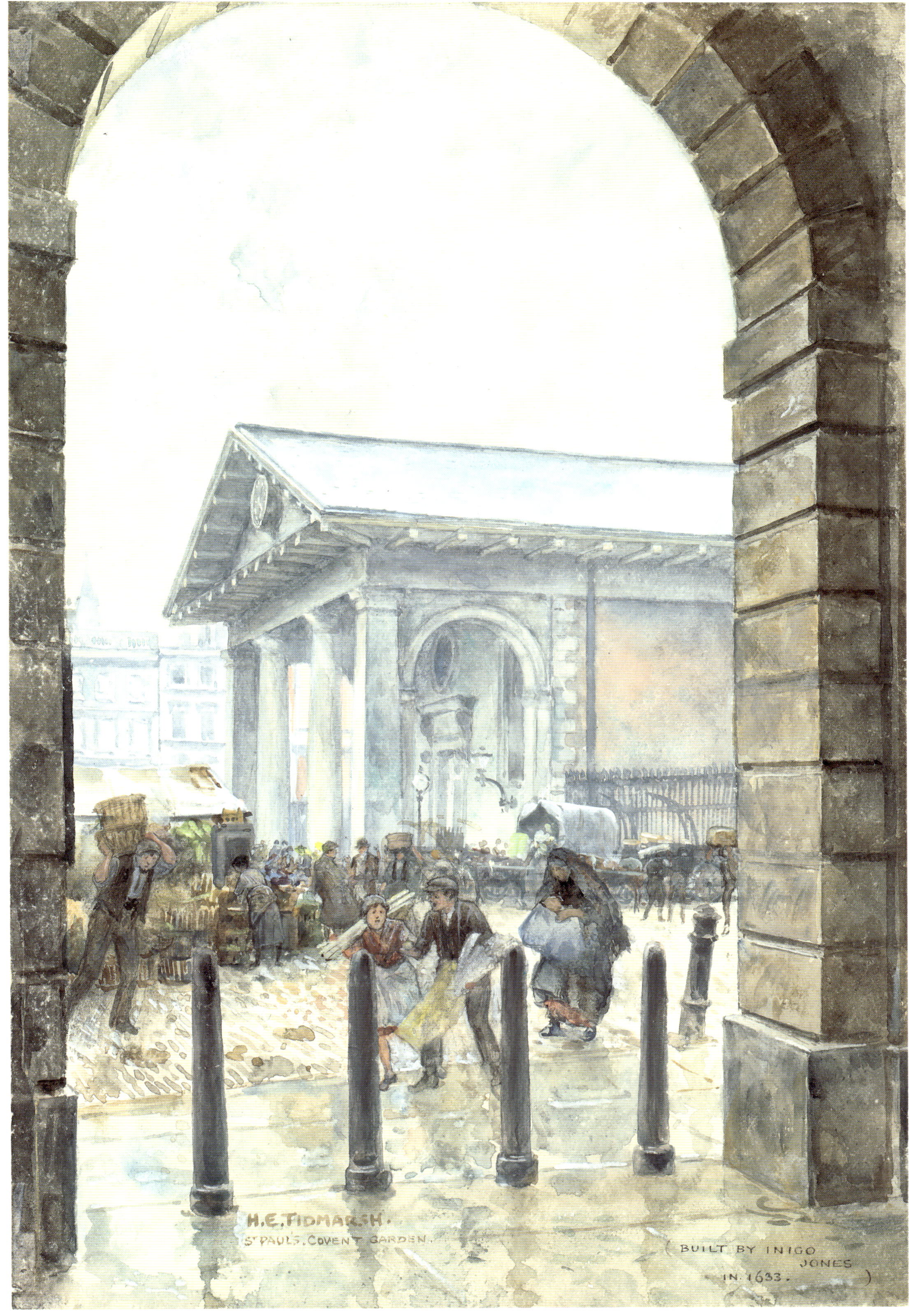
H.E. TIDMARSH.
St PAULS, COVENT GARDEN.
(BUILT BY INIGO JONES IN 1633.)

St George Bloomsbury

c.1920

ST GEORGE'S CHURCH, BLOOMSBURY, LONDON

South view of the church showing the portico, tower, and curious stepped steeple. St George's, designed by Nicholas Hawksmoor and completed in 1731, was described by Horace Walpole as 'a masterpiece of absurdity.' *Staffage:* a policeman, a hawking greengrocer with his barrow, and various pedestrians including women carrying baskets.

[79] *Watercolour drawing 390 × 280 mm*

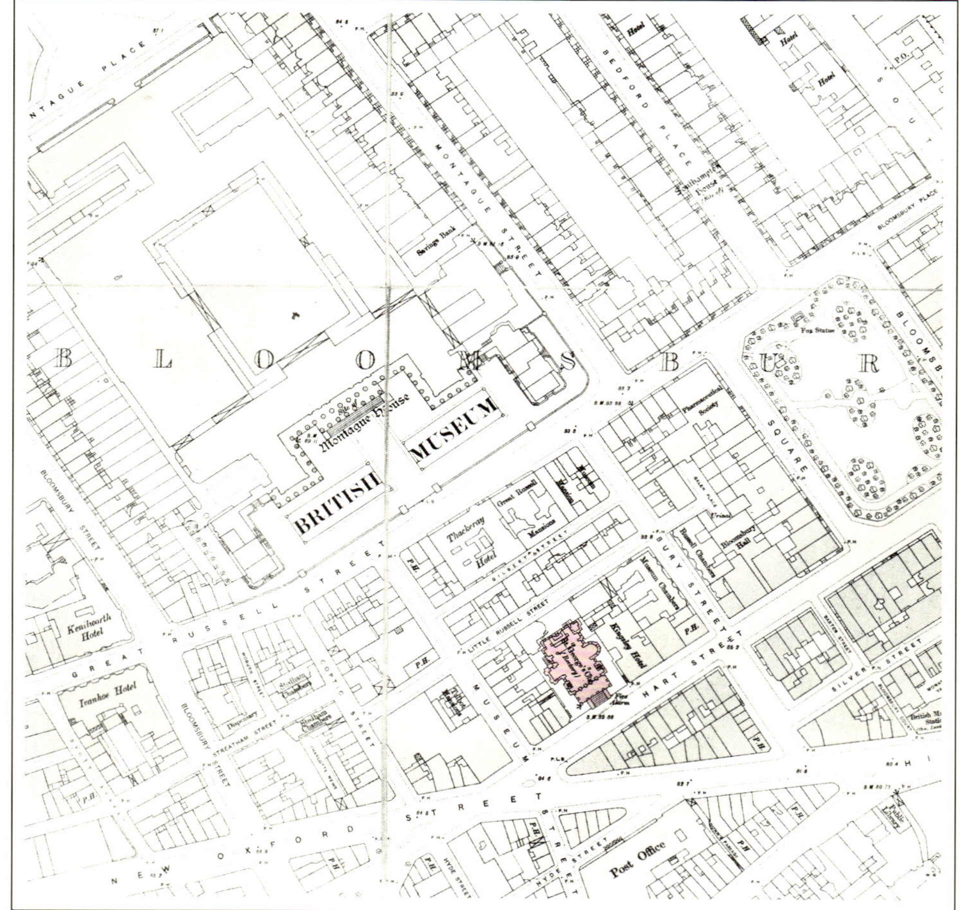

Detail from the Ordnance Survey Five Feet to One Mile Plan of London, V11.53, published 1912

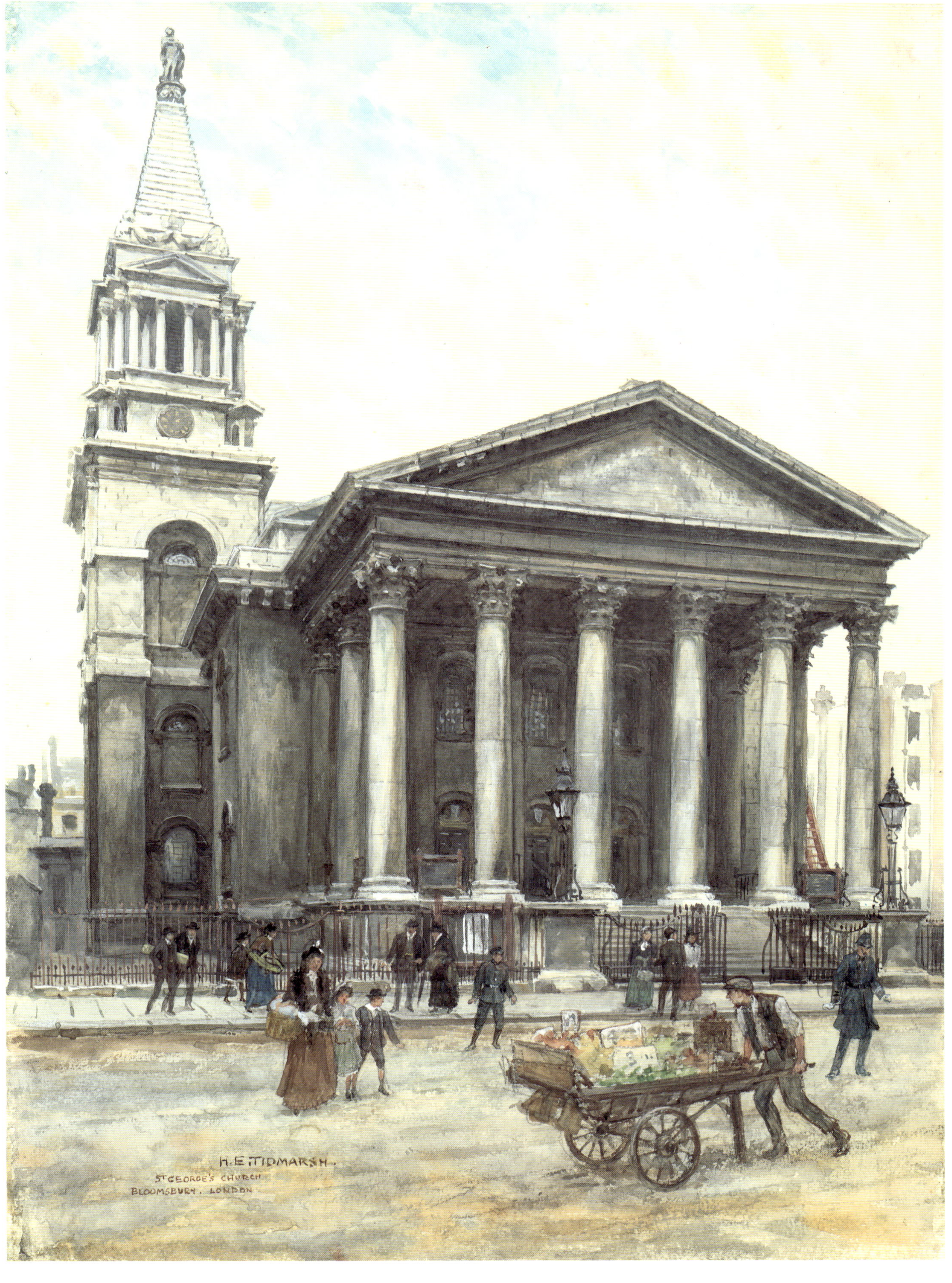
H.E.TIDMARSH.
St GEORGE'S CHURCH
BLOOMSBURY. LONDON

Trafalgar Square

1912

[UNTITLED]

On the right is Morley's Hotel, built in 1831, and the church of St Martin-in-the-Fields, built by James Gibbs in 1722-1724. *Staffage:* traffic including motor buses, taxis, and horse-drawn vehicles - a hansom cab, a coal cart, and tradesmen's carts. In the centre of the square is a cab-rank. A multitude of pedestrians are carefully drawn. The style of this watercolour differs from Tidmarsh's usual style. It resembles that adopted by Camille Pissaro in the 1890s when painting Paris streets looking down from hotel windows.

[80] *Watercolour drawing 526 × 335 mm*

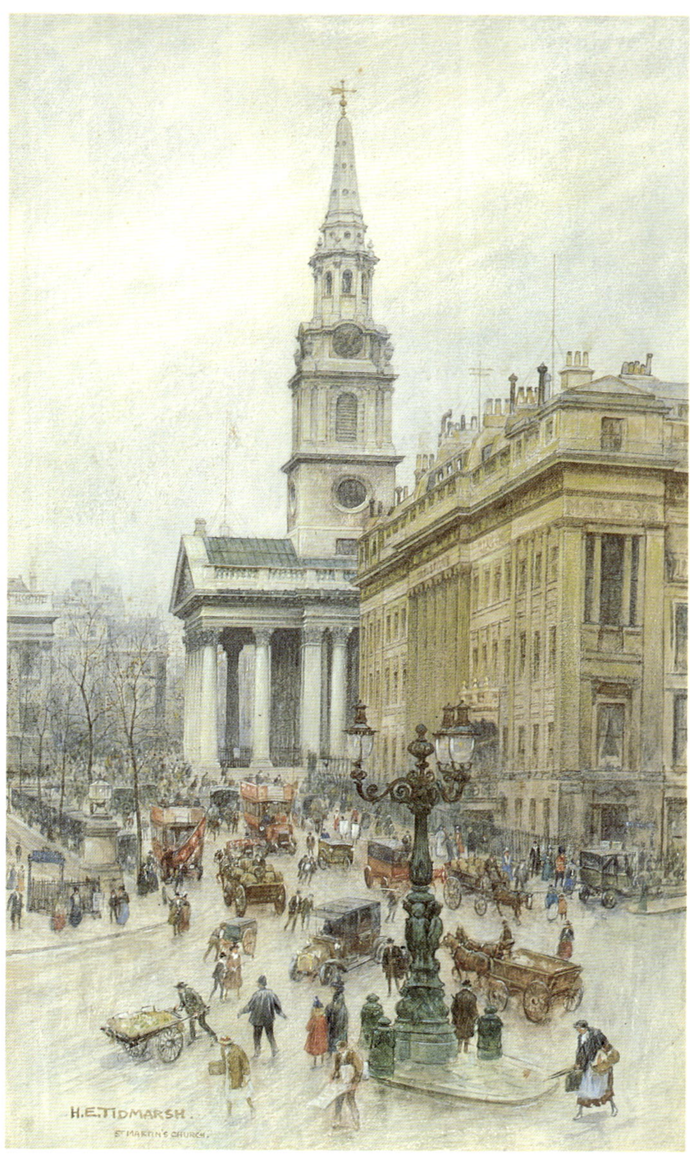

Trafalgar Square

Another version of the same image, perhaps drawn a few days later: there is less foliage on the trees. The staffage also varies.

[81] *Watercolour drawing, 556 × 324 mm (sight)*

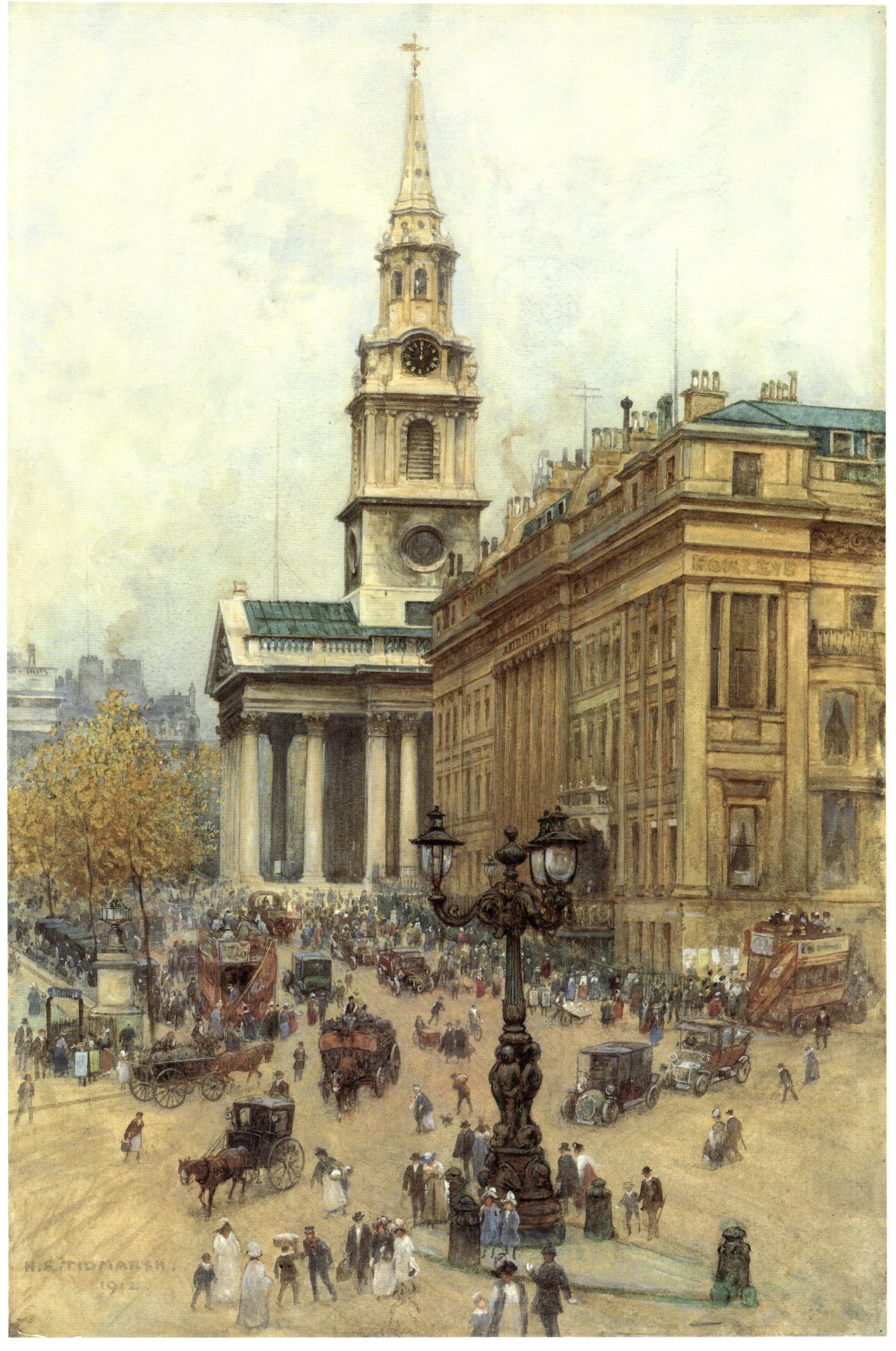
H.E. TIDMARSH.
1912

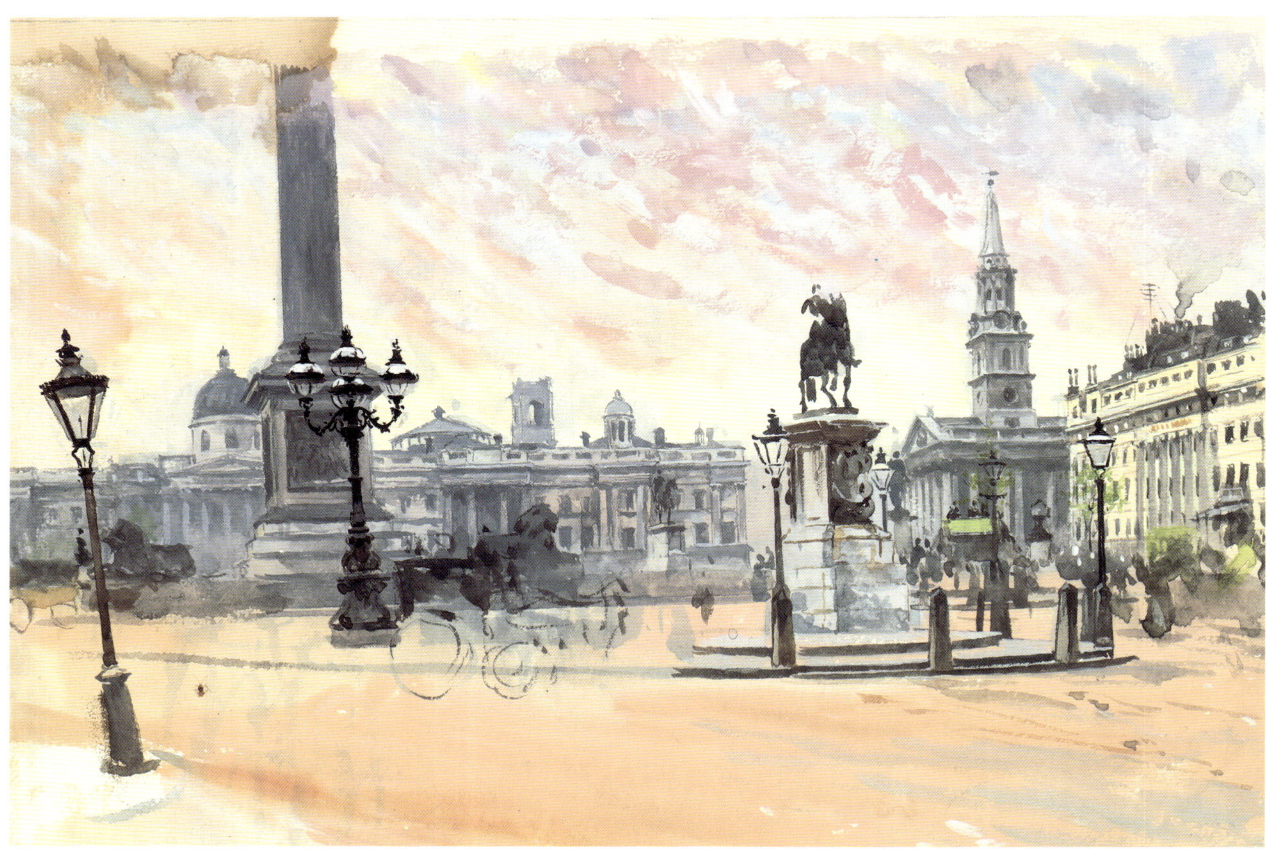

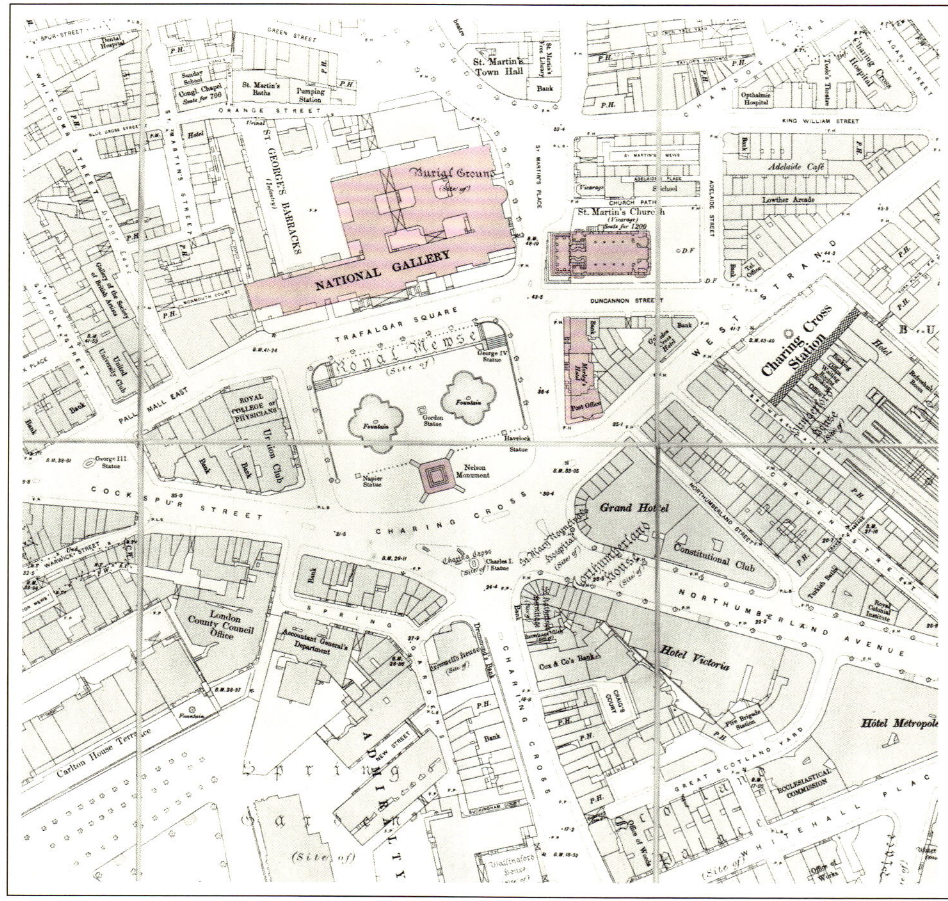

Trafalgar Square, c.1890
(above)

Looking towards Nelson's Column, Le Sueur's equestrian statue of Charles I, St Martin-in-the-Fields, and Morley's Hotel.

[82] *Watercolour sketch, 205 × 302 mm*

The National Gallery, c.1883
(above right)

An ostler leans on the bollard near his two horses.

[83] *Wash drawing, heightened with body colour, 173 × 238 mm*

The stairs of the National Gallery
(right)

[84] *Wash drawing, heightened with body colour, 120 × 175 mm*

Detail from the Ordnance Survey Five Feet to One Mile Plan of London, V11.73, published 1895

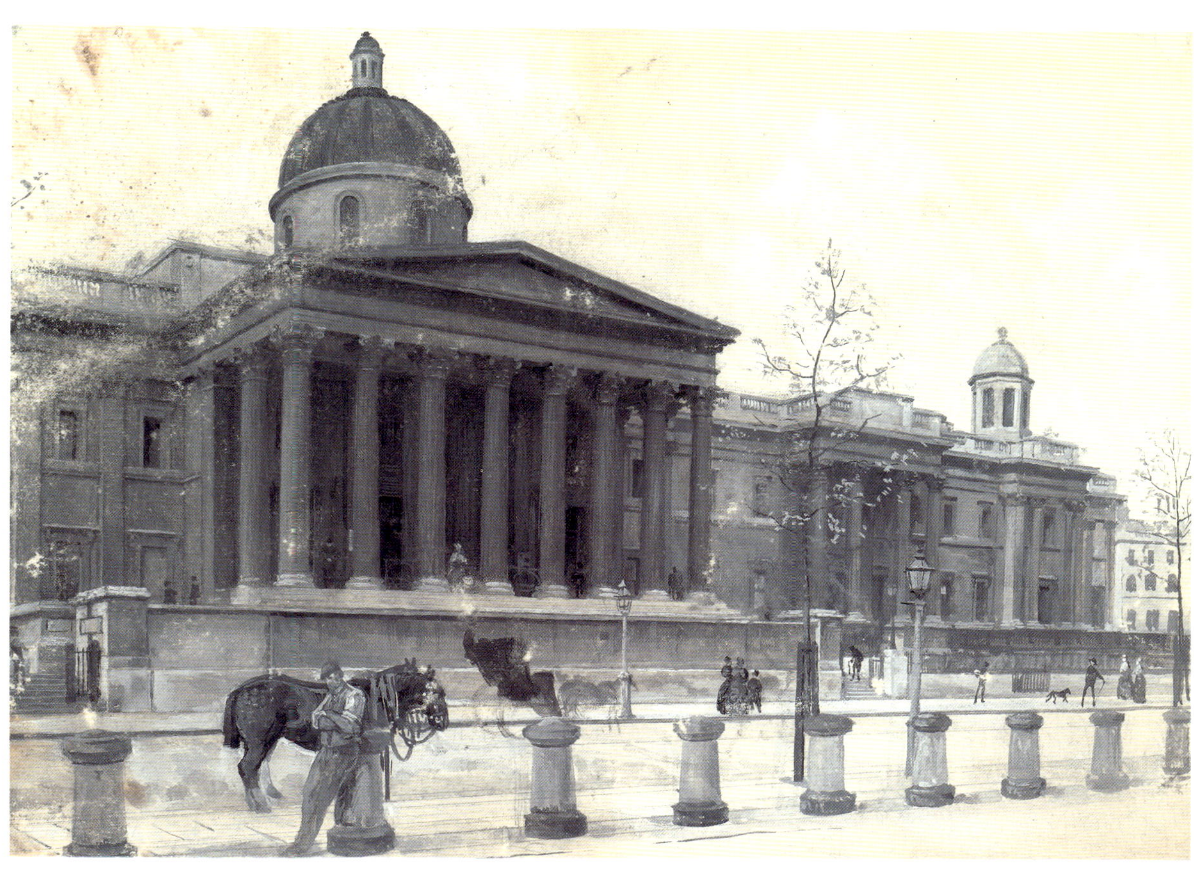

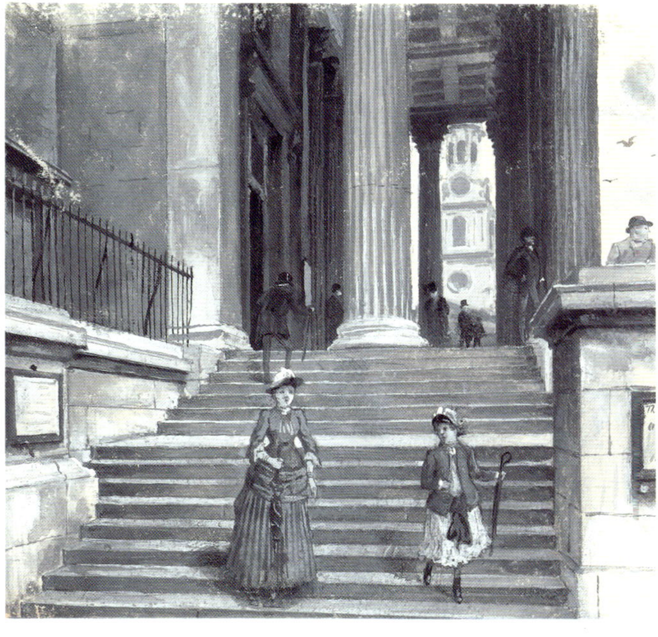

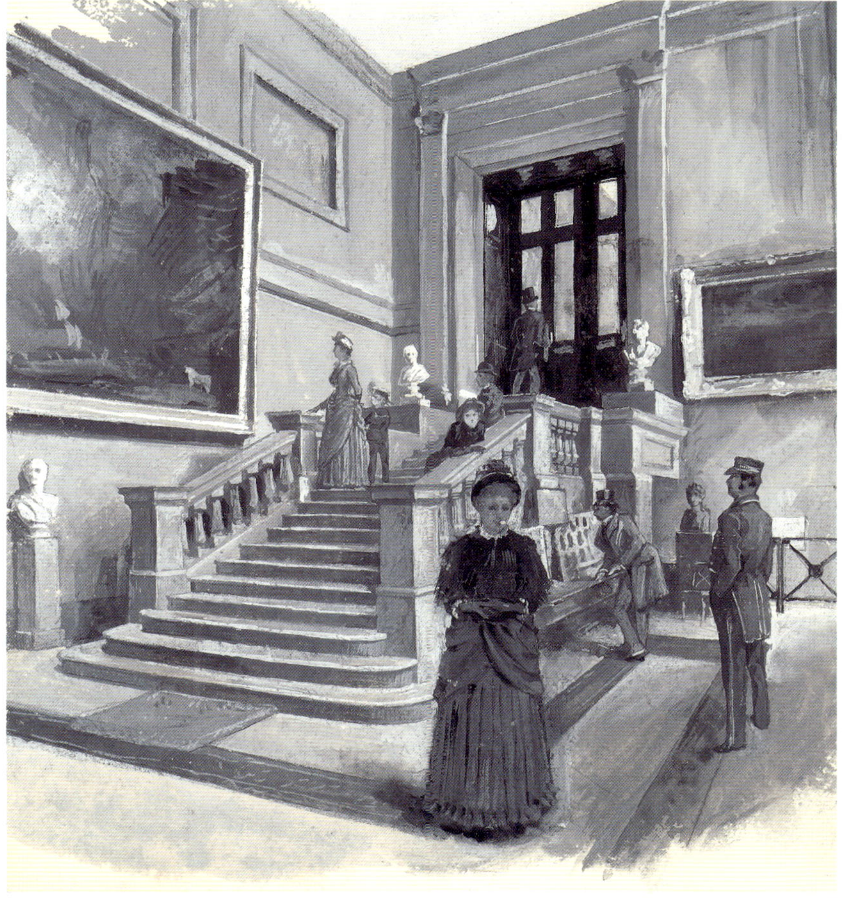

Stone stairs leading up to an exit

The painting hanging on the stairs is James Ward's colossal 'Gordale Scar' which the Gallery had purchased in 1878. It is now in the Tate Gallery.

[85] *Wash drawing, heightened with body colour, 180 × 160 mm*

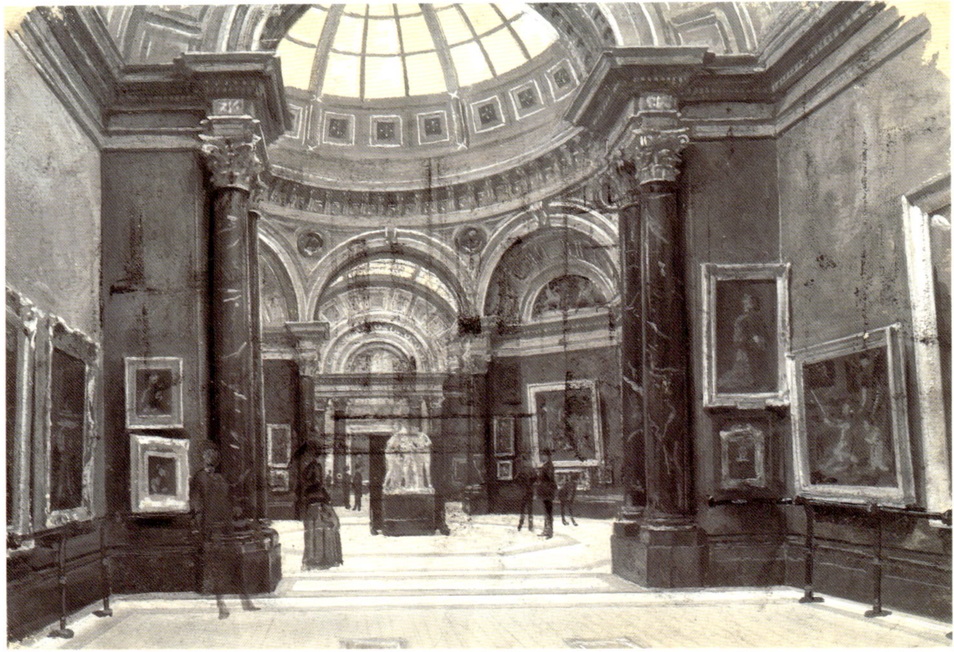

View into the Dome Room from one of the vestibules

Velazquez's 'Christ after the Flagellation' and Zurbaran's 'St Francis at Meditation' can be identified on the right.

[86] *Wash drawing, heightened with body colour, 155 × 218 mm*

Raphael's 'Ansidei' Madonna exhibited on a specially draped screen
(below left)

[87] *Wash drawing, heightened with body colour, 100 × 128 mm*

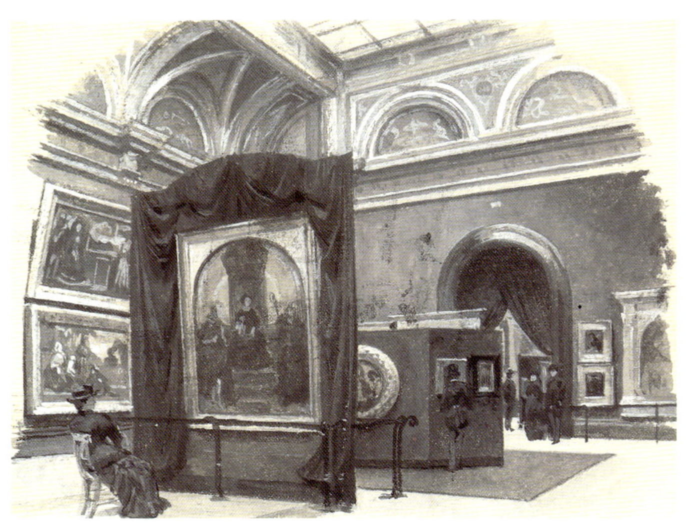

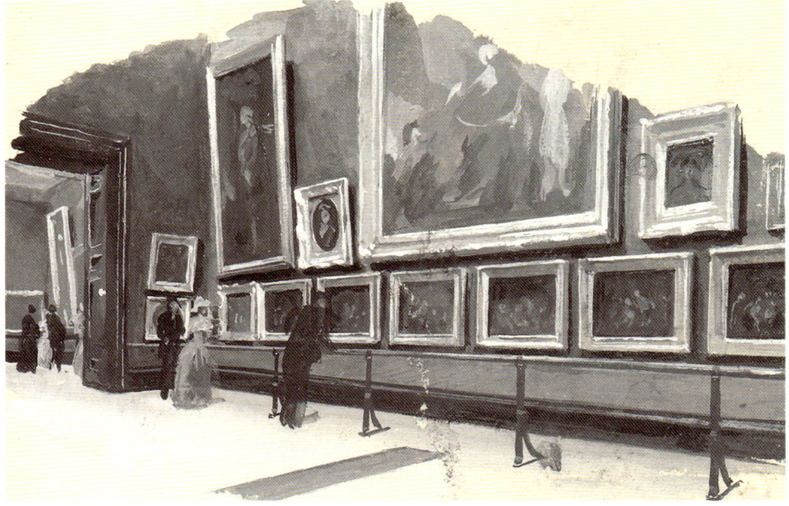

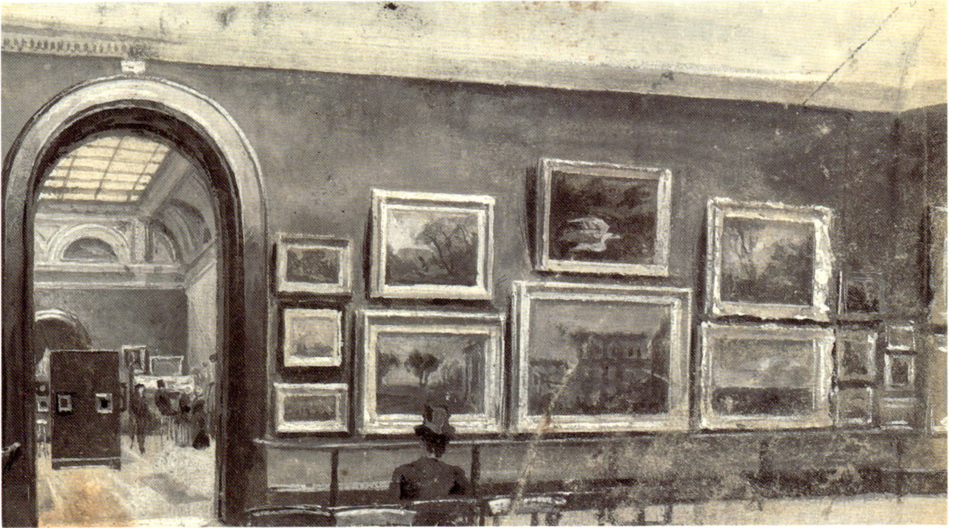

'The Shrimp Girl' by William Hogarth can be identified in the upper rank of paintings. Below are the six paintings that make up Hogarth's 'Marriage a la Mode.'
(above)

[88] *Wash drawing, heightened with body colour, 110 × 150 mm*

Identifiable pictures in this room include Claude's 'Aeneas at Delors' and Canaletto's 'Feast Day of St Roch.'

[89] *Wash drawing, heightened with body colour, 100 × 170 mm*

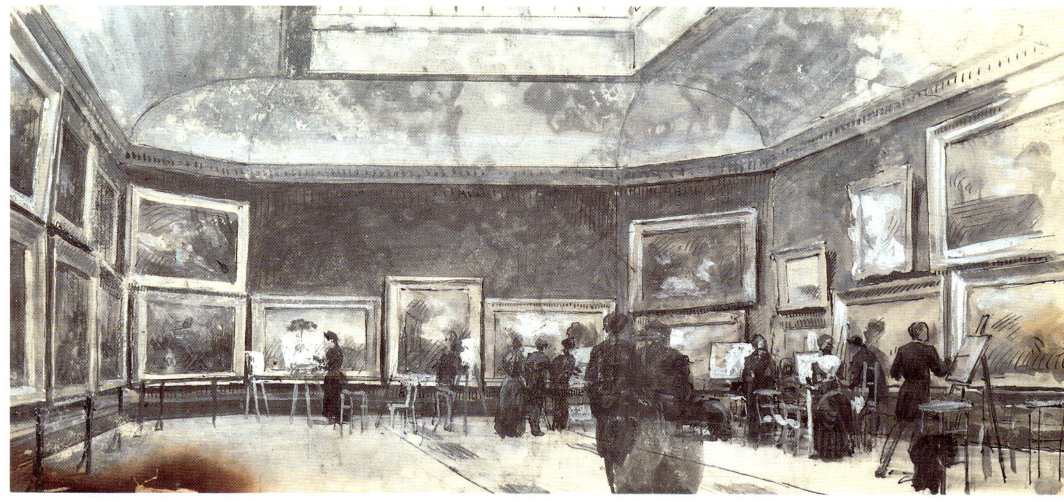

The National Gallery's Turner Room

With pictures in serried ranks, and students and copyists at work.

[90] *Wash drawing, heightened with body colour, 85 × 176 mm*

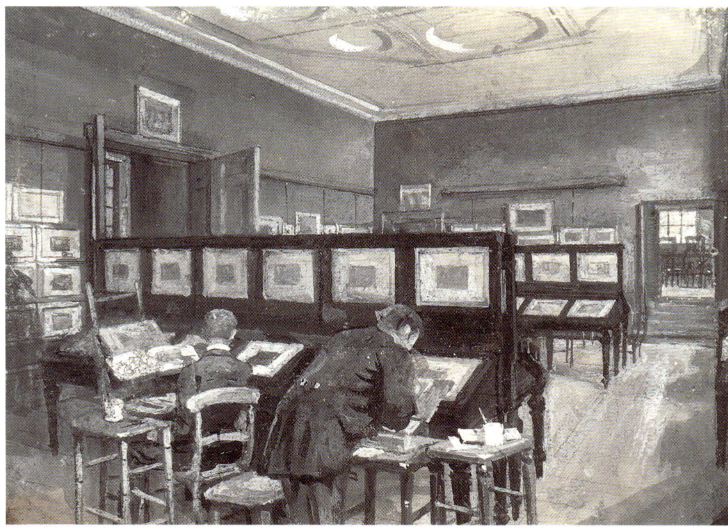

The basement of the Turner Room

Two copyists at work.

[91] *Wash drawing, heightened with body colour, 100 × 135 mm*

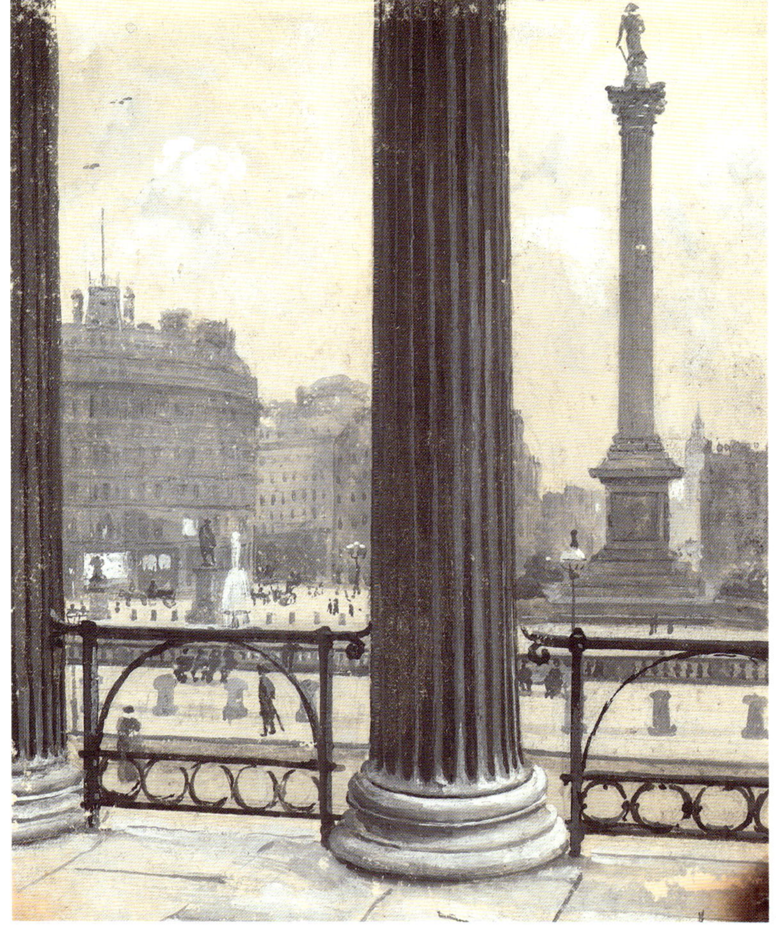

View southward

From the portico of the National Gallery towards Nelson's Column and the Houses of Parliament.

[92] *Wash drawing, heightened with body colour, 150 × 120 mm*

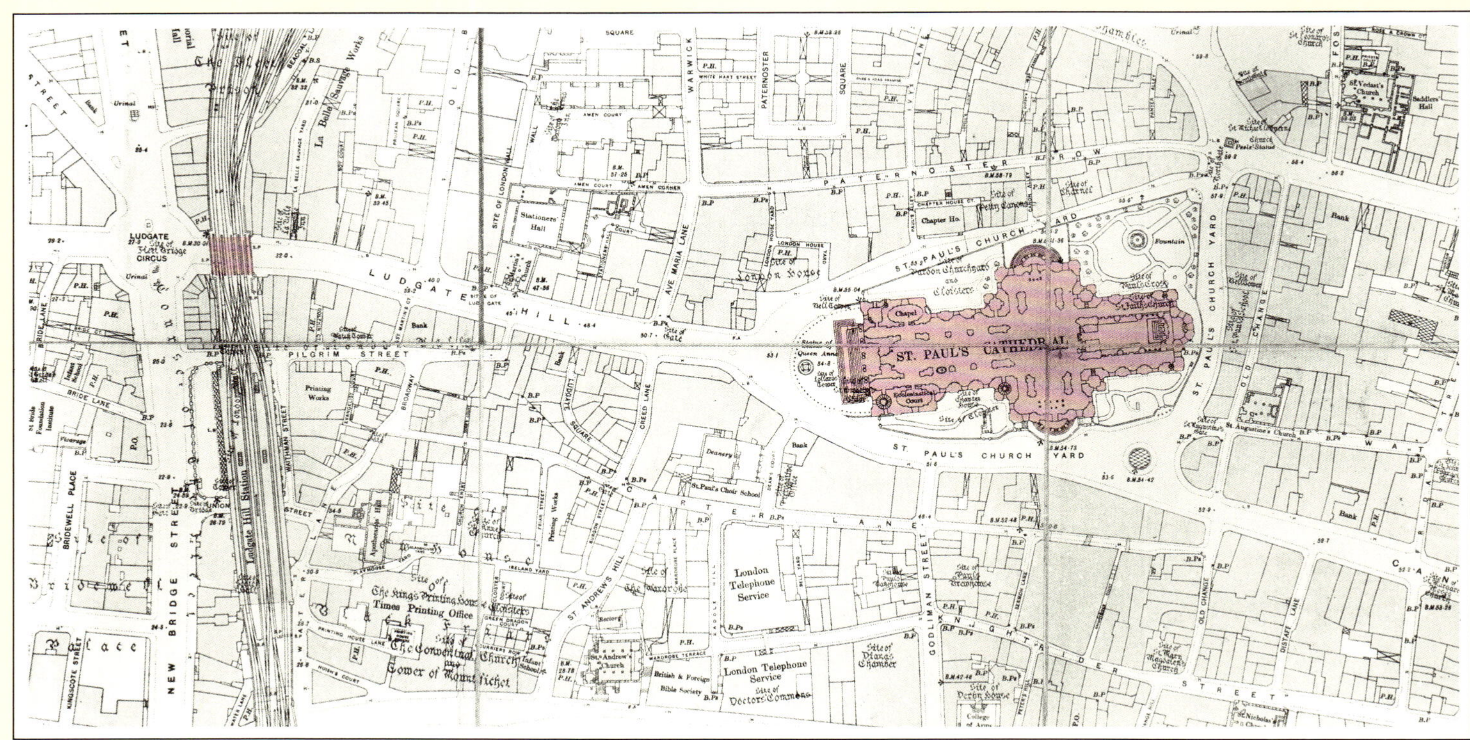

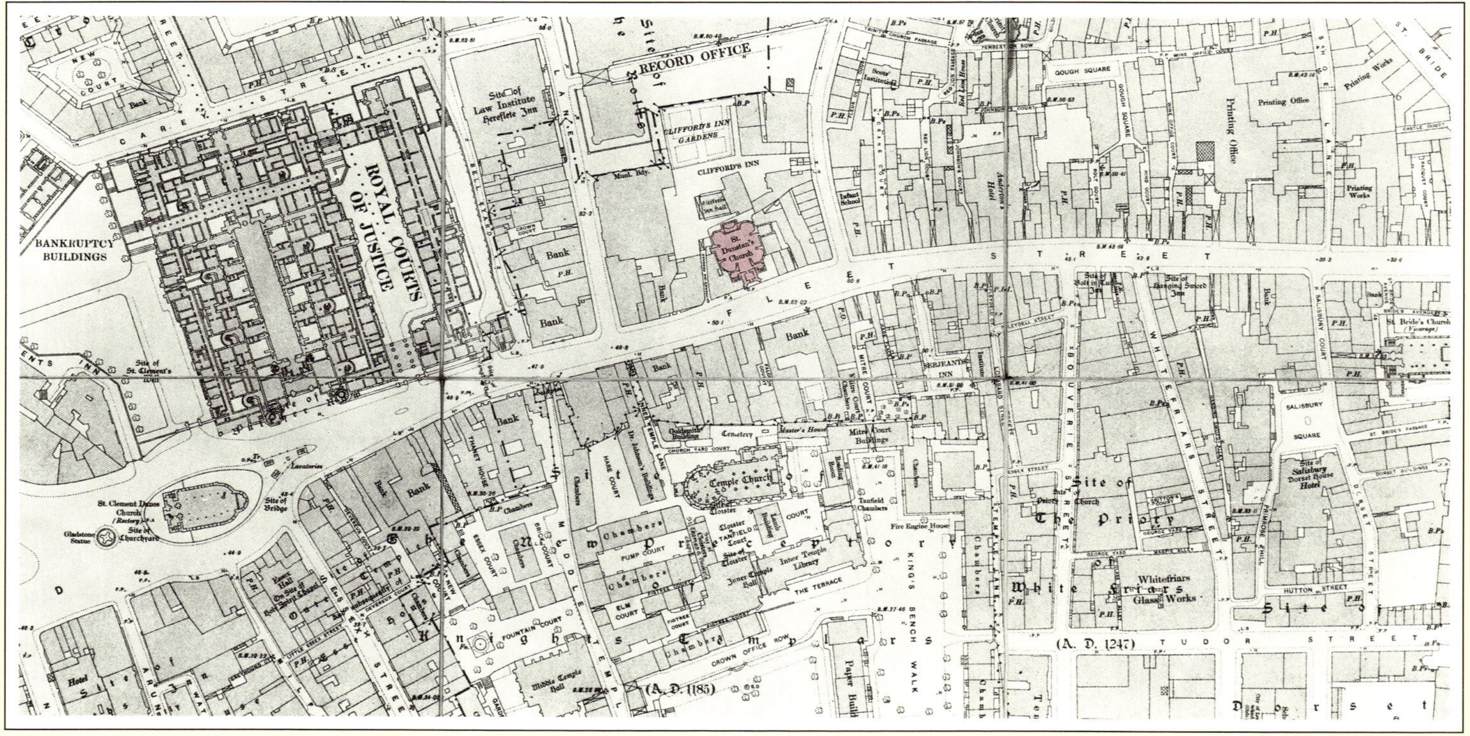

Fleet Street and St Paul's

Details from the Ordnance Survey Five Feet to One Mile Plan of London, V11.64/65, published 1912/19

Fleet Street looking West *(right)*

[93] *Detail, from plate 99*

Fleet Street and St Paul's

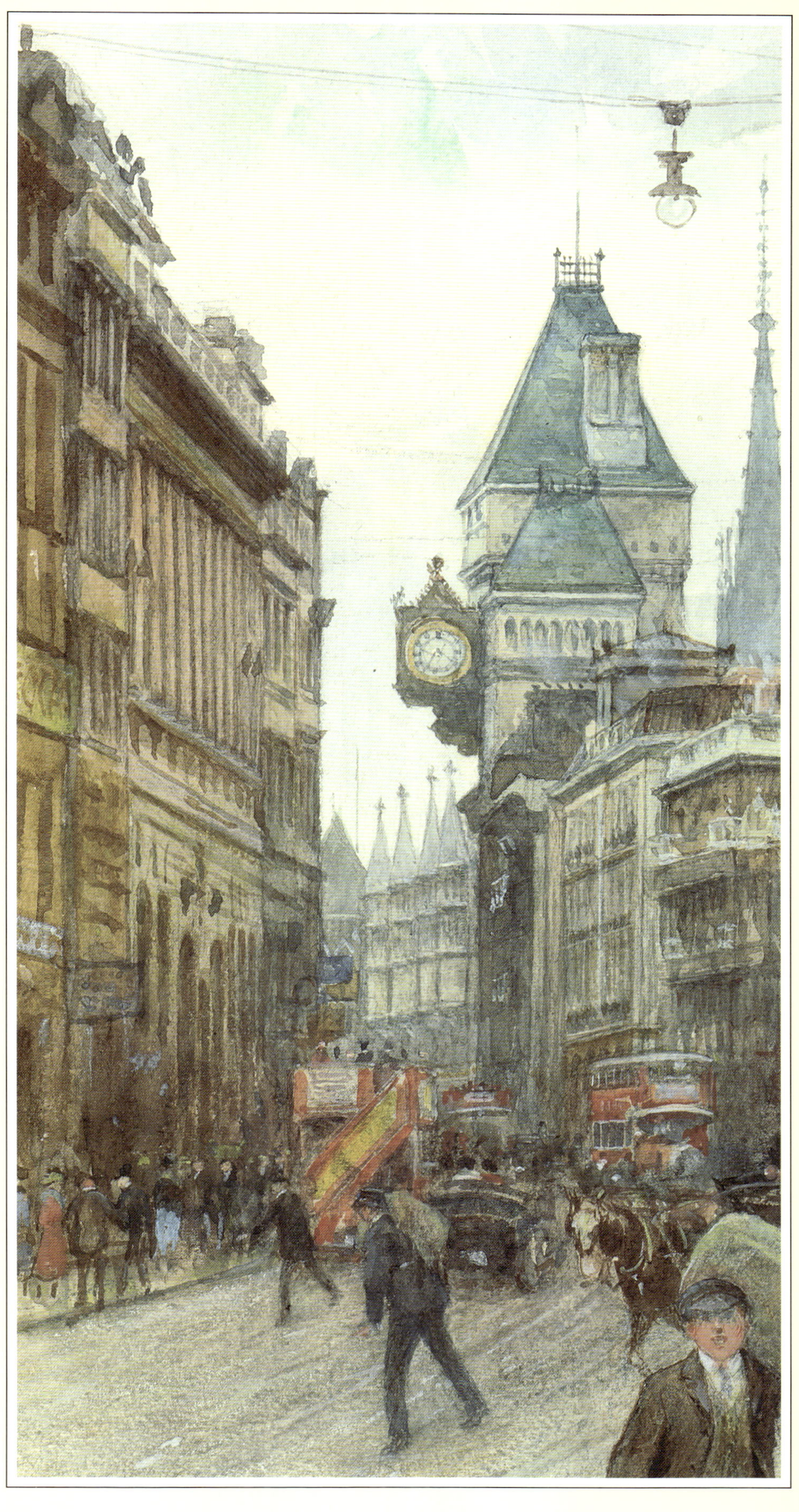

Fleet Street looking East

1898

[UNTITLED]

Scene looking east down Fleet Street towards Ludgate Circus, Ludgate Hill, St Martin Ludgate church, and St Paul's Cathedral. Until the 1980s Fleet Street was the centre of the newspaper industry. On the right are the premises of the *Southern Daily Echo.* The style of this view and its companion, plate 96, differs from Tidmarsh's other views. Though watercolours they are painted in the manner of oil paintings and the figures are somewhat contrived. It was exhibited at the Royal Academy summer show in 1898. *Staffage:* a lady wearing a muff, a railway porter (from nearby Ludgate Hill Station?) who, in contrast, has rolled-up sleeves, a distinguished-looking gentleman, a lavender-seller, a street orderly removing horse manure, a costermonger, hansom cabs, and two omnibuses.

[94] *Watercolour drawing 760 × 500 mm*

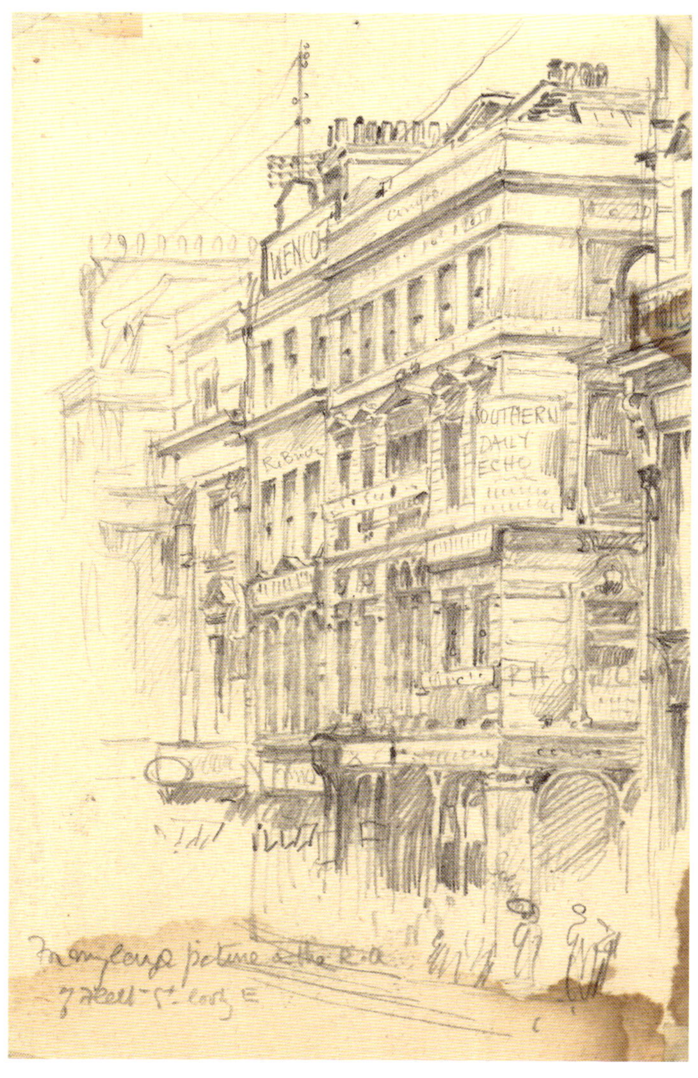

Sketch for the view of Fleet Street looking east, 1898

It is inscribed with colour and material notes.

[95] *Pencil sketch, 177 × 113 mm*

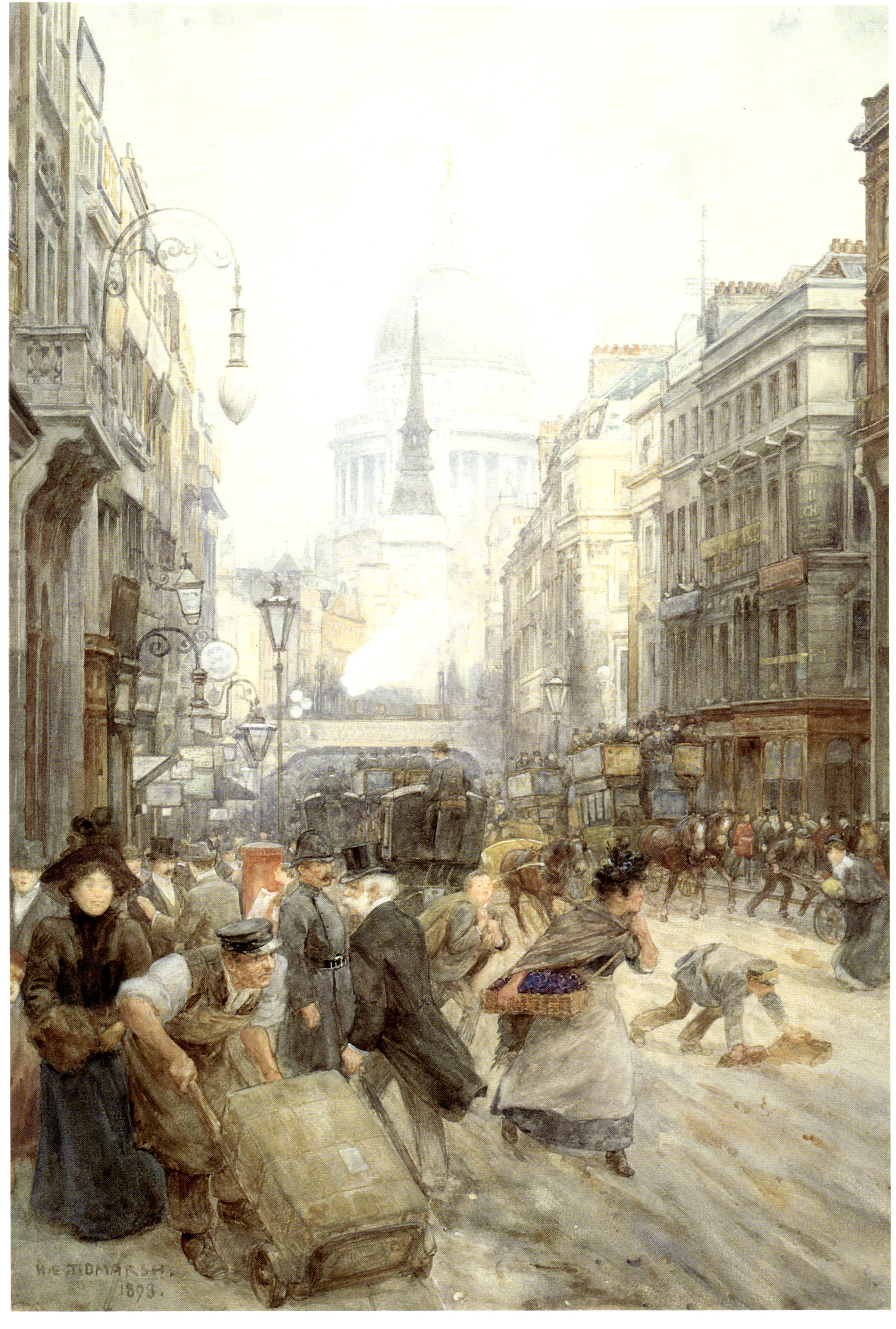
H.E.TIDMARSH.
1898.

94 Fleet Street looking West

1899

[UNTITLED]

View up Fleet Street looking west towards the church of St Dunstan in the West and the Law Courts. In the foreground are the London offices of the *Irish Times. Staffage:* a costermonger, an omnibus, hansom cabs, a messenger, a lavender-seller (the same lady appears in Tidmarsh's companion view looking east), and window shoppers.

[96] *Watercolour drawing 765 × 500 mm*

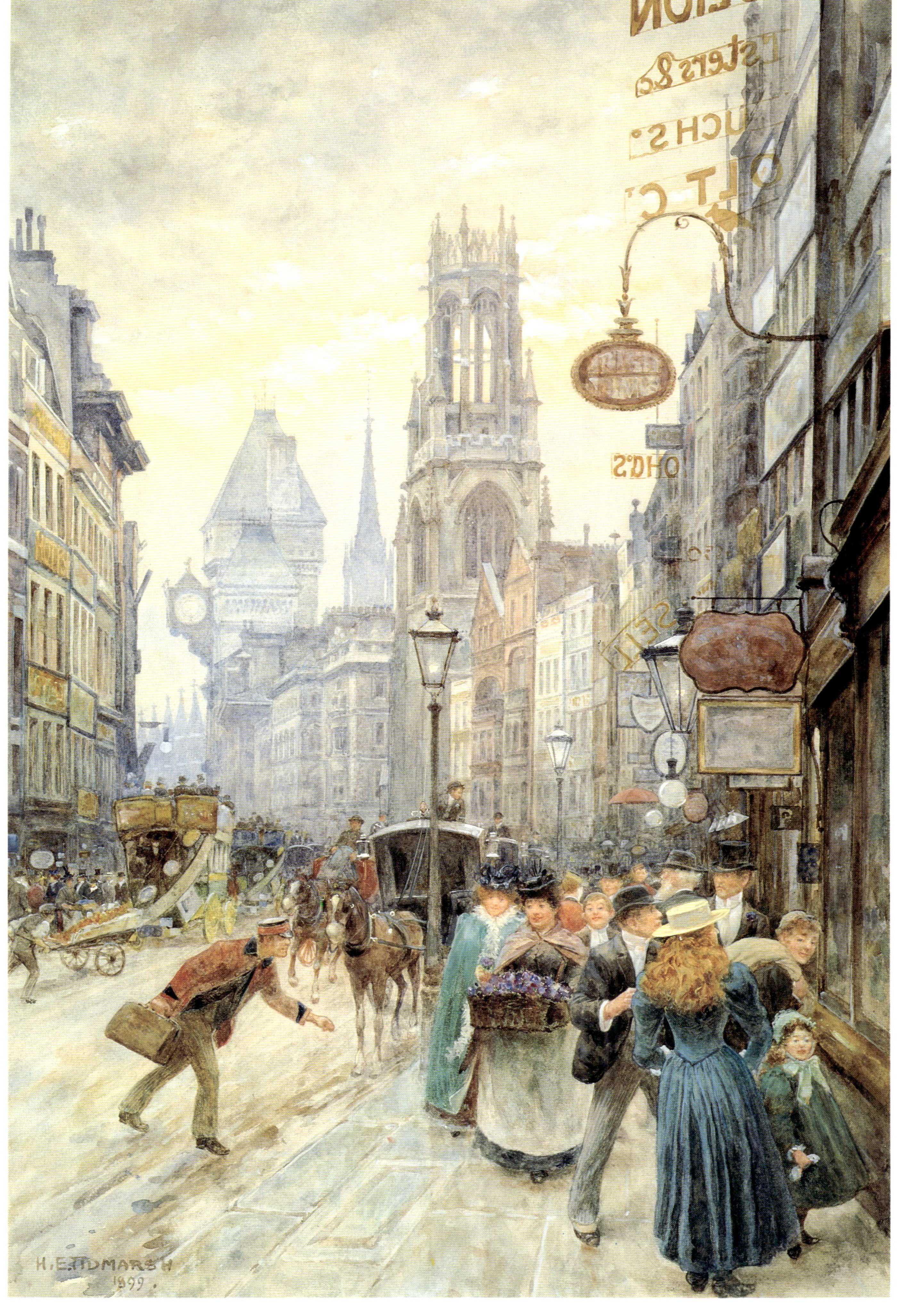
H.E.TIDMARSH
1899

96 Fleet Street and St Paul's

c.1920

[UNTITLED]

Fleet Street is viewed looking east across Ludgate Circus and up Ludgate Hill. The west towers of St Paul's Cathedral and the spire of St Martin Ludgate dominate the scene. At the foot of Ludgate Hill is the railway bridge to Ludgate Hill Station. This bridge was demolished in 1990. *Staffage:* motor buses, open motor cars, and a hawker's cart, newspaper staff, and other pedestrians.

[97] *Watercolour drawing 325 × 160 mm*

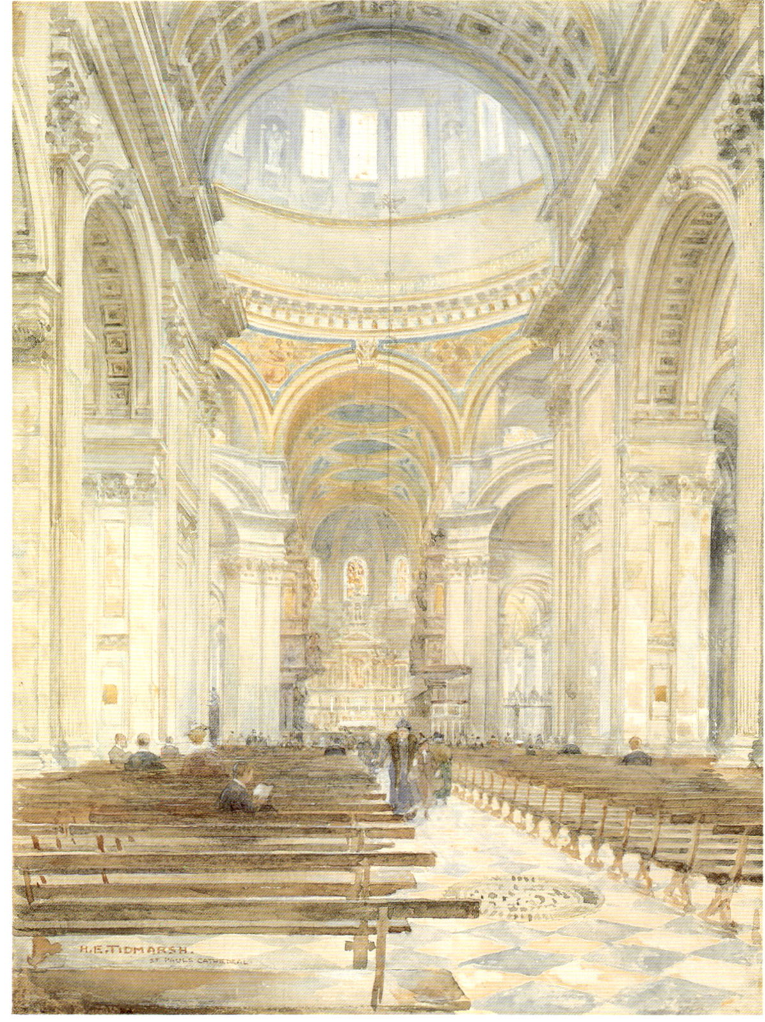

Interior of St Paul's Cathedral, looking towards the High Altar, c.1905

[98] *Watercolour drawing, 389 × 280 mm*

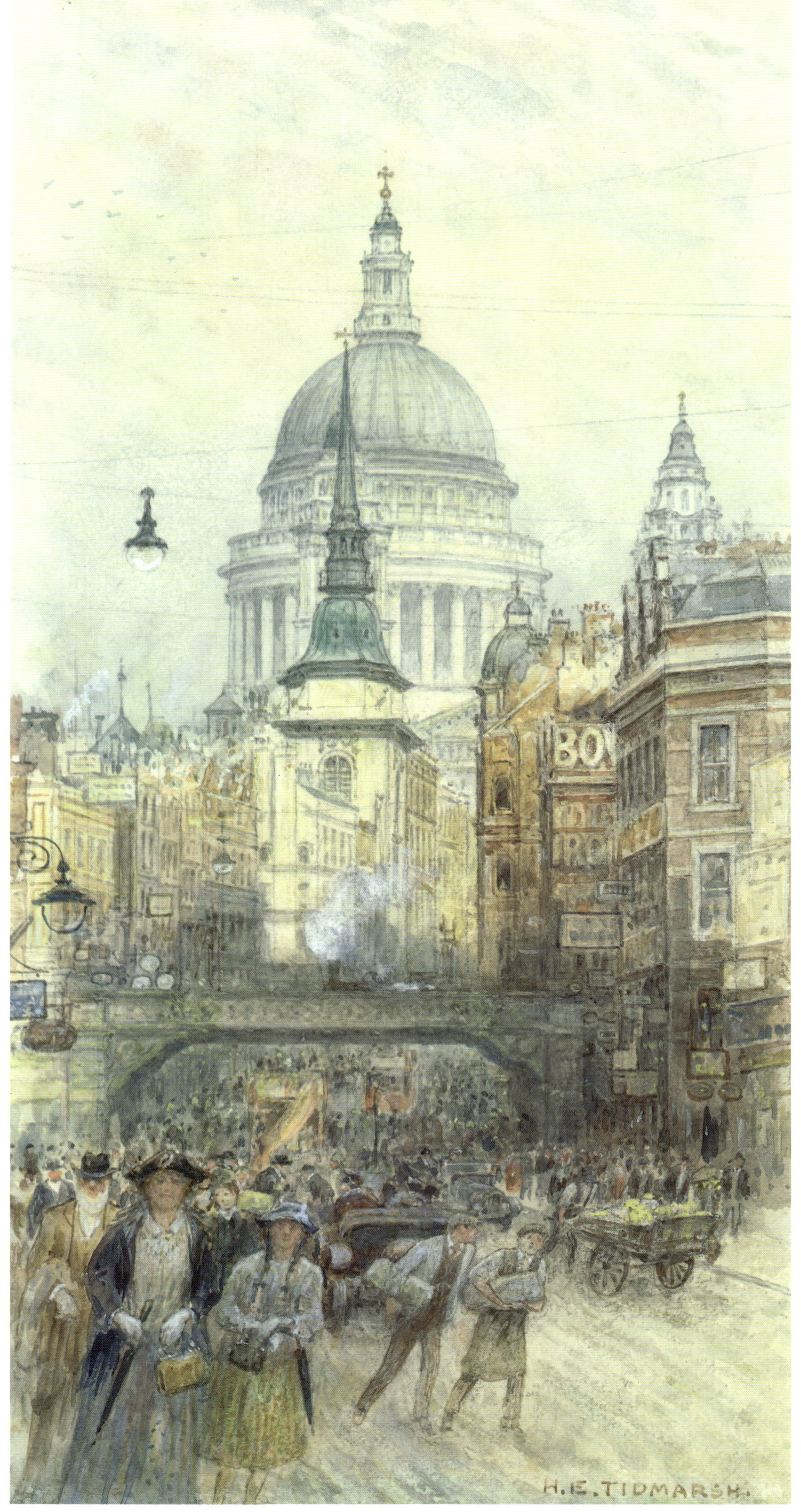
H.E.TIDMARSH.

98 Fleet Street looking West

1922

ST. DUNSTAN FLEET ST

Scene looking west towards the church of St Dunstan in the West, and the clock tower and fleche of the Law Courts. In the foreground are various hanging signs, including 'Accumulators Charged', and 'Yorkshire Post' (whose offices were at no. 171). *Staffage:* a tradesman's cart and horse, an open motor car, and four motorbuses (including one with a covered upper deck, a type banned from London streets until 1925 when four experimental models were put into service). Also numerous pedestrians, a messenger boy, and a uniformed postman.

[99] *Watercolour drawing 440 × 268 mm*

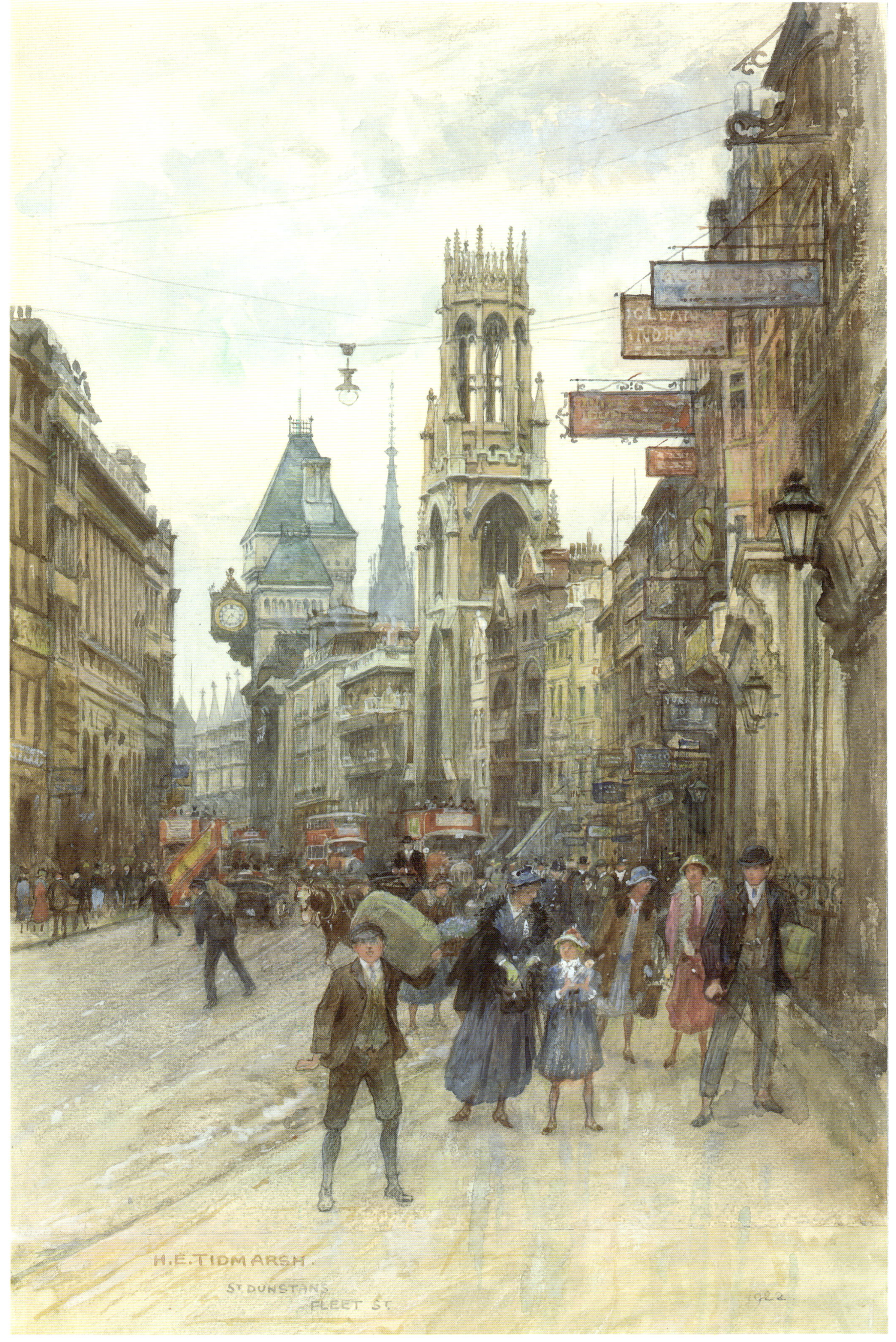
H.E. TIDMARSH.
ST. DUNSTANS
FLEET ST.
1922

100 St Bride Fleet Street

1902

[UNTITLED]

St Bride's, named after St Bridget, a 6th-century Irish saint, is viewed looking west from Bride Lane. Its famous wedding cake steeple is shown under repair. *Staffage:* a small girl with her doll, two errand boys, a delivery cart, and a number of pedestrians.

[100] *Watercolour drawing 423 × 185 mm*

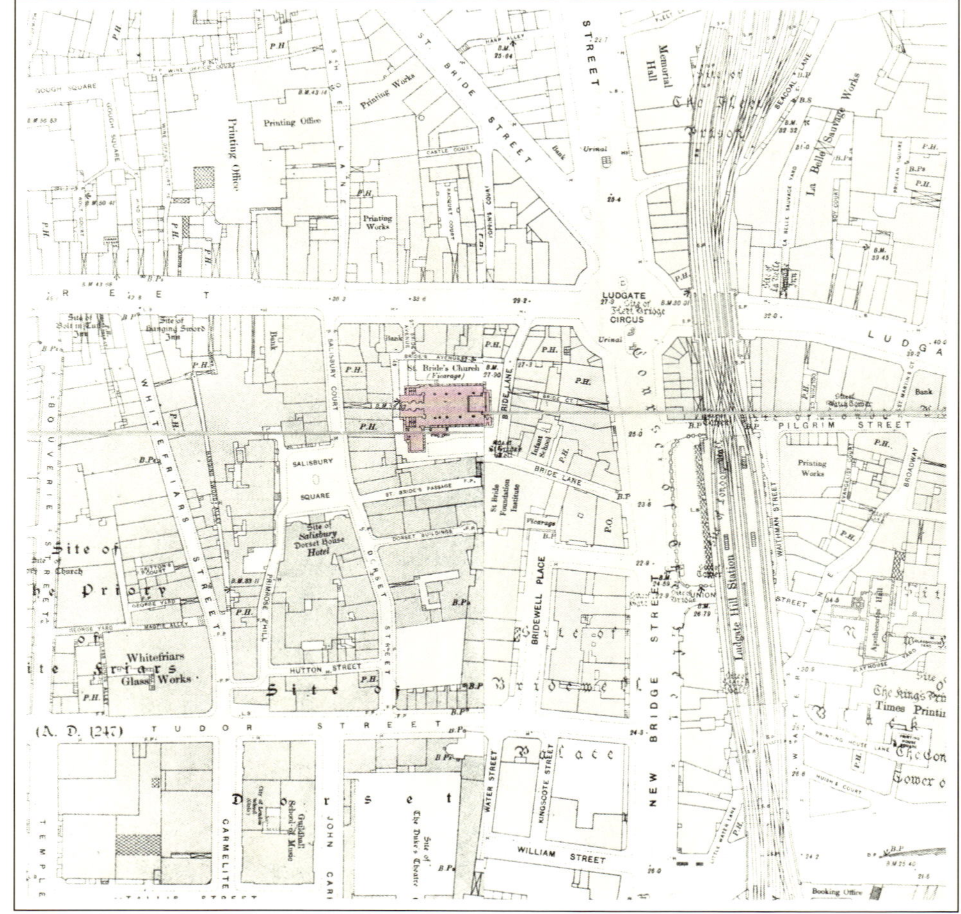

Detail from the Ordnance Survey Five Feet to One Mile Plan of London, V11.64/65, published 1912/19

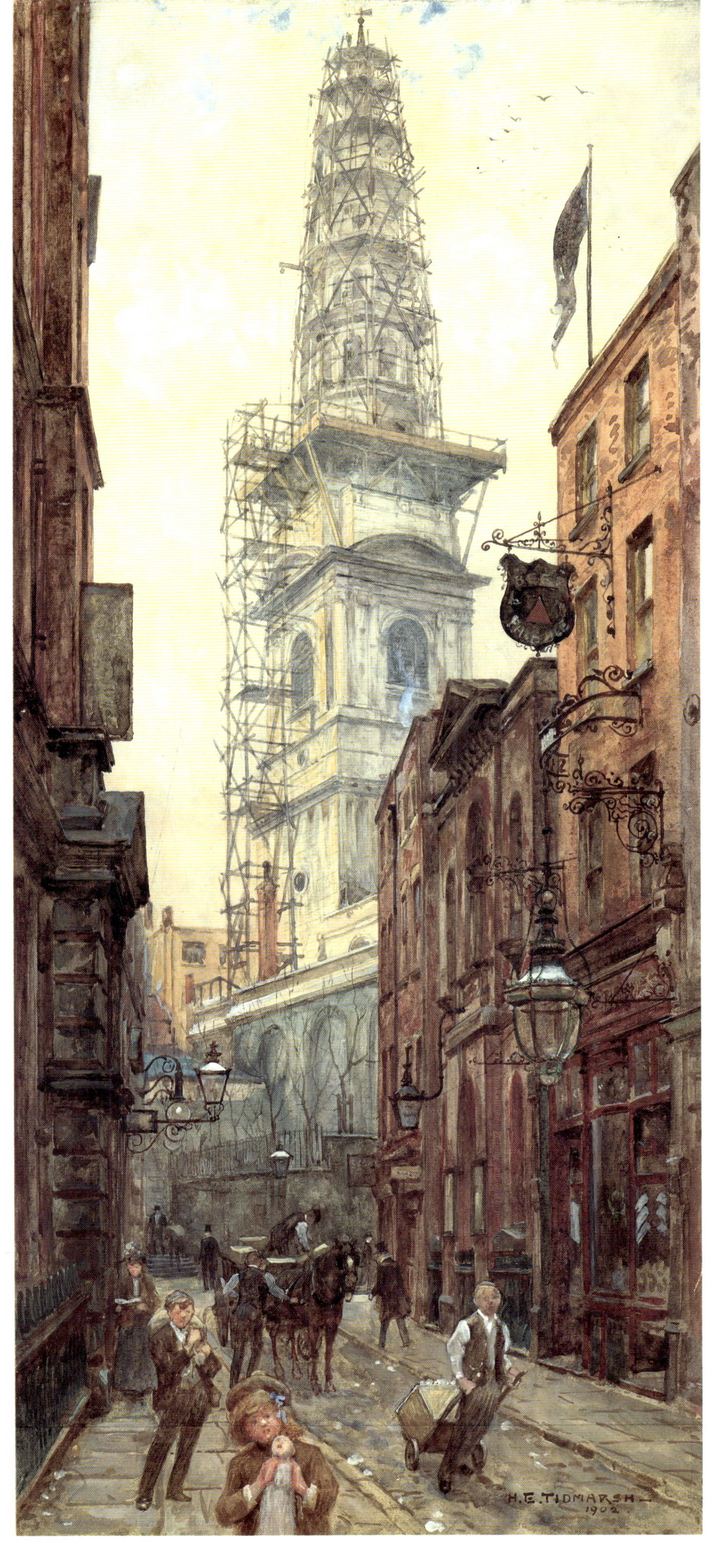
H.E. TIDMARSH
1902

102 St Bride Fleet Street

1925

ST BRIDE'S FLEET ST.
(A WREN SPIRE, FINISHED 1701)

The scene is viewed from Bride Lane looking west, a position identical to that taken by Tidmarsh for his 1902 view. *Staffage:* a horse and cart and pedestrians, including a schoolboy and a smart City lady with an attaché case.

[101] *Watercolour drawing 447 × 210 mm*

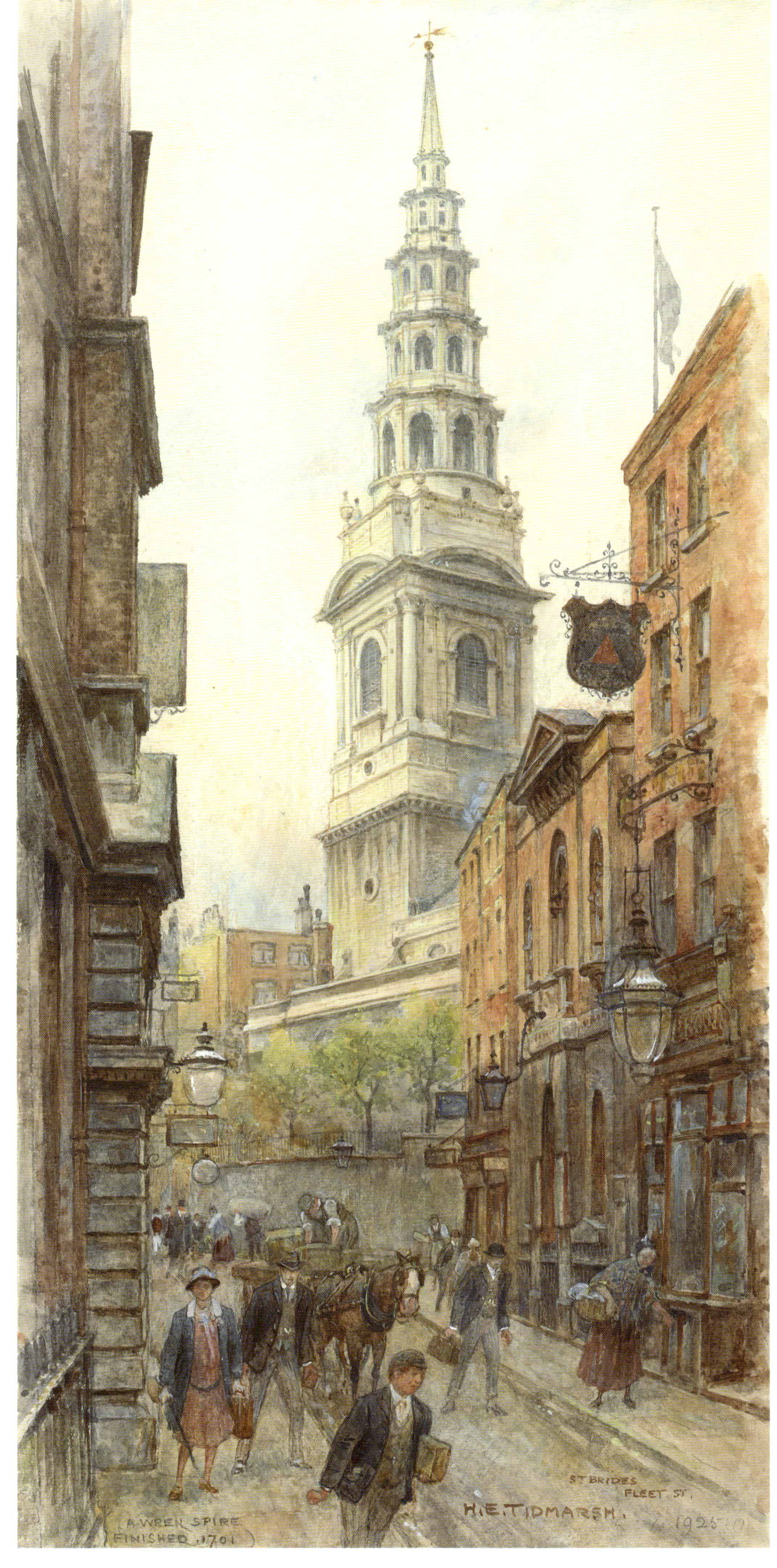
ST BRIDES
FLEET ST.
H.E.TIDMARSH.
1925
A WREN SPIRE
FINISHED 1701

104

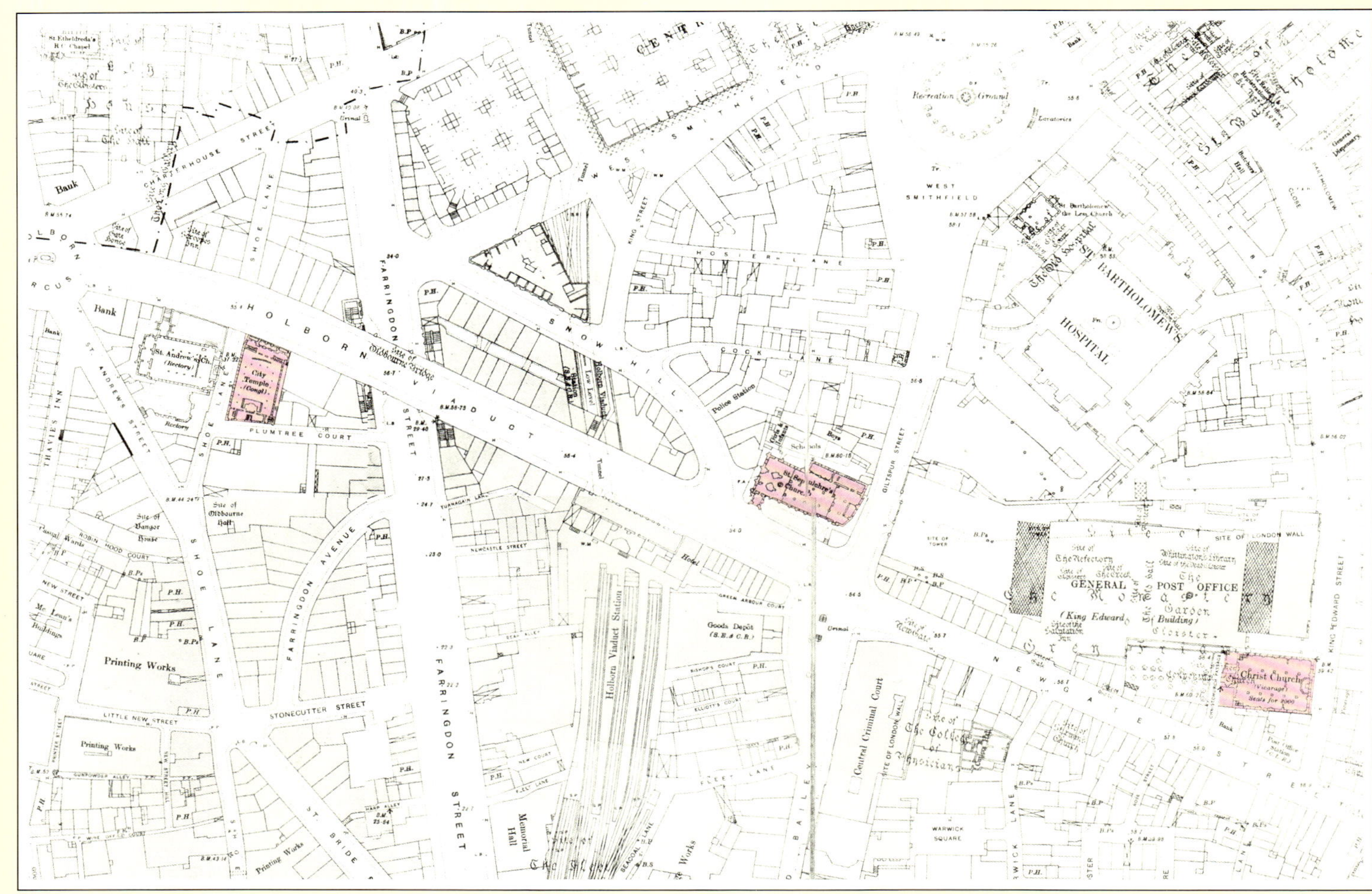

Exploring North of St Paul's

Detail from the Ordnance Survey Five Feet to One Mile Plan of London, V11.54/55/64/65, published 1912-19

St Sepulchre looking up Giltspur Street *(right)*

[102] *Detail from plate 104*

Exploring North of St Paul's

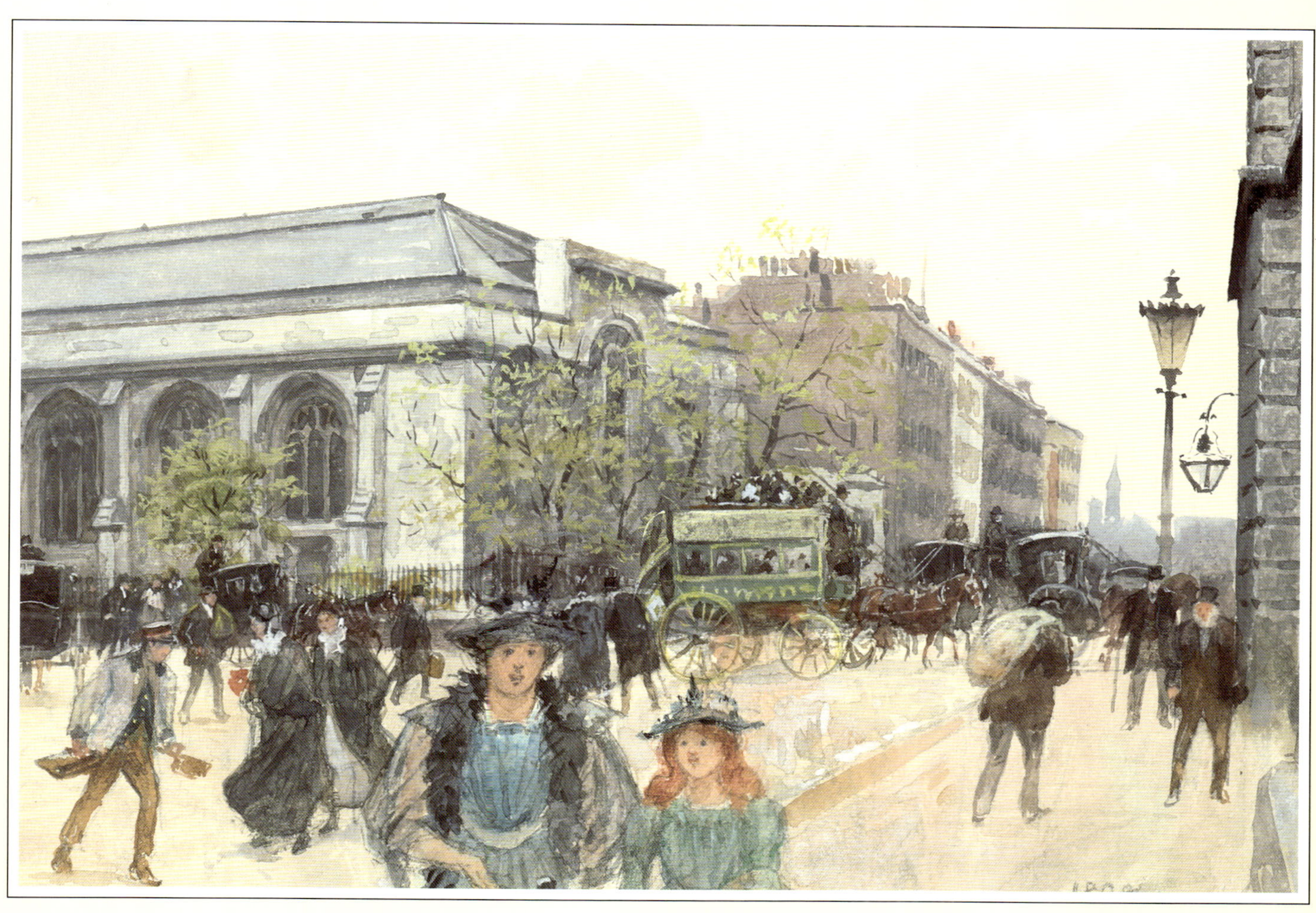

106

The City Temple

c.1899

THE 'CITY TEMPLE' (MODERN) HOLBORN
ST ANDREW, HOLBORN. ST ANDREW (REBUILT BY WREN 1686)

The City Temple, one of London's most important nonconformist chapels, was built in 1874. Beyond it is the Wren church of St Andrew Holborn. A balloon floats in the sky. Above Holborn Circus is a network of telegraph wires. *Staffage:* a horse omnibus, a hansom cab, a uniformed street sweeper, a messenger boy, porters, and pedestrians of both sexes.

[103] *Watercolour drawing 390 × 280 mm*

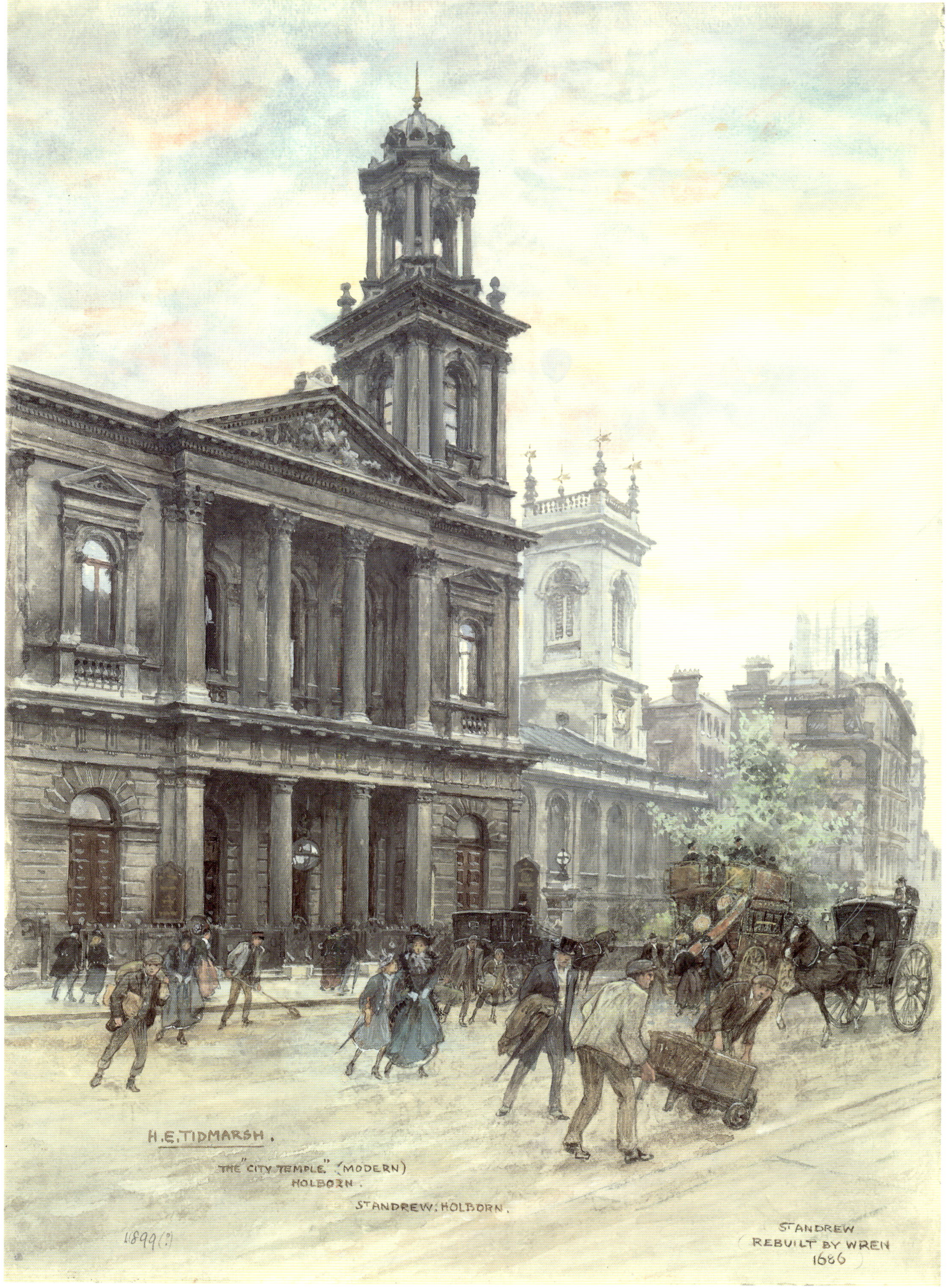
H.E.TIDMARSH.
THE "CITY TEMPLE" (MODERN)
HOLBORN.
ST ANDREW: HOLBORN.
1899(?)
ST ANDREW
REBUILT BY WREN
1686

St Sepulchre

c.1898

ST SEPULCHRE'S HOLBORN
REBUILT 1440 AFTER FIRE, REPAIRED BY WREN, 1670

St Sepulchre church as seen from the Old Bailey. On the right is the wall of Newgate Prison (demolished 1902). Beyond lies Giltspur Street. To the left, on the corner of Holborn Viaduct, is the Imperial Hotel (closed by 1900). *Staffage:* well-dressed pedestrians, including a pair of nannies with beribboned bonnets, a street-cleaner in uniform, and a postman. Outside the hotel is a cab rank with four-wheelers plying.

[104] *Watercolour drawing 275 × 390 mm*

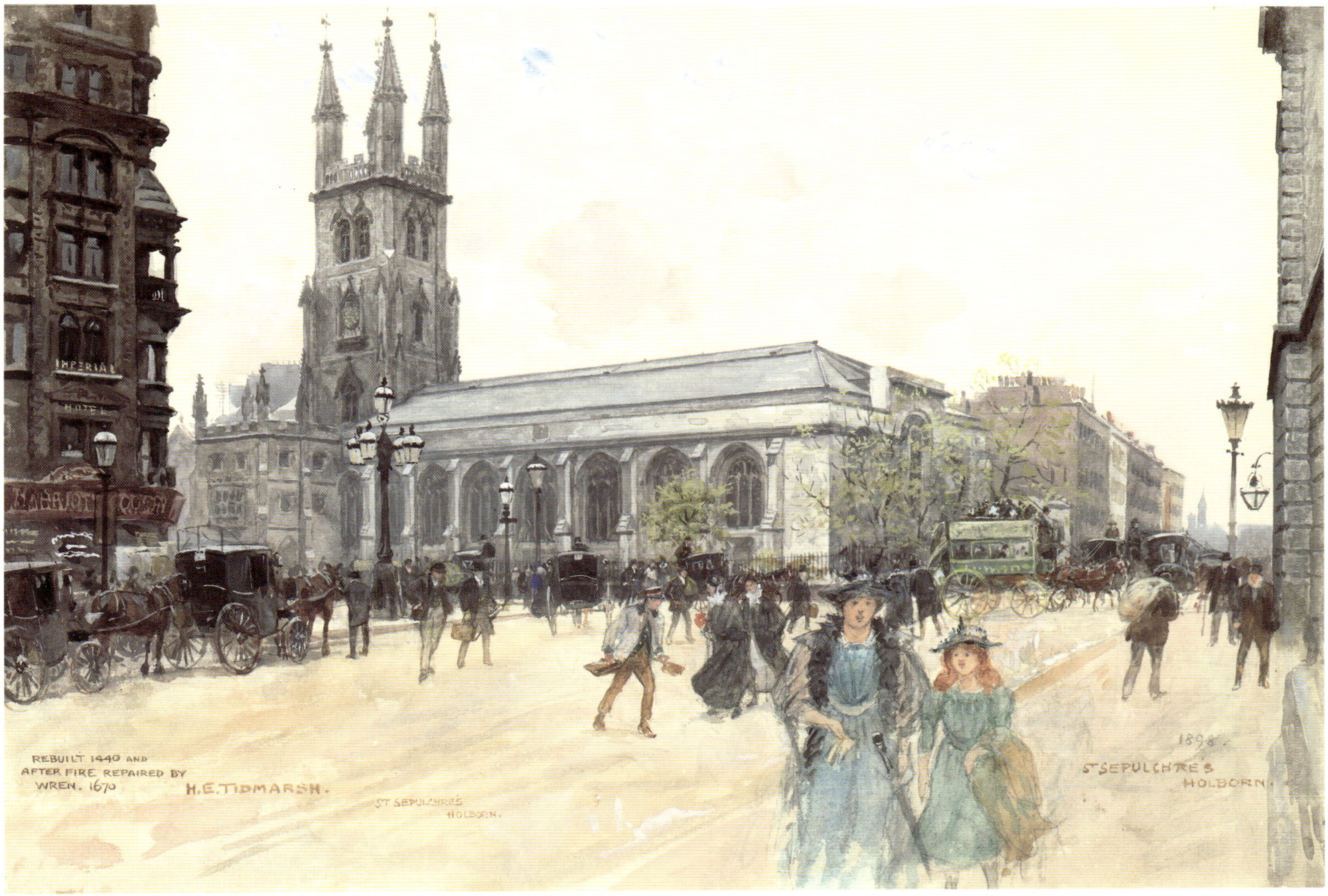

REBUILT 1440 AND
AFTER FIRE REPAIRED BY
WREN. 1670
H.E.TIDMARSH.
St SEPULCHRES
HOLBORN.
1898
St SEPULCHRES
HOLBORN.

Christ Church Newgate Street

1900

CHRISTCHURCH BY WREN
AND CHRIST'S HOSPITAL, NEWGATE ST. (REBUILT 1675)

Scene looking north towards the red brick gateway of Christ's Hospital school. On the right is the west door of the Church. The school moved to Horsham in Sussex two years later; the church was severely damaged by enemy action in World War II, and only its shell remains. *Staffage:* includes a boy in Christ's Hospital livery feeding pigeons.

[105] *Watercolour drawing 390 × 225 mm*

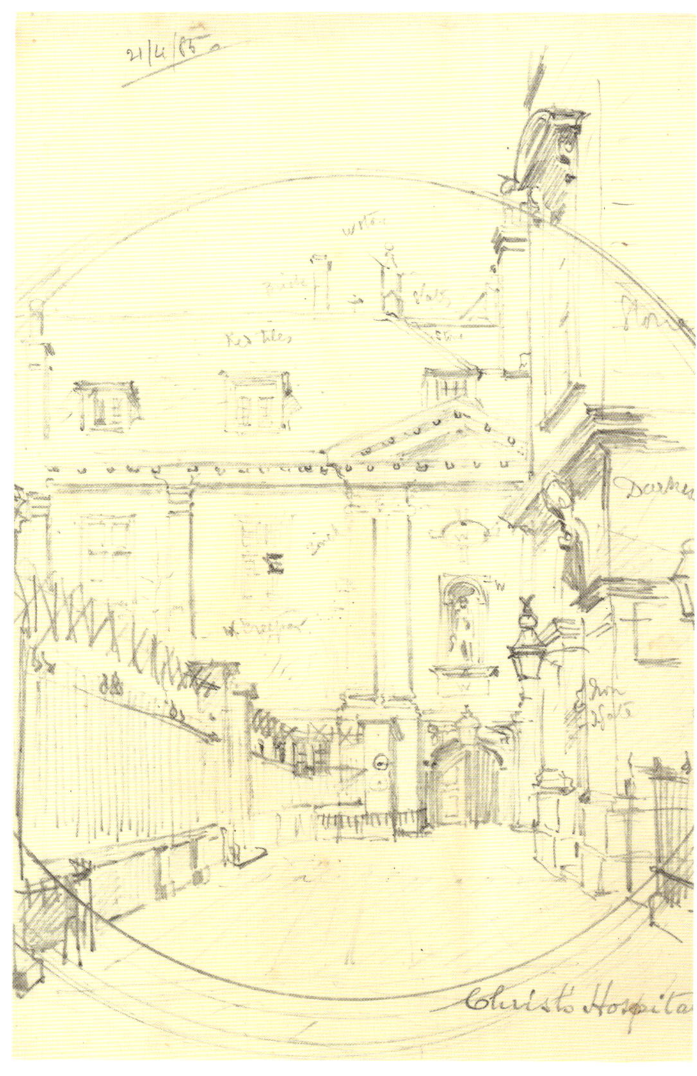

Christ's Hospital, 1885

The image is inscribed with material notes. Perhaps intended for an engraved roundel.

[106] *Pencil sketch, 175 × 110 mm*

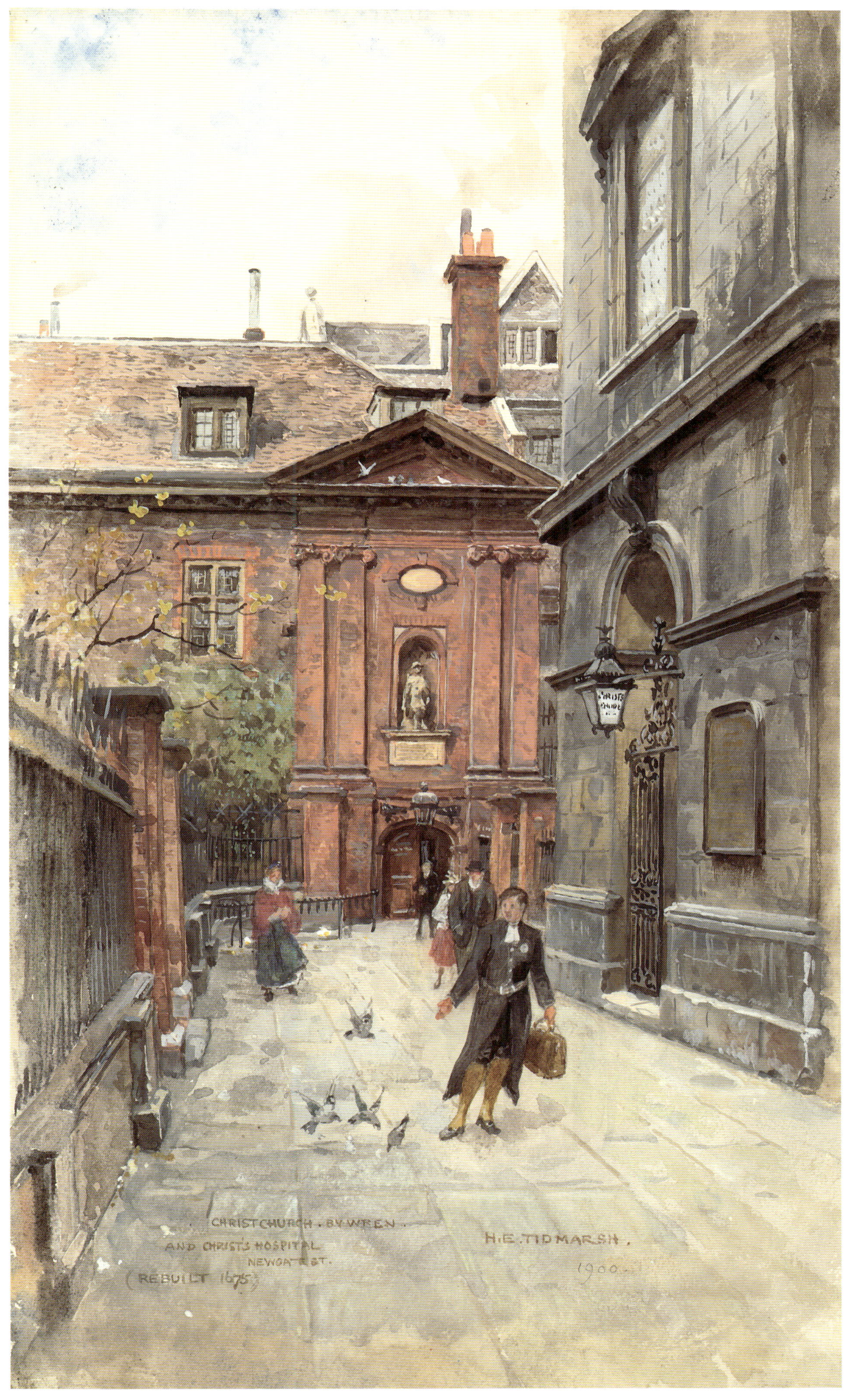
CHRISTCHURCH . BY WREN .
AND CHRIST'S HOSPITAL
NEWGATE ST.
(REBUILT 1675)
H.E. TIDMARSH.
1900.

Fore Street

1895

ST GILES CRIPPLEGATE, 1895
REBUILT AFTER A FIRE, 1545
IN 1903 THE SHOPS AND 'QUEST HOUSE' WERE REMOVED

View looking south down Redcross Street to where it met Fore Street. Facing us in Fore Street are four 17th-century houses, one with an archway which led through to St Giles Cripplegate Churchyard. Rising above these houses is the north face of the tower of the church. This area was badly burnt in World War II. The Barbican Development now stands on the site. *Staffage:* a cart heaped with kegs, and its carters; a horse manure scavenger; a policeman; porters; and pedestrians.

[107] *Watercolour drawing 392 × 220 mm*

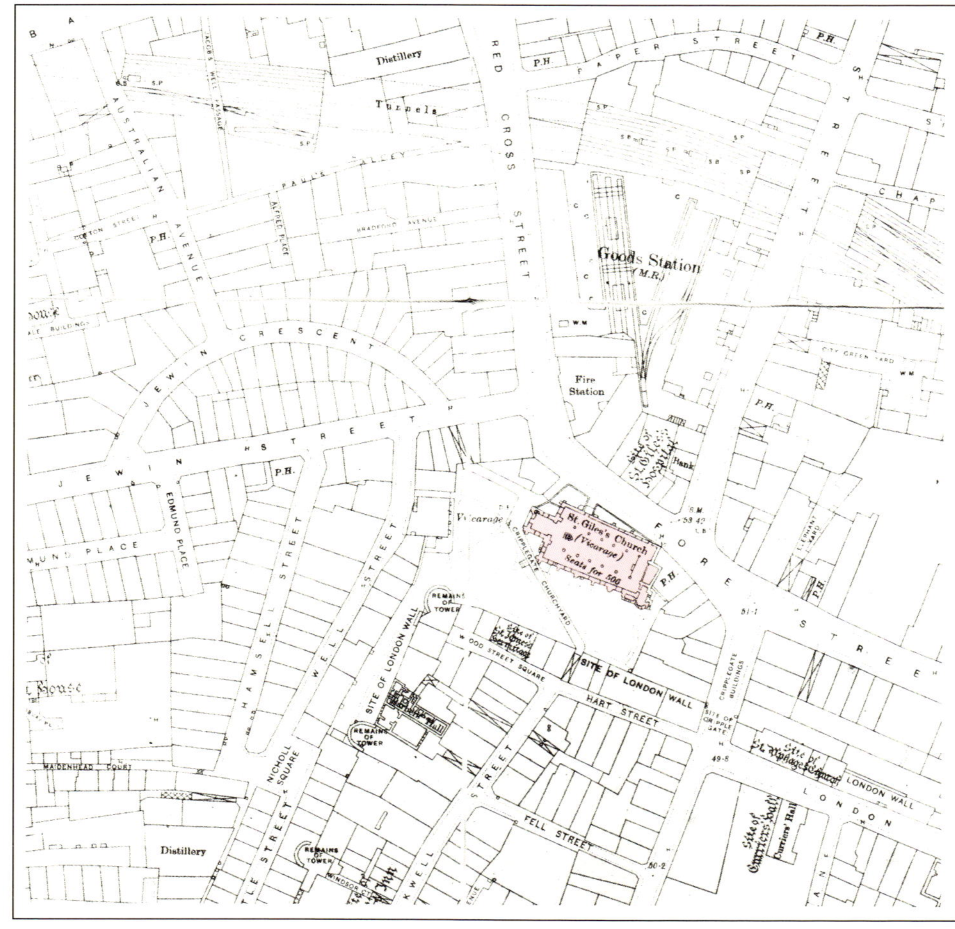

Detail from the Ordnance Survey Five Feet to One Mile Plan of London, V11.55, published 1916

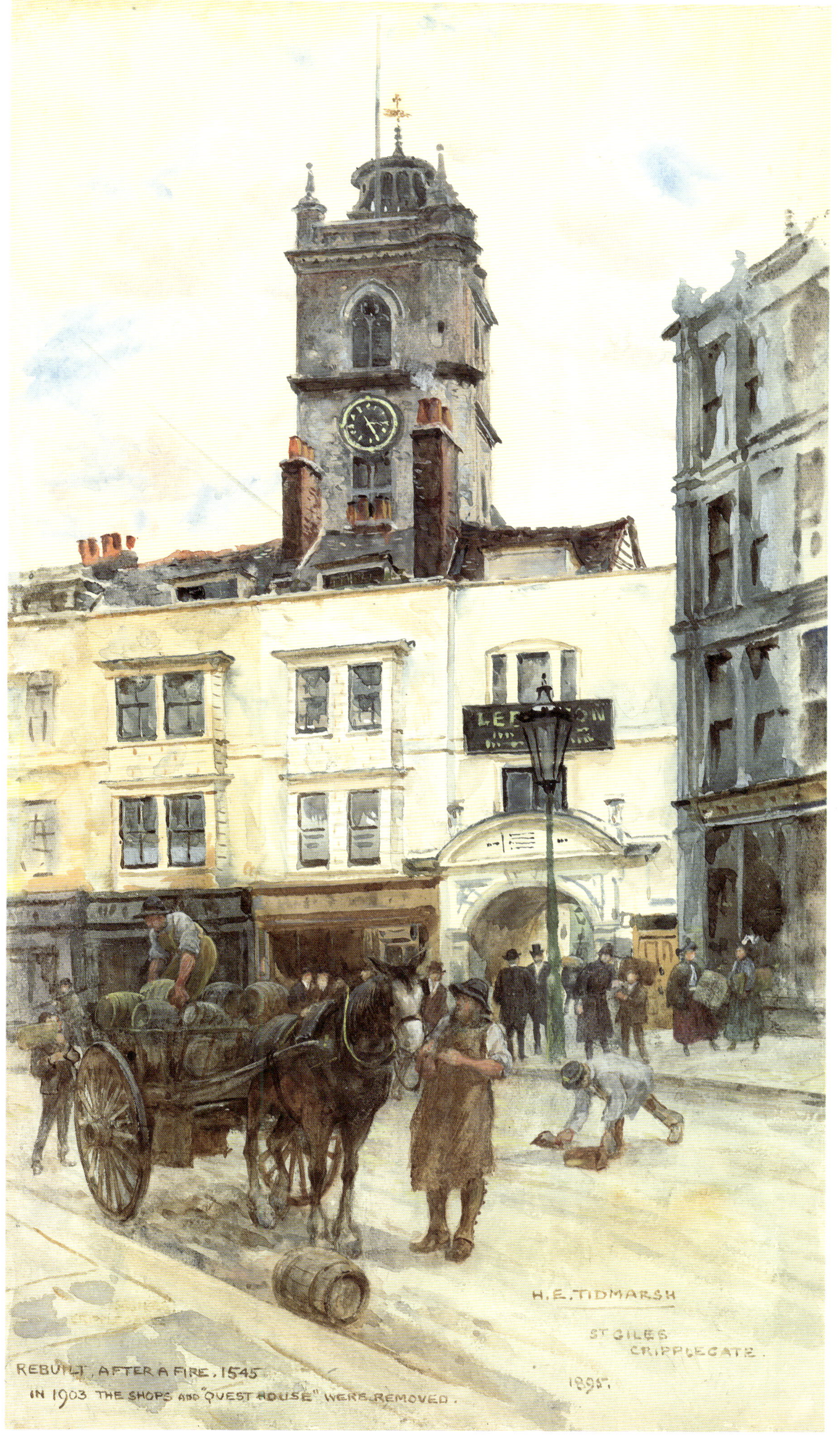
H. E. TIDMARSH
ST GILES
CRIPPLEGATE.
REBUILT, AFTER A FIRE. 1545
IN 1903 THE SHOPS AND "QUEST HOUSE" WERE REMOVED.
1895.

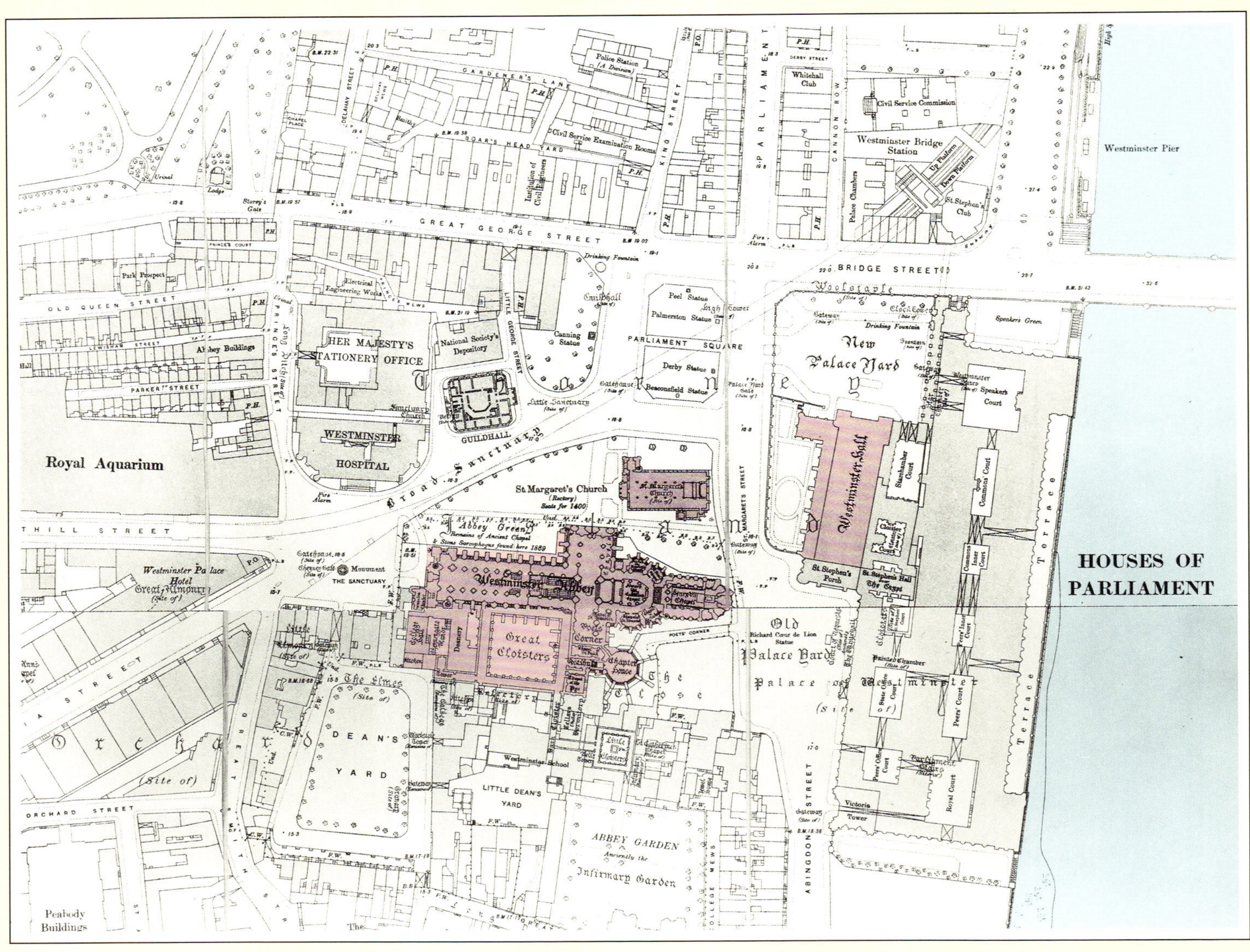

Whitehall and Westminster

Detail from the Ordnance Survey Five Feet to One Mile Plan of London, V11.83/93, published 1896/1915

Westminster Abbey *(right)*

[108] *Detail from plate 116*

Whitehall and Westminster

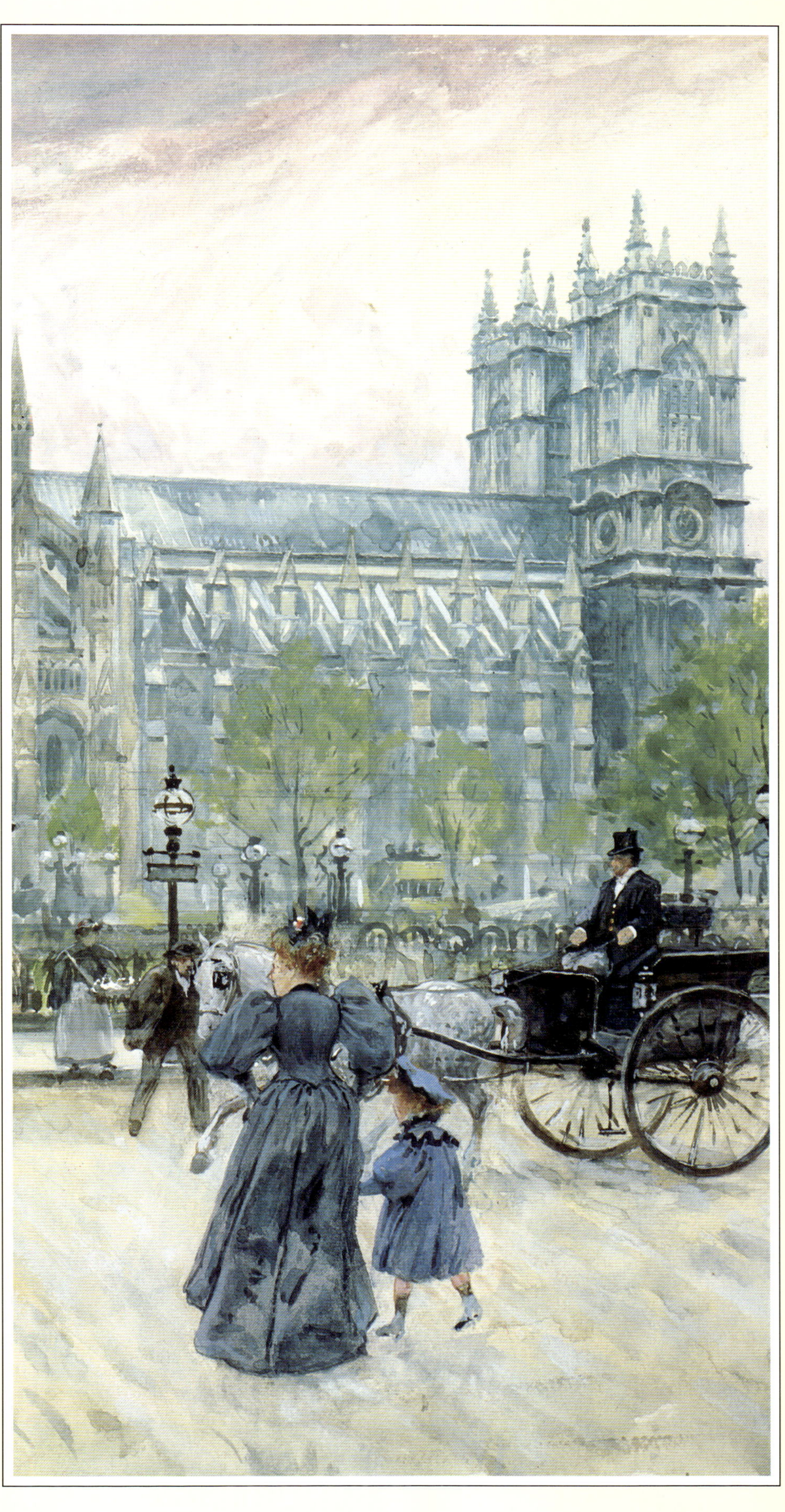

116

Banqueting House, Whitehall

c.1898

[UNTITLED]

An oblique view of the Banqueting House, the only part of Whitehall Palace that survives. Designed by Inigo Jones for James I, it was the first Renaissance building to be erected in London. Charles I was executed here in 1649. Immediately beyond the Banqueting House is a much foreshortened Gwydir House. The vista is closed by the clock tower of the Houses of Parliament. *Staffage:* many pedestrians of both sexes on the pavement. A man is wheeling a cart along the street.

[109] *Watercolour drawing 390 × 275 mm*

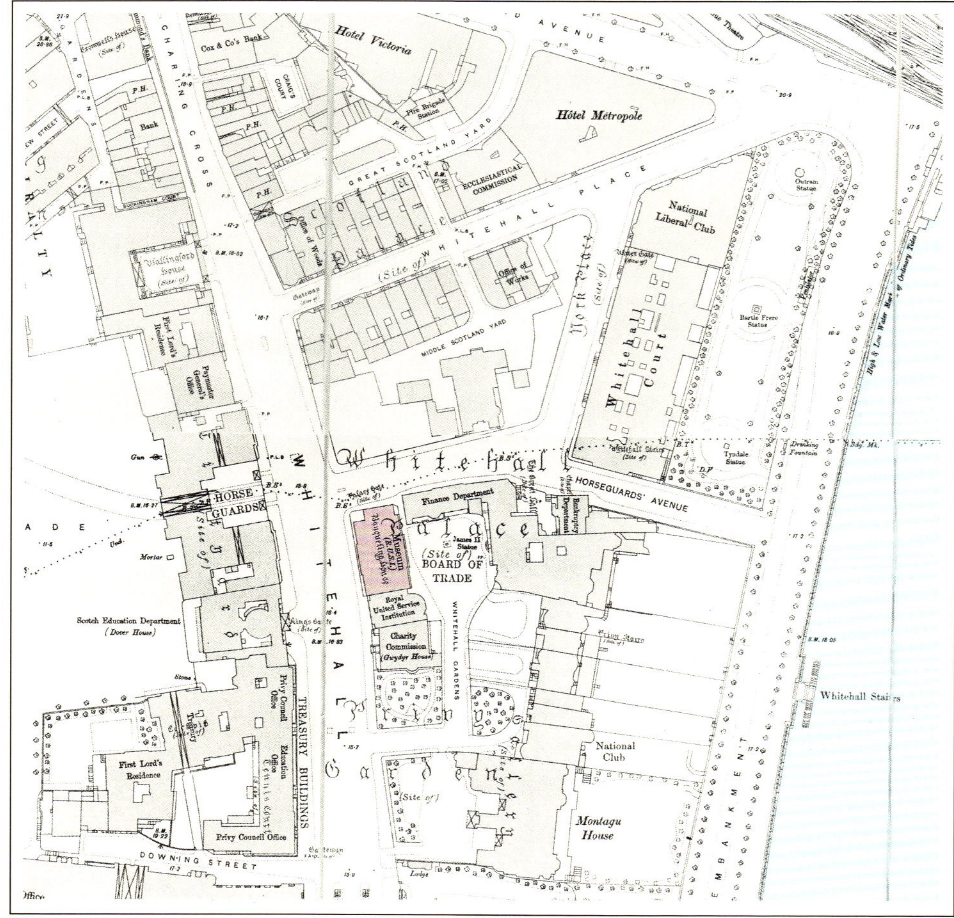

Detail from the Ordnance Survey Five Feet to One Mile Plan of London, V11.73/83, published 1895/6

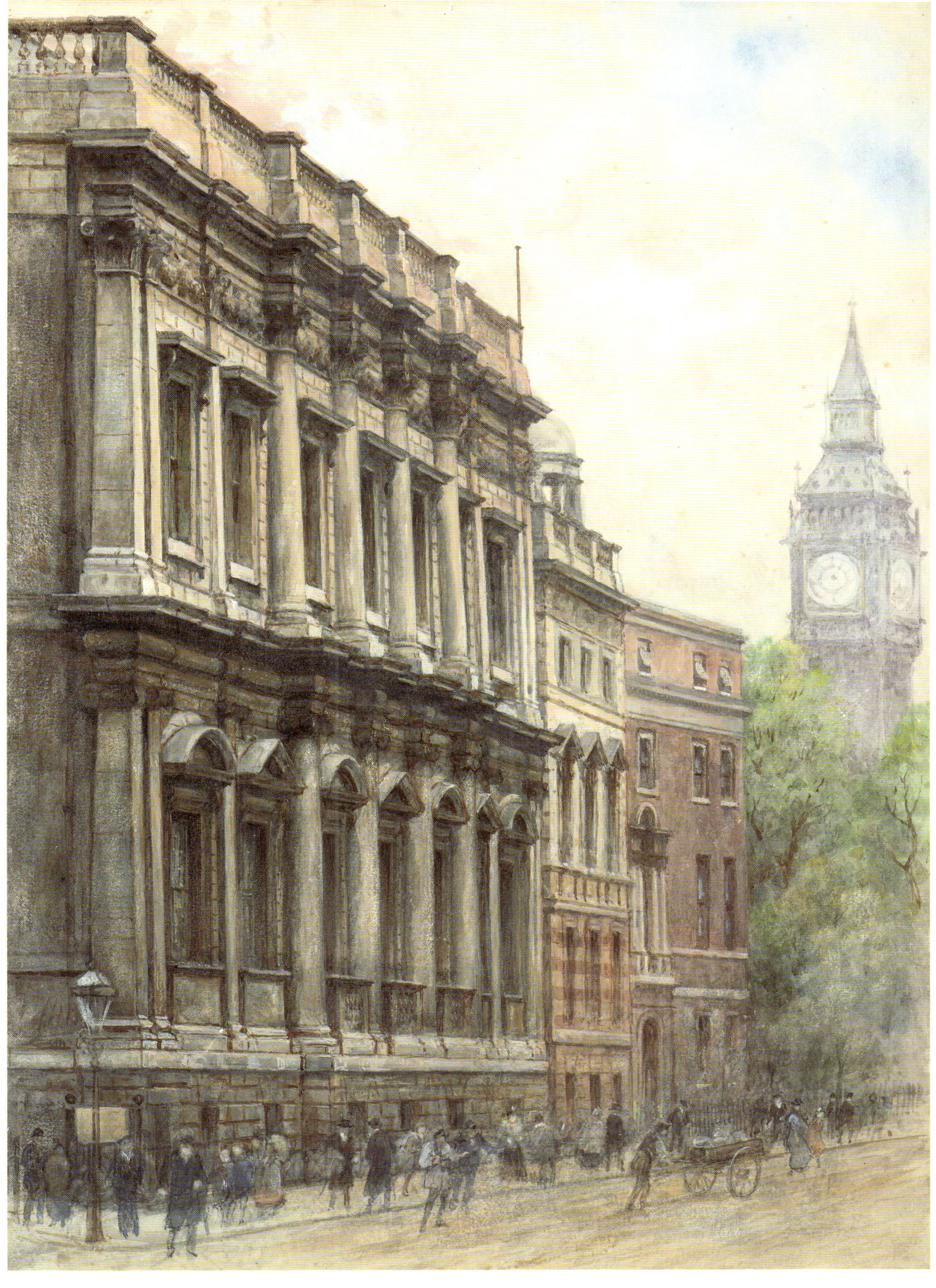

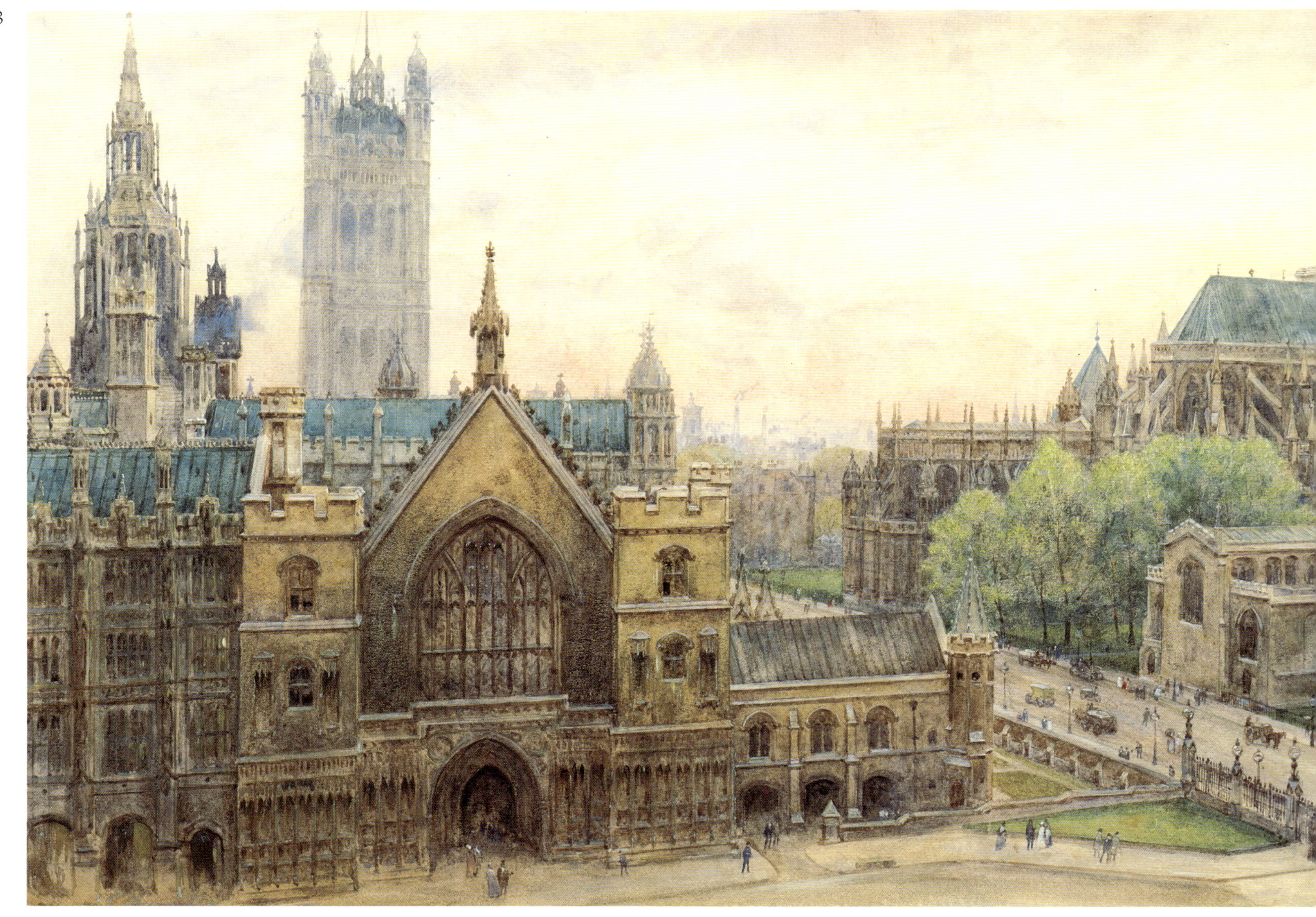

Parliament Square

1913

[UNTITLED]

On the left is Westminster Hall, and beyond it the ventilator tower and Victoria Tower. In the centre is Westminster Abbey and St Margaret Westminster. And on the right can be seen Victoria Street, with the campanile of Westminster Cathedral on the horizon, Middlesex Guildhall, and Wesleyan Central Hall (from 1932 called Methodist Central Hall). In a note on the support Tidmarsh has written: '... The painting was made on many visits from the roof of the office building opposite Palace Yard' (i.e. an office in Bridge Street).

[110] *Watercolour drawing 305 × 864 mm sight*

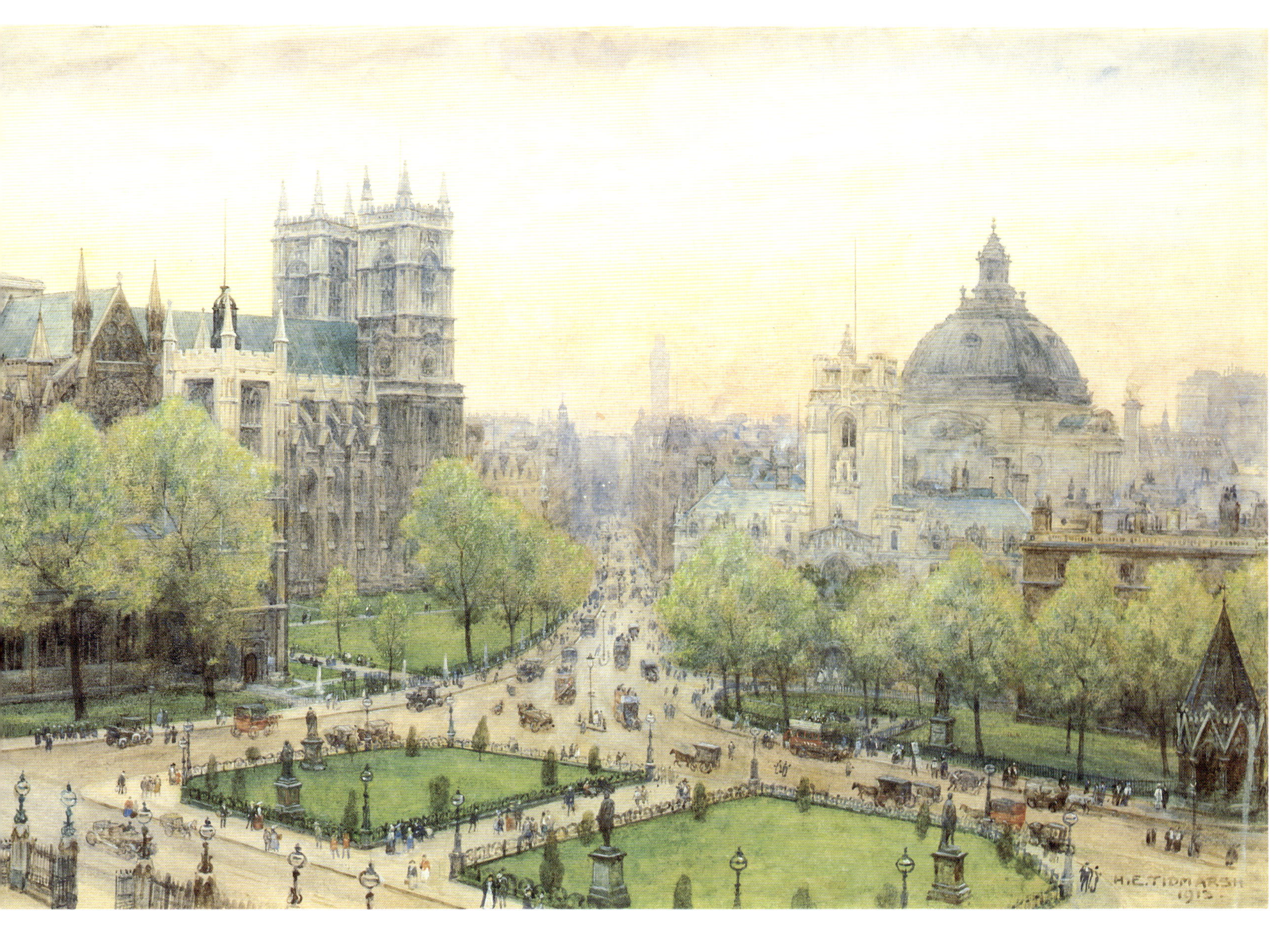
H.E. TIDMARSH
1915

Westminster Hall

1914-1928

WESTMINSTER HALL

The north front of Westminster Hall is seen from New Palace Yard. Built in 1394-1401 and famed for its oak hammer-beam roof, the Hall represents the only surviving part of the original Palace of Westminster. It now forms a vestibule of the House of Commons. To the south is Victoria Tower. The statue of Oliver Cromwell by Sir William Hamo Thornycroft was erected in 1877.

[111] *Watercolour 282 × 388 mm sight*

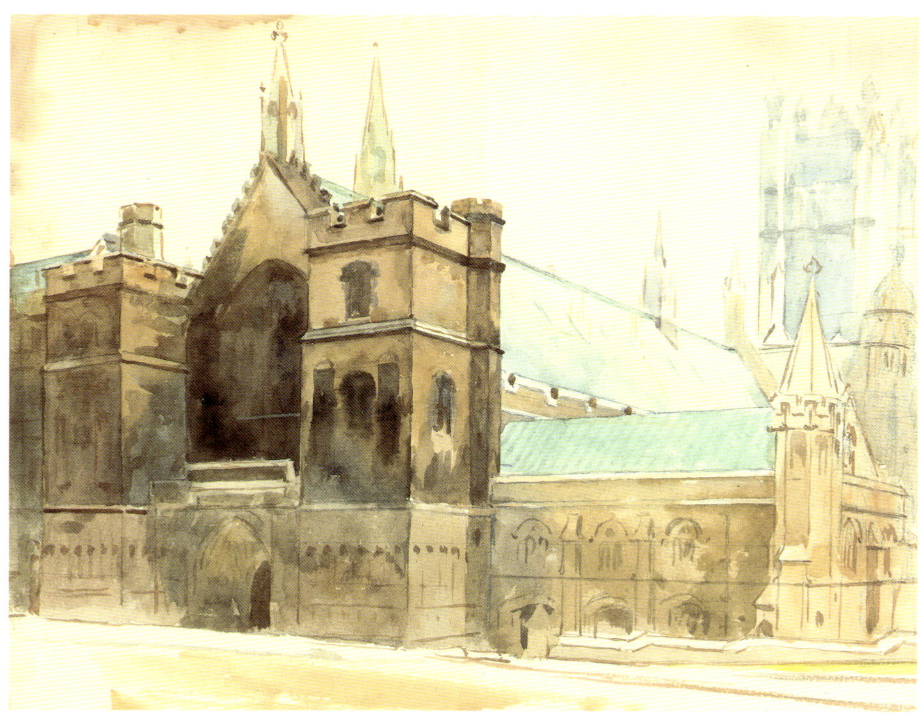

Study for 'Westminster Hall', c.1914

[112] *Watercolour sketch, 235 × 295 mm*

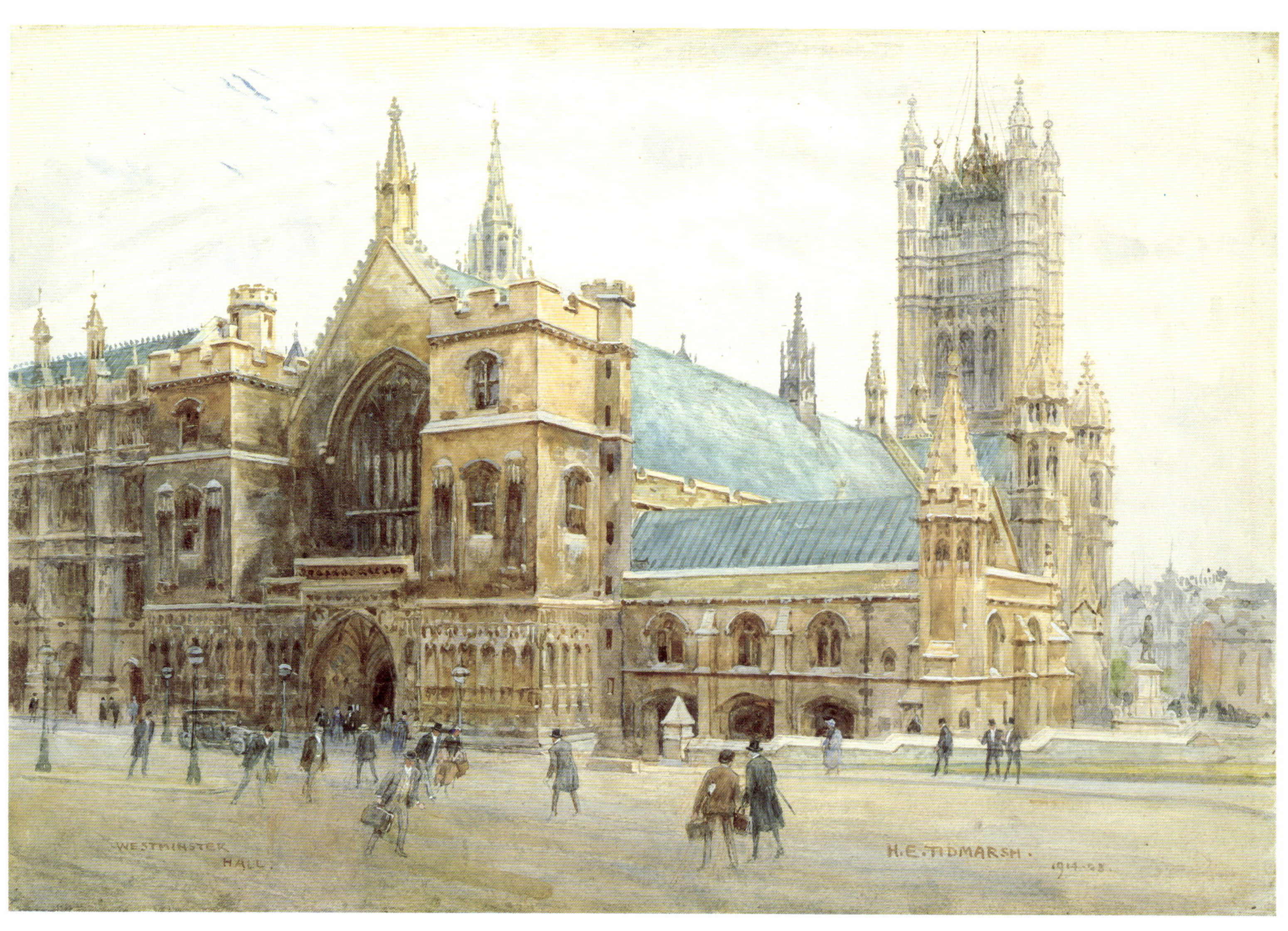
WESTMINSTER
HALL.
H.E. TIDMARSH.

Westminster Abbey

1913

[UNTITLED]

Shows the Chapter House, the South Transept, the Chevet, and a south east view of the Henry VII Chapel. *Staffage:* a chauffeur-driven open motor car, a dust cart, and pedestrians, including a top-hatted and red-faced cleric accompanied by a smart youth.

[113] *Watercolour drawing 262 × 391 mm*

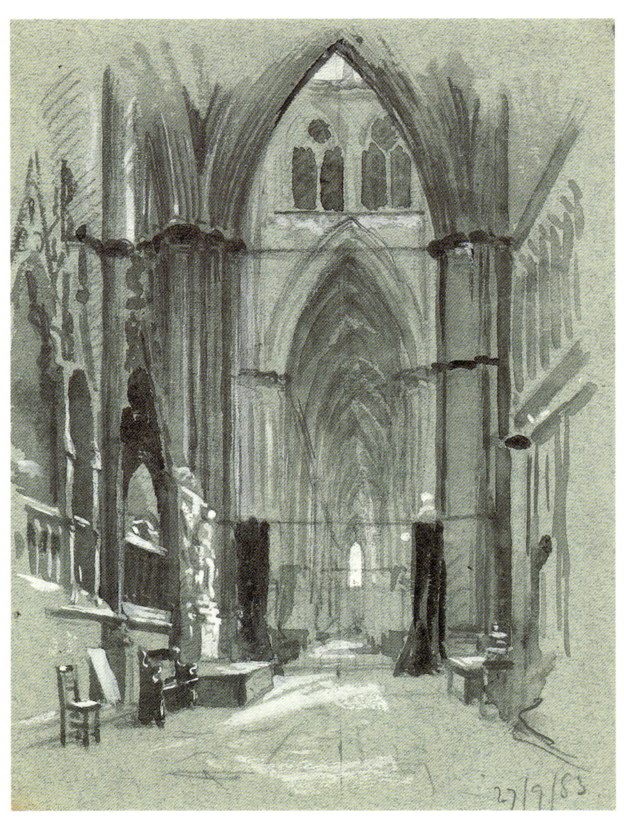

Henry VII Chapel, looking east, 1883

[114] *Wash drawing, heightened with body colour, 170 × 135 mm*

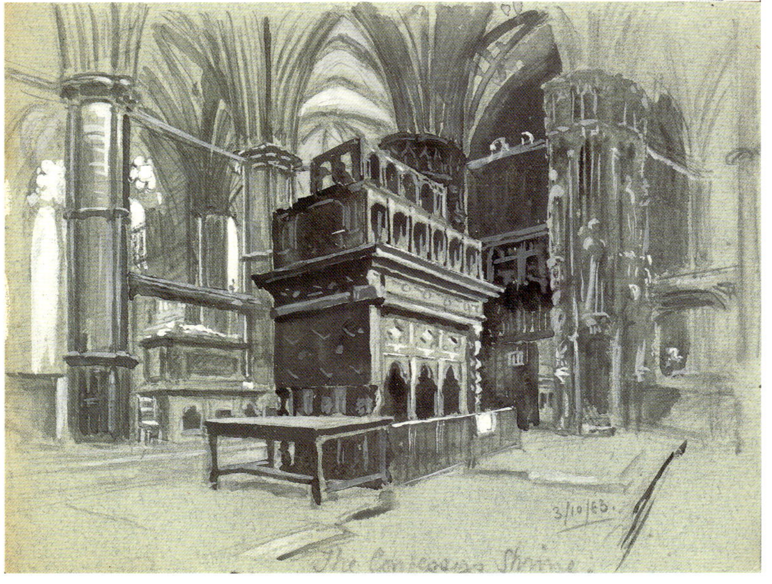

The shrine of Edward the Confessor in Westminster Abbey, viewed from the south west, 1883

[115] *Wash drawing, heightened with body colour, 135 × 175 mm*

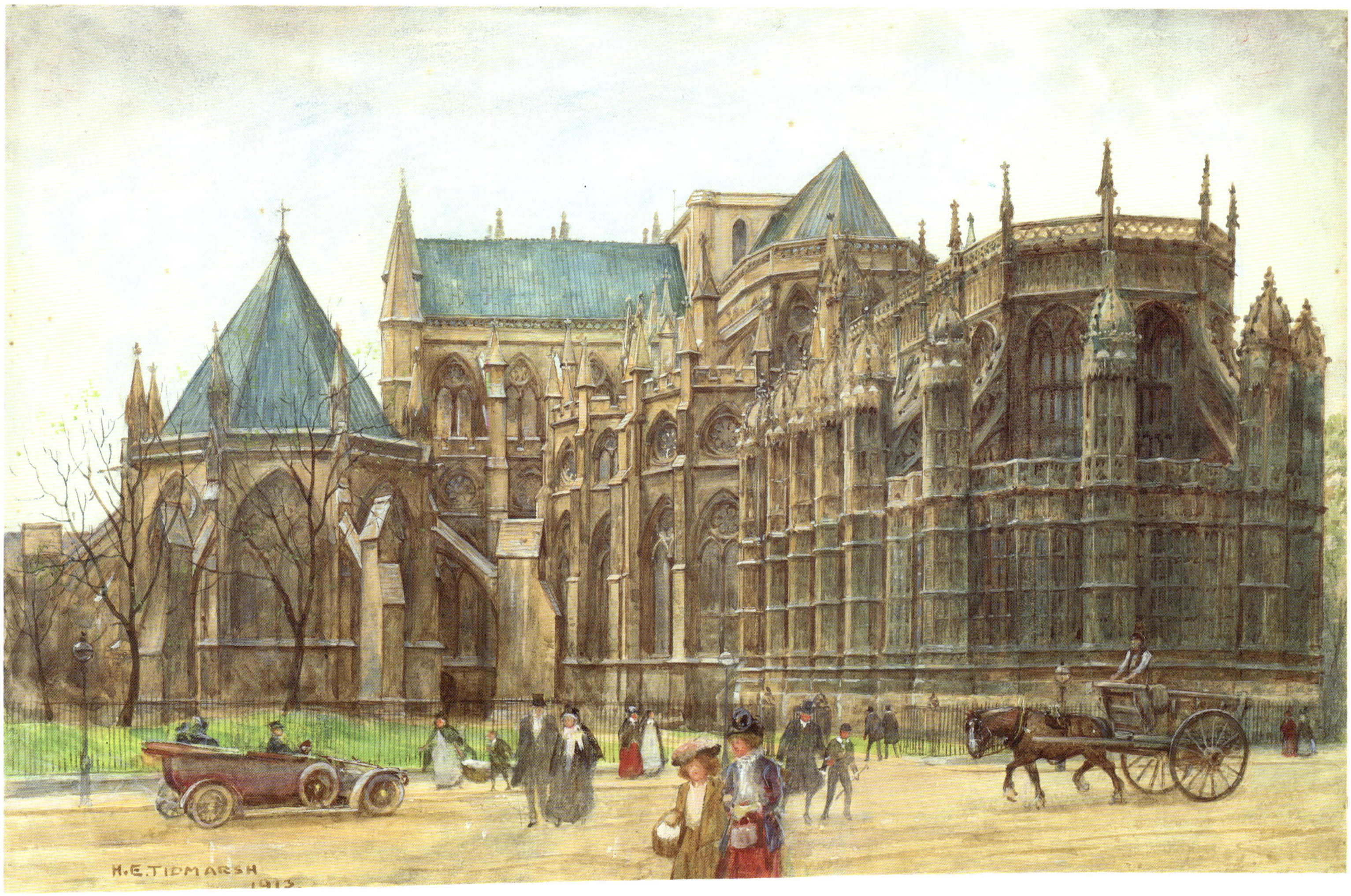

124 **Westminster Abbey**

1896

[UNTITLED]

It is ten o'clock in the morning on a spring day. On the left is St Margaret Westminster, and behind it Westminster Abbey. The statue on the left is of Lord Palmerston, that in the centre is of Sir Robert Peel. *Staffage:* a growler awaiting customers, a children's nanny in characteristic cape, and a footman riding a trap, who seems to have been sent out shopping. Tidmarsh exhibited this watercolour at the Royal Academy summer show of 1896 (see page 9).

[116] *Watercolour drawing 265 × 380 mm sight*

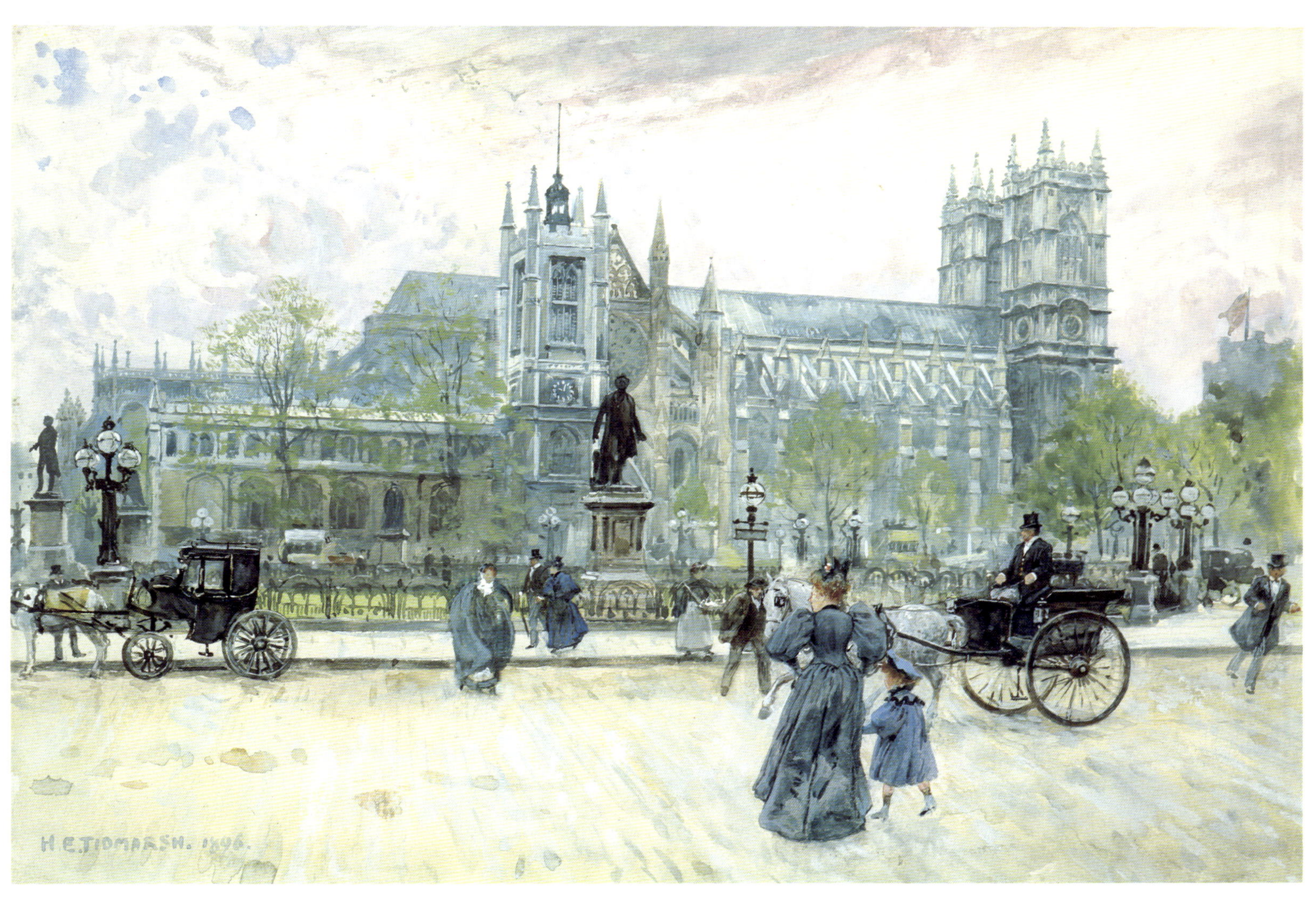
H.E.TIDMARSH. 1896.

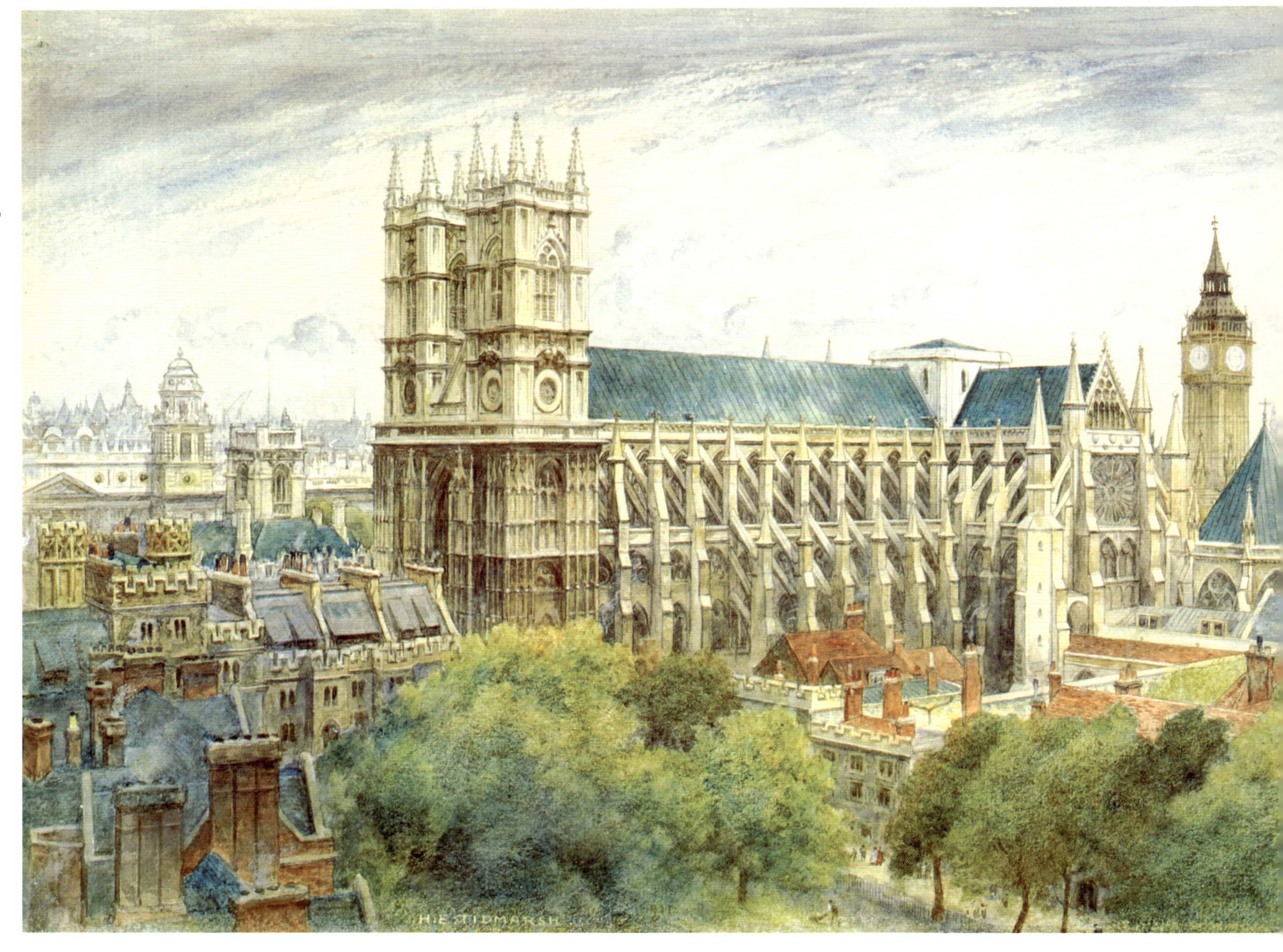

Roof-Top View of Westminster looking North East
c.1913

[UNTITLED]

The view is taken probably from the tower of St Matthew's in Great Peter Street. In the mid-distance is the Home Office, designed by J. M. Brydon and completed in 1907; the tower of the Middlesex Guildhall, built by J. S. Gibson & Partners, 1906-1913; Westminster Abbey; and the Houses of Parliament. The dome of St Paul's and Tower Bridge appear on the horizon. The Gothic building on the right is the chapel of old Church House, demolished 1936-1937.

[117] *Watercolour drawing 335 × 863 mm sight*

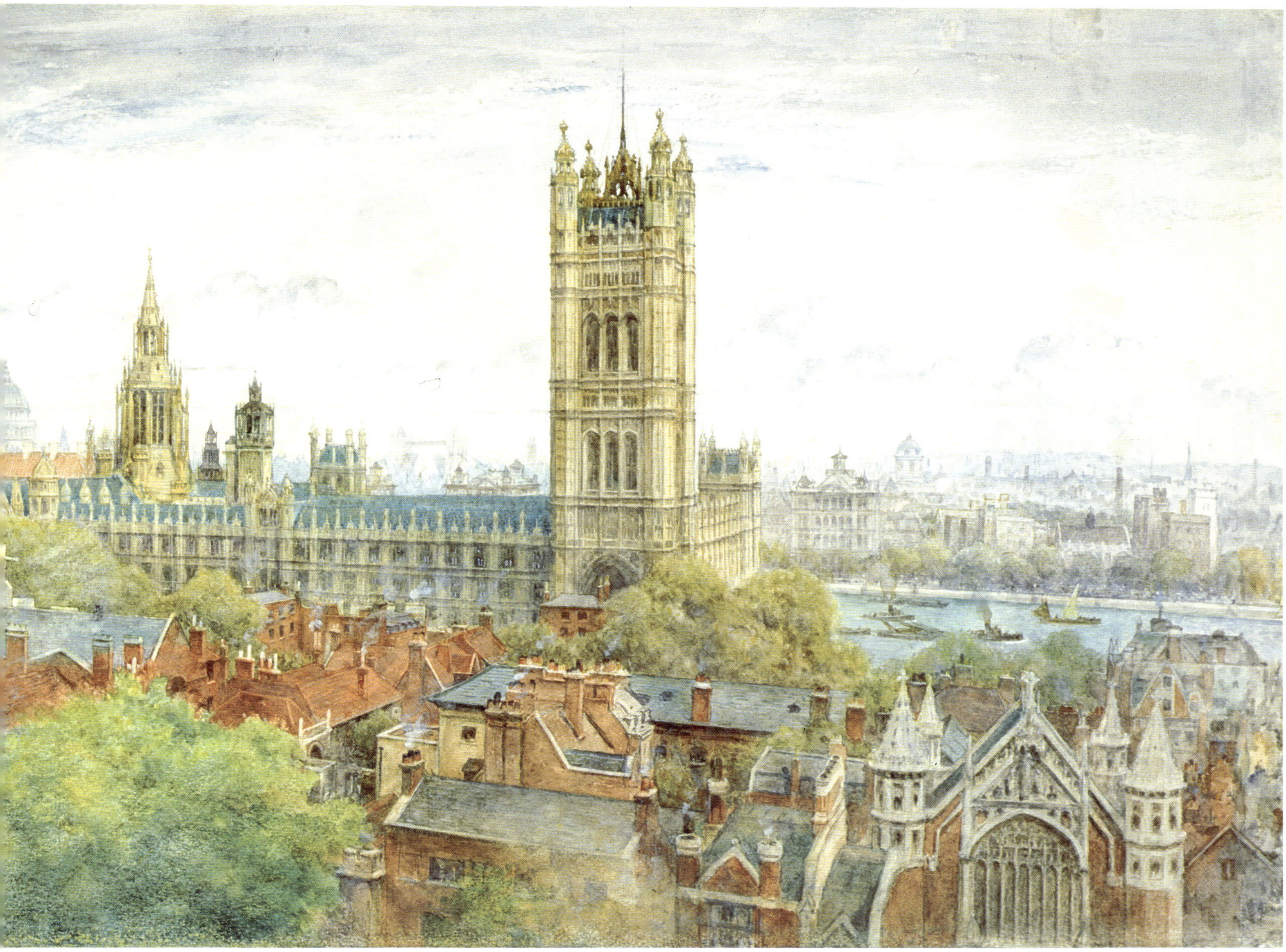

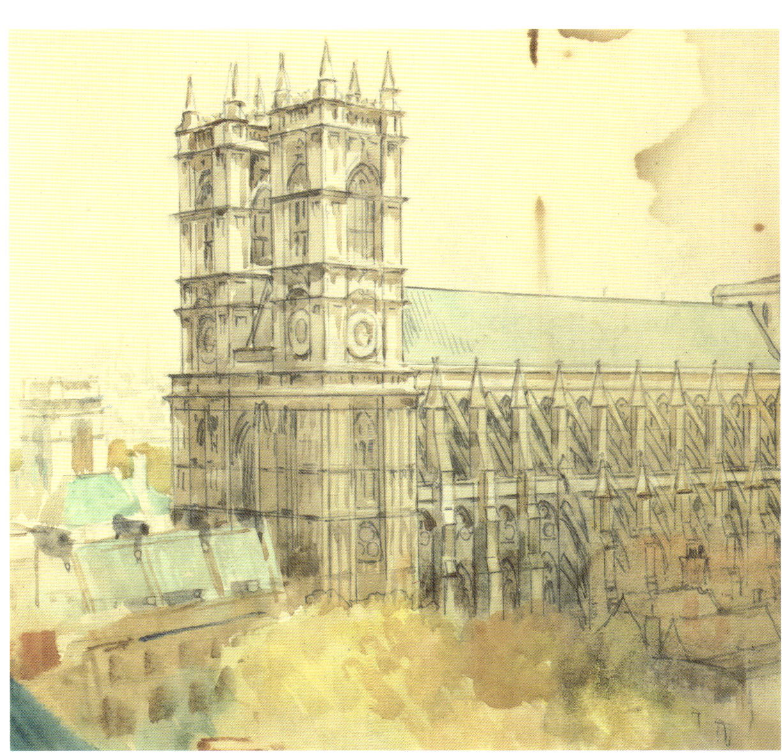

Study for the Westminster Abbey detail in Tidmarsh's roof-top view of Westminster, 1913

[118] *Watercolour sketch, 233 × 242 mm*

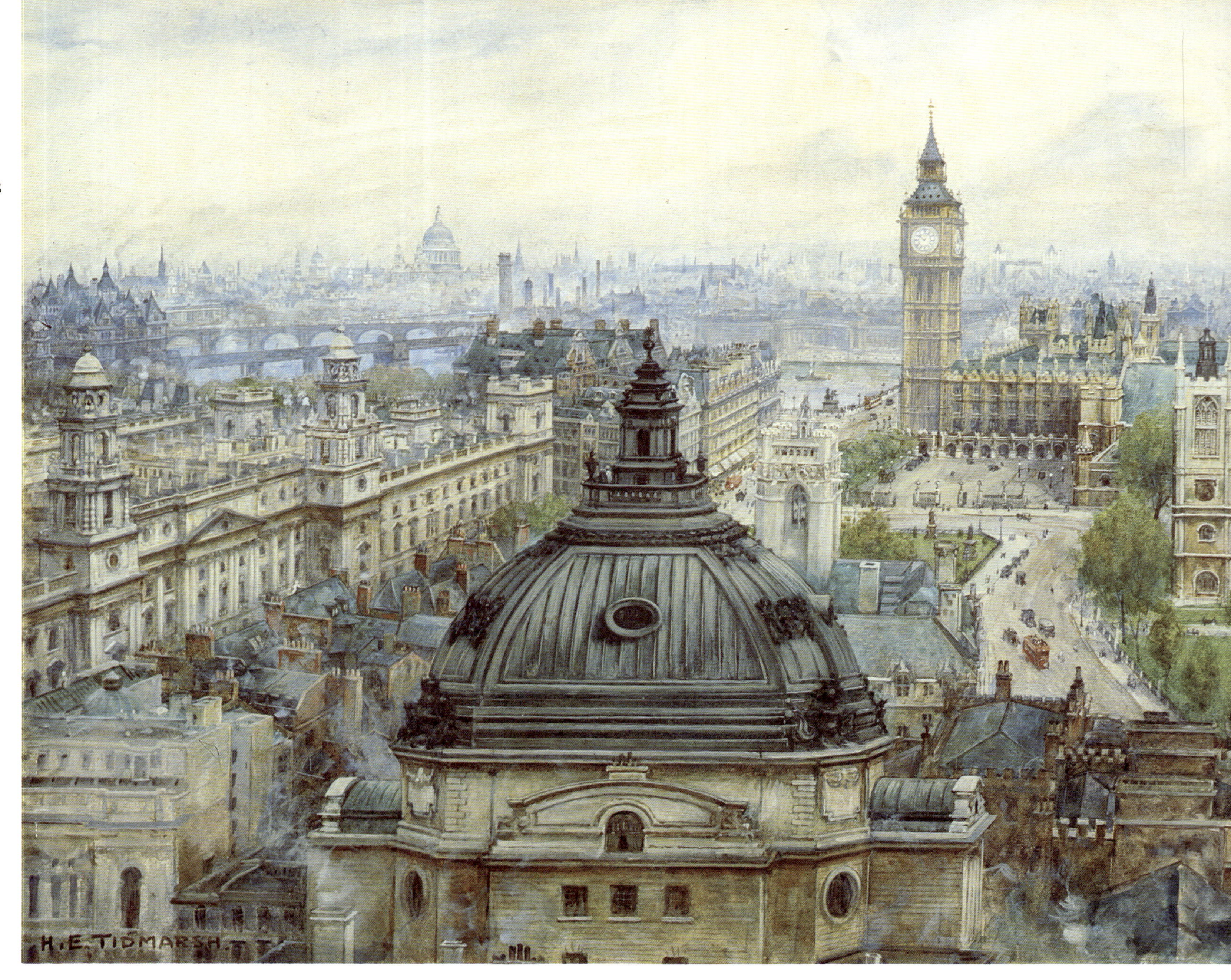

Roof-Top View of Westminster looking West

c.1912

[UNTITLED]

The view was taken from the dome of the Wesleyan Central Hall. Not wanting to leave out this new and important Methodist landmark, Tidmarsh placed it in the foreground. The Hall, designed by Lanchester & Rickards, was built on the site of the Royal Aquarium. It was completed in 1911. To the left of it, on the north side of Great George Street, is the new Home Office. On the right of it is St Margaret Westminster, Westminster Abbey, and Westminster School. In the distance can be seen St Paul's Cathedral, County Hall under construction, Tower Bridge, and the Houses of Parliament. On the extreme right are Lambeth Palace and Doulton & Co.'s pottery works in Lambeth, and St John Smith Square in Westminster.

[119] *Watercolour drawing 360 × 910 mm sight*

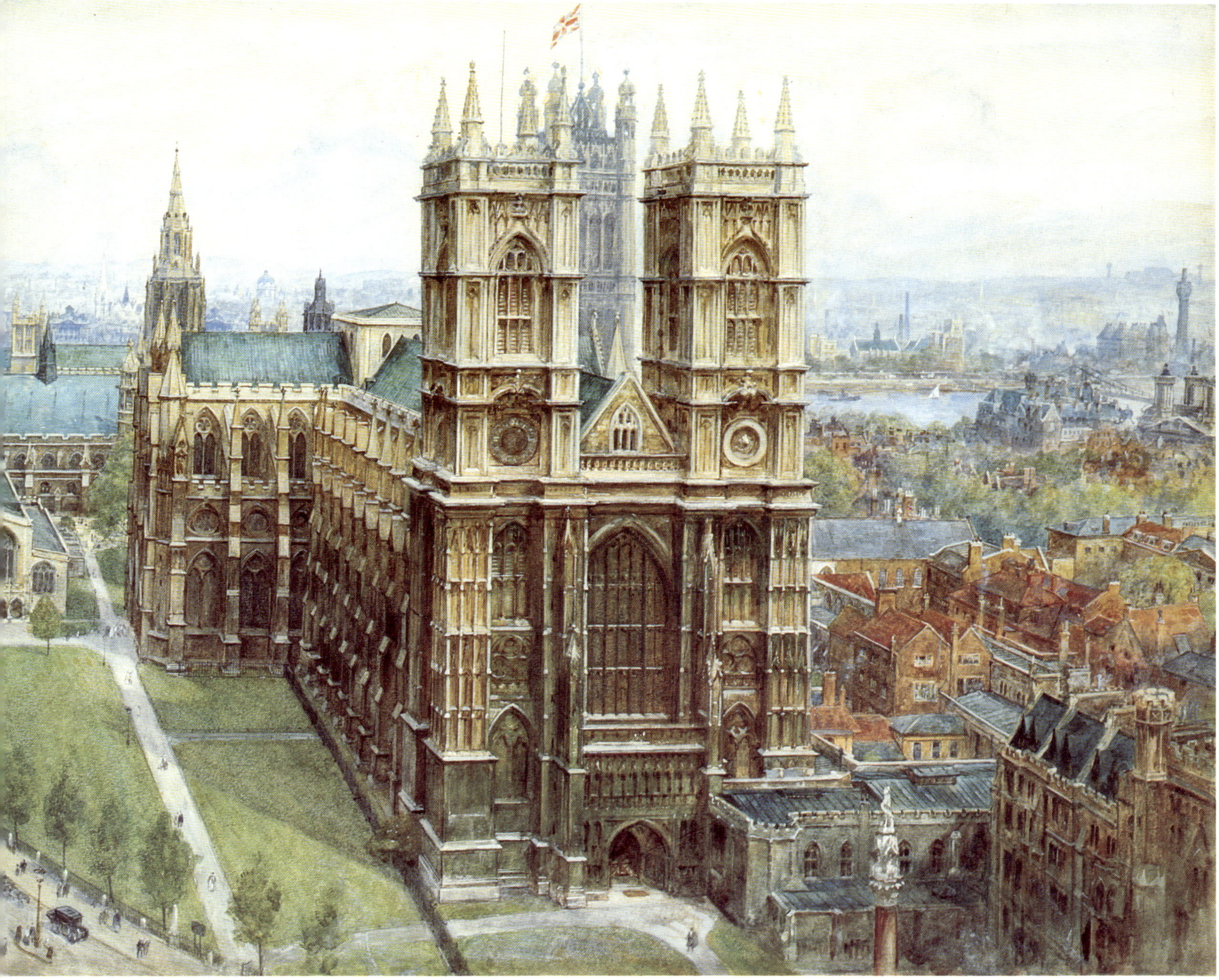

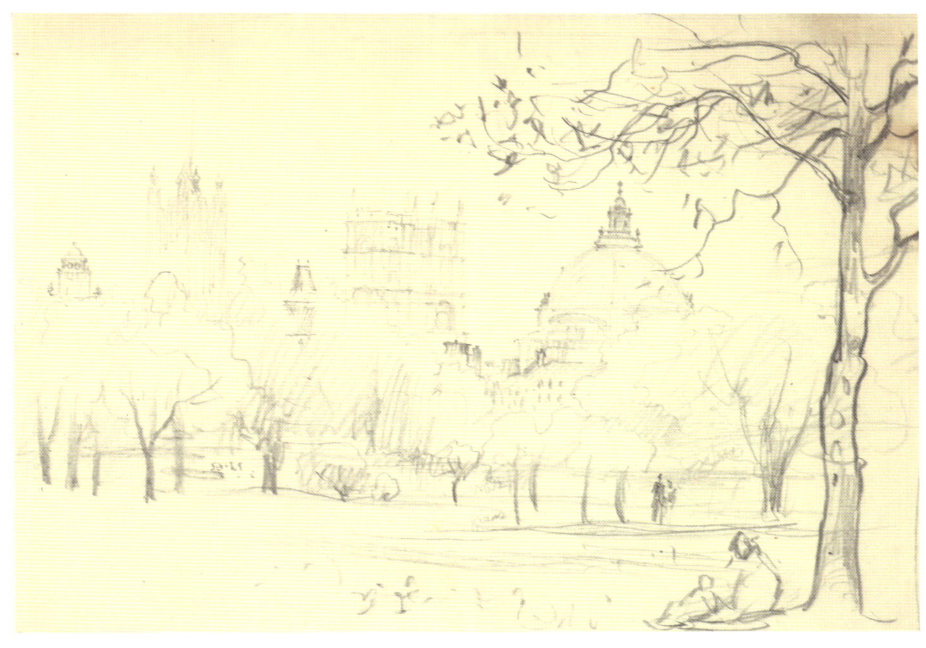

View towards Parliament, Westminister Abbey, and the Wesleyan Central Hall, from St James's Park, c.1912

[120] *Pencil sketch, 230 × 335 mm*

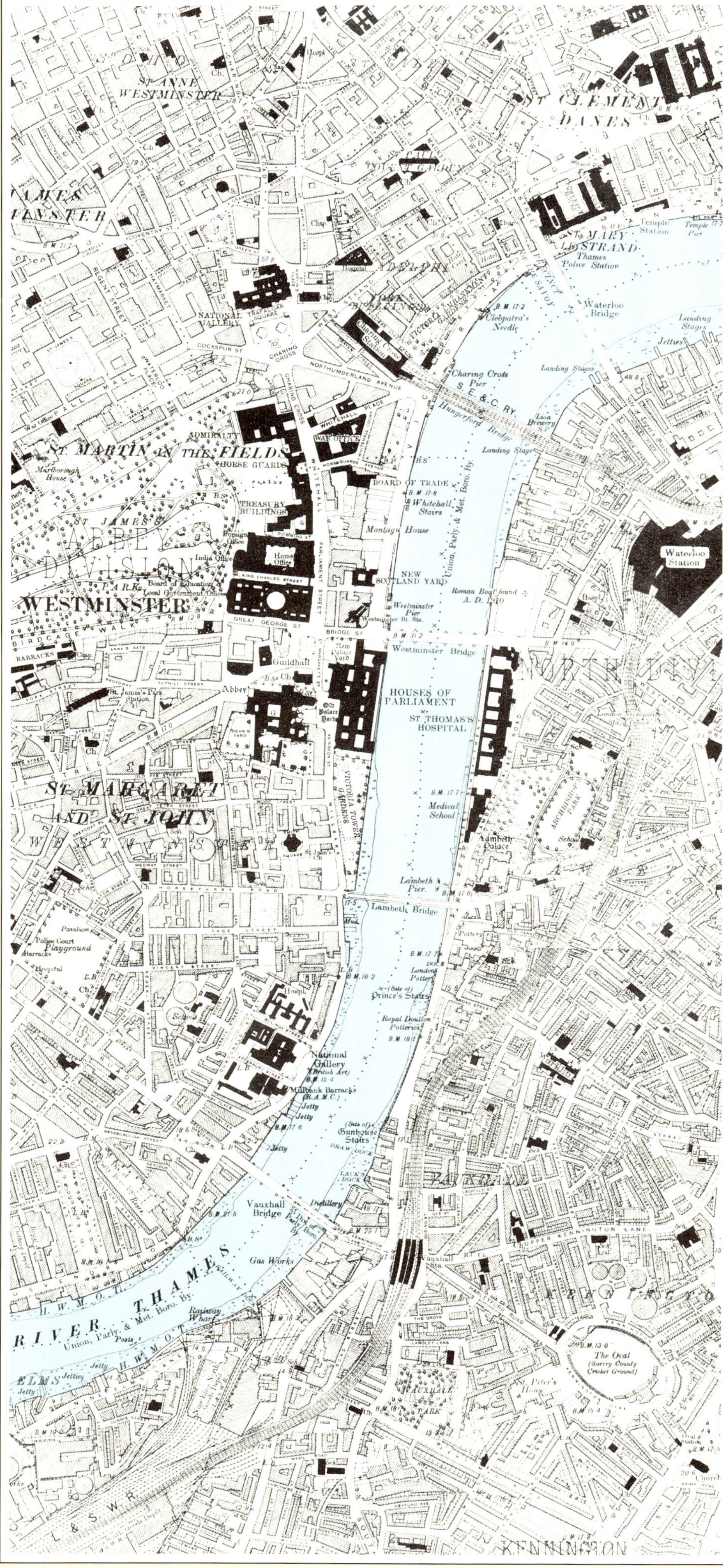

River Thames

Detail from the Ordnance Survey Six Inch to One Mile Plan of London, as revised 1913/14

London Bridge from Southwark *(right)*

[121] *Detail from plate 135*

River Thames

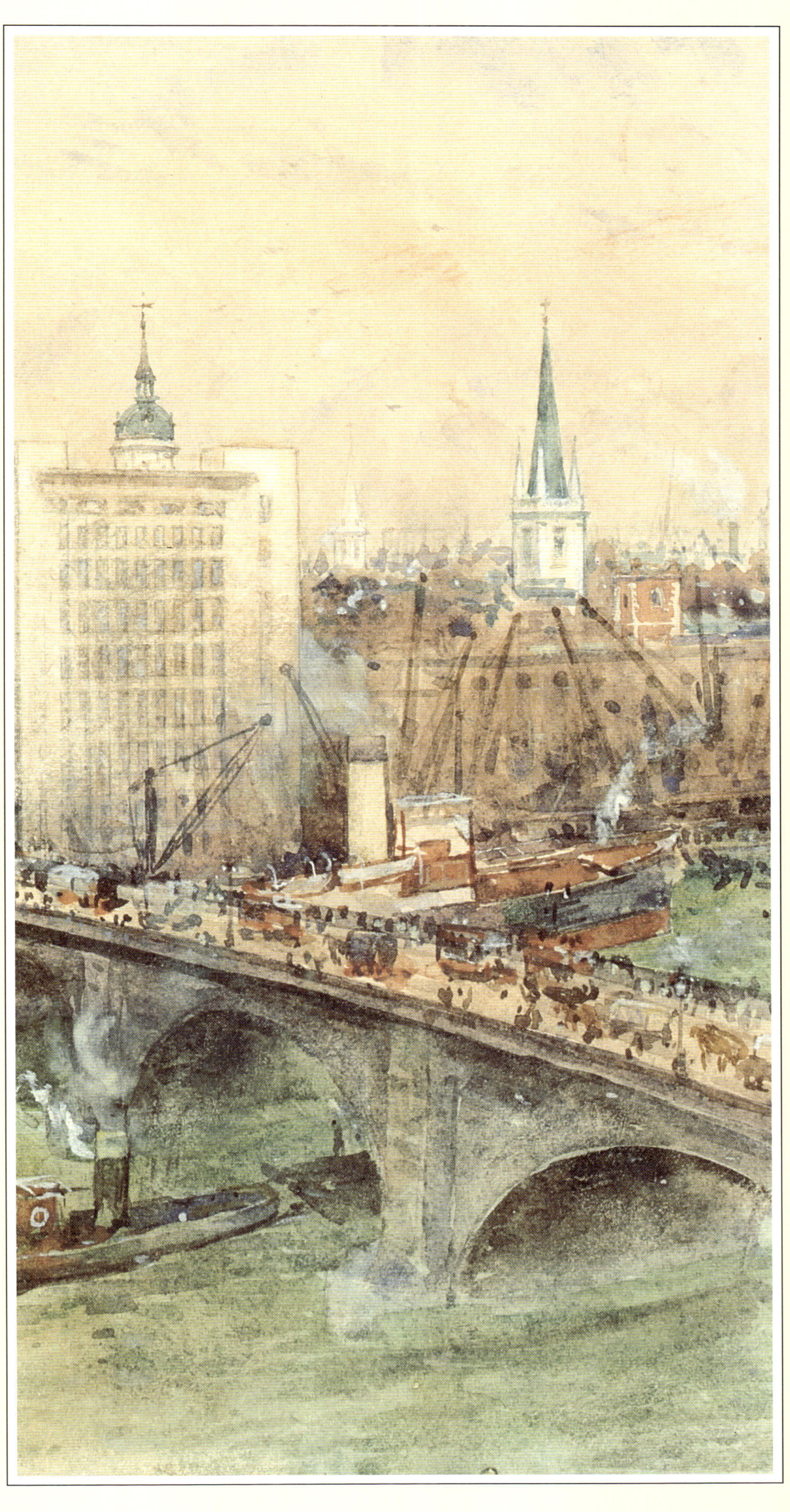

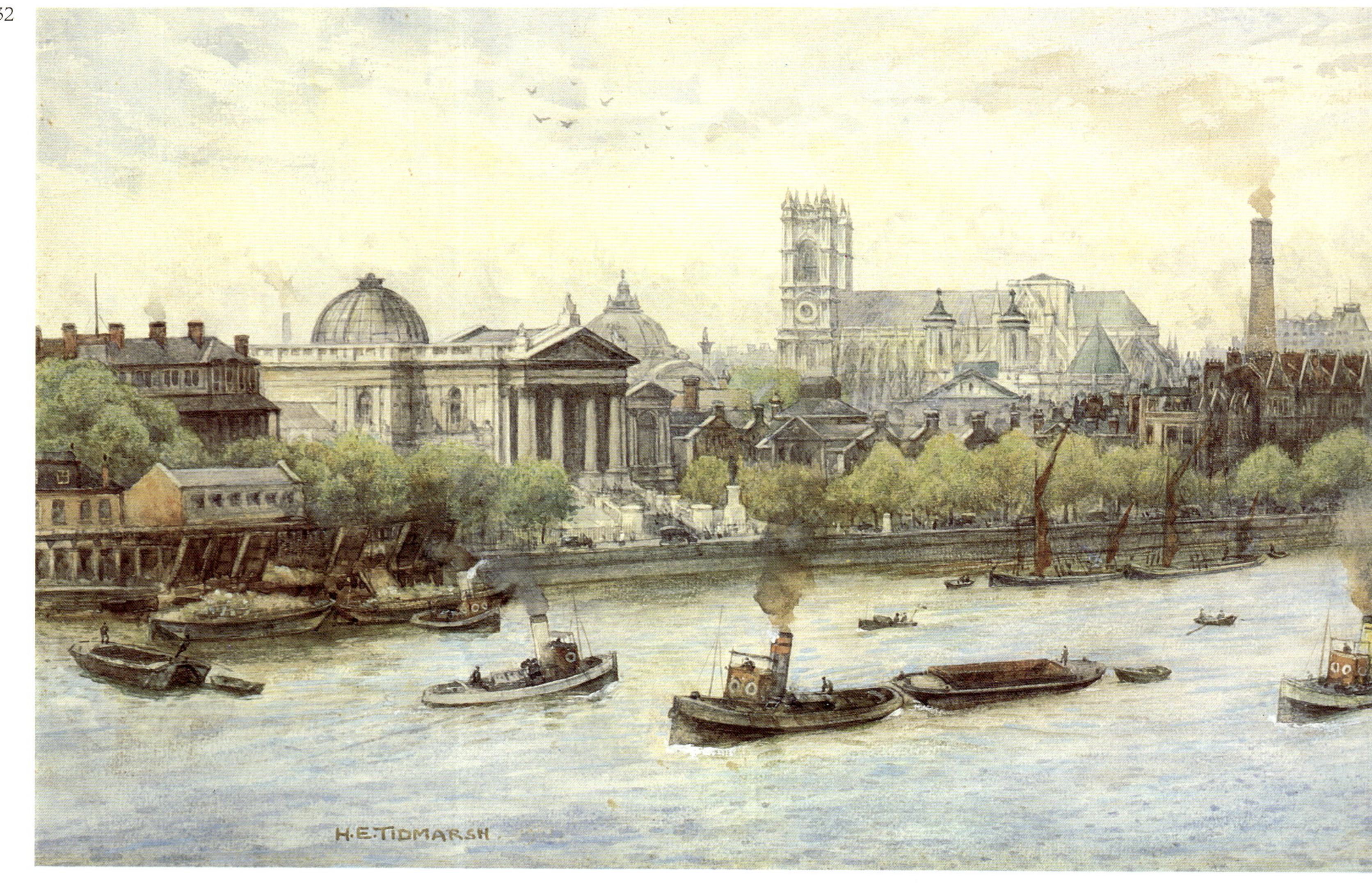

The Thames looking North from Lambeth

c.1921

[UNTITLED]

From left to right can be seen Grosvenor Road wharves, the Tate Gallery, the dome of Wesleyan Central Hall, Westminster Abbey, the Houses of Parliament, Lambeth Bridge, County Hall, St Thomas's Hospital, and Lambeth Palace. Tidmarsh has ruthlessly foreshortened the scene between the Tate and Parliament, and exaggerated the scale of Central Hall and Westminster Abbey. The lattice-stiffened Lambeth Suspension Bridge was replaced by Sir George Humphreys' three-span bridge in 1929-1932. On the Thames are sailing barges, lighters, and tugs.

[122] *Watercolour drawing 253 × 772 mm sight*

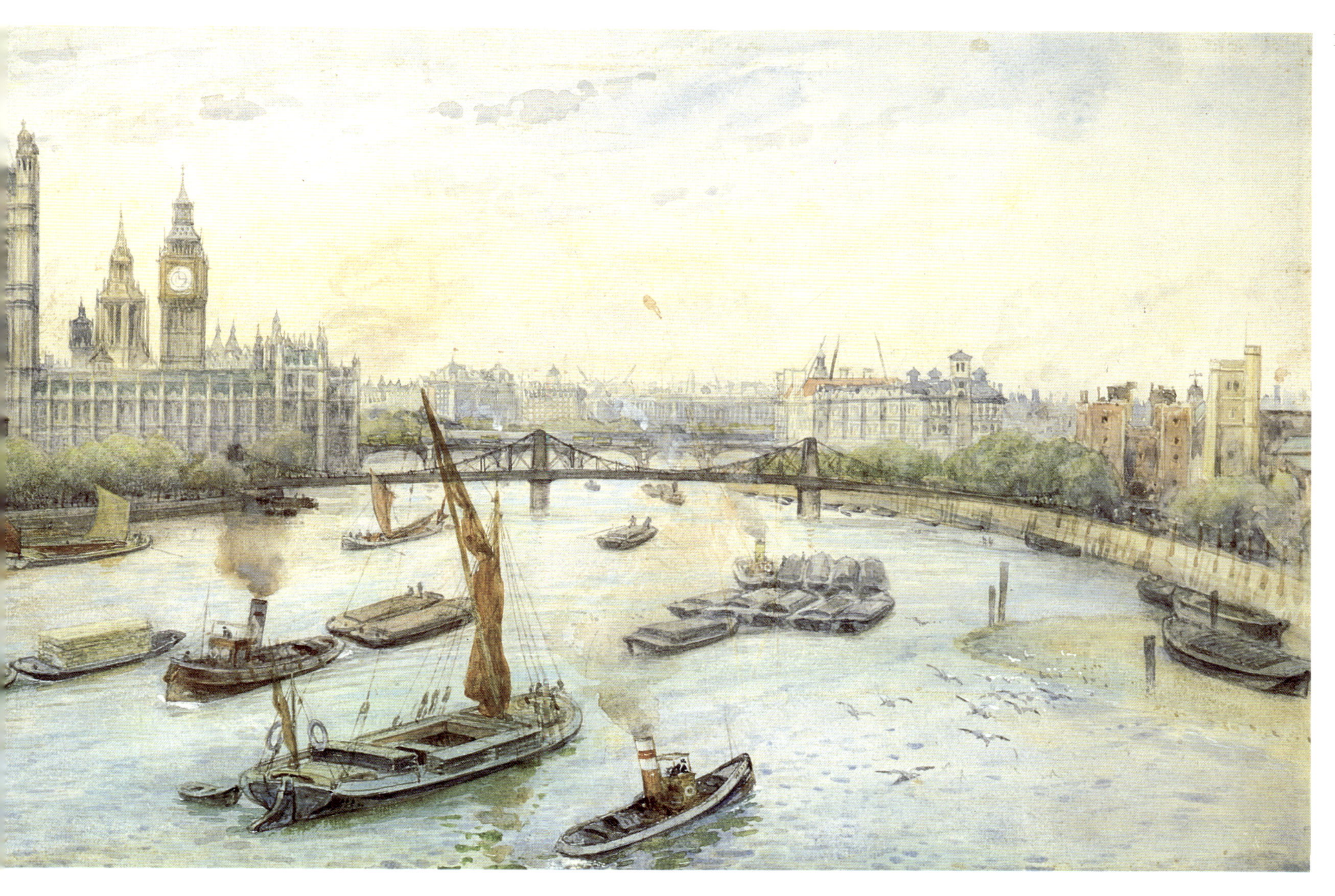

Lambeth Palace

c.1909

LAMBETH PALACE, AND CHURCH

Lambeth Palace, the official residence of the Archbishop of Canterbury, viewed from Millbank. In the foreground is a steam tug and a rowing boat; other boats are moored downstream of Lambeth Pier. Tidmarsh had drawn a series of views of Lambeth Palace for the *Graphic*, published 31 July 1886.

[123] *Watercolour drawing 198 × 300 mm*

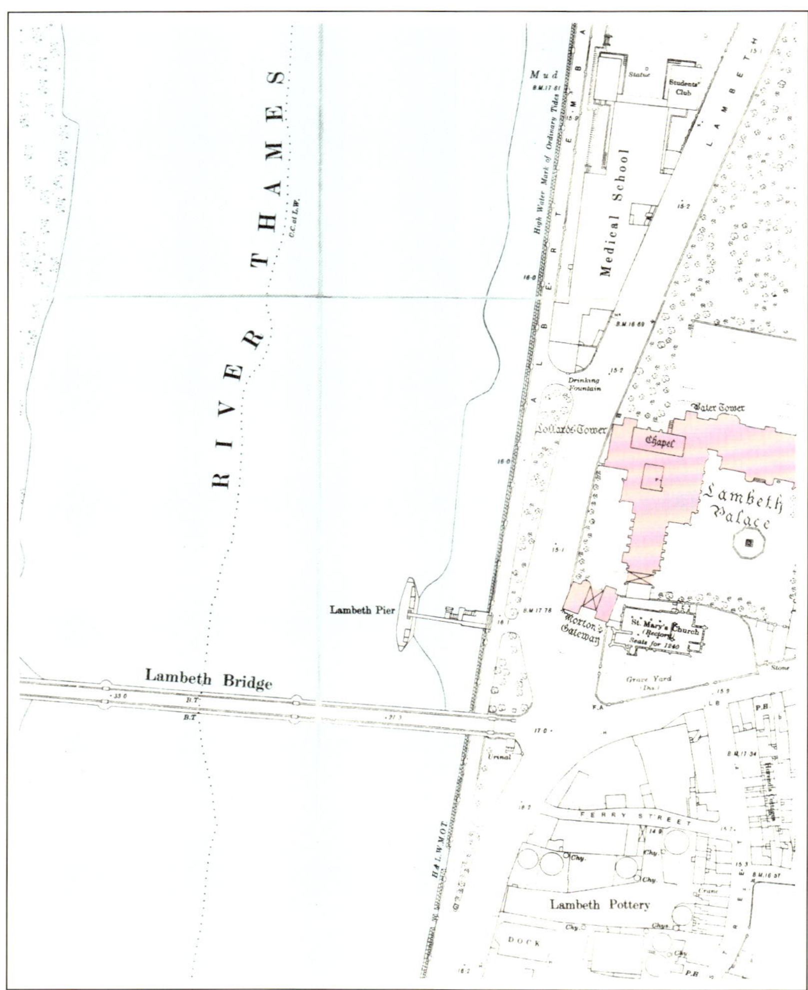

Detail from the Ordnance Survey Five Feet to One Mile Plan of London, V11.93, published 1915

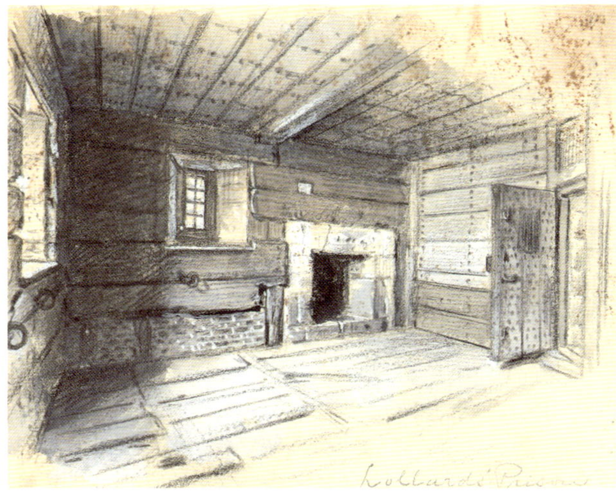

Lollards' Tower, Lambeth Palace, c.1886

Built as a water tower in 1342, legend has it Lollards were imprisoned there.

[124] *Wash drawing, heightened with body colour, 128× 155 mm*

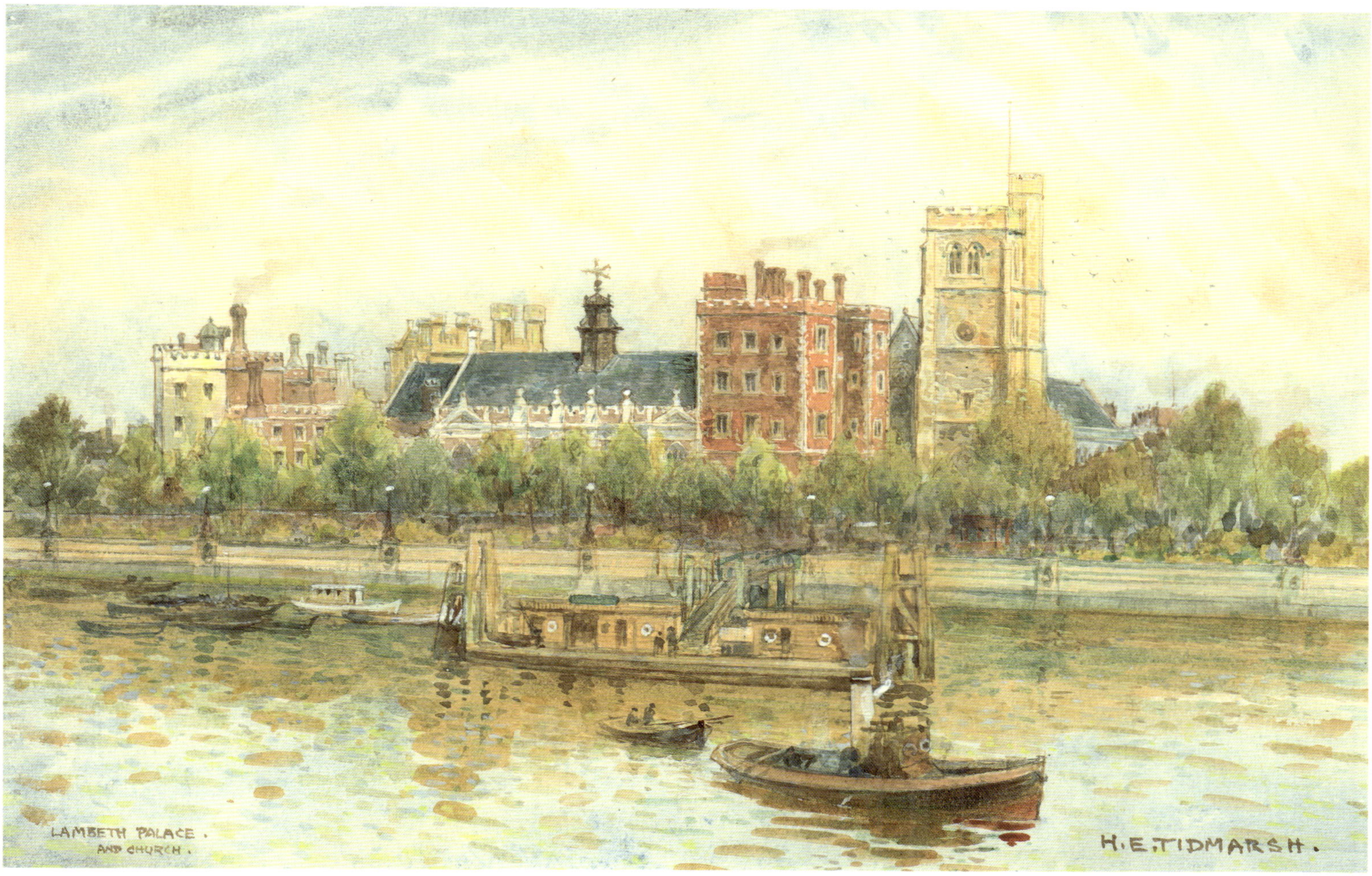

LAMBETH PALACE.
AND CHURCH.
H.E.TIDMARSH.

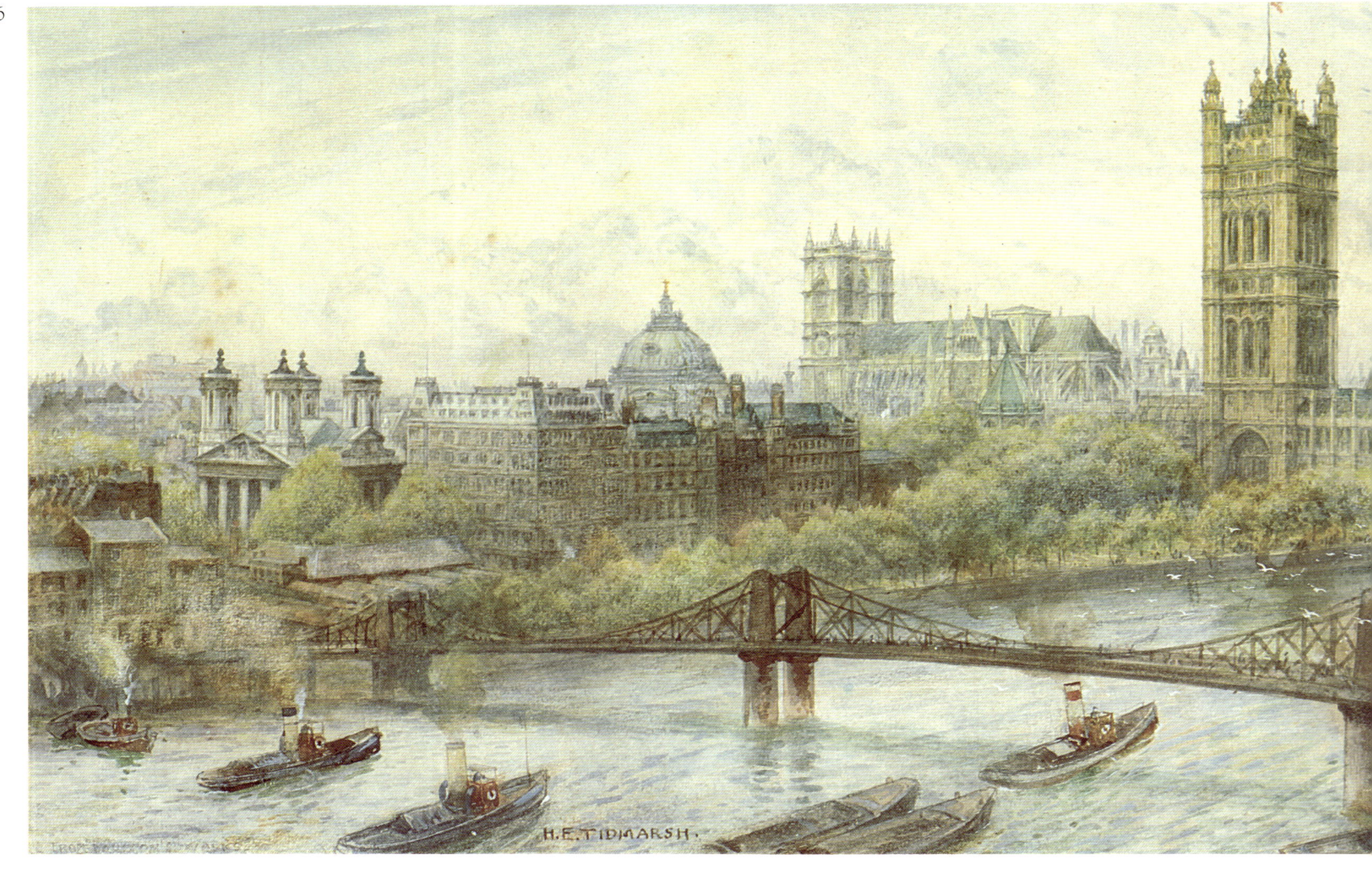

The Thames looking North West from Lambeth

1921

LAMBETH OLD SUSPENSION BRIDGE

The view is taken from Doulton & Co.'s pottery works. The principal landmarks from left to right are: St John Smith Square, Lambeth Suspension Bridge (replaced 1929-1932), Ecclesiastical Commissioners, the dome of Wesleyan Central Hall, Westminster Abbey, the Houses of Parliament, Westminster Bridge, and Lambeth Palace. On the Thames are tugs, lighters, and a pleasure steamer.

[125] *Watercolour drawing 260 × 795 mm (sight)*

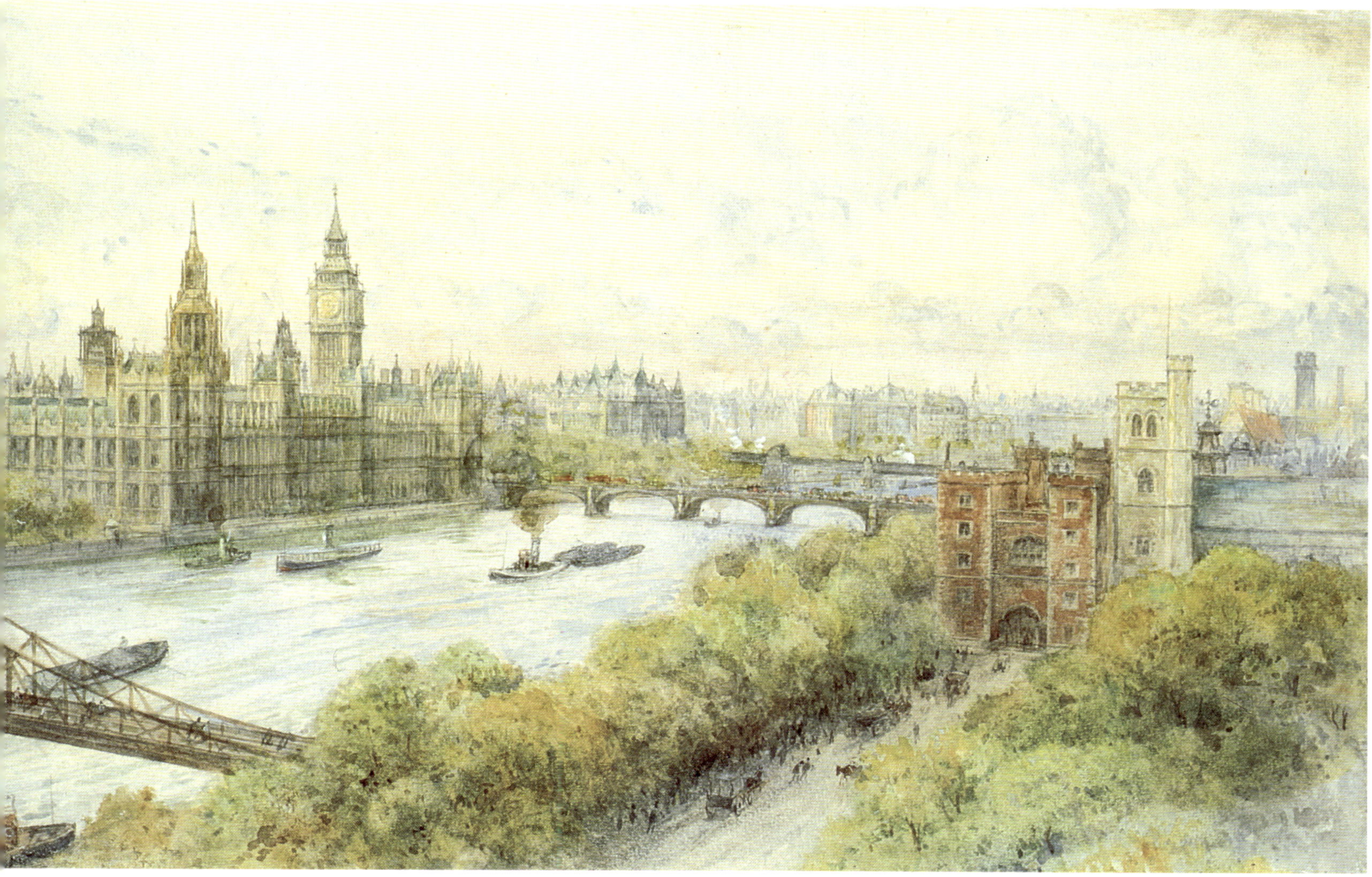

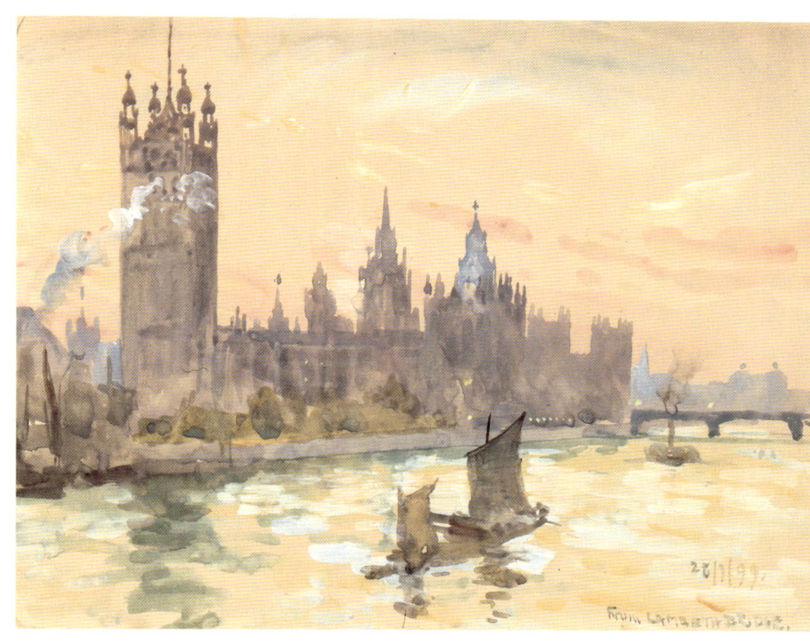

The Houses of Parliament, sketched from Lambeth Bridge, 1899

[126] *Watercolour sketch with body colour, 240 × 305 mm*

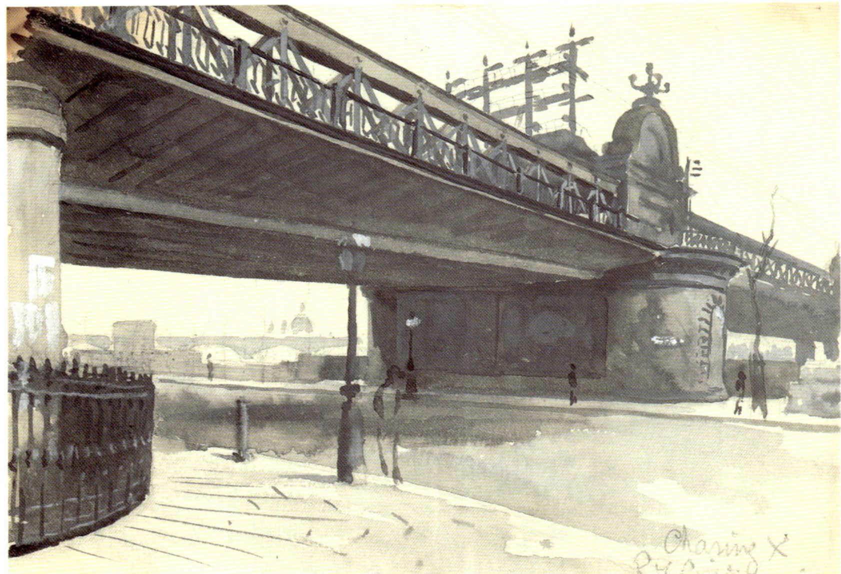

Charing Cross Railway Bridge from Northumberland Avenue, c.1885

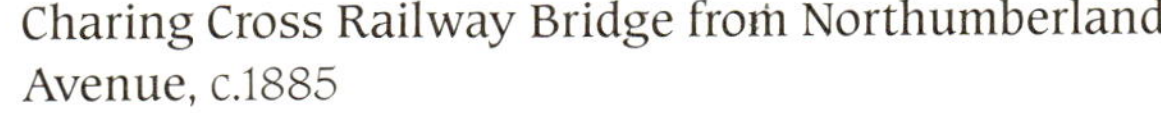

[127] *Wash drawing, heightened with body colour, 130 × 182 mm*

The Floating Swimming Bath, Victoria Embankment, 1883

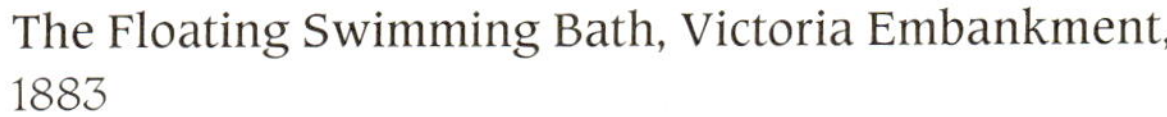

(below left)

This bath, enclosed in glass with flanking domes, was moored just west of the Charing Cross Railway Bridge. It was removed when the bridge was widened in 1886.

[128] *Wash drawing, heightened with body colour, 123 × 155 mm*

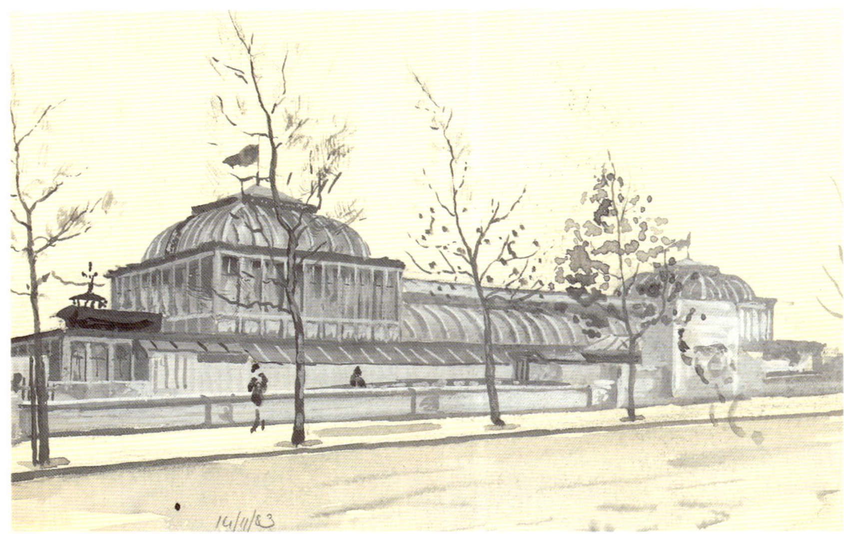

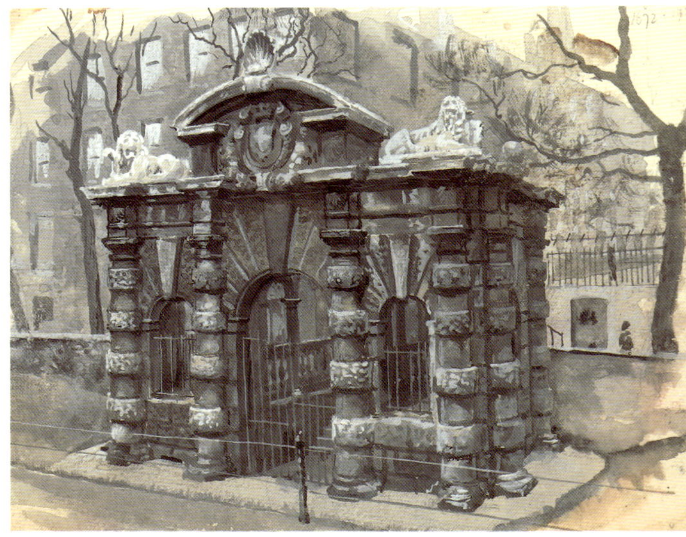

York Watergate, c.1890

(above)

The gate had formerly been the entrance from the river stairs to the Duke of Buckingham's garden at York House. It became separated from the Thames when land was reclaimed for building the Victoria Embankment in the 1860s.

[129] *Wash drawing, heightened with body colour, 128 × 162 mm*

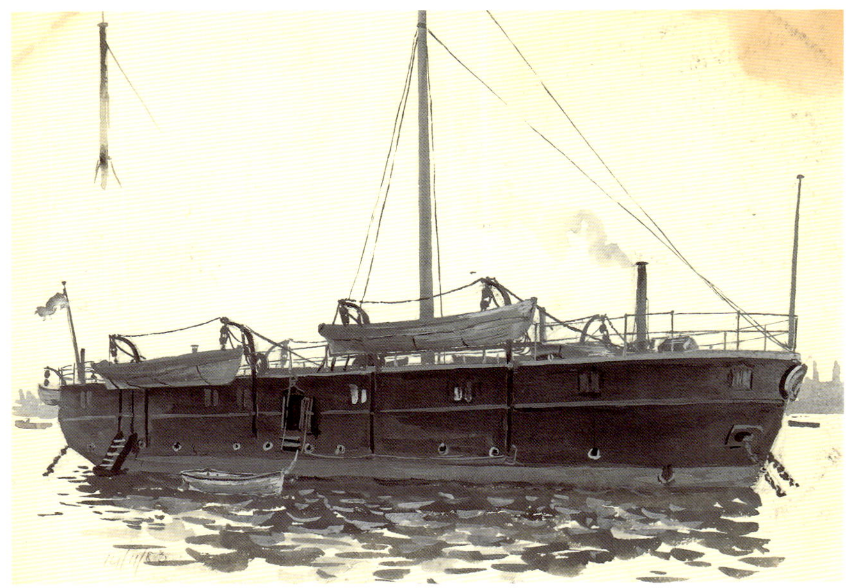

Screw gunboat belonging to the Royal Navy Artillery Volunteers, 1883

This boat had been built by Laird at Birkenhead in 1856.

[130] *Wash drawing, heightened with body colour, 130 × 180 mm*

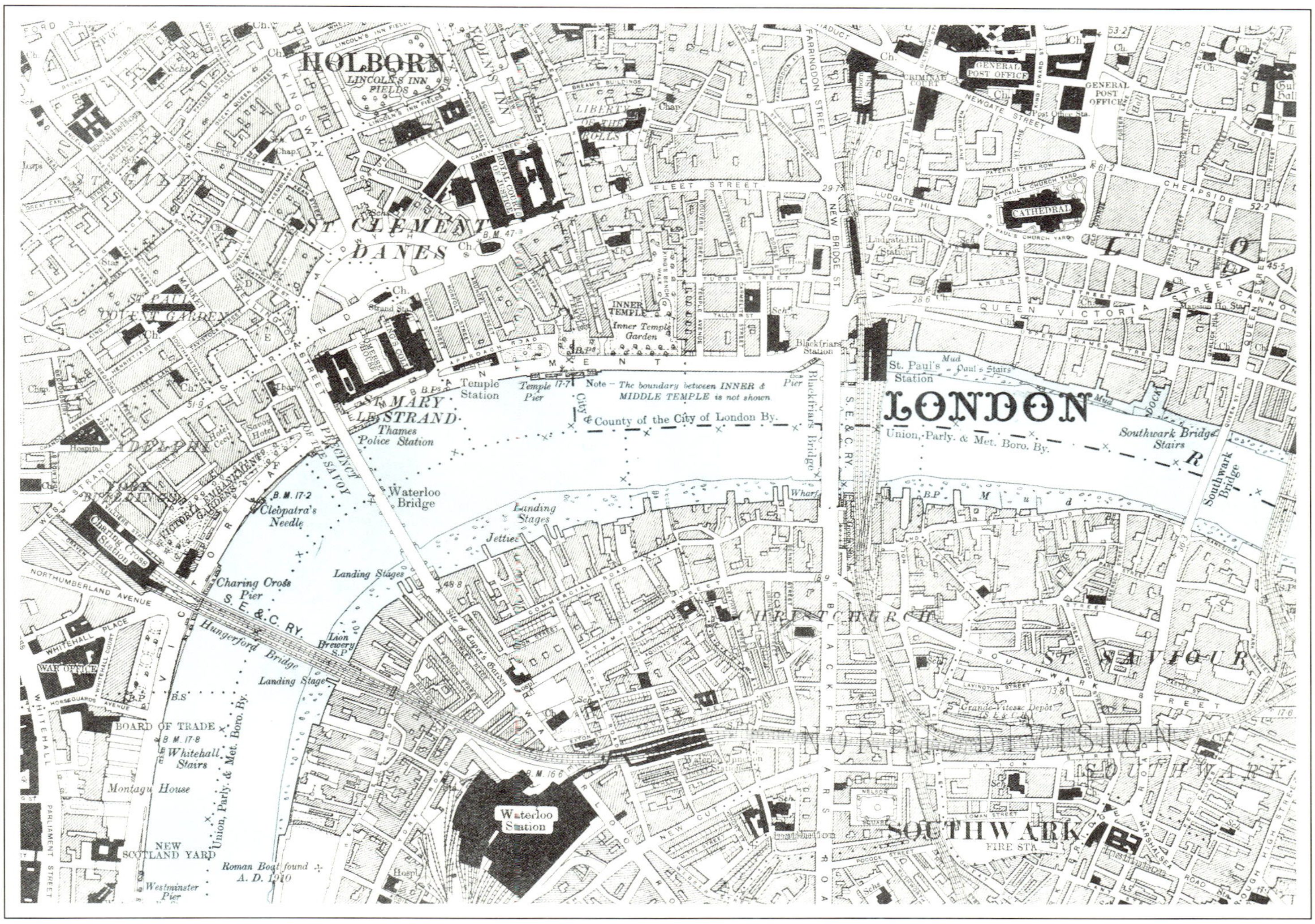

Detail from the Ordnance Survey Six Inch to One Mile Plan of London, as revised 1913/14

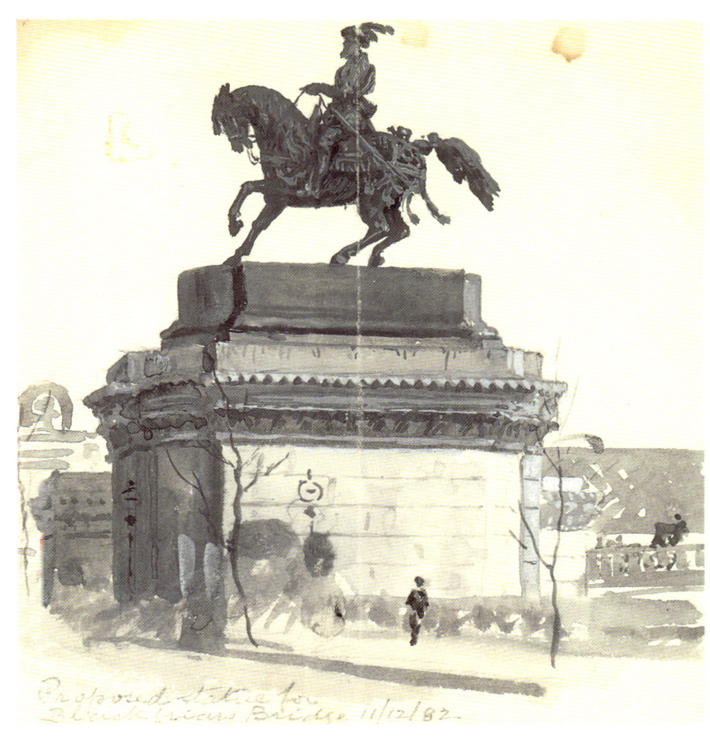

Proposed statue for Blackfriars Bridge, 1882

The horseman in 16th-century costume, is mounted on a richly caparisoned horse. In the event it was a seated statue of Queen Victoria which was erected in 1896.

[131] *Wash drawing, heightened with body colour, 130 × 125 mm*

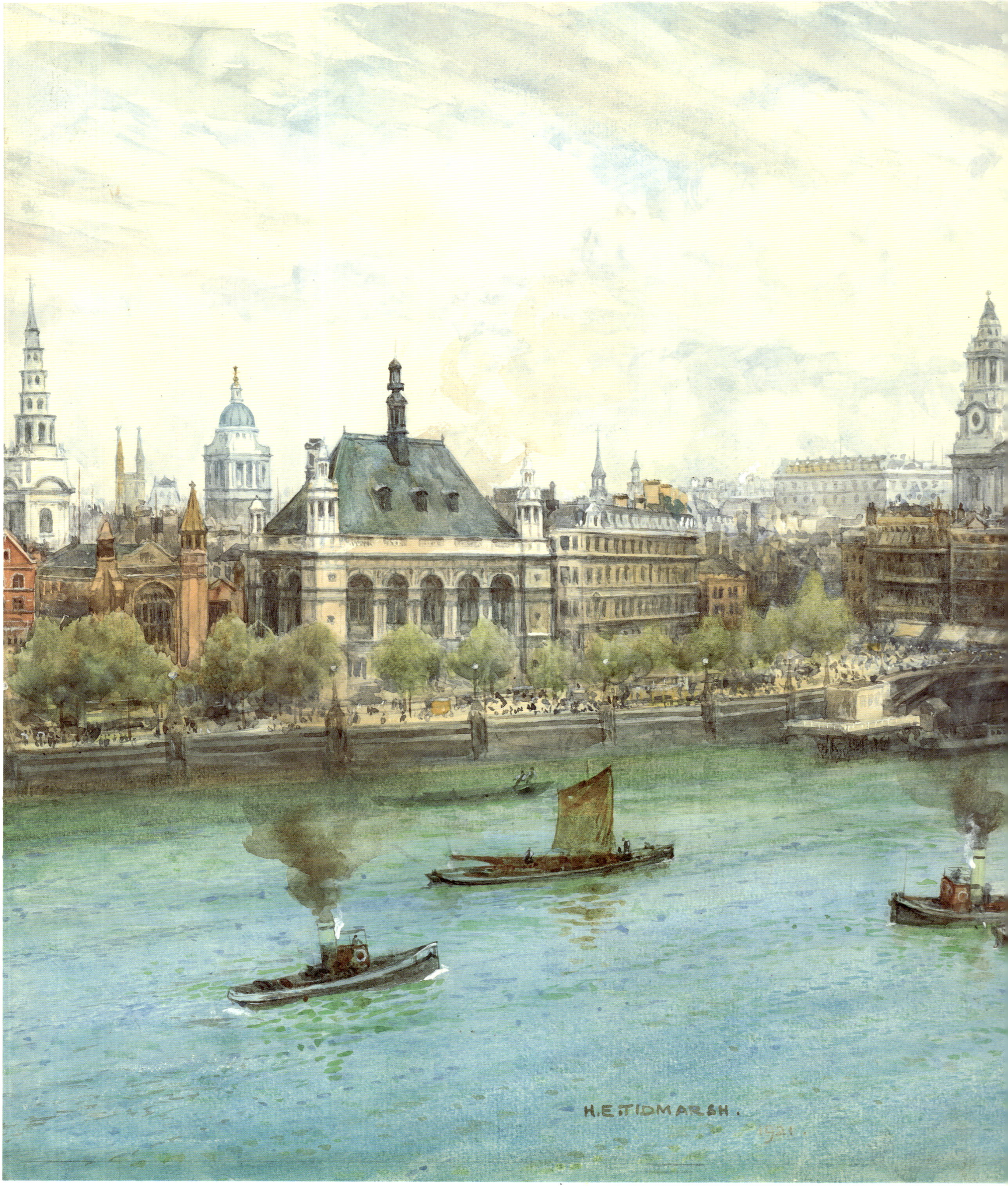

Caption on page 143

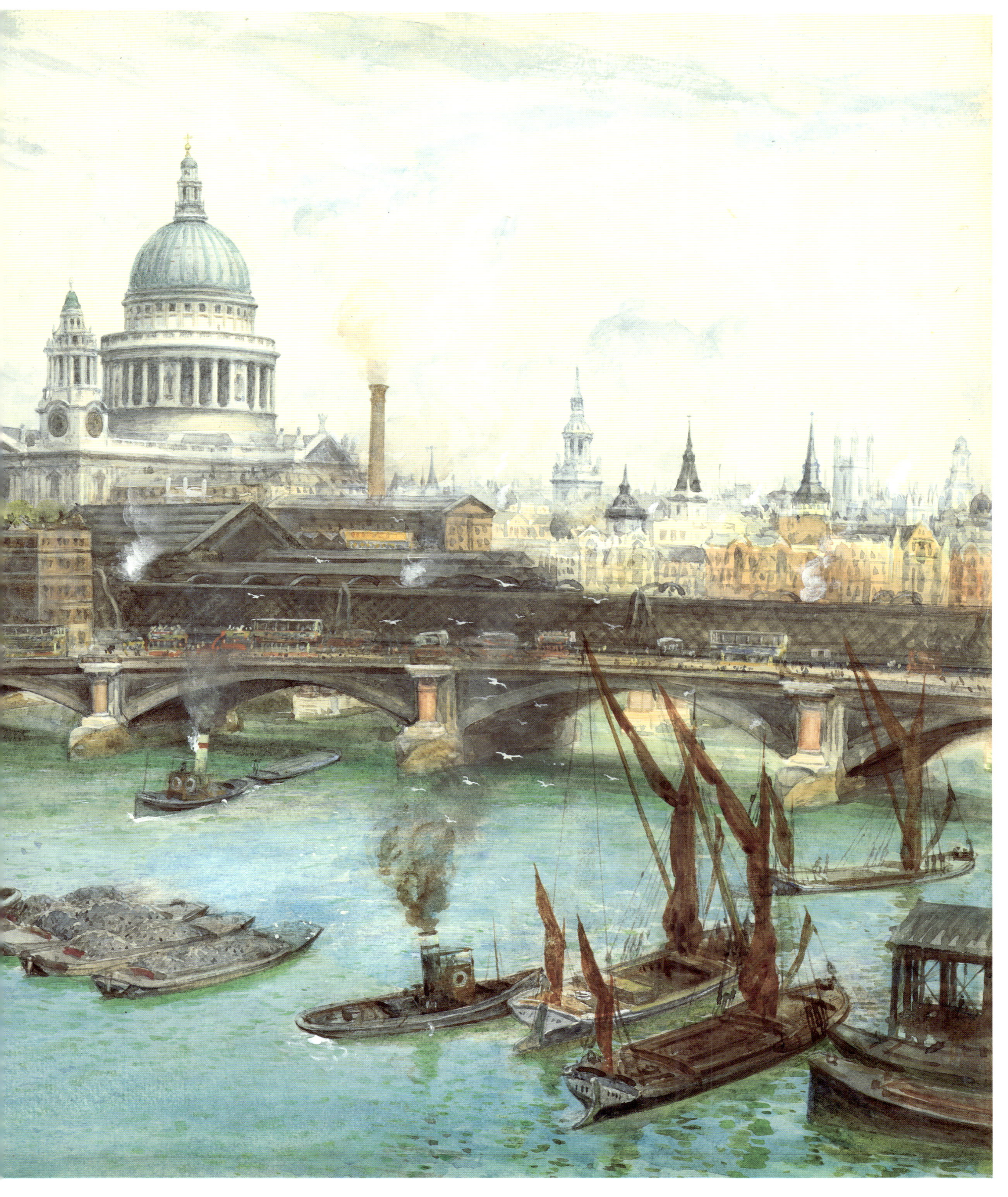

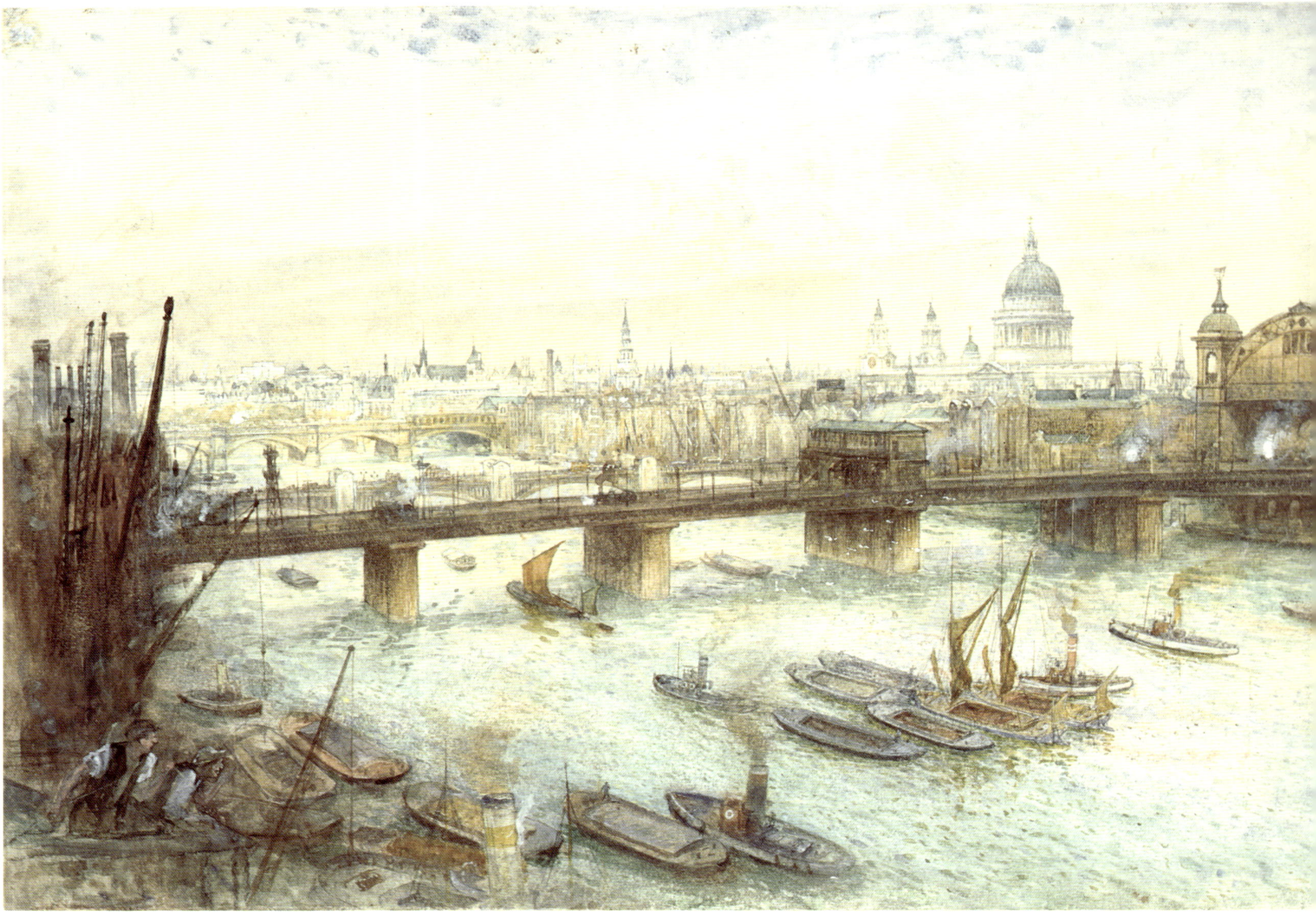

The Thames looking North West from Southwark

1921-1927

LONDON, WITH CANNON ST. RY.

View taken from the tower of the Anglican Southwark Cathedral. The bridges shown, going upstream, are London Bridge, Cannon Street Railway Bridge, Southwark Bridge, and the Southern Railway's Railway Bridge at Blackfriars. Significant landmarks from left to right include the City of London School, St Paul's Cathedral, Cannon Street Station, the City of London Brewery, Fishmongers' Hall, and Adelaide House designed by Sir John Burnett and completed in 1924. Cannon Street Station was designed by John Hawkshaw and completed in 1866. Its roof was destroyed in the Second World War and has never been replaced. Note the signal box on Cannon Street Railway Bridge. On the river two of the spritsailed barges have set smaller jury, or 'bridge' lug sails.

[133] *Watercolour drawing 312 × 880 mm sight*

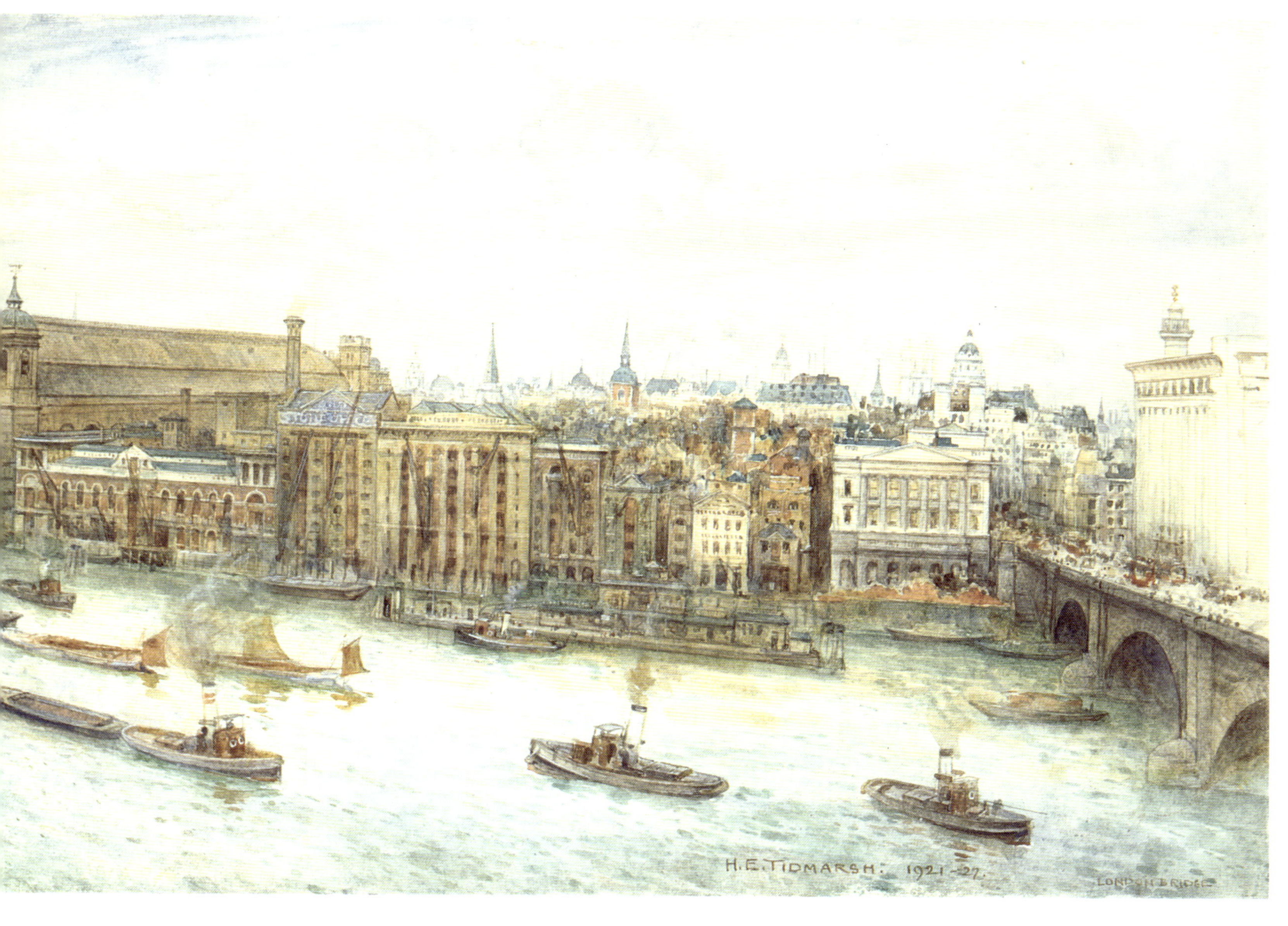

The City of London

1921

[UNTITLED]

A view looking towards the City, taken from Nelson's Wharf, Lambeth. From west to east various spires and towers can be identified: St Bride Fleet Street, St Sepulchre, the Old Bailey, St Paul's Cathedral, St Mary-le-Bow, St Benet Paul's Wharf, St Nicholas Cole Abbey, St Mary Aldermary, St Mary Somerset, and the Royal Exchange. Bordering the river on the left are Sion College (a theological library), and the City of London School. To right of centre the river is crossed by the Blackfriars road and rail bridges. At the north end of the road bridge is Blackfriars Pier. The river is occupied by tugs and barges.

[132] *Watercolour drawing 340 × 568 mm* *See pages 140-141*

Southwark Cathedral

1899

ST SAVIOURS SOUTHWARK. LONDON BRIDGE
(THE EAST END IS EARLY ENGLISH, 1207)

St Saviour's church was raised to the dignity of a pro-Cathedral in 1897. Tidmarsh's drawing of the east end is taken from the corner of Duke Street, with the London Bridge Tavern on the left. On the right is the London & Westminster Bank and Bank Chambers. *Staffage:* a horse bus making for Borough High Street, while another, and a vacant hansom cab, make for London Bridge. Two women hawkers offer flowers to a Homburg-hatted man, a newsboy shouts his wares, and a gaitered and top-hatted cleric crosses the road from the church.

[134] *Watercolour drawing 390 × 277 mm*

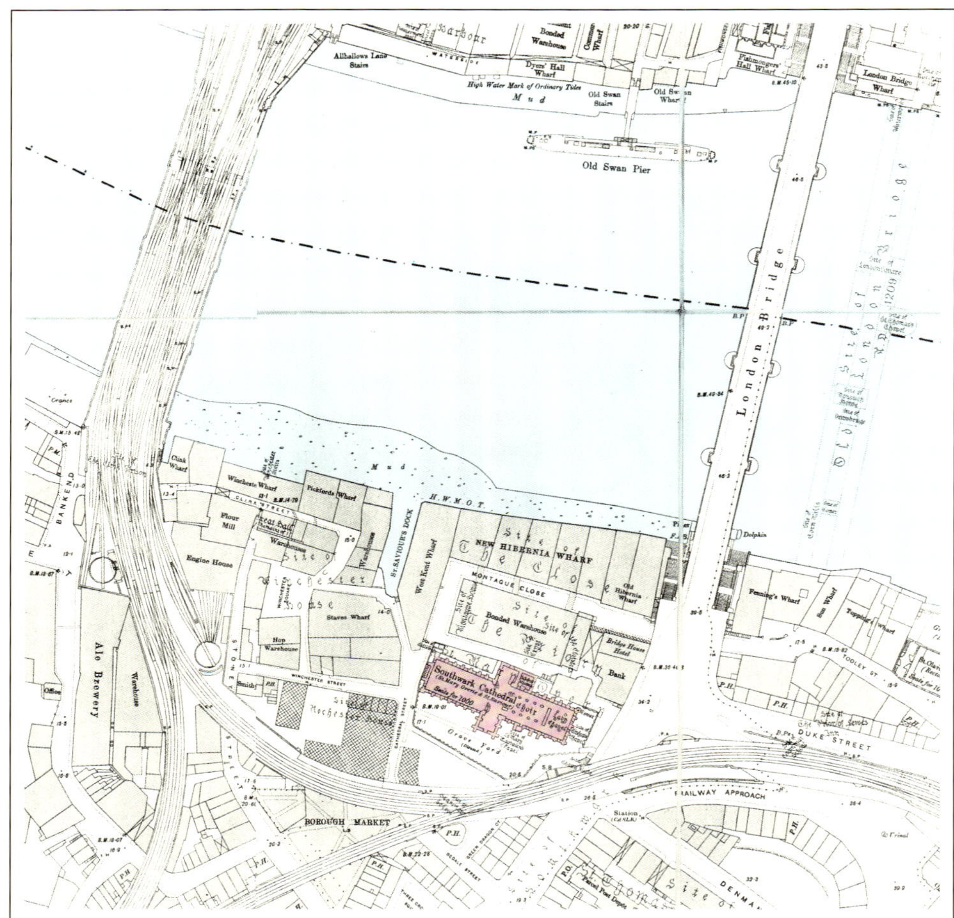

Detail from the Ordnance Survey Five Feet to One Mile Plan of London, V11.75/96, published 1919/20

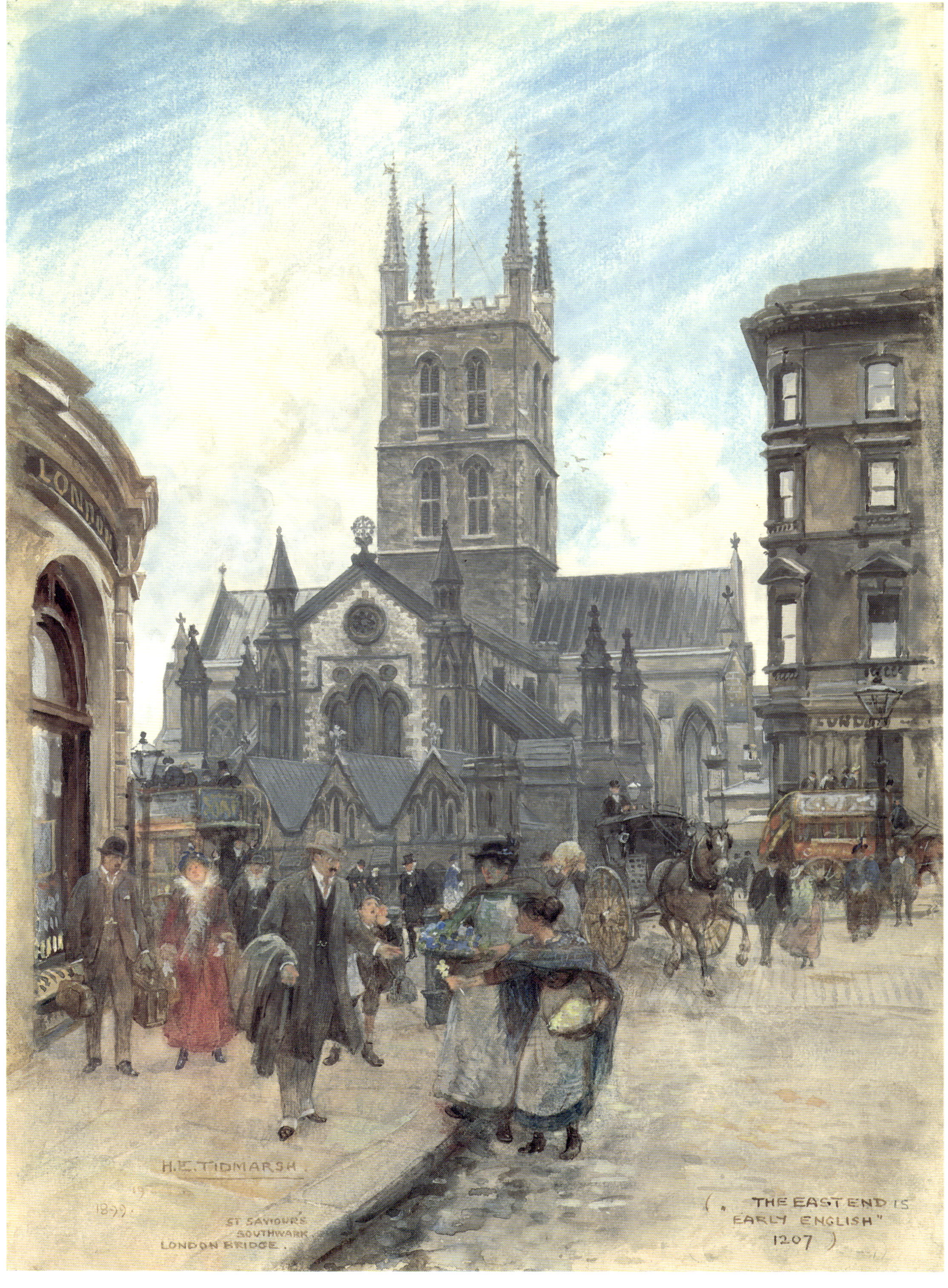
LONDON
H.E. TIDMARSH.
1899.
ST SAVIOUR'S
SOUTHWARK
LONDON BRIDGE.
(. "THE EAST END IS
EARLY ENGLISH"
1207)

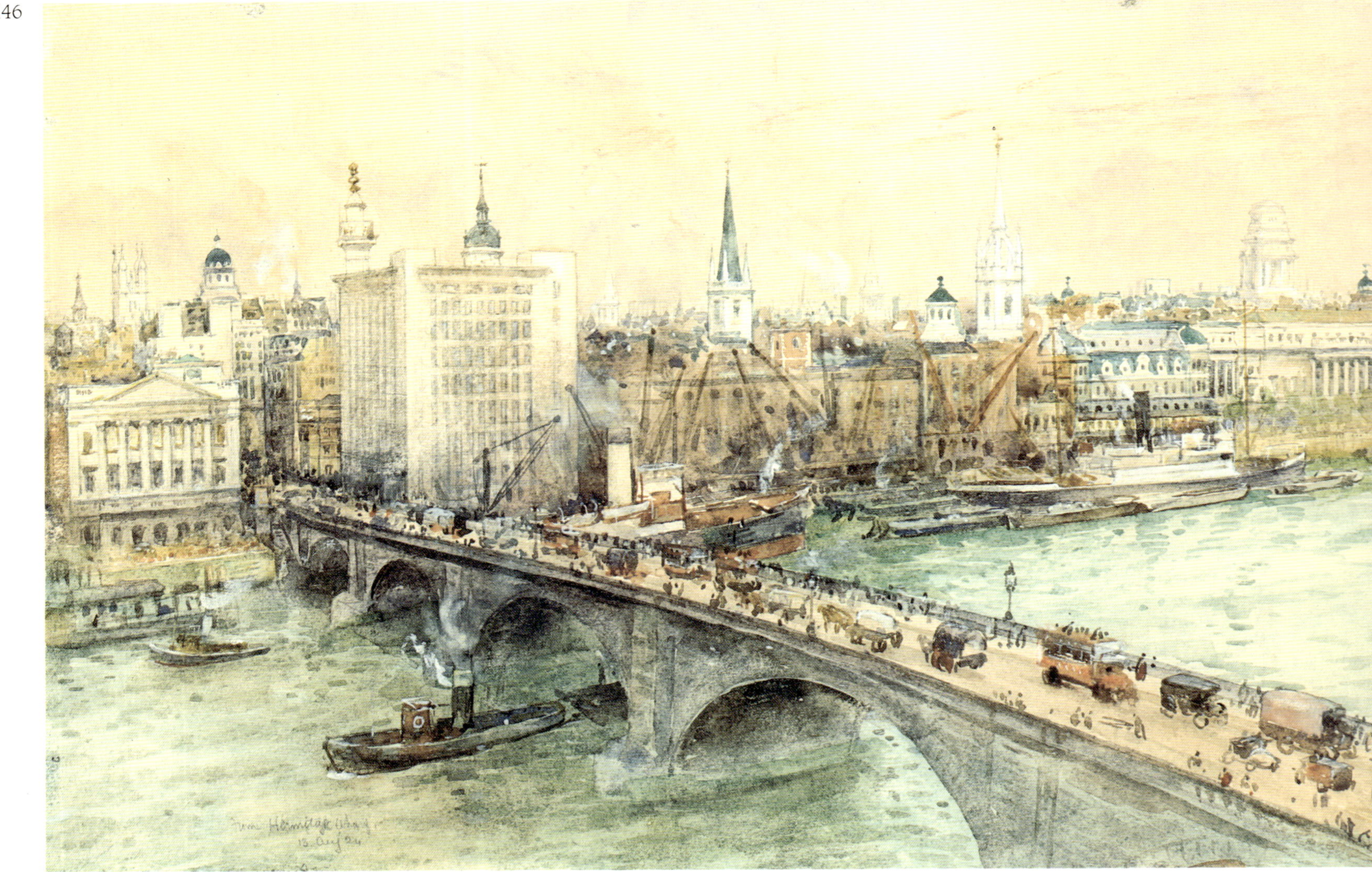

The Thames looking North East from Southwark

1924

[UNTITLED]

A pencil note on the watercolour states that the view was taken from Hermitage Wharf, though in fact it seems to have been from Old Hibernia Wharf. Recent buildings include Adelaide House, and the Port of London Authority building, designed by Sir Edwin Cooper, and completed in 1922. On the extreme right is St Olave Tooley Street, demolished 1927-1928. Hay's Wharf offices were built on the site. The Southwark warehouses formed what was called 'the larder of London' since it was here that most of the capital's imported dairy products were stored. The bascules of Tower Bridge are shown open. On the river are tugs, lighters (some sailed), and various cargo ships.

[135] *Watercolour drawing 265 × 788 mm sight*

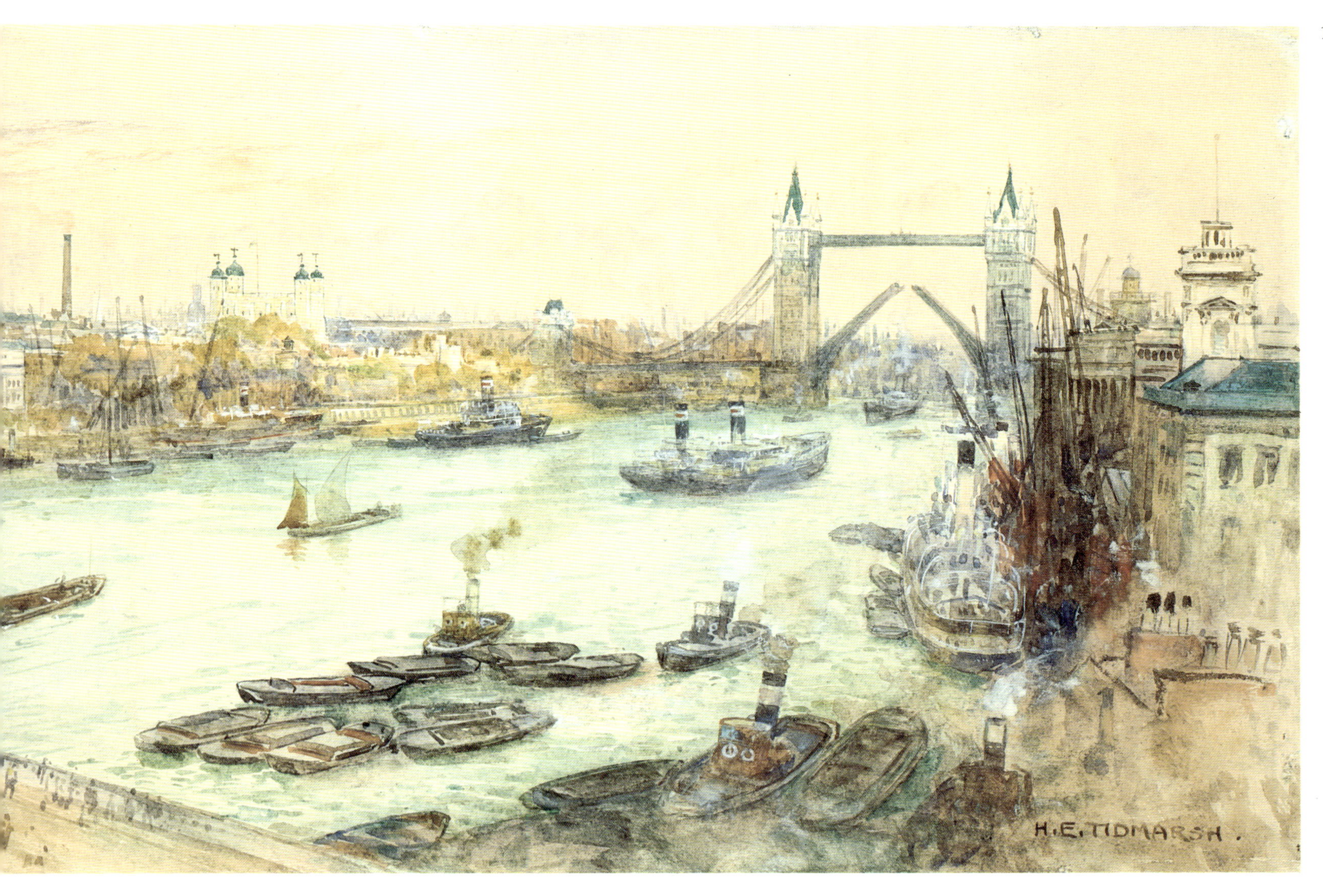
H.E. TIDMARSH.

The Tower of London

1915

[UNTITLED]

This view of the Tower is taken from the Wakefield Tower looking towards the Bell Tower and the Byward Tower. At the extreme left is the St Thomas More Tower above Traitors' Gate. On the Thames near the Tower can be seen various cargo vessels, all of them European traders. Those steam ships off the Tower carried cargoes to Antwerp, those across the river traded to the Baltic ports. There are lighters and Thames barges a little further upstream. Staffage: A yeoman warder addresses three visitors. The girl holds a cane. A gardener is to be seen at work in a garden that had been created in the drained moat.

Tidmarsh drew a large number of views of the Tower of London, including a series for an article by D. H. Parry, 'The Tower and its Traditions', in *Cassell's Magazine*, (1904).

[136] *Watercolour drawing 272 × 384 mm sight*

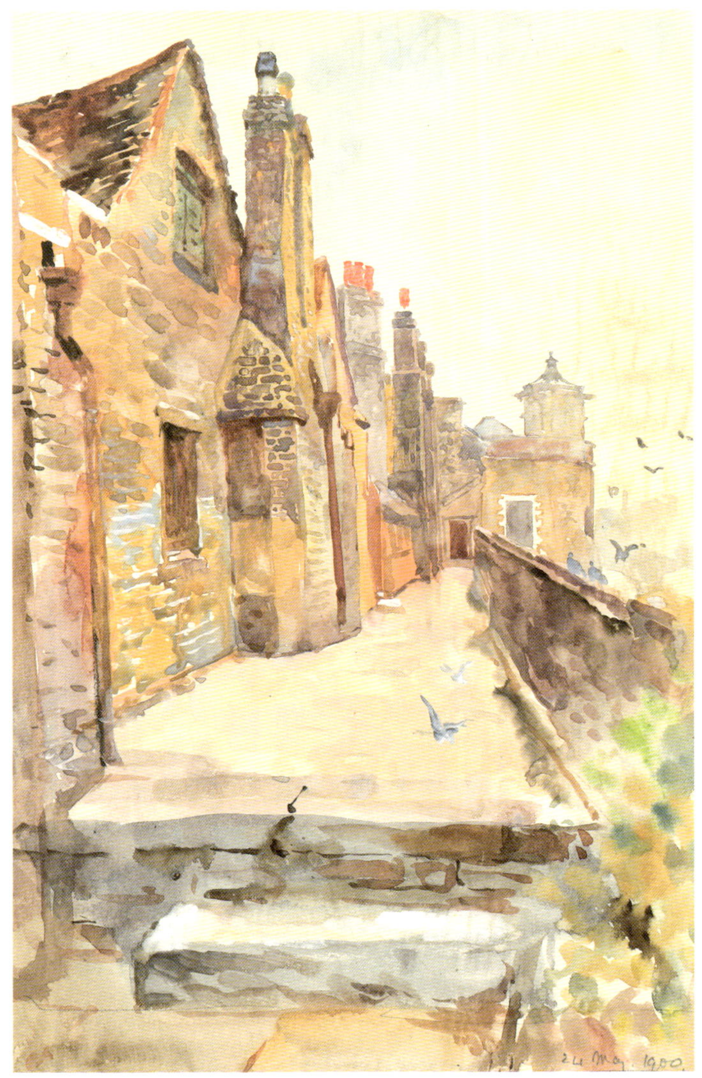

Prisoners' Walk, outside the Beauchamp Tower

The view is looking south towards the Bell Tower.

[137] *Wash drawing, 275 × 175 mm*

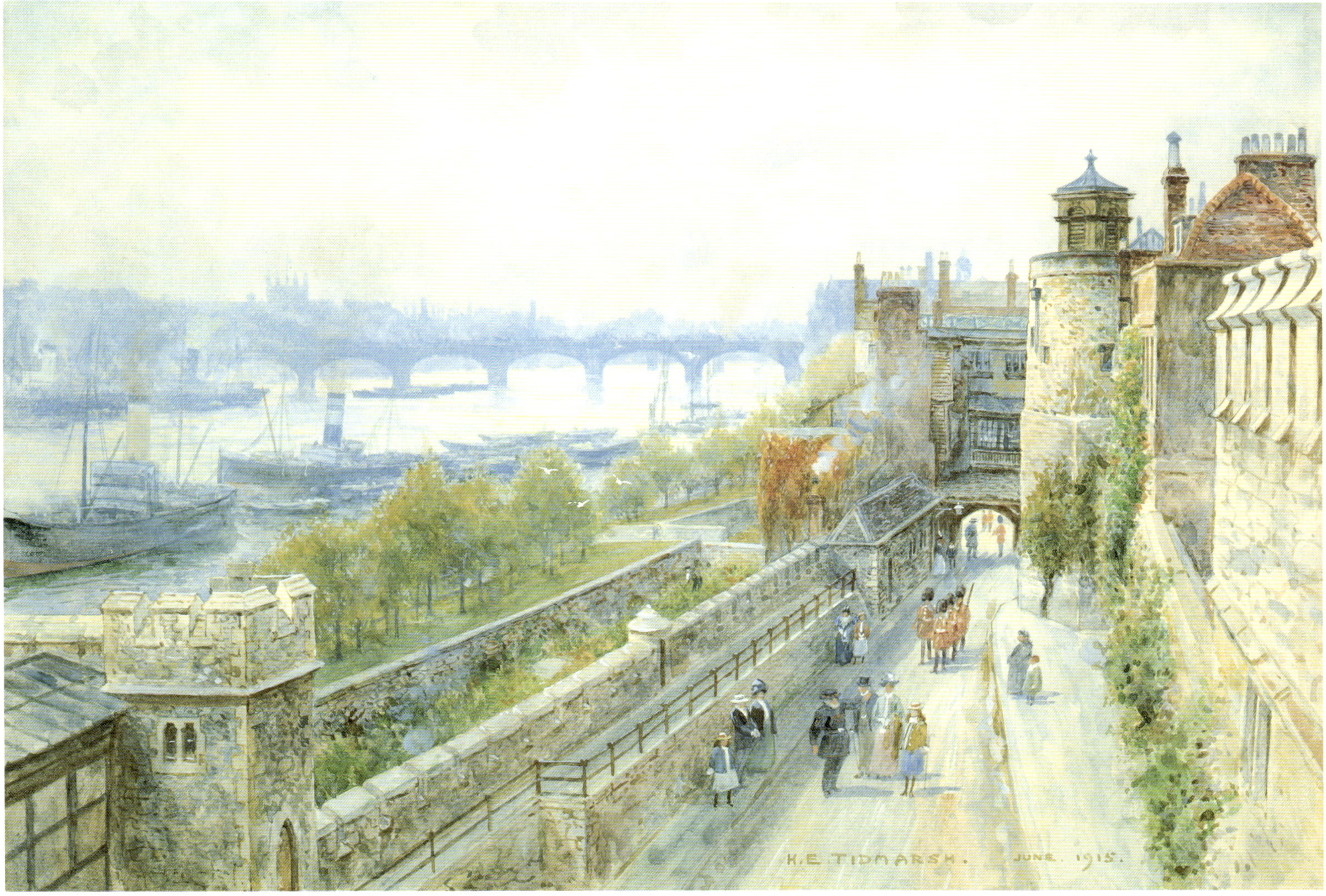

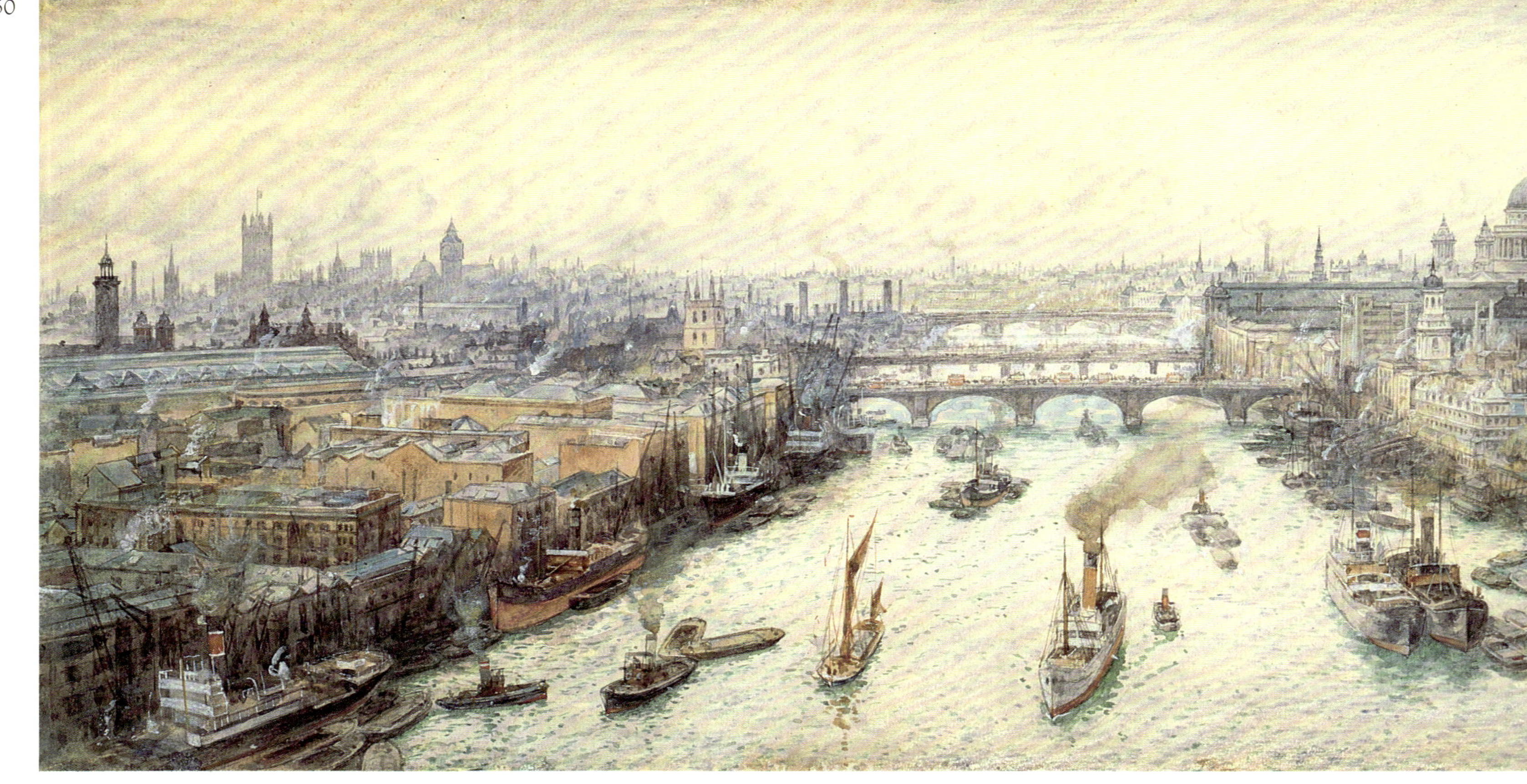

The Thames looking West

1925

LONDON DEPICTED FROM THE TOWER BRIDGE

Identifiable landmarks include from left to right: London Bridge Station, the Houses of Parliament and behind them Westminster Abbey, and Southwark Cathedral. Advancing upstream London Bridge, Cannon Street Railway Bridge, and Southwark Bridge. Then Cannon Street Station, St Magnus the Martyr, St Paul's Cathedral, the Monument, the Custom House, St Mary le Bow, St Dunstan-in-the-East, St Margaret Pattens, St Michael Cornhill, the Port of London Authority, and the Tower of London. Between the Custom House and the Tower can be seen Brewers' Quay, occupied at this time by the General Steam Navigation Company whose steamships traded with Continental Europe. Tower Bridge in the 1920s opened thirteen or fourteen times a day to let ships through to the Pool, such was the volume of trade. On the Thames are cargo ships of various sorts, and a Thames barge left of centre.

[138] *Watercolour drawing 242 × 898 mm*

Detail from the Ordnance Survey Six Inch to One Mile Map of London, as revised 1913/14

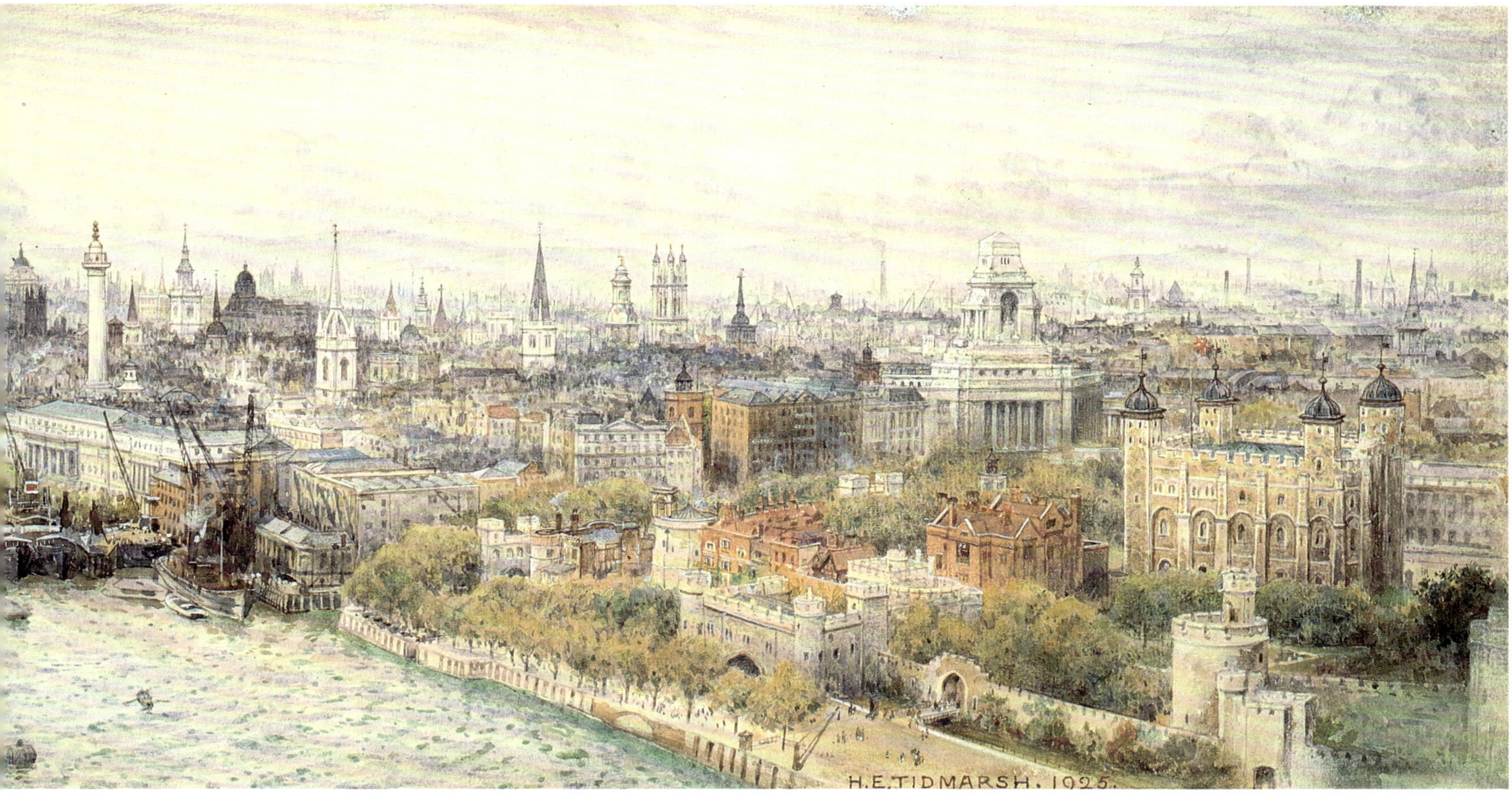

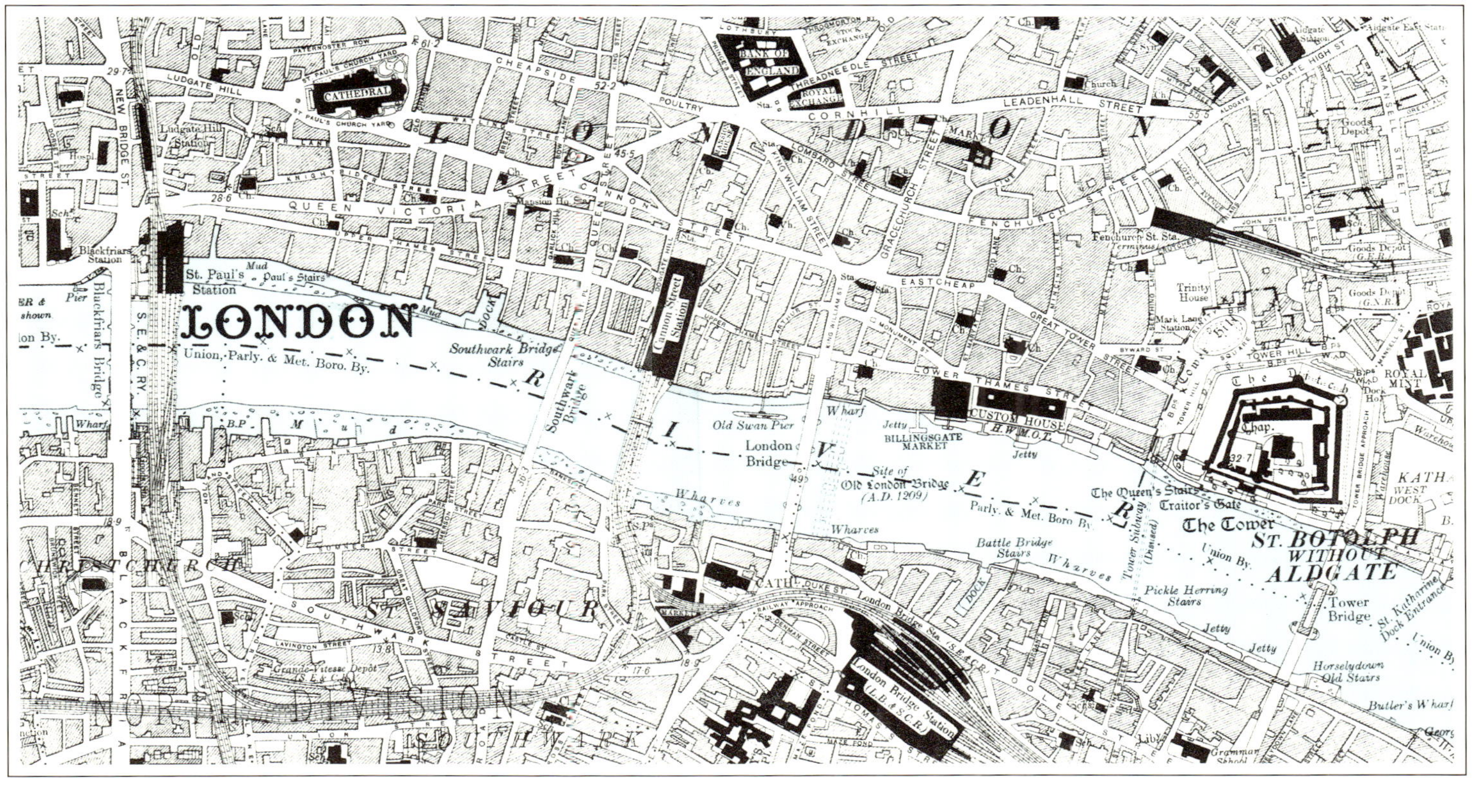
LONDON
Union, Parly. & Met. Boro. By.
CATHEDRAL
BANK OF ENGLAND
ROYAL EXCHANGE
LUDGATE HILL
CHEAPSIDE
POULTRY
CORNHILL
LEADENHALL STREET
THREADNEEDLE STREET
QUEEN VICTORIA STREET
FENCHURCH STREET
EASTCHEAP
GREAT TOWER STREET
LOWER THAMES STREET
CUSTOM HOUSE
BILLINGSGATE MARKET
Ludgate Hill Station
St. Paul's Station
Blackfriars Station
Blackfriars Bridge
Southwark Bridge
Southwark Bridge Stairs
Cannon Street Station
Fenchurch St. Sta.
Mark Lane Station
Trinity House
Old Swan Pier
London Bridge
Site of Old London Bridge (A.D. 1209)
Wharves
Wharf
Jetty
Battle Bridge Stairs
Tower Subway (Disused)
The Queen's Stairs
Traitor's Gate
The Tower
The Ditch
Chap.
ST. BOTOLPH WITHOUT ALDGATE
Tower Bridge
Pickle Herring Stairs
Horselydown Old Stairs
Butler's Wharf
St. Katharine Dock Entrance
ROYAL MINT
Goods Depot
Parly. & Met. Boro. By.
Union By.
L O N D O N
R I V E R
CHRISTCHURCH
ST. SAVIOUR
NORTH DIVISION
SOUTHWARK
London Bridge Station
S.E. & C. RY.
NEW BRIDGE ST.
BLACKFRIARS

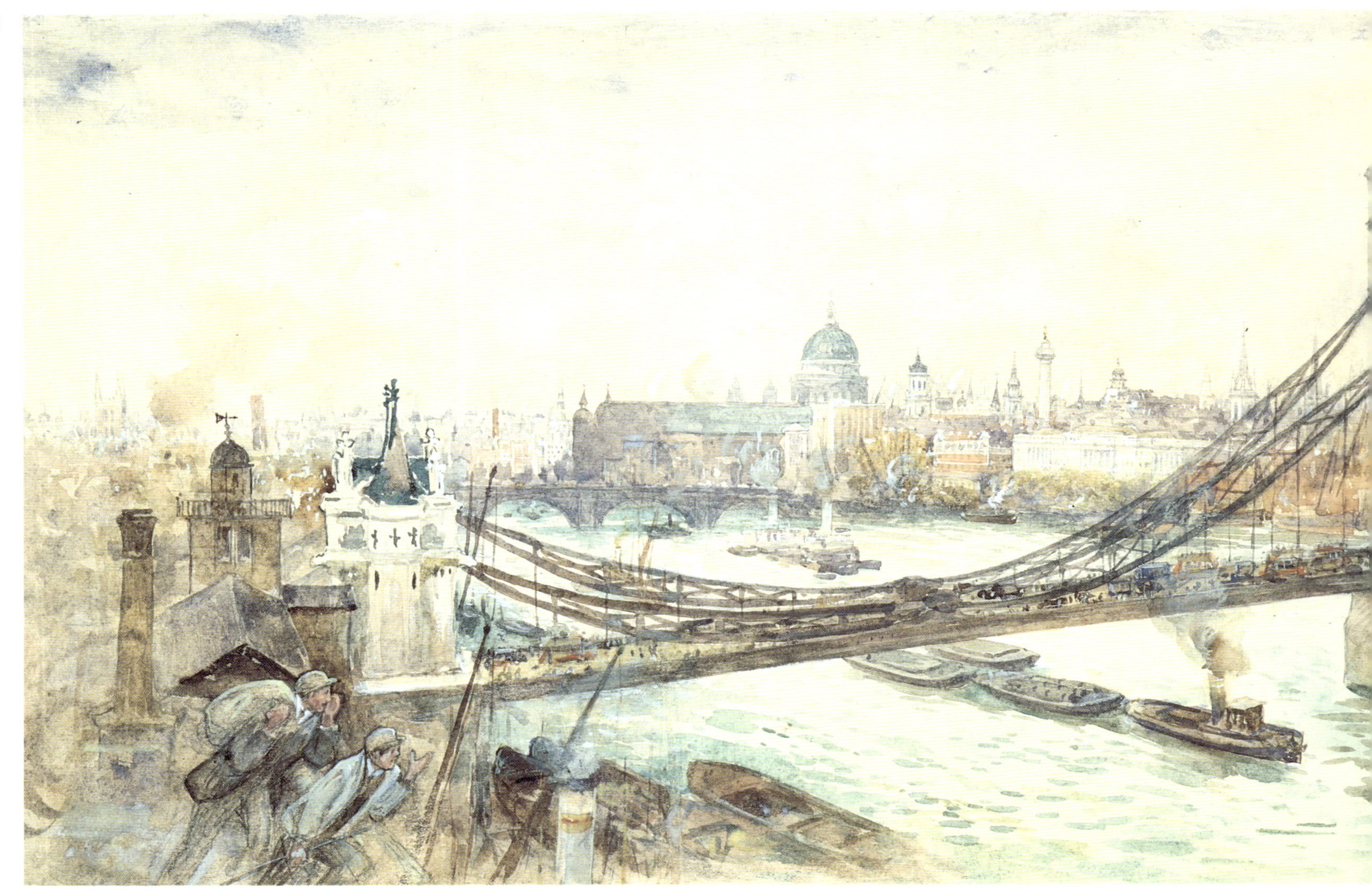

Tower Bridge

1930

TOWER BRIDGE AND LONDON

View taken from a wharf in Bermondsey. Principal landmarks shown from left to right: Southwark Cathedral, Courage's Brewery, London Bridge, Cannon Street Station, St Magnus the Martyr, the Monument, the Custom House, St Dunstan-in-the-East, Tower Bridge, the Port of London Authority, Tower of London, and St Katherine's Dock. The tug with red bands on its funnel was one of the Tower Bridge tugs. Its purpose was to give assistance to any shipping at that point in the river. A pencil note to the right of bottom centre reads: 'First study for the careful drawing afterwards reproduced in "three colour."'

[139] *Watercolour drawing 255 × 775 mm*

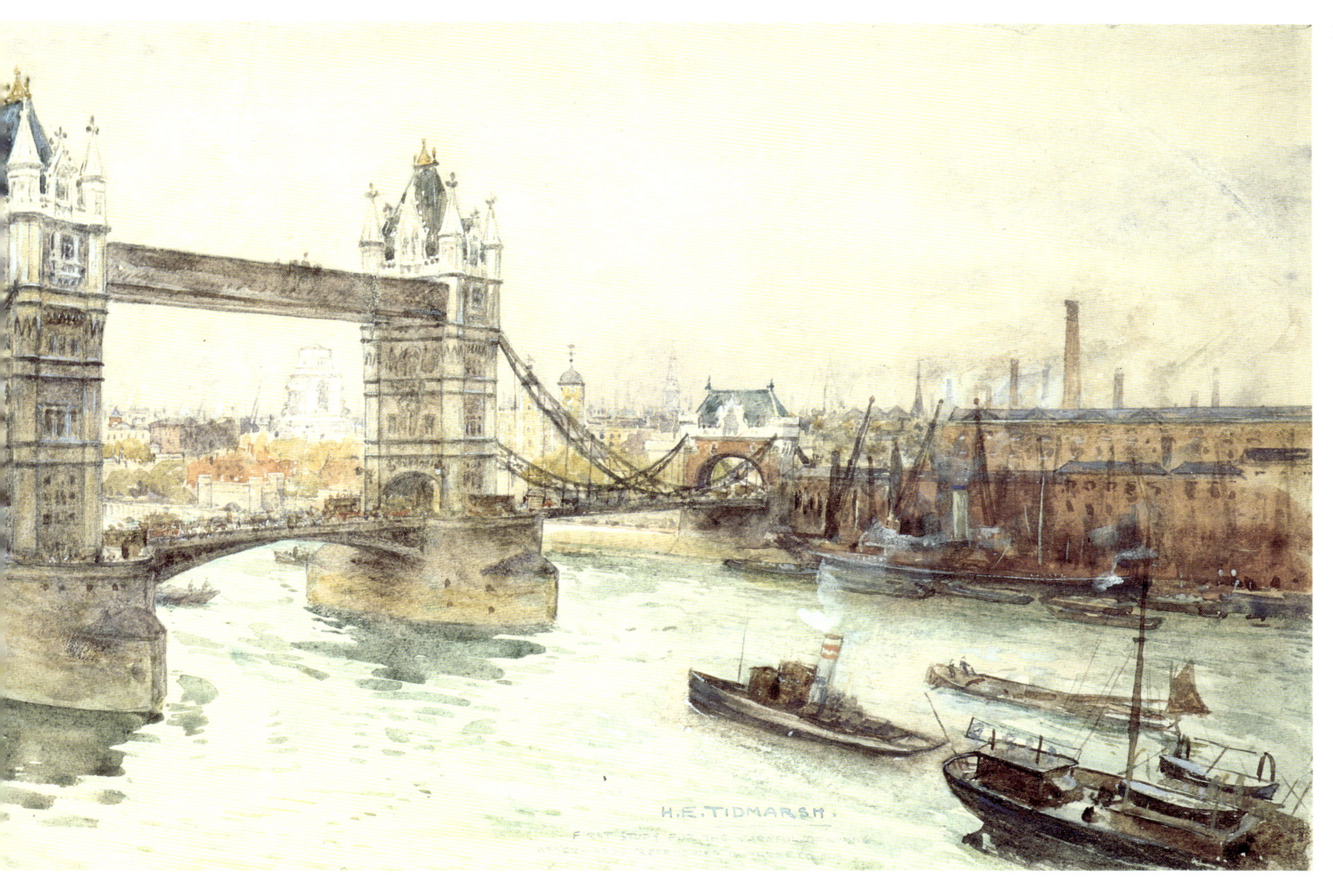
H.E. TIDMARSH.

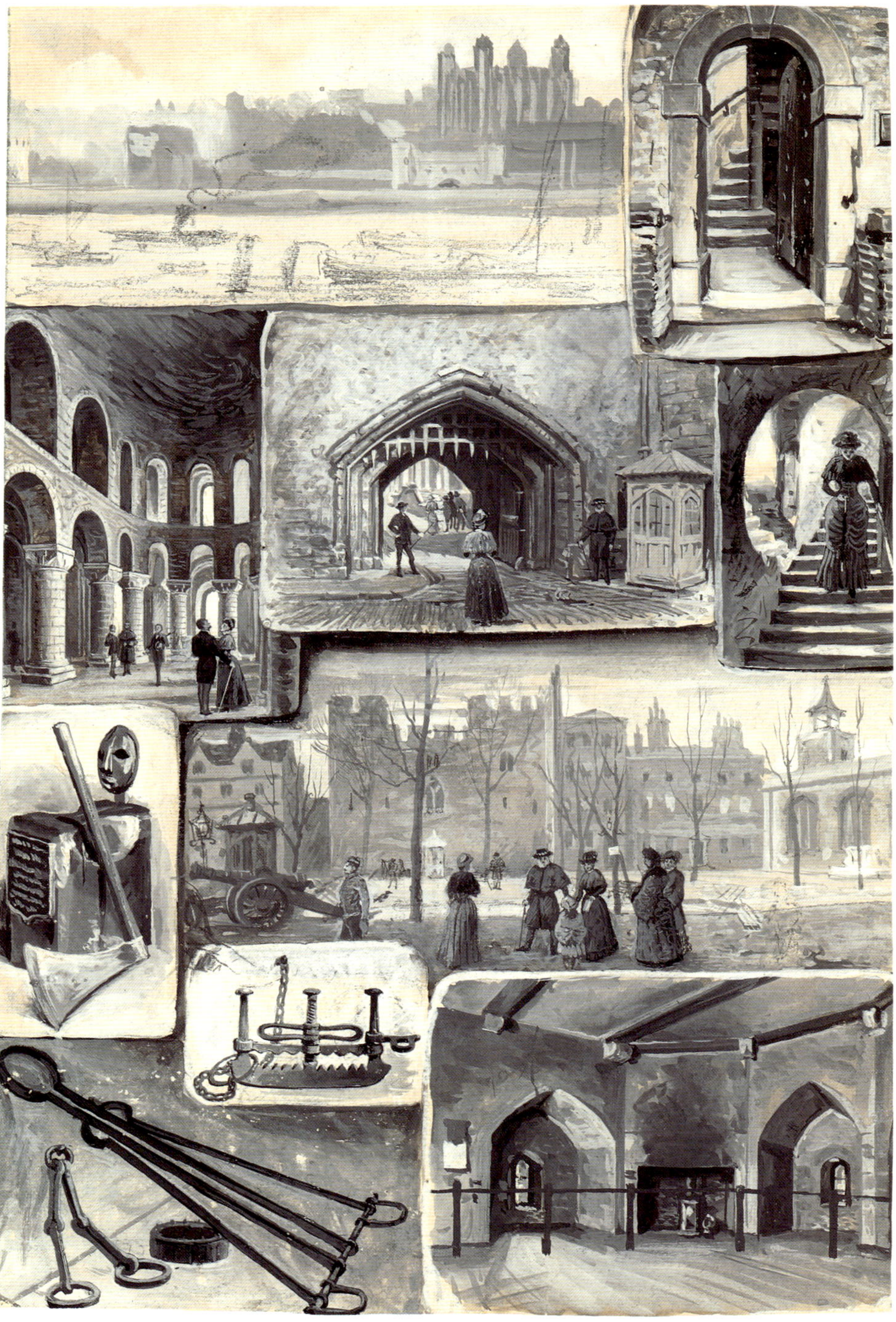

Trompe l'oeil of drawings of the Tower of London, c.1900

a. The White Tower from the Thames;
b. Staircase in Bloody Tower
c. St John's Chapel
d. Gateway to Bloody Tower
e. White Tower staircase
f. Beauchamp Tower, St Peter ad Vincula, and the site of the execution block
g. Block and heading axe, with metal scold's mask
h. Thumbscrew
i. Fetters, Tudor iron collar, and 'Skeffington's daughter' (a crushing instrument)
j. Interior of Beauchamp Tower

[140] *Wash drawing with body colour, 220 × 145 mm*

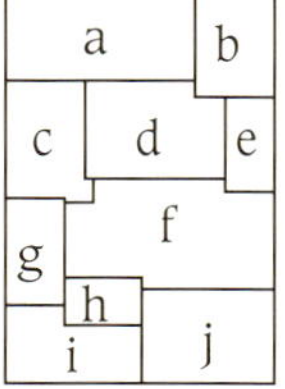

St George Hanover Square *(right)*

[141] *Detail from plate 142*

Further Afield

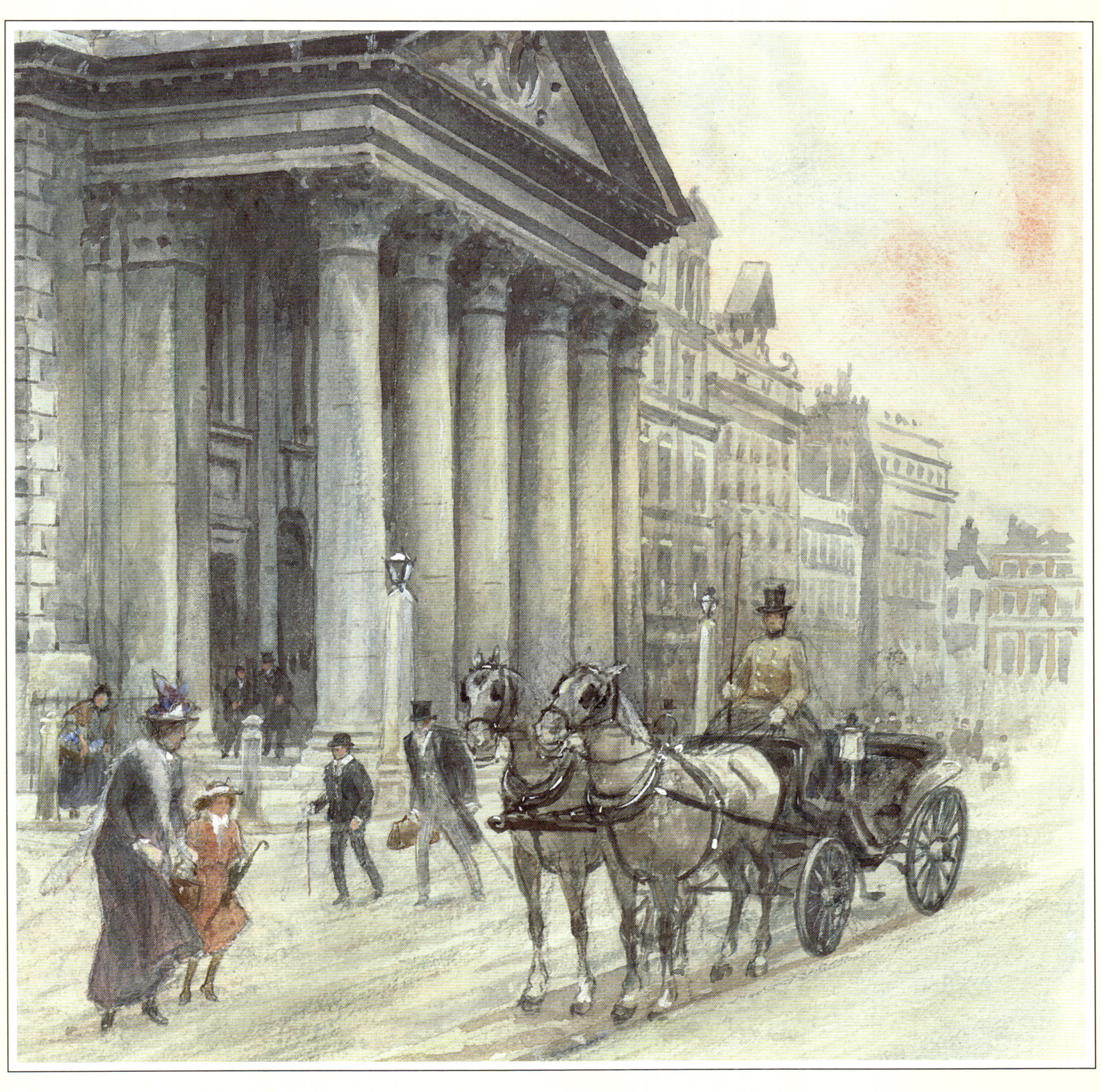

St George Hanover Square

c.1920

ST GEORGE'S HANOVER SQUARE

The scene looking down St George Street with Maddox Street running eastward. The tower and cupola of the church are enveloped in scaffolding carrying a contractor's signboard. St George's, a very fashionable church, was built by John James in 1712-1724. *Staffage:* a victoria drawn by two horses under the control of a top-hatted and cockaded coachman, a policeman, a bonneted flower-seller, and well-heeled pedestrians.

[142] *Watercolour drawing 380 × 280 mm*

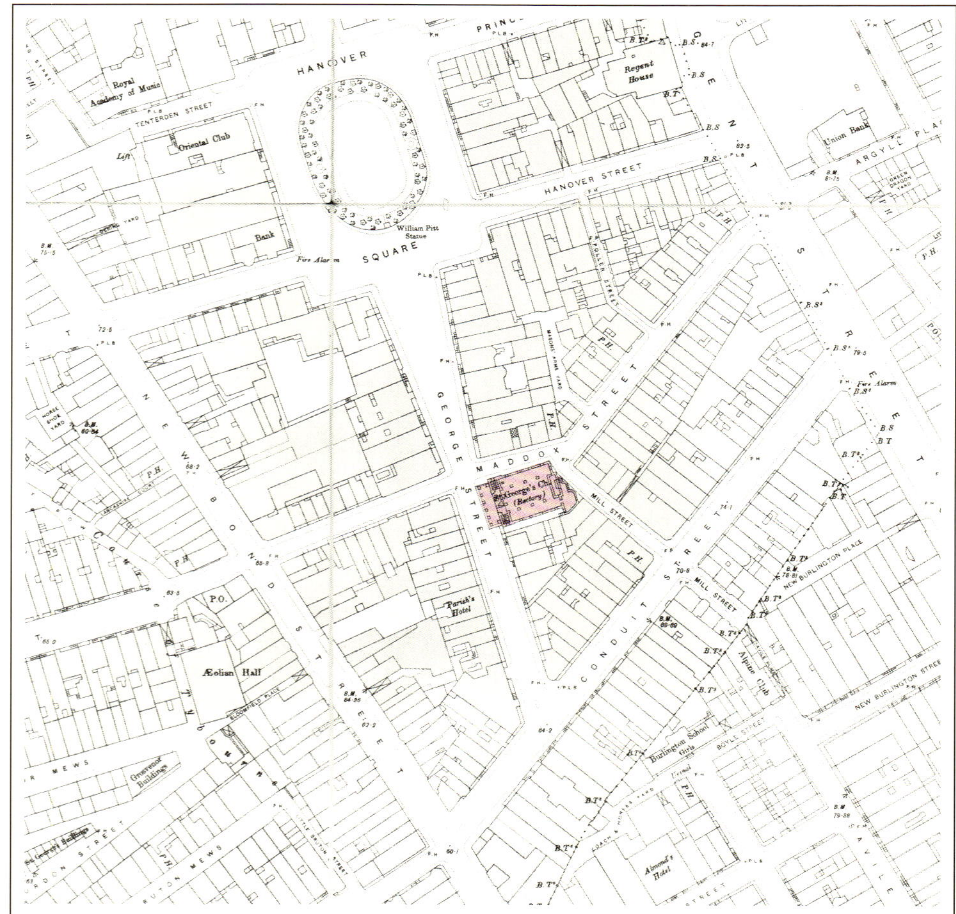

Detail from the Ordnance Survey Five Feet to One Mile Plan of London, V11.62, published 1910

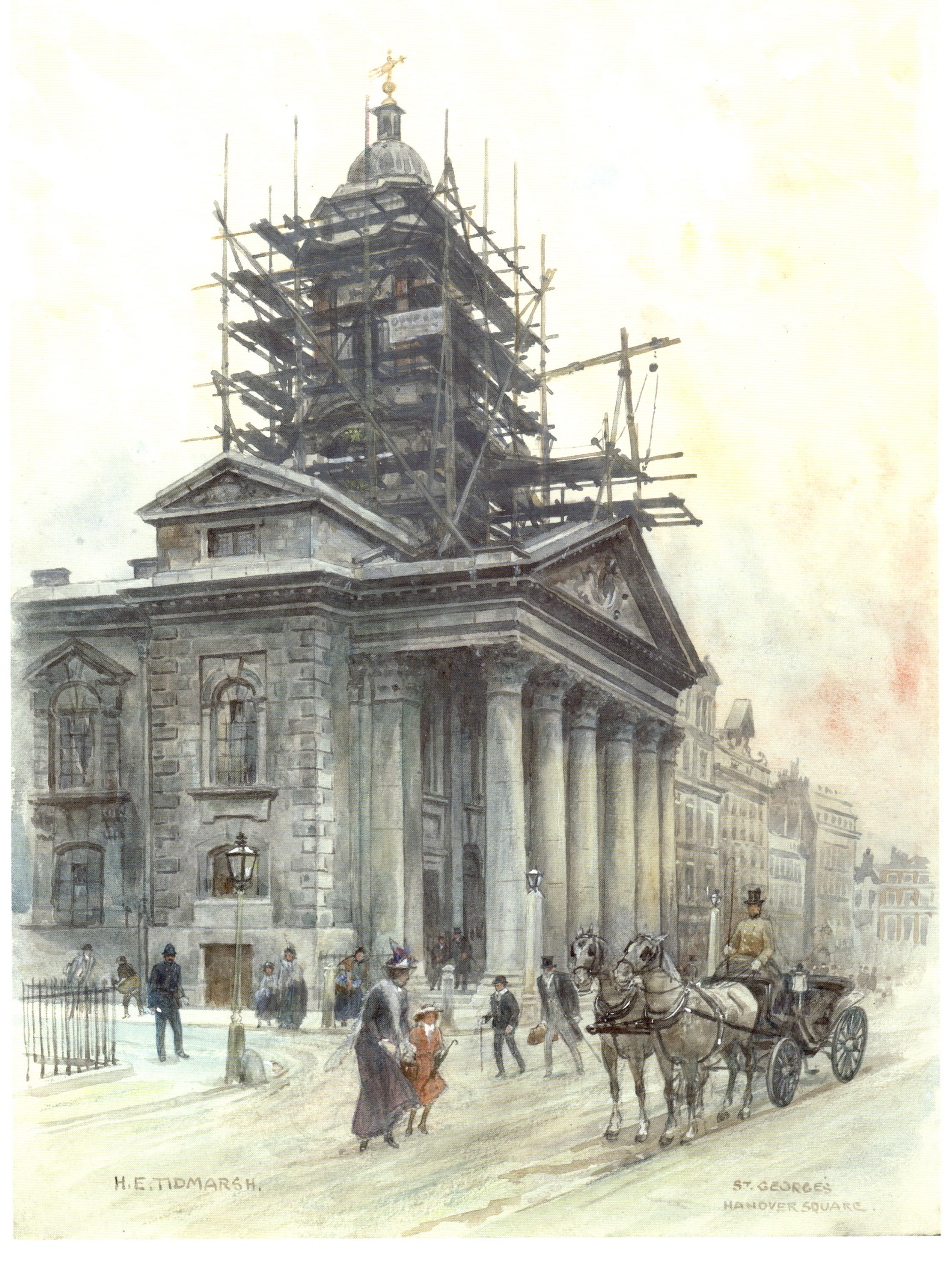
H.E.TIDMARSH.
ST. GEORGES
HANOVER SQUARE.

The Metropolitan Tabernacle

c.1908

SPURGEON'S TABERNACLE

The Metropolitan Tabernacle, on the west side of Newington Butts, was built by W. Pocock, 1859-1861, for the popular preacher, C. H. Spurgeon. A placard on the railings reads, 'Thos. Spurgeon', and on a building to the north, 'Rabbits' (i.e. Rabbits & Son, boot and shoe makers, no. 22 Newington Butts until 1908, after which the site was occupied by the Ministry of Works and Public Buildings). *Staffage:* a victoria and many pedestrians.

[143] *Watercolour drawing 279 × 354 mm*

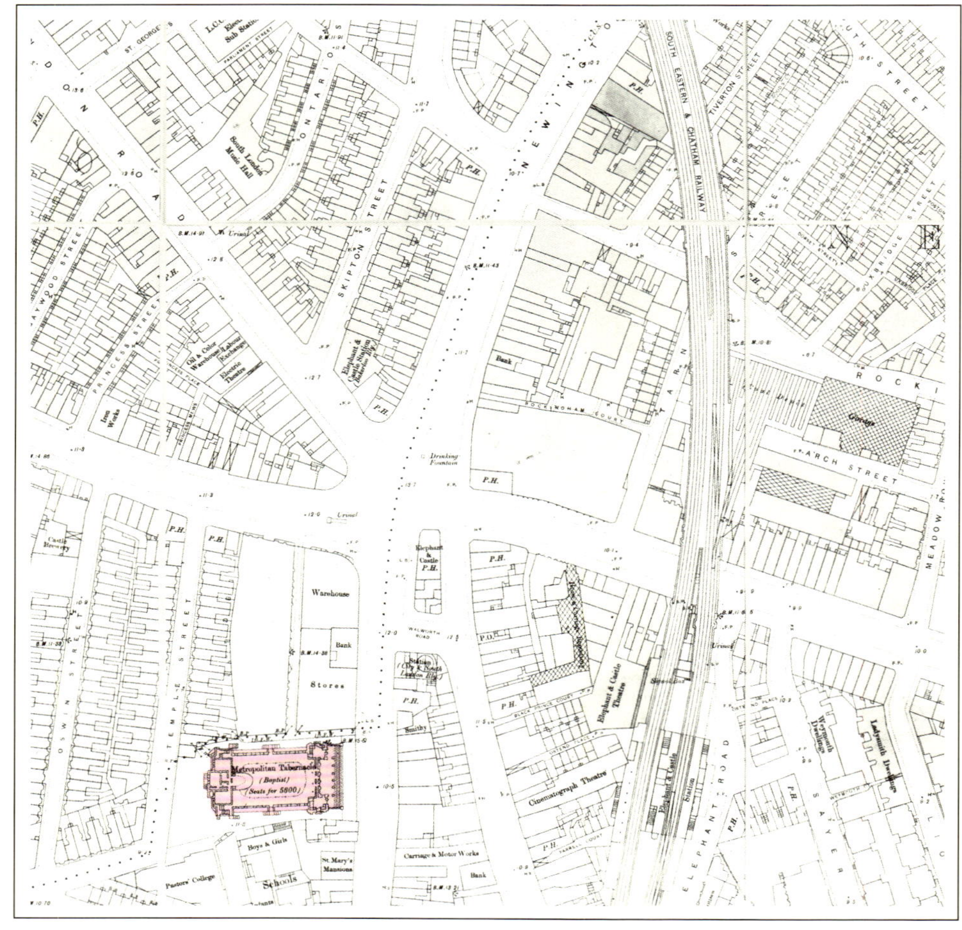

Detail from the Ordnance Survey Five Feet to One Mile Plan of London, V11.95, published 1912

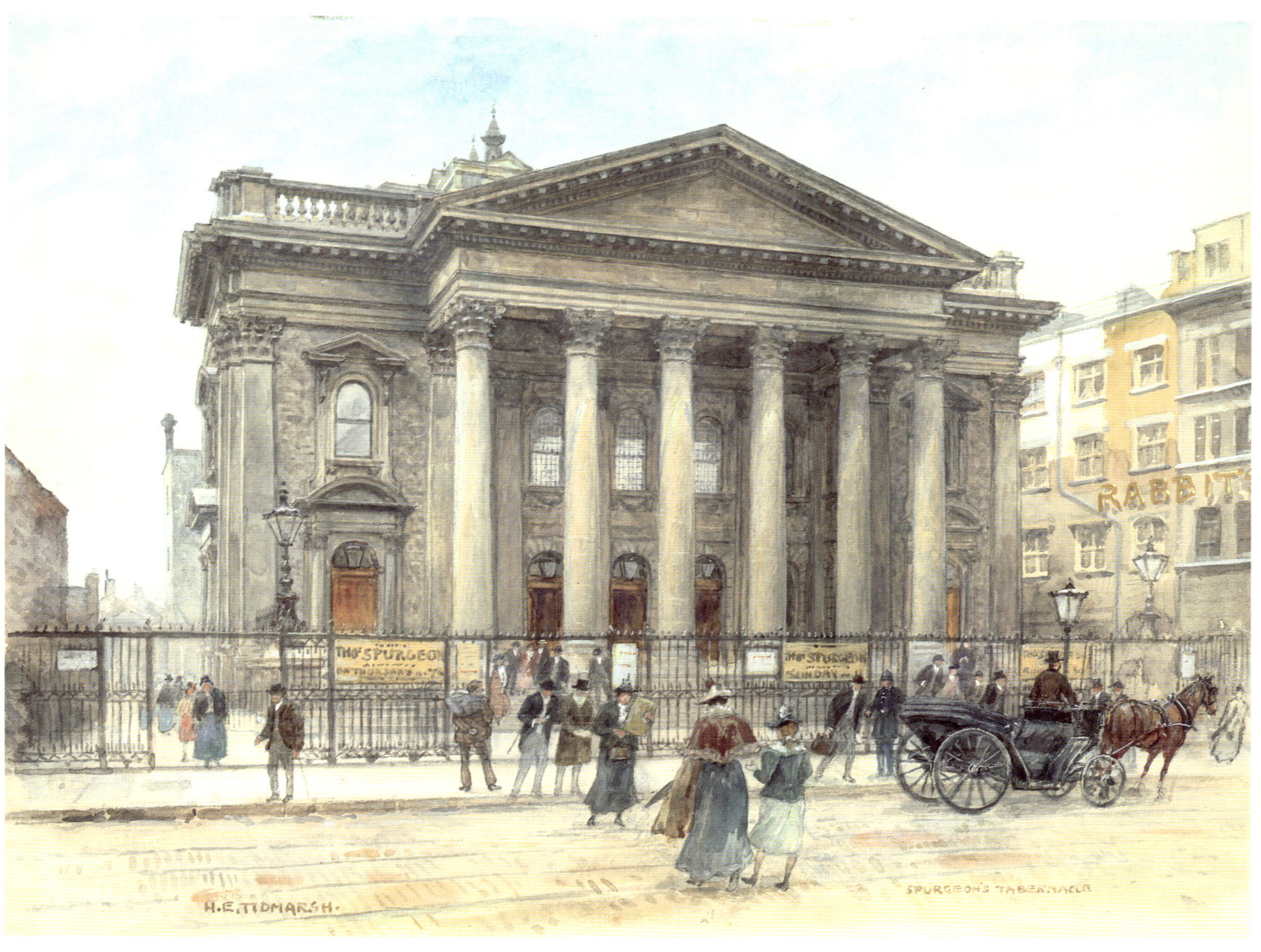
THO^S SPURGEON
THO^S SPURGEON
SUNDAY
H.E.TIDMARSH.
SPURGEON'S TABERNACLE

Wesley's Chapel

c.1900

WESLEY'S CHAPEL, CITY ROAD

This eighteenth-century chapel (at no. 47 City Road, just north of the City) is considered to be the Mother Church of world Methodism. Built in 1777-1778, it was damaged by fire in 1879 and considerably altered in 1891, the centenary of John Wesley's death. It was restored between 1972 and 1978.

[144] *Watercolour drawing 230 × 283 mm*

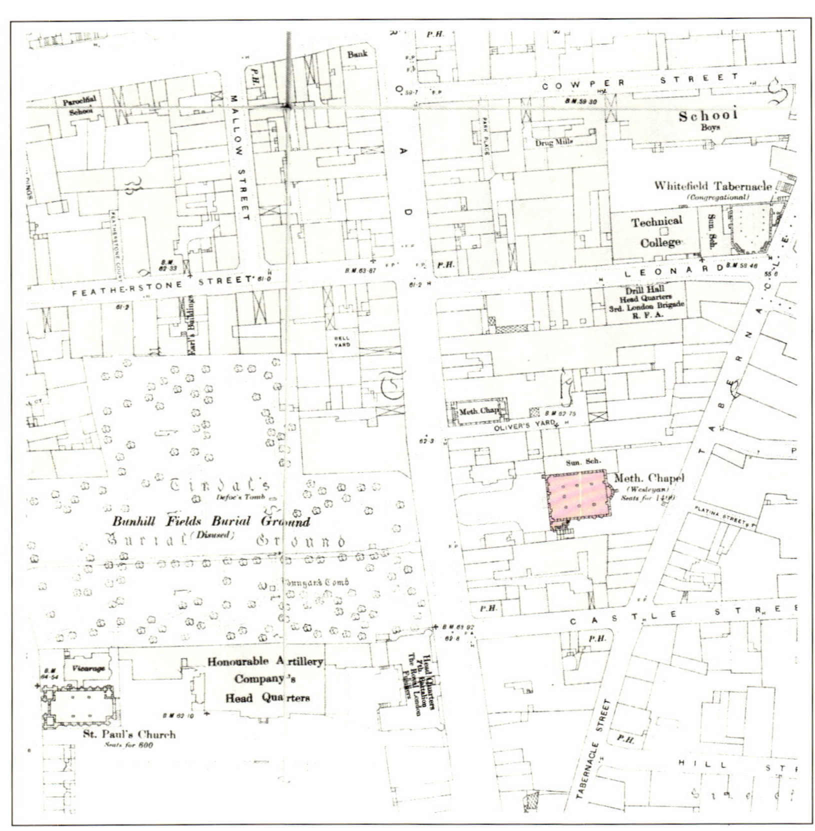

Detail from the Ordnance Survey Five Feet to One Mile Plan of London, V11.46, published 1913

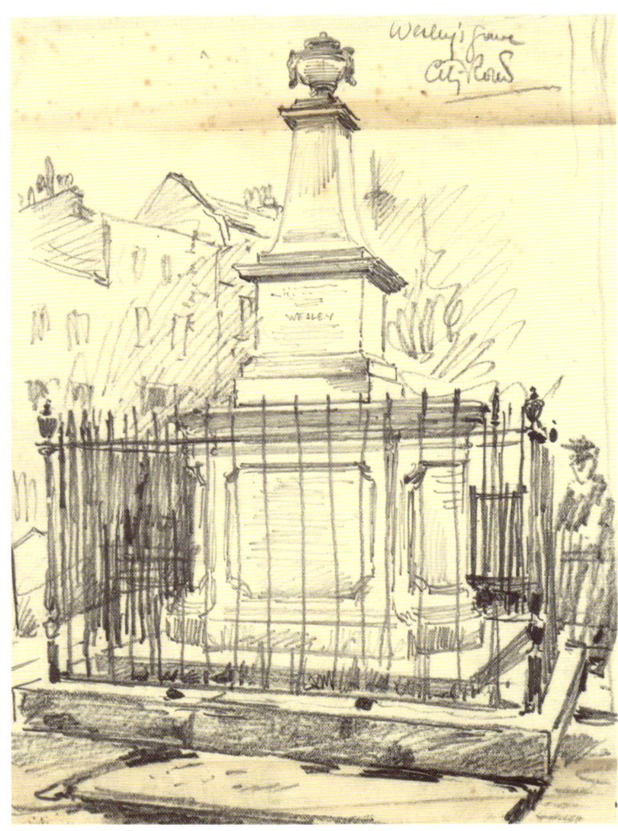

John Wesley's grave, in the grounds of Wesley's Chapel, City Road

[145] *Pencil drawing, 235 × 170 mm*

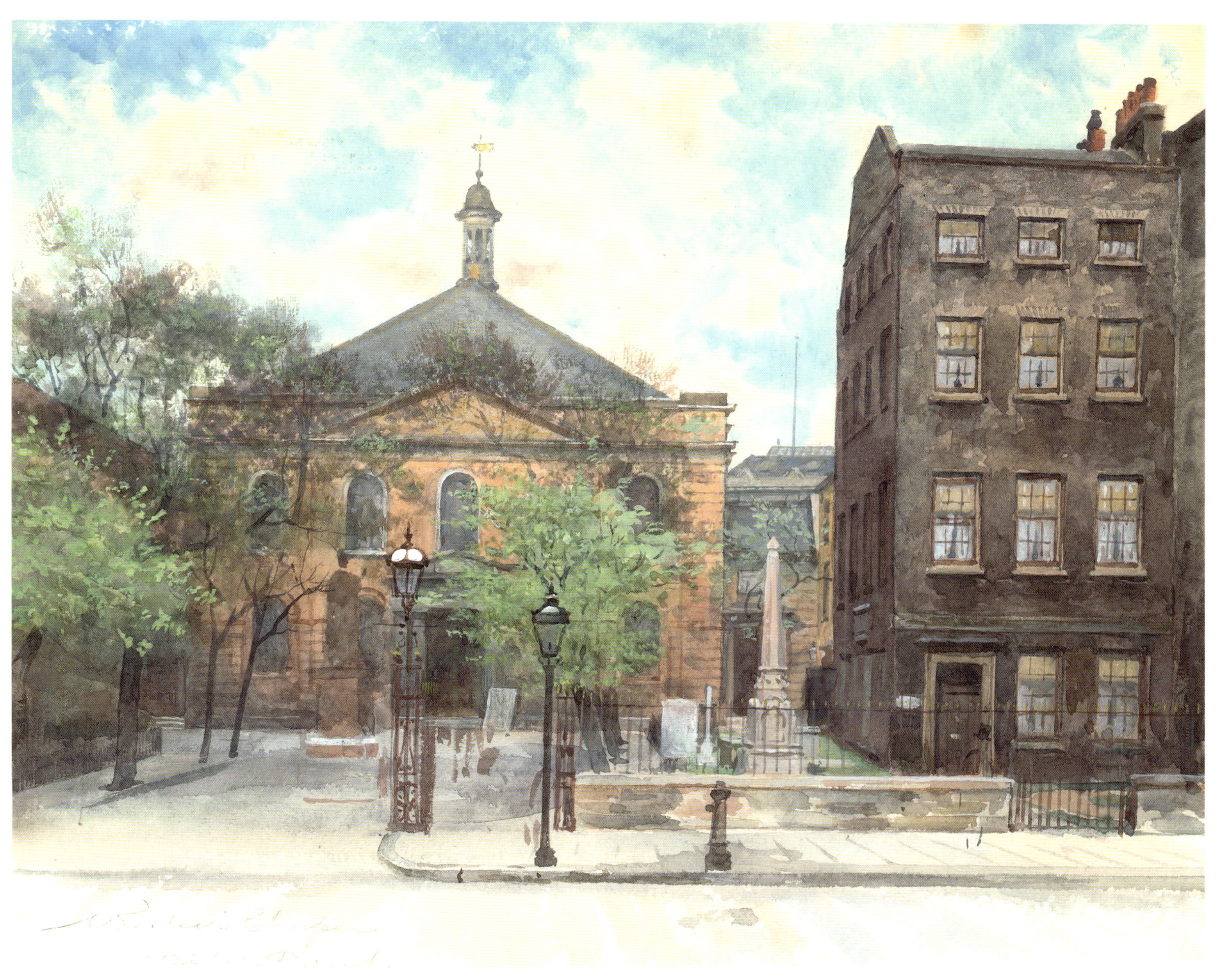

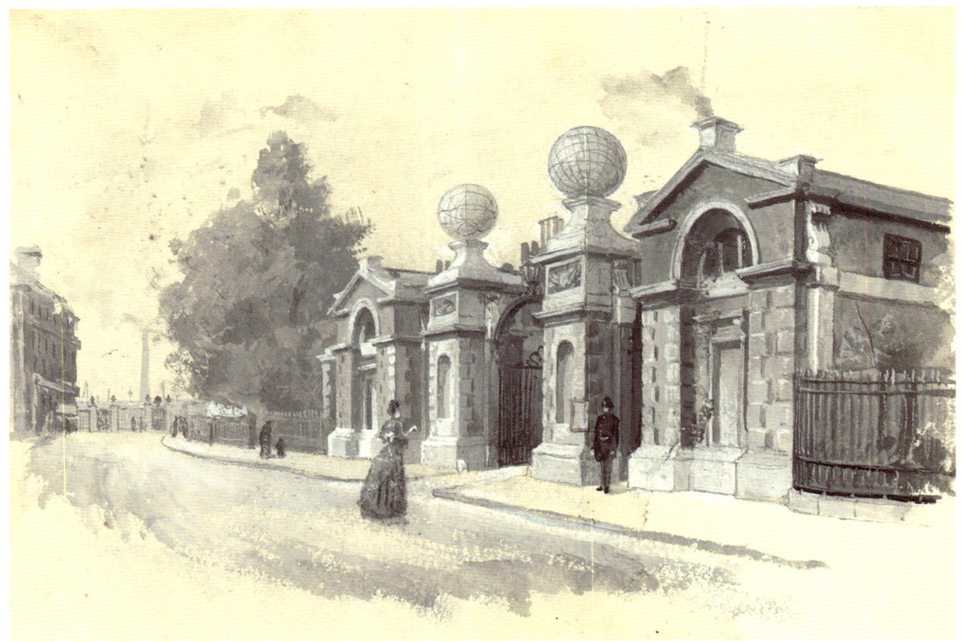

The entrance to the Royal Naval College from King William Walk, c.1885

The gate was erected by Richard Oliver, mathematical master to Greenwich Hospital School, in 1752-1754. The gate is surmounted by two stone globes, on the left a terrestrial globe, with the track of Anson's circumnavigation on the *Centurion*, and on the right a celestial globe.

[146] *Wash drawing with body colour, 128 × 183 mm*

View of the Royal Naval College from the north east, c.1885
(below)

On the left is the corner of the chapel colonnade, on the right the northern facade of the Painted Hall, surmounted by its dome.

[147] *Wash drawing with body colour, 172 × 260 mm*

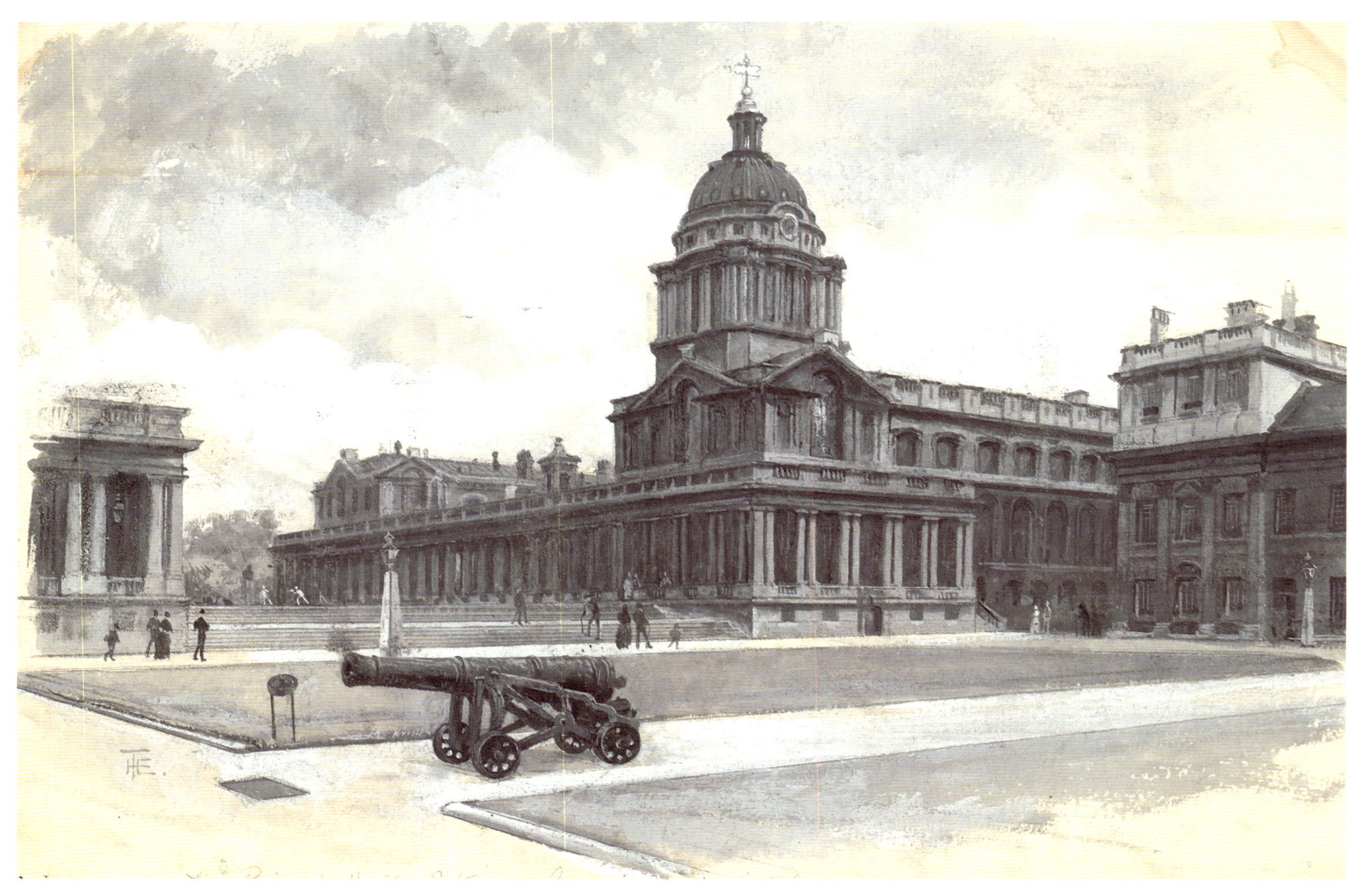

The interior of the museum at the Royal Naval College, 1885

The museum consisted of a suite of rooms in the Queen Anne block. The exhibits now form part of the National Maritime Museum collection.

[148] *Wash drawing with body colour, 155 × 215 mm*

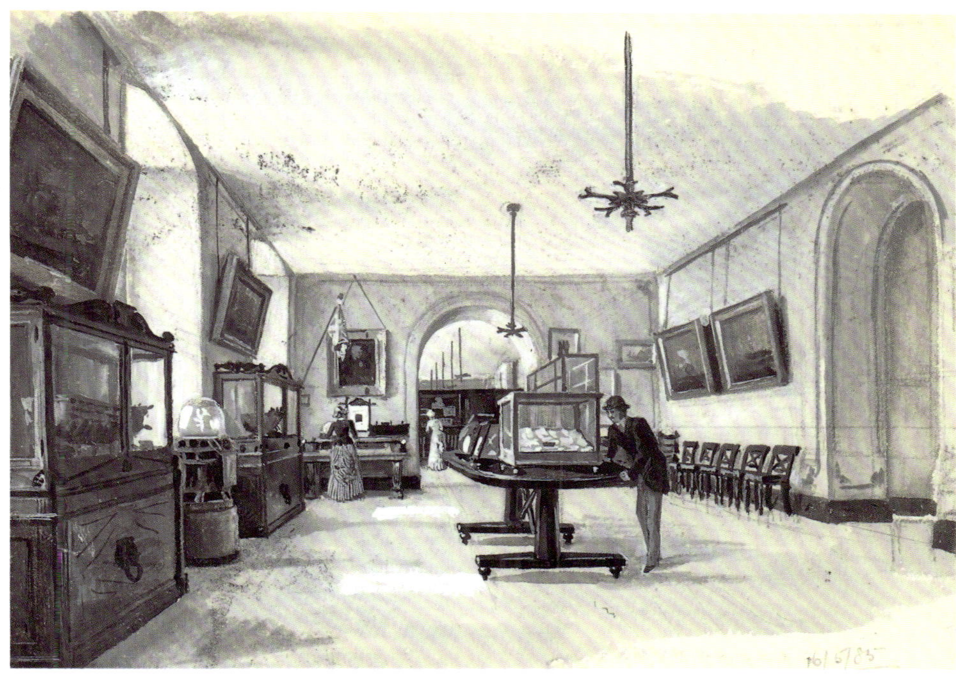

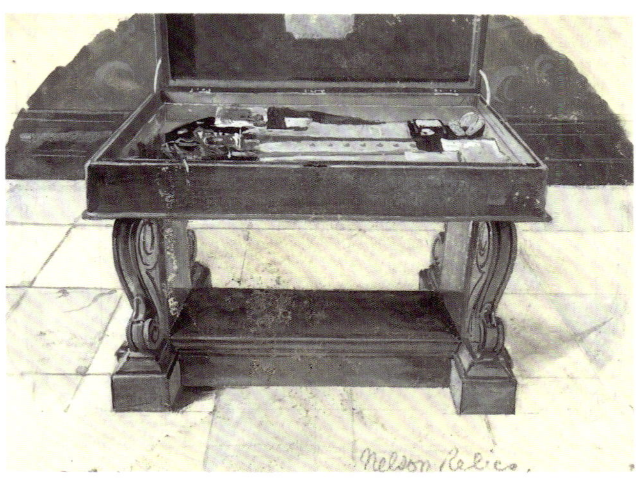

Display case with Nelson's relics, in particular, his Trafalgar coat with the bullet hole

The exhibits are now in the National Maritime Museum collection.

[149] *Wash drawing with body colour, 130 × 165 mm*

View from the vestibule through the Ionic screen into the Painted Hall, c.1885
(right)

The walls are hung beneath window level with a triple row of naval paintings. These constituted the 'National Collection of Marine Paintings', assembled to commemorate 'the eminent services of the Royal Navy in England.' They now form part of the National Maritime Museum's collection.

[150] *Wash drawing with body colour, 240 × 175 mm*

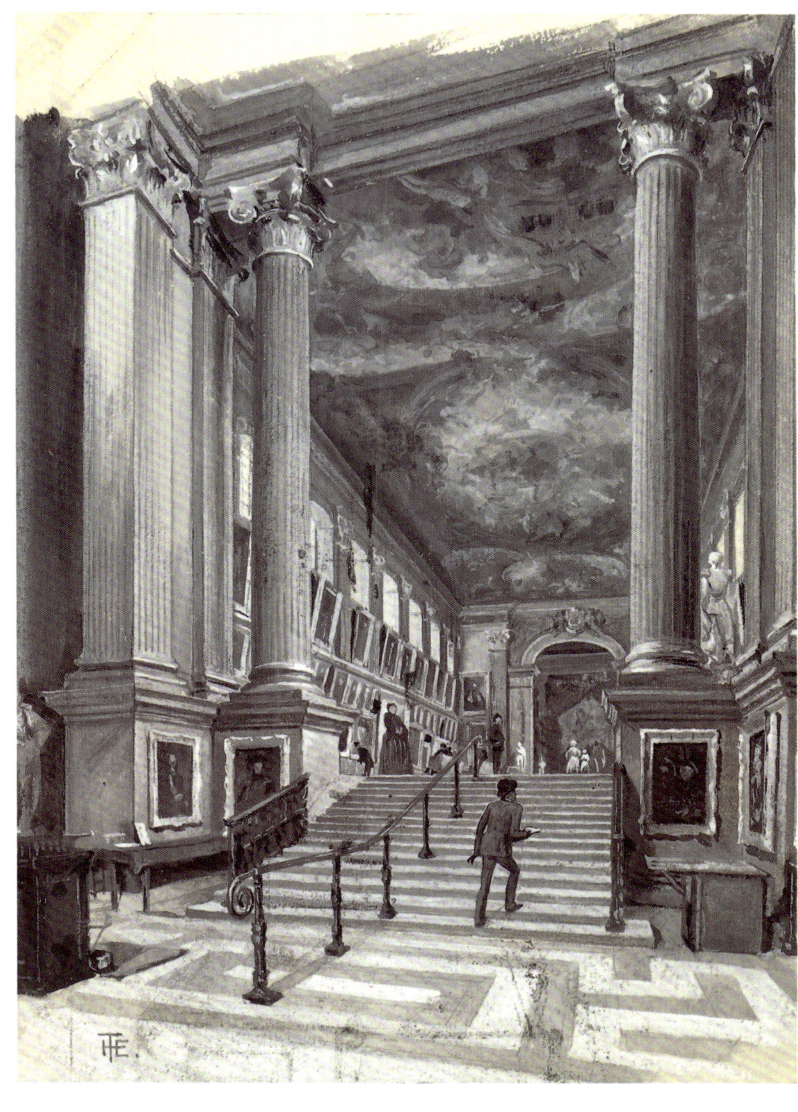

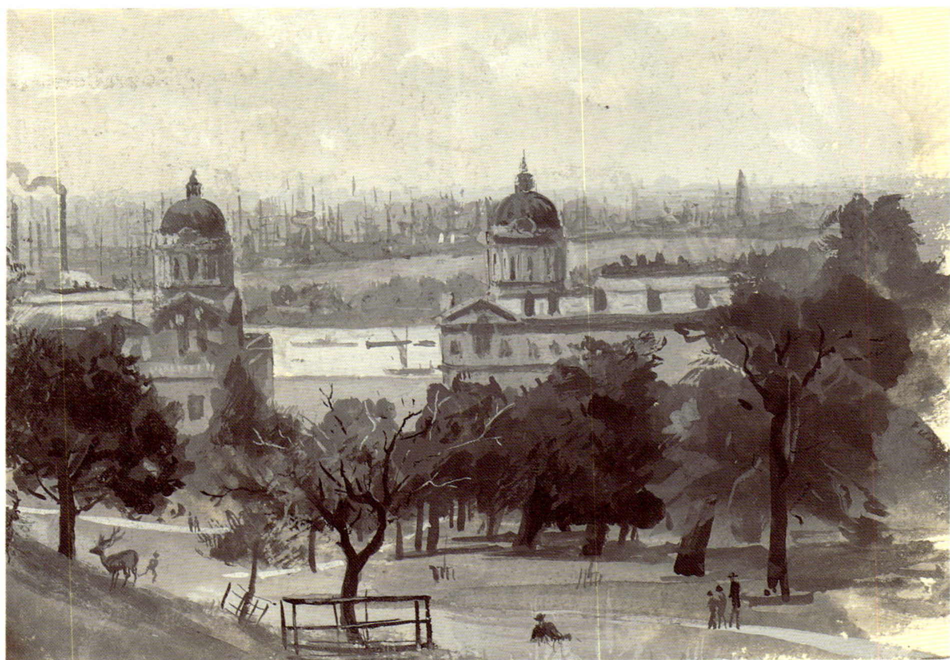

View from Flamsteed House of the Royal Naval College, looking across the Thames to the Isle of Dogs and London beyond, c.1885

[151] *Wash drawing with body colour, 100 × 143 mm*

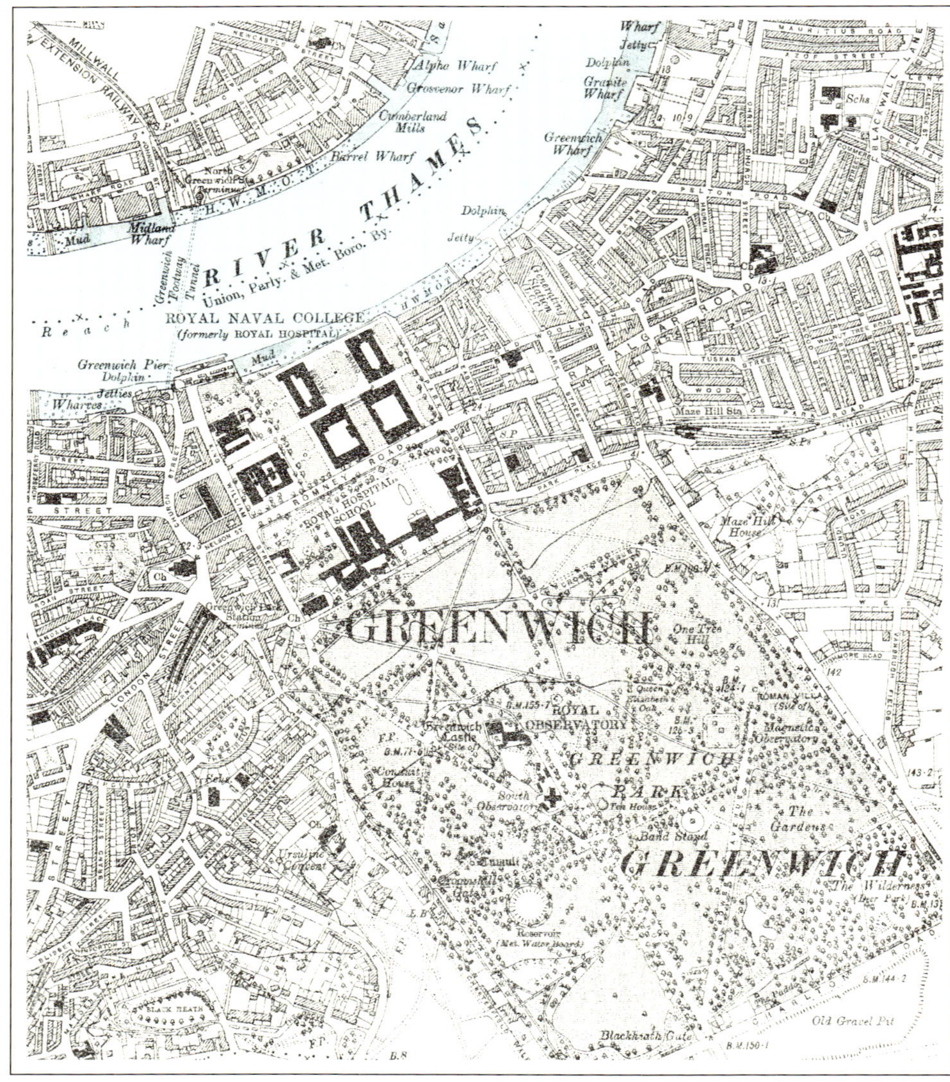

Detail from the Ordnance Survey Six Inch to One Mile Map of London, as revised 1913/14

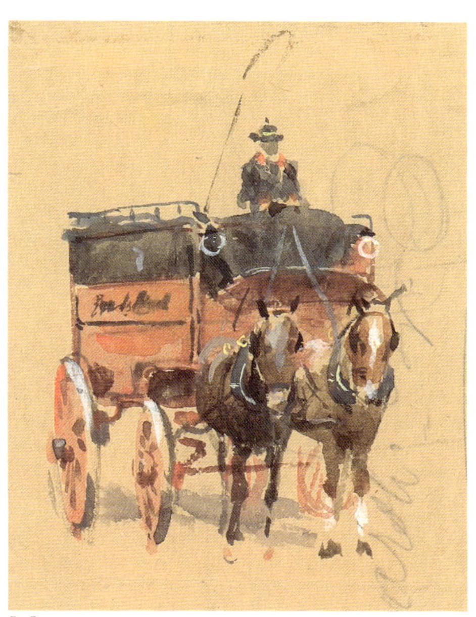

[a]

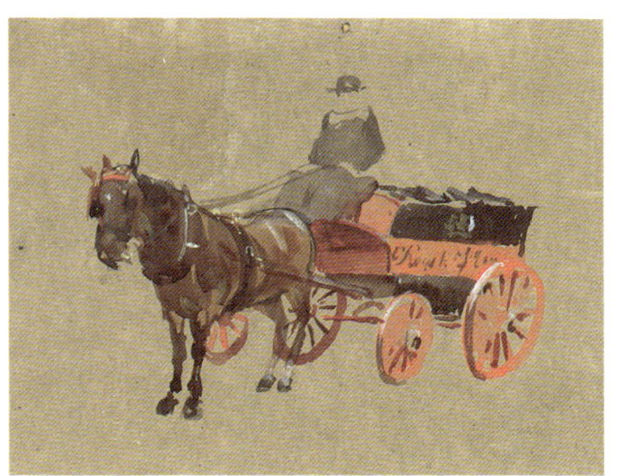

[b]

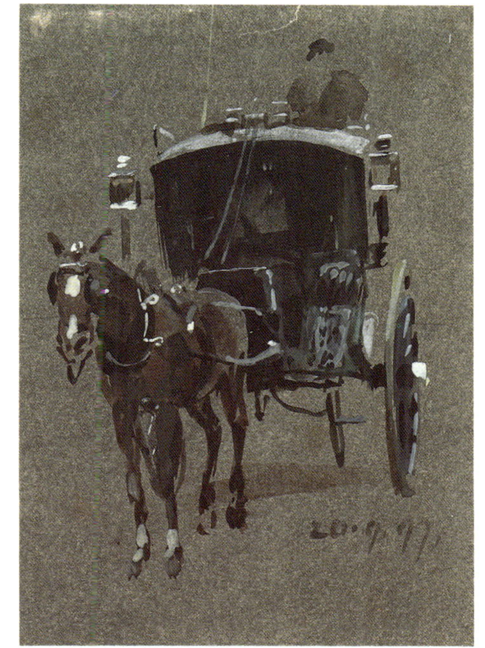

[c]

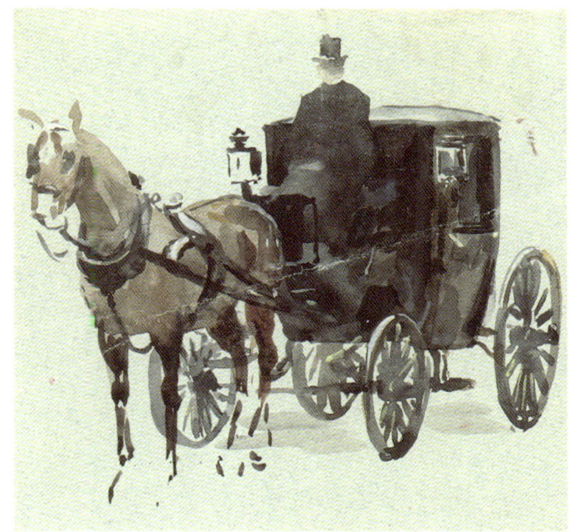

[d]

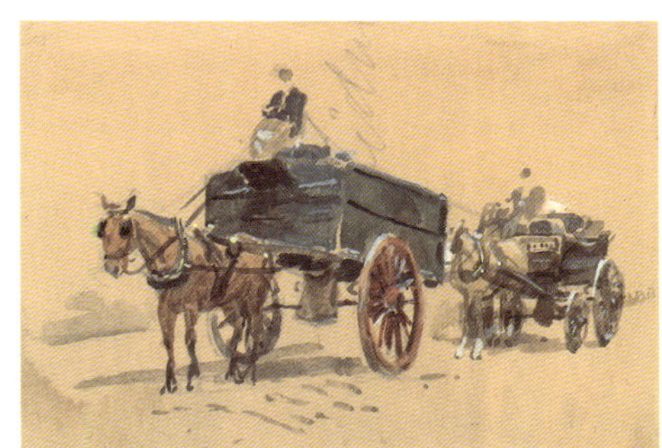

[e]

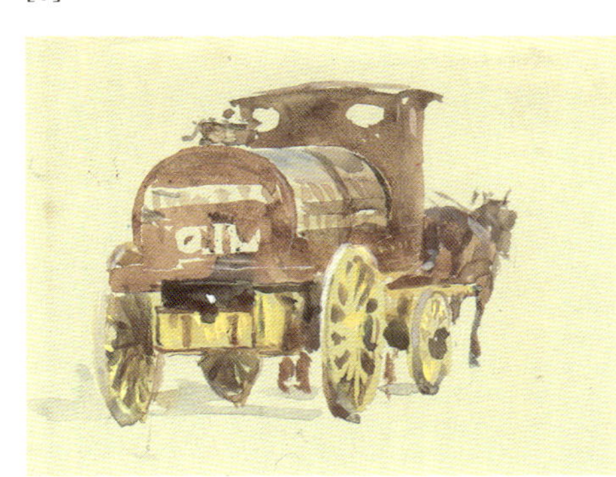

[f]

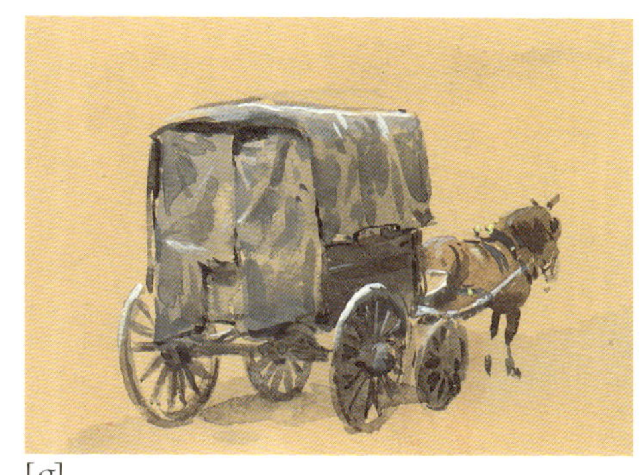

[g]

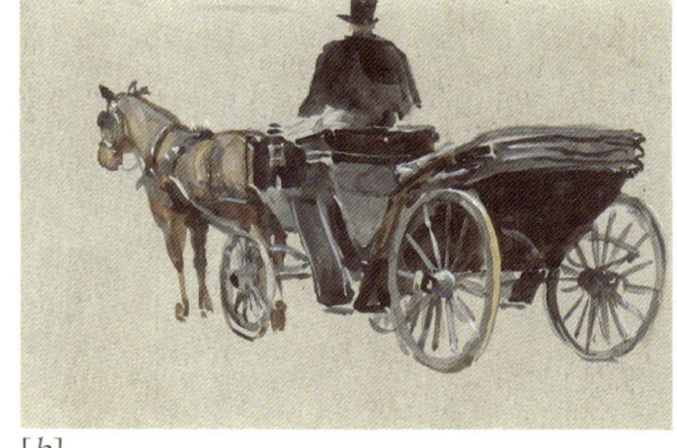

[h]

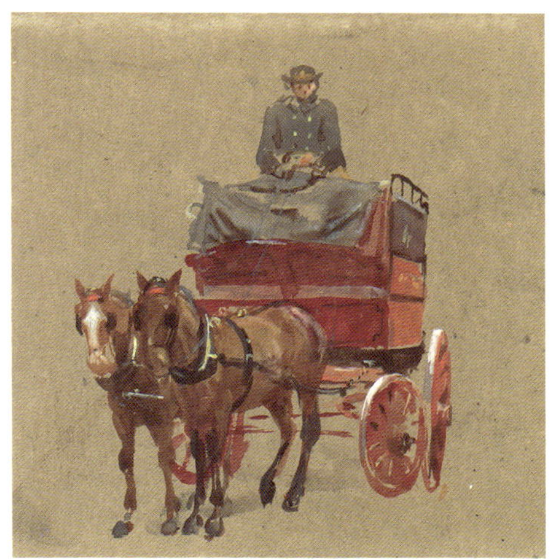

[i]

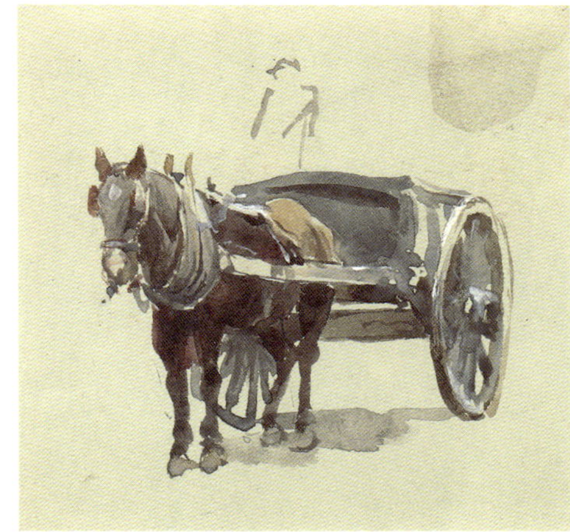

[j]

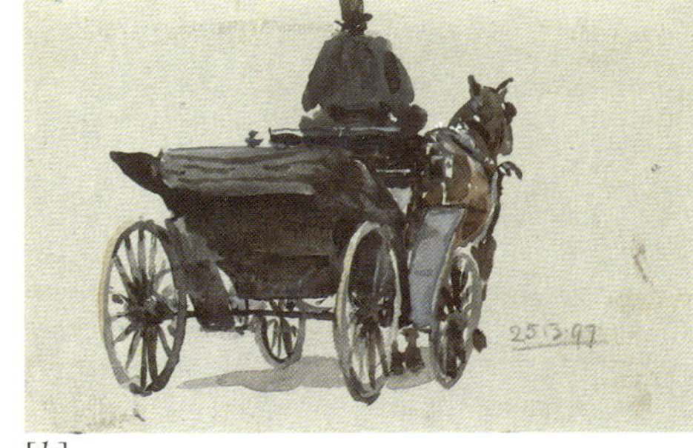

[k]

Various London vehicles, c.1897

No doubt intended for staffage in street views.

[152] *Watercolour sketches heightened with body colour on coloured papers.*

a. *Two-horse Royal Mail van, 114 × 115 mm*
b. *Single-horse Royal Mail van, 95 × 115 mm*
c. *Hansom cab, 126 × 85 mm*
d. *Single-horse Brougham, 120 × 122 mm*
e. *Horse and dust cart, with a four-wheeled vehicle in the background, 96 × 135 mm*
f. *Horse-drawn oil-tanker (used for delivering domestic oil door-to-door), 138 × 108 mm*
g. *Four-wheeled covered van, 80 × 105 mm*
h. *Victoria with lowered hood, 88 × 120 mm*
i. *Two-horse Royal Mail van, 110 × 82 mm*
j. *Horse-drawn dust cart, 95 × 95 mm*
k. *Victoria with lowered hood, 95 × 128 mm*

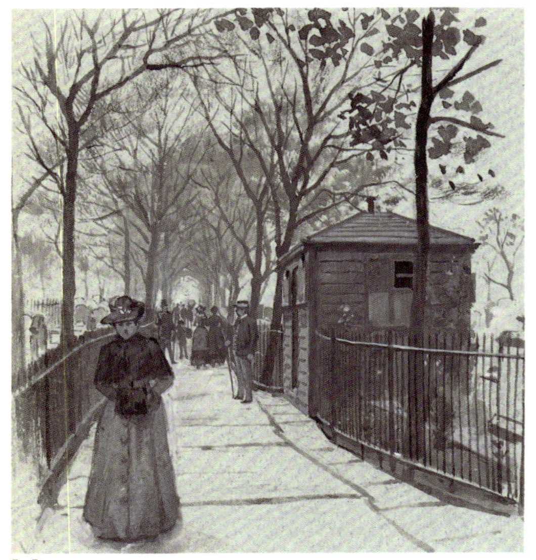

[a]

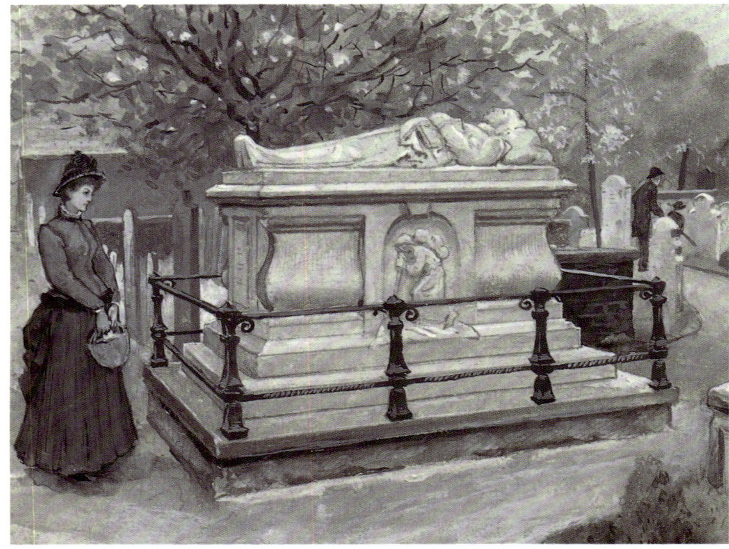

[d]

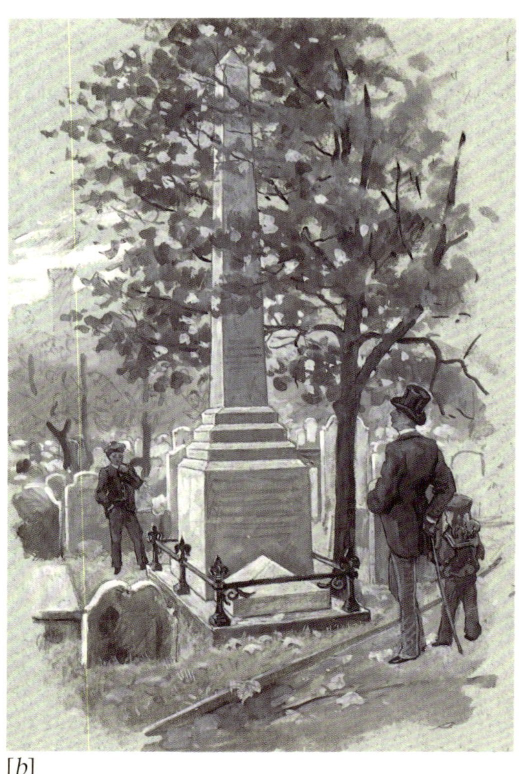

[b]

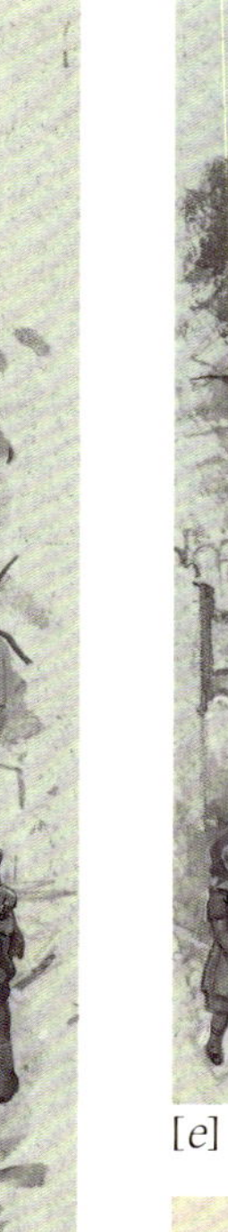

[e]

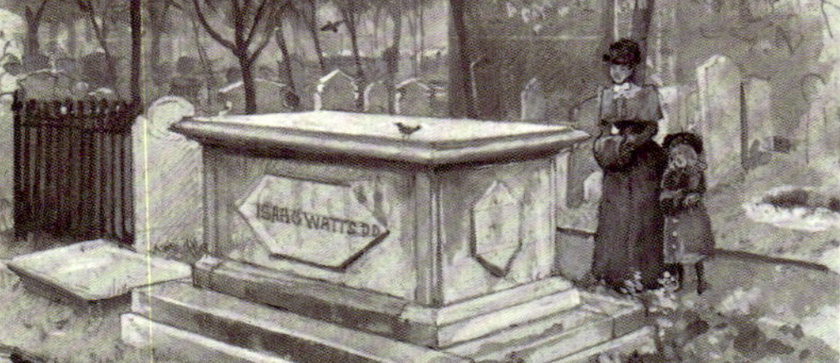

[c]

[f]

A selection of graves, tombs and memorial stones in Bunhill Burial Ground, Bunhill Fields, c.1900

[153] *Wash drawings heightened with body colour on grey paper.*

a. *Railed off pedestrian way through Bunhill Fields, 140 × 128 mm*
b. *Obelisk to Daniel Defoe, died 1731, 175 × 115 mm*
c. *Tomb of Isaac Watts, hymn writer, died 1748, 102 × 130 mm*
d. *Tomb of John Bunyan, died 1688, 106 × 136 mm*
e. *Obelisk surrounded by railings, probably the memorial to Revd Joseph Hughes, died 1833, 130 × 75 mm*
f. *Tomb of Richard Cromwell. It attracts the attention of a man in a shovel hat, possibly a self-portrait of H. E. Tidmarsh, 95 × 110 mm*

Headstone of Thomas Stothard R.A., died 1834
(endpiece)

[154] *Wash drawing heightened by body colour [check], 100 × 60 mm*

INDEX

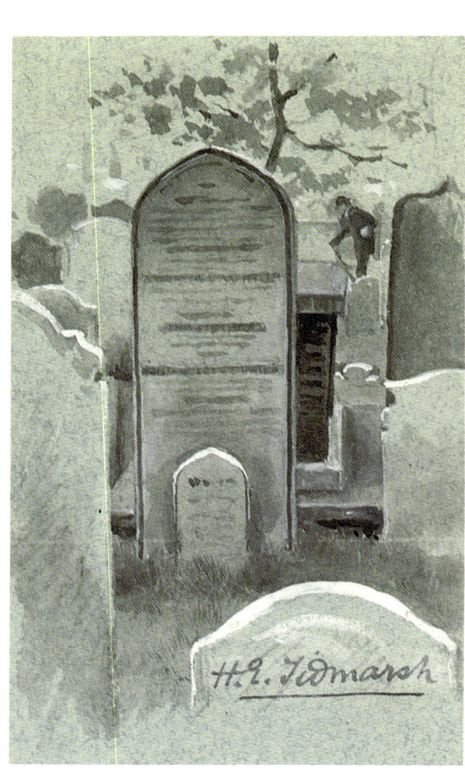
H.E. Tidmarsh

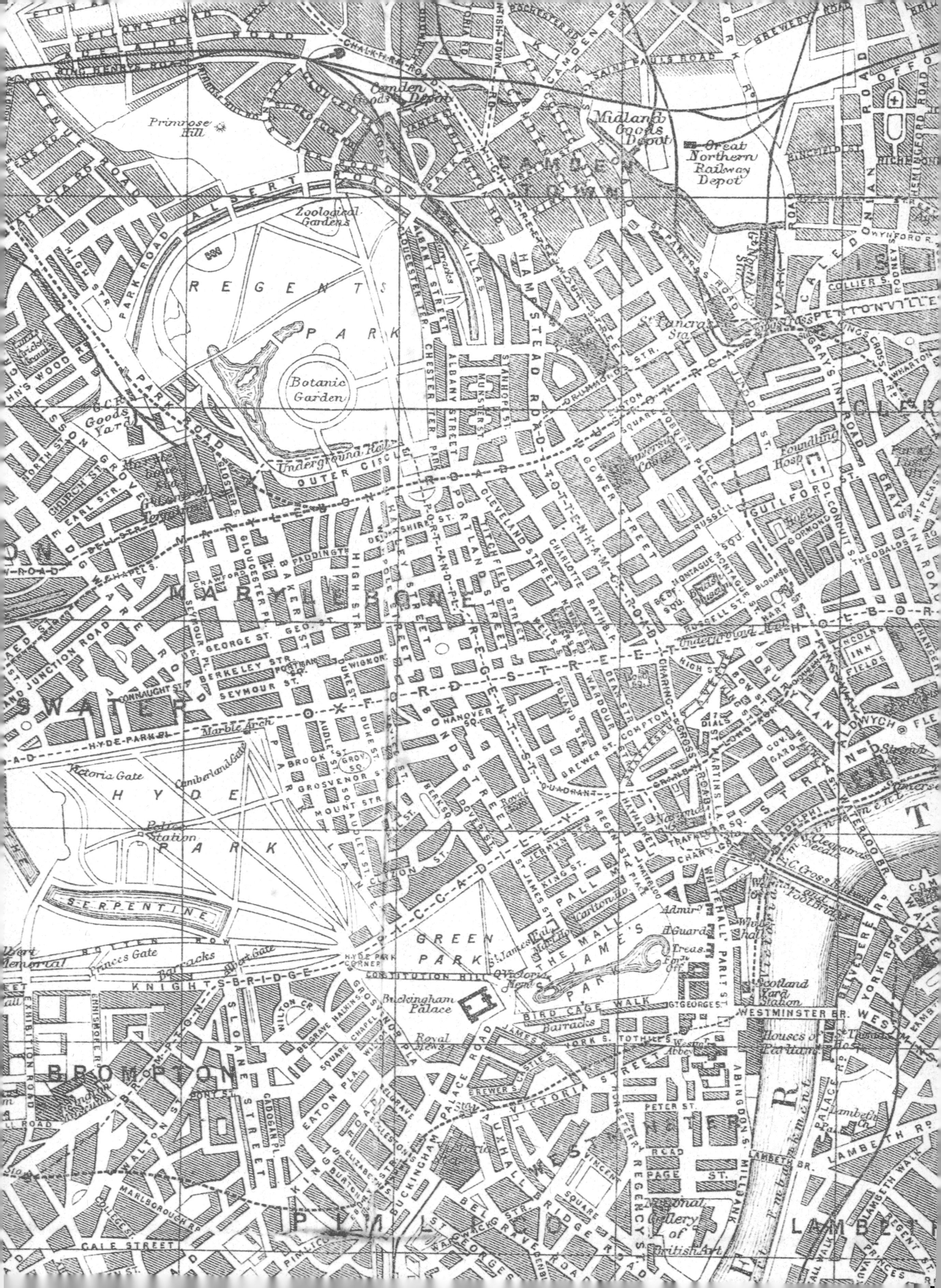
Primrose Hill
Camden Goods Depot
Midland Goods Depot
Great Northern Railway Depot
CAMDEN TOWN
Zoological Gardens
REGENTS PARK
Botanic Garden
Underground Rail
OUTER CIRCLE
ALBERT ROAD
PARK ROAD
HAMPSTEAD ROAD
St Pancras Sta.
PENTONVILLE
CALEDONIAN ROAD
Foundling Hosp
GUILFORD ST.
EUSTON ROAD
MARYLEBONE ROAD
MARYLEBONE
GOWER STREET
TOTTENHAM C. ROAD
RUSSELL SQ.
British Museum
OXFORD STREET
REGENT STREET
BAKER ST.
PORTLAND PL.
CLEVELAND STREET
CHARLOTTE STREET
HIGH HOLBORN
LINCOLNS INN FIELDS
DRURY LANE
STRAND
ALDWYCH
EDGWARE ROAD
HYDE PARK PL.
Marble Arch
HYDE PARK
Victoria Gate
Cumberland Gate
Police Station
SERPENTINE
ROTTEN ROW
Princes Gate
Albert Gate
Barracks
KNIGHTSBRIDGE
HYDE PARK CORNER
CONSTITUTION HILL
GREEN PARK
PICCADILLY
GROSVENOR SQ.
BERKELEY SQ.
HANOVER SQ.
BOND STREET
PARK LANE
CURZON ST.
JERMYN ST.
PALL MALL
HAYMARKET
TRAFALGAR SQ.
CHARING CROSS
WHITEHALL
Admiralty
H. Guards
Treasury
THE MALL
ST JAMES'S PARK
BIRD CAGE WALK
Buckingham Palace
Royal Mews
WESTMINSTER BR.
Houses of Parliament
Scotland Yard Station
WATERLOO BR.
Cleopatra's Needle
BROMPTON
SLOANE STREET
EATON PLA.
BELGRAVE SQUARE
GROSVENOR PLA.
VICTORIA STREET
VAUXHALL BRIDGE ROAD
PIMLICO
WESTMINSTER
National Gallery of British Art
LAMBETH BR.
LAMBETH RD.
Lambeth Palace
LAMBETH
MARLBOROUGH RD.
CALE STREET
PAGE ST.
REGENCY ST.
MILLBANK
YORK ROAD
BAYSWATER